Fodor's

D1551218

WALT DISNEY WORLD®
FOR
ADULTS

The Only Guide with a Grown-Up Point of View

RITA AERO

Fodor's Travel Publications, Inc.
New York • Toronto • London • Sydney • Auckland

The information in this guide originated with the author and has not been authorized or endorsed by The Walt Disney Company or any of its affiliates.

While every care has been taken to ensure the accuracy of the information in this guide, the passage of time will always bring changes, and consequently the publisher cannot accept responsibility for errors that may occur. All prices and operating schedules quoted herein are based on information available to us at press time. Operating hours, maps, resort policies, coming attractions, and admission fees and other costs may change, however, and the prudent will avoid inconvenience by calling ahead.

Walt Disney World is a registered trademark of The Walt Disney Company. Some of the attractions, products, and locations written about in this guide are registered trademarks of The Walt Disney Company and other trademark owners. The use in this guide of trademarked names, including those listed below, is strictly for editorial purposes, and no commercial claim to their use, or suggestion of sponsorship or endorsement, is made by the author or publisher. Those words or terms that the publisher has reason to believe are trademarks are designated as such by the use of initial capitalization and trademark symbols, where appropriate. However, no attempt has been made to identify or designate all words or terms to which trademark or other proprietary rights may exist. Nothing contained herein is intended to express a judgment on, or to affect the validity or legal status of, any word or term as a trademark, service mark, or other proprietary term.

Adventureland	Audio-Animatronics	Captain EO	Circle-Vision 360	Disneyland	EPCOT
EPCOT® Center	Fantasyland	Magic Kingdom	Magic Kingdom® Park	Mickey Mouse	Mickey's Starland
PeopleMover	Space Mountain	Typhoon Lagoon	Walt Disney	Walt Disney World	Walt Disney World® Resort

Jim Henson's Muppet*Vision 3D is copyright © 1991 Henson Associates, © Disney. Teenage Mutant Ninja Turtles is a registered trademark of Mirage Studios, based on characters and comic books created by Kevin Eastman and Peter Laird. copyright © 1991 Mirage Studios.

Map Design: Harry Driggs

Art Director: Rita Aero

Senior Editors: Stephanie Rick, Maribeth Riggs, Monica Baltz

Associate Editors: Jan Haag, Cynthia VanEvery, Suzanne Lipsett

Research Editor: Jane Cartelli

Internet Research: George Csiscery, Richard Brzustowicz, Jr., Steevie Klein

Research Associates: Robin Clauson, Steve Haight, Janet Teich, Jack Teich

Copy Editor: Carolyn Miller

Art and Editorial Intern: Sara Keough

Index: Jerry Stanton

Fodor's Editor: Michael Spring

Electronic Prepress: Dan Everard, RR Donnelley & Sons Co.

Jacket Design: Fabrizio LaRocca

Jacket Photos: Flamingo, Bill Nosh/FPG International; Water, Color Box/FPG International; Lemon, Color Box/FPG International; Golf, John Callanan/Image Bank; Fireworks, Philip M. Derenzis/Image Bank

Symbol Font Design: Bill Tchakirides, U-Design Type Foundry, Hartford, CT

Travel Coordinator: Rebecca Gardener, Travel Advisors, Mill Valley, CA

Premium Representative: Ken Berger, Random House, Inc., San Francisco, CA

Legal Counsel: Sheldon Fogelman, Richard Rosenberg, Diana Frost

Special Contributions: Kristina Peterson, Vicki Valentine, Jane Gottlieb, David Obst, Candice Fuhrman, Michelle Sidrane, Chuck Bloodgood, Jim Keough, Linda Sparrowe, Bill Lucerne, Peg Lucerne, Sean Maytum, Esther Mitgang, Diana Rick, Larry Cartelli, Howard Rheingold, Wendy Justus.

CONTENTS

Walt Disney World for Adults

Walt Disney World for Adults began with a family reunion many years ago. It somehow fell to me to plan the activities during our stay for our all-adult group. Since this would be my first visit to Walt Disney World, I flew to Orlando several days ahead of everyone else to review the attractions, select restaurants that our diverse group would enjoy, and plan a schedule we could follow together. The only book available at the time was *Birnbaum's Official Guide to Walt Disney World* and, as informative as it was, it did not indicate which attractions adults would enjoy or which hotels had the amenities they needed. There was also no information on what entrees were actually served in the various restaurants.

Like most visitors who have spent time at Disneyland, I arrived unprepared for Walt Disney World. I expected an amusement park and found a universe. In a frenzy of activity, I reserved time on the PGA courses for the golfers in the family; investigated how to join the studio audience of a popular television show in production; found a fishing excursion for the anglers; discovered a delightful way to explore the architecture of the themed resorts by boat; and found a perfect, secluded picnic spot for an afternoon getaway while touring Discovery Island. I looked at menus from all the restaurants to find dining spots that would satisfy everyone's tastes and discovered how to order meals in advance for those in our group on special diets. I explored the public transportation systems, looking for the most convenient ride to the nearest attractions, and discovered parking areas that would reduce the physical strain on the older members in our group. I also toured as many resorts as I could and quickly discovered where we *should* have stayed (we already had booked rooms elsewhere), and the perfect area of the hotel for groups like ours.

By the time the rest of the group arrived, I had secured dinner show and restaurant reservations and had written out a day-by-day itinerary for everyone. I had even selected the attractions we would see together, based on my assessment of how our adult group would enjoy them. I must admit the itinerary was a bit ambitious, but it made our family reunion a memorable, stress-free event. I was careful to leave the afternoons free, knowing that several of the older members of our group would want to rest, and now I've come to realize how essential that afternoon break is for *any* visitor. Most significantly, however, I learned how important it is to have a vacation strategy for Walt Disney World, the world's most complex playground.

Unexpectedly, I became something of an expert on adult vacations at Walt Disney World, and with each subsequent trip that I planned for friends, acquaintances, and friends of friends, I learned more about the activities, entertainments, and pleasant diversions that adult visitors have available to them. Meanwhile, on my own trips and tours, I noticed much to my surprise that at least half of the visitors at Walt Disney World were adults touring *without* children. There were retirees and young couples, singles traveling in groups, adults who were attending conventions and business seminars, and even young parents touring together in the afternoons and evenings after leaving their children with Disney babysitters or at Disney day camps. The folks at Walt Disney

World also saw this phenomenon and began launching their own campaign to entertain this huge adult audience. They opened Pleasure Island, with its late-night music and dance clubs, and built two additional PGA golf courses and several world-class resorts.

Walt Disney World is now the number-one honeymoon destination in the world, and the enormous number of visitors who flock to it each year suggests it is the world's most popular *adult* vacation destination as well. With nearly twenty-five thousand hotel rooms and five PGA golf courses, Walt Disney World is the largest golf resort on the planet and hosts hundreds of professional tournaments each year, including the world's biggest, the PGA Tour's Walt Disney World/ Oldsmobile Golf Classic. To enhance its range of activities for adults, Walt Disney World is currently positioning itself as a premier sports vacation destination, with televised marathons and other competitions, fantasy sports camps for adults, and expanded recreation facilities.

Walt Disney World for Adults is the book I wish I'd had when I was planning those early visits. It contains all the information I have sought out over the years: detailed descriptions of all the resorts, their room amenities, recreation facilities, and access to transportation, along with ratings on just how fresh the rooms really are; restaurant reviews that explain exactly what's on the menu and what kind of dining experience to expect; a complete overview of all the sporting and outdoor activities available to both resort guests and day visitors; concise descriptions of the menus and entertainment presented at each dinner show; and all those essential and hard-to-get insider tips on everything from navigating the Orlando International Airport and selecting ground transportation to Walt Disney World, to car parking strategies for adults and older travelers. There's also useful information for travelers with disabilities, and tips on how to get discounts at hotels, shop for necessities, and pack what you need to survive the rigors of touring the theme parks.

Most important, *Walt Disney World for Adults* contains easy-to-use maps of all the recreation areas — maps designed especially for adult travelers — including areas that have yet to show up on any maps published by Disney. Each map indicates the locations of the best telephones and rest rooms, as well as cocktail lounges, cafes, banking services, and much more. The complex legends and unnecessary details that make most maps so difficult to use have been eliminated. I would have loved to have had these maps when I began touring Walt Disney World, and I'm glad I have them now because sometimes I still get lost.

The heart and soul of this book, however, are the adult vacation itineraries and half-day tours. There are many to choose from, and they are the key to an enjoyable, carefree vacation at Walt Disney World. They have been extensively field-tested by adults of all ages, including first-time visitors. Use the mini-tours and itineraries to make *your* Walt Disney World adult vacation the best it can possibly be. (They're ideal for families with older children, too.) And let all of us who were involved in this book know how it worked for your trip. Fill out the Reader Survey on the last page and send it to us with your opinions and any tips you may have discovered that we can pass on to fellow travelers. Have a great vacation! ◆

How to Use This Book

First-time visitors to Walt Disney World can be easily overwhelmed by its size and the vast number of entertainment and recreation choices available to guests. Many arrive assuming WDW is something like Disneyland with hotels, so they are unprepared to take advantage of their options and take control of their vacation time. They end up following the crowds, standing in long lines, being turned away from already booked restaurants and dinner shows, and remaining unaware of the many recreation possibilities that are offered. Repeat visitors, too, can get caught up in the herd because they do not have a preplanning strategy.

This book will give you the tools you need to take full advantage of your Walt Disney World vacation and get the most out of the time and money you will spend there. It will allow you to know ahead of time where you will be spending each day, so that you can make advance reservations for restaurants, tours, and sporting and entertainment events. The sections of the book are arranged in an order that will help you to quickly see what your choices are and to plan your vacation efficiently by preselecting the attractions, hotels, restaurants, and activities that will enhance your overall experience.

ATTRACTIONS

Begin by glancing through the first section, "Attractions." Familiarize yourself with the theme parks and recreation areas and decide in advance what you would like to see and do. Notice, too, the mini-tours included with each attraction. By combining these tours, you can design your own custom vacation. For example, you make want to combine a morning tour and lunch at Disney-MGM Studios with an evening tour and dinner at the World Showcase.

VACATION ITINERARIES

Continue to the next section, "Vacation Itineraries," which has five special-interest tours for adults. Each Vacation Itinerary covers four days and can be expanded or modified, and each recommends a range of hotels that are convenient for that itinerary. If you find a Vacation Itinerary that matches your special interests, simply follow the schedule with its preplanning and reservations countdown to departure. When you arrive, your reservations will all be made, so you can relax and have a good time. If you do not find a Vacation Itinerary that works for you, if you are staying for only three nights or less, or if you are attending a convention demanding part of your day, use the half-day tours in "Attractions" to design your own itinerary. Create a schedule that shows where you will be each day, so you can follow up with restaurant and entertainment reservations. The phone numbers you will be calling from outside the Orlando area indicate a 407 area code in the text; all phone numbers require a 407 area code if you call from outside the area.

TICKETS & TIMING

Once your vacation schedule has taken shape, turn to "Tickets & Timing" to make sure you're traveling at a time when the weather is pleasant and the parks are not crowded. If you are traveling during a time of peak attendance, you will not be able to see as many attractions, although during crowded times there are many more special events, celebrity appearances, parades, and fireworks shows to take advantage of and enjoy. This section also indicates the value seasons, those times of year when resort rates are at their lowest.

HOTELS

If you know when you're traveling, move on to "Hotels," which presents complete reviews of each resort at Walt Disney World. Stay on WDW property if you possibly can; it will make your vacation a simpler and more complete experience, and only Walt Disney World resort guests can make advance reservations at restaurants, dinner shows, and golf courses. Select a hotel in a resort area that provides easy access to the activities and attractions you will be visiting most. Consult the map on page 10 for hotel locations, and book your accommodations well in advance of your trip.

RESTAURANTS AND DINNER SHOWS

The next sections, "Restaurants" and "Dinner Shows," will help you decide where and when to dine. Remember, WDW is spread out over many miles, so choose restaurants at locations where you will be touring, dine at a nearby resort, or dine at your own resort if you're returning to rest. If you are staying at a WDW resort, you can secure dinner show and theme-park restaurant reservations in advance. Take advantage of this privilege — restaurant reservations fill quickly, particularly at busy times.

SPORTING ACTIVITIES

If you prefer an active vacation or enjoy outings in nature, you can find out about your options in "Sporting Activities." There are plenty of choices including boating, bicycling, tennis, waterskiing, and nature walks. If you plan to play at one of Walt Disney World's PGA golf courses, be sure to make advance reservations.

TOURING TIPS

Finally, look through "Touring Tips," which is filled with vacation strategies from experienced WDW visitors. Here, you'll find tips on discount travel, group vacations, family reunions, holidays, local transportation, parking, babysitting, and much more. There is also a description of services available for travelers with disabilities.

READER SURVEY

The tours and itineraries have been field-tested at various times of the year, and the ratings that appear throughout this book came from a consensus of adult visitors. We are interested in your experiences and opinions, as well. If you would like to add your voice to the ratings and touring tips, fill out the Reader Survey on the last page when you return from your vacation and tell us about your trip. ◆

ATTRACTIONS

The Walt Disney World attractions are located throughout the forty-three-square-mile resort, separated by miles of forests, wilderness areas, lakes, and waterways. One hundred and twenty-five miles of road traverses Walt Disney World, with more than twenty unique resort hotels clustered near the major theme parks. Although the land, like all of Florida, is flat, the landscaping is such that visitors never really see their recreation destination until they actually arrive there. One striking exception is Epcot Center, whose immense eighteen-story silver geosphere is visible from many areas of Walt Disney World.

The major attractions include the Magic Kingdom (a replica of the familiar Disneyland theme parks in California, Tokyo, and France), Disney-MGM Studios, and Epcot Center (which is divided into two theme parks, the World Showcase and Future World). The other attractions described in this chapter are Typhoon Lagoon, Pleasure Island, Discovery Island, Disney Village Marketplace, and Fort Wilderness & River Country. In each attraction, all entertainment events are rated for adult tastes and all full-service restaurants are described (for complete restaurant reviews see "Restaurants," page 167). Services at each attraction are also listed, including pertinent information for visitors with disabilities. Each attraction (with the exception of Disney Village Marketplace) also includes one or more half-day tours for adults.

✳

HOW TO USE THE HALF-DAY TOURS

The half-day tours are designed especially for first-time visitors to Walt Disney World, although return visitors will also find the touring strategies useful. At the Magic Kingdom, World Showcase at Epcot, Future World at Epcot, and Disney-MGM Studios, the half-day tours are oriented to either the morning or evening, since lines tend to be long in the afternoons. At Discovery Island, Fort Wilderness & River Country, and Typhoon Lagoon, there are morning tours *and* afternoon tours, since these attractions are ideal for mid-day getaways. At Pleasure Island, there is an evening tour of the nightclubs and entertainment events. Almost all tours include lunch or dinner as part of the overall experience, and each tour specifies the best time of year to take it. In general, most tours will work best during low- to moderate-attendance times (see "Crowds & Weather," page 140). Most theme parks charge admission, so you will want to plan your ticket purchase based on the length of your stay and how much you would like to see and do (see "Admissions," page 139).

The half-day tours allow you to design and plan a custom vacation at Walt Disney World based on your interests and past experiences. Because most are designed in three- to five-hour modules, you can mix and match two or more attractions that appeal to you in a single day. You can also combine one half-day tour with entertainment events and activities that are available outside the theme parks (see "Dinner Shows," page 209, and "Sporting Activities," page 217). If you're visiting WDW for a convention, seminar, or special event, you will find that the half-day tours allow you to experience the best that a particular attraction offers in the limited time available to you. If you are planning to stay four days or longer, you may want to follow one of the five special-interest Vacation Itineraries that begin on page 97. These itineraries incorporate most of the attractions as well as the entertainment and recreation options that are available throughout Walt Disney World. ◆

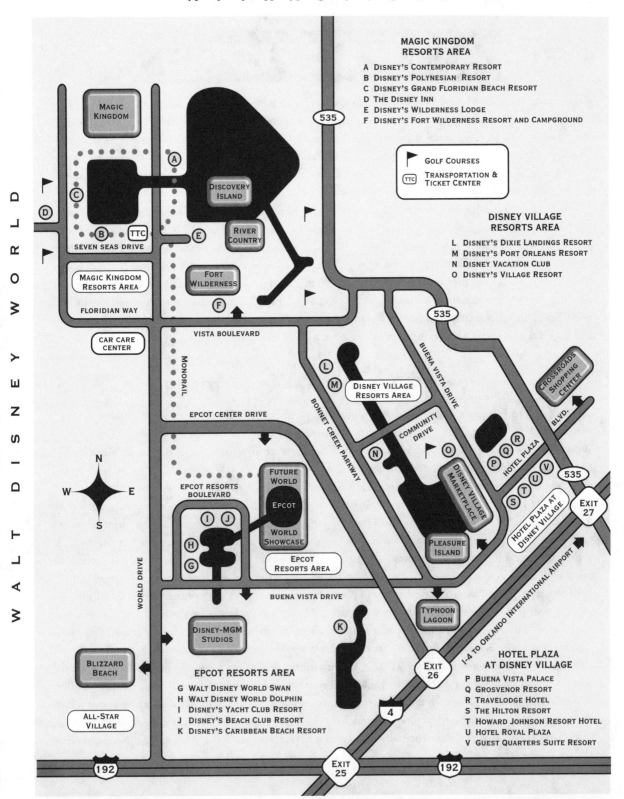

WALT DISNEY WORLD

MAGIC KINGDOM RESORTS AREA

A DISNEY'S CONTEMPORARY RESORT
B DISNEY'S POLYNESIAN RESORT
C DISNEY'S GRAND FLORIDIAN BEACH RESORT
D THE DISNEY INN
E DISNEY'S WILDERNESS LODGE
F DISNEY'S FORT WILDERNESS RESORT AND CAMPGROUND

⚑ GOLF COURSES
TTC TRANSPORTATION & TICKET CENTER

DISNEY VILLAGE RESORTS AREA

L DISNEY'S DIXIE LANDINGS RESORT
M DISNEY'S PORT ORLEANS RESORT
N DISNEY VACATION CLUB
O DISNEY'S VILLAGE RESORT

EPCOT RESORTS AREA

G WALT DISNEY WORLD SWAN
H WALT DISNEY WORLD DOLPHIN
I DISNEY'S YACHT CLUB RESORT
J DISNEY'S BEACH CLUB RESORT
K DISNEY'S CARIBBEAN BEACH RESORT

HOTEL PLAZA AT DISNEY VILLAGE

P BUENA VISTA PALACE
Q GROSVENOR RESORT
R TRAVELODGE HOTEL
S THE HILTON RESORT
T HOWARD JOHNSON RESORT HOTEL
U HOTEL ROYAL PLAZA
V GUEST QUARTERS SUITE RESORT

WALT DISNEY WORLD OVERVIEW

Walt Disney World lies south of Orlando on Interstate 4, about a thirty-minute drive from the Orlando International Airport. This sprawling forty-three-square-mile playground contains nine distinct theme parks and recreation areas, more than twenty luxury resorts, a dozen lakes with miles of interconnected waterways, and five PGA golf courses — all separated by wilderness areas, wetlands, forests, and conservation areas. It's a self-contained, self-sustaining world with its own telephone system, power plant, waste management and recycling center, transportation system, medical center, and earth station linked with three Disney-owned space satellites that coordinate every aspect of this vacation paradise. There are five main resort areas in Walt Disney World, each with themed resort accommodations spanning a range of prices and amenities.

MAGIC KINGDOM RESORTS AREA: At the northernmost point of Walt Disney World, this area incorporates the Magic Kingdom, Fort Wilderness, River Country, Discovery Island, Magnolia Golf Course, and Palm Golf Course. Bay Lake, the largest lake on the property, is located here, along with Seven Seas Lagoon and the Fort Wilderness Waterways. The fourteen-mile monorail system connects most of the resorts in this area with the Magic Kingdom and Epcot Center. The resorts located here are The Disney Inn, Disney's Contemporary Resort, Disney's Grand Floridian Beach Resort, Disney's Fort Wilderness Resort and Campground, and Disney's Wilderness Lodge, the newest luxury resort.

EPCOT RESORTS AREA: Located in the center of Walt Disney World, the Epcot Resorts Area incorporates Epcot Center, including the World Showcase and Future World. This area is adjacent to Disney-MGM Studios, and water launches provide transportation between most of the Epcot resorts and Disney-MGM Studios. The area has three small recreational lakes: Barefoot Bay, Crescent Lake, and Stormalong Bay. The resorts located here are Disney's Beach Club Resort, Disney's Caribbean Beach Resort, Disney's Yacht Club Resort, Walt Disney World Dolphin, and Walt Disney World Swan.

ALL-STAR VILLAGE: The resorts in this new area will be open in 1994. The area lies at the farthest point south in Walt Disney World, just beyond Disney-MGM Studios and adjacent to the new Blizzard Beach water park. It is also the site of Walt Disney World's fourth major theme park, Animal Kingdom, scheduled for completion in 1997. The resorts here are serviced by Walt Disney World buses, although a continuation of the monorail system to the area is included in the master plan. The resorts located here are Disney's All-Star Sports Resort, Disney's All-Star Music Resort, and Disney's Fiesta Resort.

DISNEY VILLAGE RESORTS AREA: The Disney Village Resorts Area incorporates Pleasure Island, Typhoon Lagoon, Disney Village Marketplace, Osprey Ridge Golf Course, Eagle Pines Golf Course, and Lake Buena Vista Golf Course. Water launches provide transportation between the resorts in this area and Pleasure Island and Disney Village Marketplace. Buena Vista Lagoon is located here and feeds into the meandering Disney Village Waterways. The resorts located here are Disney Vacation Club, Disney's Dixie Landings Resort, Disney's Port Orleans Resort, and Disney's Village Resort.

HOTEL PLAZA AT DISNEY VILLAGE: Hotel Plaza is located adjacent to the Disney Village Resorts Area and enjoys the same attractions and recreation facilities. Transportation is provided solely by Walt Disney World buses. Crossroads Shopping Center is located at one end of Hotel Plaza Boulevard. The resorts located here are Buena Vista Palace, Grosvenor Resort, Guest Quarters Suite Resort, The Hilton Resort, Hotel Royal Plaza, Howard Johnson Resort Hotel, and Travelodge Hotel. ◆

WALT DISNEY WORLD

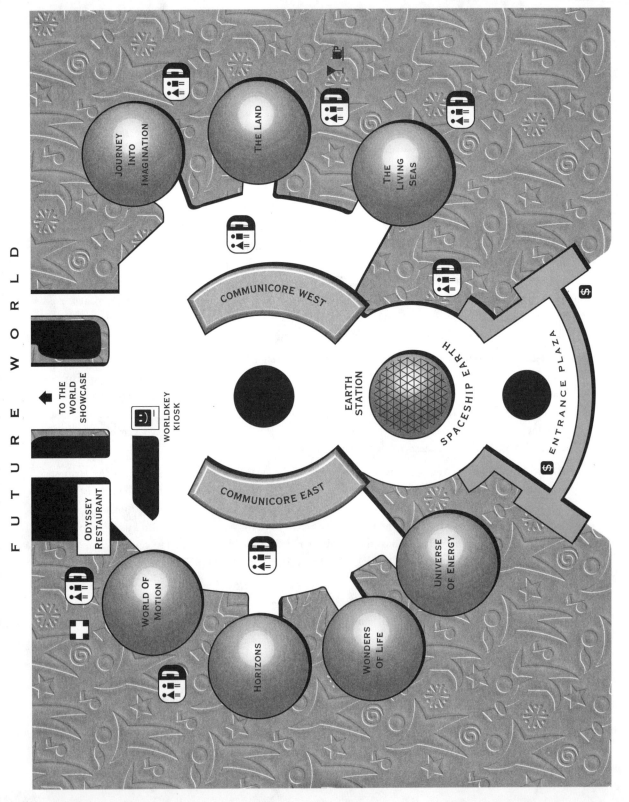

FUTURE WORLD

JOURNEY INTO IMAGINATION

THE LAND

THE LIVING SEAS

COMMUNICORE WEST

EARTH STATION

SPACESHIP EARTH

ENTRANCE PLAZA

TO THE WORLD SHOWCASE

WORLDKEY KIOSK

ODYSSEY RESTAURANT

COMMUNICORE EAST

WORLD OF MOTION

HORIZONS

WONDERS OF LIFE

UNIVERSE OF ENERGY

FUTURE WORLD AT EPCOT

Future World occupies the front half of Walt Disney's Experimental Prototype Community of Tomorrow, better known as Epcot Center. Epcot is distinguished by its landmark silver geosphere, and its theme is technology and the future. Future World's eight theme pavilions and two CommuniCore buildings contain informative, entertaining exhibits and attractions in the areas of transportation, energy, communication, agriculture, and health, and most are of considerable interest to adults. A number of pavilions are actually ongoing experiments designed to test innovations in energy management, waste and water recycling, and food production. Many of these innovations have been incorporated into day-to-day operations at Future World and throughout Walt Disney World.

WHEN TO GO: The Future World pavilions and attractions are most accessible and enjoyable after 5 PM, when crowds begin to migrate to the World Showcase restaurants or return to their hotels. If you prefer a morning visit, arrive at the entrance gate about half an hour before the scheduled opening time, so you can enjoy some of the popular attractions during the first hour and a half, before the park fills. Opening and closing times vary throughout the year, so check ahead at Guest Services in your resort, or call 407 824-4321. The Spaceship Earth attraction frequently opens one half hour before the rest of the park.

HOW TO GET THERE: Future World is located at the main entrance to Epcot Center. The large parking lot at Epcot is free to guests at WDW resorts (day visitors are charged a nominal fee). The parking lot is serviced by trams. WDW buses and monorails stop at Epcot's main entrance. The buses service all WDW resorts. The monorail system services the Transportation and Ticket Center, the Magic Kingdom, and the following resorts: Contemporary, Polynesian, and Grand Floridian. Future World can also be entered by way of the World Showcase through the International Gateway from the following resorts: Dolphin, Swan, Yacht Club, and Beach Club.

✴

ATTRACTIONS

✖✖✖ – Good entertainment. ✖✖ – Enjoyable if you have the time and interest. ✖ – Of limited appeal.

EPCOT'S ENTRANCE PLAZA: As visitors enter the sprawling Entrance Plaza and pass by its sleek tripod sculpture fountain, they face the huge, multifaceted, 180-foot-high silver geosphere housing Spaceship Earth. The geosphere, clearly visible from any part of Epcot, serves as a point of orientation. The Entrance Plaza is the site of many of Epcot's services, including the tour desk, bank, wheelchair rentals, lockers, camera center, and American Express financial services.

✦ *Spaceship Earth* — This ride, which actually travels inside the Epcot geosphere, was created in a collaboration between Disney designers and world-renowned science fiction writer Ray Bradbury. Visitors journey through the history of communication, from the earliest cave paintings to the printing press, and from the age of radio to the future of satellite communications. The lifelike Audio-Animatronic figures, carefully researched dioramas, and dazzling star dome overhead make Spaceship Earth one of Future World's not-to-be-missed experiences for both students and adults. Duration: 16 minutes. ✖✖✖

EARTH STATION: Located behind Spaceship Earth, this information lobby is a spacious open room where visitors can ask for information at Guest Relations, use the WorldKey Information Service to make restaurant reservations, pick up the day's schedule of Epcot events, make WDW resort reservations, or leave and retrieve messages at the Message Center.

COMMUNICORE EAST: One of a pair of large, semicircular buildings facing the huge multilevel fountain in the center of Future World, CommuniCore East houses a number of entertaining exhibits that focus on the use of computers for engineering, design, and storing and retrieving vast and varied types of information. Computerized games and information modules, many with touch-screen monitors, present a range of topics — for example, designing a personal roller coaster, determining the population of any state, and picking up tips on energy conservation. It's a waste to take just a quick walk through the CommuniCore East exhibits; almost all of them are participatory and require some time. Early morning and evening are the best times to explore this pavilion, since the exhibits attract crowds of children during the afternoon. CommuniCore East also houses a gift shop that sells high-tech items and Disney merchandise.

✦ *Backstage Magic* — While standing in line for the Backstage Magic attraction, visitors see a well-crafted preshow on overhead video monitors that explains the development of the computer and how it works. Visitors then enter the exhibit, where they embark on an engaging tour of the electronic technology at work in Walt Disney World, culminating with a peek into the operations center itself. Duration: 18 minutes. ✗✗

✦ *Energy Exchange* — Touch-screen monitors and displays in this attraction present a broad range of energy-related exhibits, including methods for generating energy and energy conservation tips. In a "hands-on" section, visitors can turn a hand-cranked generator to light up a bulb and pedal a bicycle to see how much energy they can generate. ✗

COMMUNICORE WEST: On the other side of the Fountain of Nations, across from CommuniCore East, is a mirror-image structure, CommuniCore West. Here the focus is on robotics and telecommunications. Impressive exhibits include robots in action, communications devices and systems, and computerized games and information kiosks, many with touch-screen monitors. In the center is the Fountain of Information, a large, colorful kinetic sculpture made up of neon signs, video monitors, books, iridescent laser discs, maps, and many other types of information media. Early morning and evening are the best times to explore this pavilion, since it is filled with children in the afternoons. Like CommuniCore East, the CommuniCore West exhibits are almost all participatory. CommuniCore West also houses a gift shop that sells high-tech toys, computer goodies, robot-created personalized tee-shirts, and Disney merchandise.

✦ *Expo Robotics* — This large exhibit area showcases sophisticated robotics in action. On a small stage, five robotic arms of the type used in auto assembly lines put on a brief show, juggling, balancing, and spinning tops. The Portrait Drawing Robots use computer imaging techniques to create unique, free souvenir portraits of visitors. These portrait drawing robots were designed for the 1985 International Science Exposition in Tsukuba, Japan. The image capturing takes only a few seconds, and the execution of the portraits by robotic arms holding pens takes about three to five minutes. ✗

✦ *FutureCom* — From a family-sized phone booth to video teleconferencing by satellite, Future-Com showcases telecommunications systems once only dreamed of in science fiction stories. The exhibits include games that challenge visitors to unscramble images of their faces or to control a network of long-distance phone calls. Touch-screen computers display current events in any state, and live demonstrations allow visitors to experience video teleconferencing in action. To demonstrate online database technology, visitors can log on to the birth databank and find out what important events happened on their birthdays, how much food they have consumed in their lifetimes, how much time they have spent sleeping, and a number of other fascinating facts about themselves. ✗✗

✦ *Epcot Outreach* — CommuniCore East and West were originally envisioned as centralized electronic town halls, where people could gather to retrieve information electronically from numerous sources. Epcot Outreach embodies this idea by offering background and technical information on many of the exhibits at WDW. Interested visitors can request data from the attendant at the desk, who has access to a massive databank on specific topics, such as how many people Walt Disney World employs or how WDW's three space satellites function at the park. Perhaps not surprisingly, the most commonly asked question is, "Where are the nearest rest rooms?" ✗

✦ *Teacher's Center* — Designed for educators as well as parents, the Teacher's Center is a specialized information source that provides printed educational materials, previews of educational software, and professional education journals. A working computer network allows teachers to exchange ideas with other professionals in the field. ✗

UNIVERSE OF ENERGY PAVILION: With its pyramidal shape and mirrored surface, the Universe of Energy is a traveling theater that is part ride, part film, and total technical marvel. There is always a crowd at this popular pavilion, but its interior accommodates about six hundred people at a time, so lines disappear quickly. During peak hours, longer waits are the norm.

✦ *Universe of Energy* — Just inside the pavilion, visitors watch a short film about the types of energy in use today. They are then seated in what seems to be a large theater. Here, a second film begins, but at this point, all similarity to a theater ends. The room breaks apart into six large traveling vehicles that take visitors on a journey through a primeval world populated with prehistoric beasts wallowing in swampy waters, flapping ominously overhead, or locked in mortal combat. Erupting volcanoes spew lava, and thick fog wafts across the vehicles' paths. The Audio-Animatronic figures, some of the largest ever built, are stunning in their detail, and ambient special effects include whiffs of sulfur at the volcanic eruption and warm tropical air. Duration: 45 minutes. ✗✗✗

WONDERS OF LIFE PAVILION: Just beyond the Universe of Energy pavilion, where a steel DNA sculpture looms near a gigantic golden dome, is the Wonders of Life pavilion. This pavilion houses the Fitness Fairground exhibition center, the AnaComical Players theater, and three popular attractions: Body Wars, Cranium Command, and *The Making of Me.*

✦ *Body Wars* — In this thrill ride, visitors are miniaturized and injected into a human body to retrieve a technician investigating the effects of a splinter. Naturally, problems develop and visitors find themselves hurtling along in the circulatory system, hoping to be rescued themselves. The theater is actually a flight simulator that moves, tilts, and bucks dramatically during the show. The seat belts provided are a definite necessity for this ride, which is not for those prone to motion sickness. Some health restrictions are enforced. Long lines are the norm at almost any hour. Duration: 5 minutes. ✗✗✗

✦ *Cranium Command* — One of the funnier attractions in Future World, this show opens with a preshow cartoon introducing the Cranium Command, a specialized corps of Brain Pilots trained to run the systems that make up the human body. Those who fail get stuck running the bodies of chickens, as the loudmouth training sergeant continually reminds his cadets. Visitors then enter a multimedia theater, where they follow Buzzy, the youngest Cranium Command cadet, on his first venture into a truly frightful environment — the body and mind of a twelve-year-old boy on a typical school day. The clever humor strikes on an adult level. Cranium Command is hidden in the back of the pavilion, so lines are generally short. The animated preshow helps to make the rest of the show clear. Duration: 18 minutes. ✖✖

✦ *The Making of Me* — This light and humorous film tells all about the facts of life. Created for a younger audience, *The Making of Me* has aroused considerable controversy through its open approach to the topic of sex and reproduction, culminating with superb though graphic footage of the stages of pregnancy from initial conception through birth. Lines are common at this attraction, due primarily to the small size of the theater. Duration: 14 minutes. ✖✖

✦ *AnaComical Players* — The actors and comedians in this small open theater in the Fitness Fairground put on an improvisational comedy performance, tagging a member of the audience to appear as a contestant in a game show about health. Duration: 15 minutes. ✖

✦ *Fitness Fairground* — This large and lively exhibition center presents a collection of both serious and lighthearted exhibits focused on lifestyles and personal health. Visitors can try out the latest workout and fitness-monitoring equipment, receive personalized suggestions for improving their health and well-being, and learn about the latest medical and health breakthroughs. Despite the fact that some of the exhibits are a bit preachy and biased, this pavilion always attracts a crowd. A gift shop features health-oriented books and other items for visitors in a shopping mode. ✖

HORIZONS PAVILION: The large building next to the Wonders of Life that looks like a giant flying saucer is the Horizons pavilion. Enclosing the domed OmniSphere theater, one of the largest movie screens in the world, the pavilion is dedicated to a spectacular ride and show that explores how we will live and work in the twenty-first century.

✦ *Horizons* — Visitors board four-passenger vehicles on an exploration of past and current speculations about the future. Starting with visions from the past, such as Jules Verne's imaginary flight to the moon, visitors travel through time until they reach the present in the OmniSphere theater, where they are treated to dramatic images of new technologies in action. Turning to the future, twenty-first-century lifestyles are presented as visitors travel through convincing futuristic environments. The line for Horizons tends to move quickly, although when the Universe of Energy audience exits, Horizons can be temporarily swamped. Duration: 15 minutes. ✖✖

WORLD OF MOTION PAVILION: This massive wheel-shaped pavilion, covered in stainless steel, houses It's Fun to be Free, a ride through the past, present, and future of transportation, as well as the Trans-Center exhibition hall, where transportation-related exhibits and the latest models of GM vehicles are on display.

✦ *It's Fun to be Free* — In this charming ride, bare feet, magic carpets, ostriches, bicycles, automobiles, and airplanes are just some of the modes of transportation explored. The highly detailed sets and chaotic scenarios use props that include genuine artifacts from the eras they depict. Audio-Animatronic figures reflecting the vagaries of human nature lend realism to this ride. As they travel into the future of transportation, visitors are treated to a magnificent view of a dazzling, soaring cityscape linked by aerial trains and other exotic vehicles that seem to ascend forever. Duration: 15 minutes. ✗✗

✦ *TransCenter* — Visitors can enter this line-free exhibition center at any time through doors on the east side of the pavilion. TransCenter contains a number of transportation exhibits, including a whimsical animated film about alternatives to the internal combustion engine, displays on fuel conservation and aerodynamics, and a very clever assembly-line robot. TransCenter also gives visitors an up-close look at concept cars and lets them get into the driver's seat of the latest models of full-featured GM vehicles. ✗✗

JOURNEY INTO IMAGINATION PAVILION: This pavilion is housed in a pair of leaning glass pyramids fronted by unpredictable spurting and leaping fountains. It features the Journey Into Imagination attraction, a ride that explores the creative process; the Magic Eye Theater's special 3-D movie presentation; and The Image Works exhibition center, a hands-on electronic playground.

✦ *Journey Into Imagination* — An eccentric adventurer named Dreamfinder and his purple sidekick Figment lead visitors on a flight of fancy, exploring the realms where imagination and ideas flourish — in music, art, theater, literature, science, and technology. Huge fanciful sets are interspersed with laser effects and bursts of music. There is an underlying structure to the sequences in the ride, but it is not particularly clear to most first-time visitors, who find it fairly disjointed and even boring. This attraction is probably best enjoyed as a purely sensory experience. If you are not particularly fond of cuteness, skip it. Duration: 14 minutes. ✗

✦ *Magic Eye Theater* — Although slated to be replaced soon, the current show, *Captain EO*, was directed by Francis Coppola, using special effects created by George Lucas. Starring Michael Jackson and Angelica Huston, this 3-D film takes viewers wearing special glasses on a visual journey through an alien universe. A motley crew of strange and silly beings of questionable competence under the command of Captain EO (Michael Jackson) are under orders to find the Supreme Being (Angelica Huston) and give her a special gift that will change her gloomy planet into a place of merriment. Captain EO and his crew become embroiled in a lively adventure expressed in music, dance, comedy, and high drama. While the dance styles might seem a little dated, the video and sound effects help create one of the most realistic 3-D experiences anywhere. Duration: 20 minutes. ✗✗

✦ *The Image Works* — This high-tech electronic environment is a place to play with light, sound, color, and video. Hands-on exhibits include neon light tunnels, electronic paint boxes, areas of floor that generate musical tones to be played with the feet, and lasers that draw geometric patterns. A nearby shop sells a wide variety of film and a small selection of cameras, lenses, and videos. The Image Works appeals primarily to children, who can spend vast amounts of time in the area. However, adults who like simple razzle-dazzle and have time to spare may find it worth a look, especially if they can elbow their way to the controls of an exhibit. ✗

THE LAND PAVILION: Food and farming — past, present, and future — are explored in this largest of the Future World pavilions. The massive tri-level building, with its glass roof and greenhouses, is a combination science experiment and theme attraction. The Land pavilion houses the Harvest Theater film attraction, the Kitchen Kabaret stage show, the Listen to The Land boat ride attraction, and the

Harvest Tour of the greenhouses. Also in the pavilion are a gift shop selling gardeners' goodies, the Farmer's Market food court, and the Land Grille Room, one of the two full-service restaurants in Future World.

✦ *Listen to The Land* — Located on the lower level of the pavilion, this boat ride is a pleasant, relaxing, and informative journey through the history of agriculture. A live guide travels with visitors through three ecological biomes: a tropical rain forest; a hot, harsh desert; and a replica of the American prairie, depicting a small family farm at the turn of the century. As they cruise through The Land's impressive experimental greenhouses, visitors learn about applied future technologies in agriculture. Much of the produce and fish grown in the greenhouses is served in the Land Grille Room restaurant. Duration: 13 minutes. ✖✖✖

✦ *Harvest Theater* — In the Harvest Theater, a 70mm film entitled *Symbiosis* examines the inter-relationship between humans and the land through a series of spectacular images from around the world, some beautiful and some nightmarish. The film shows how humans have adapted the environment to suit their needs and describes some of the resulting environmental problems, touching only lightly on the solutions. Made about a decade ago, the film has a seriously dated, slightly whiny feel to it and presents some questionable or incomplete information. Perhaps the best approach is to consider it a nice air-conditioned break from standing and walking, and focus on its strong visual aspects. Duration: 19 minutes. ✖

✦ *Kitchen Kabaret* — Hostess Bonnie Appetit and a cast of singing and dancing Audio-Animatronic fruits, vegetables, and other foods — including characters like Mr. Eggz, a dreadful punster who doesn't know when to quit — present a dandy musical revue based on the basic food groups and nutrition. Although the show does not reflect the most current nutritional information, it transforms a potentially dull subject into an unexpectedly enjoyable experience. Duration: 14 minutes. ✖✖

✦ *Harvest Tour* — This walking tour takes up where the Listen to The Land boat cruise leaves off. Covering many of the same topics, the tour explores them in greater depth, with an emphasis on the experiments underway in the greenhouses. Visitors have a chance to ask questions and pick up gardening tips from the guides, all of whom hold degrees in agricultural fields. Tours are limited to ten people and leave every half hour between 9:30 AM and 4:30 PM. Reservations are required and must be made in person at the Guided Tour Waiting Area. Only same-day reservations are taken. Duration: 45 minutes to 1 hour. ✖

THE LIVING SEAS PAVILION: The rippling façade of this massive pavilion suggests a natural shore-line, complete with crashing waves. Here, visitors experience life under the oceans. The Living Seas houses one of the world's largest saltwater aquariums, a mammal research center, a living reef, and numerous exhibits on marine topics. The Living Seas Gift Shop features marine-themed gifts, and the Coral Reef Restaurant offers diners a dramatic view of the aquarium as they eat.

✦ *Caribbean Coral Reef Ride* — This is not strictly a ride, but a pavilion-wide experience. After a short dramatic film on the interrelationship between humans and the ocean, visitors descend in the Hydrolator (a simulated elevator ride) to the ocean floor, where they board Seacabs for a short ride through the twenty-seven-foot-deep tropical aquarium. The Seacab ride ends at Sea Base Alpha, an under-water research facility. Here, visitors can take some time to view the more than two hundred species of sea life in the aquarium, watch the sleepy manatees and other residents of the Marine Mammal Center, and explore the exhibits on aquaculture and ocean ecosystems. A marine biologist is on hand to answer questions. Duration: 20 minutes; visitors may explore Sea Base Alpha as long as they wish. ✖✖✖

✳

EVENTS AND LIVE ENTERTAINMENT

Live entertainment, including marching bands and other musical events, is scheduled throughout the day until about 6 PM at various Future World sites. Visitors can pick up an entertainment schedule at Earth Station, behind the Epcot geosphere. Schedules are also available at most Future World shops.

ILLUMINATIONS: This sensational fireworks, laser, music, and water show occurs over the World Showcase Lagoon nightly, between 8 and 10 PM, depending on the time of year. There is actually no really good viewing area in Future World, since the show is oriented to the World Showcase. For a good view, visitors need to arrive at the World Showcase at least half an hour before show time. Some of the best viewing locations close to Future World include Cantina de San Angel at the Mexico pavilion, along the lagoon on both sides of the United Kingdom pavilion, and on the bridge promenade in front of the France pavilion. Duration: 20 minutes. ✖✖✖

TOUR: *Guided Tour of Epcot* — This tour presents an overview of both the World Showcase and Future World. The attractions often visited in Future World include Cranium Command, Horizons, and World of Motion, with a break for lunch at the Farmer's Market in The Land pavilion, followed by two World Showcase attractions, the film *Impressions de France* and The American Adventure. (Attractions visited may vary.) The tour is limited to twenty-five people and leaves from the Tour Desk at Epcot's Entrance Plaza at 9:45 AM. No advance reservations are taken; about $5. Duration: 4 hours. ✖✖

✳

FULL-SERVICE RESTAURANTS

Guests staying at WDW resorts can make restaurant reservations up to three days in advance. Same-day reservations should be made the moment the park opens, at Earth Station, at a WorldKey Information Service kiosk, or at the restaurant itself. Smoking is not permitted in the restaurants. See "Restaurants," page 167, for detailed restaurant reviews and reservation strategies.

THE LAND PAVILION: *The Land Grille Room* — This pleasant, intimate restaurant, furnished with comfortable booths, revolves slowly, giving diners a view of three simulated environments — rain forest, desert, and prairie. The menu features regional American entrees, as well as sandwiches and salads. Beer, wine, and spirits are served. Open for breakfast, lunch, and dinner; reservations necessary.

THE LIVING SEAS PAVILION: *Coral Reef Restaurant* — The Living Seas pavilion's giant aquarium forms one wall of this atmospheric, dimly lit restaurant. Tables are arranged in tiers so that everyone has a clear view. On arrival, guests receive picture cards to help them identify the marine life they are watching. The menu features fresh seafood. Beer, wine, and spirits are served. Open for lunch and dinner; reservations necessary.

✳

COCKTAIL LOUNGES AND CAFES

A number of refreshment stands in Future World serve all-day snacks and fast-food meals. Most have menus designed to appeal to families with children. Those listed below are especially pleasant rest stops and also make ideal meeting spots for visitors who want to shop or tour separately and rendezvous later. Two are in the World Showcase, but they are directly adjacent to Future World. The lively Rose & Crown Pub in the nearby United Kingdom pavilion is a particularly good place to enjoy before-dinner cocktails.

THE LAND PAVILION: *Farmer's Market* — A wealth of fast-food booths line one side of this food court, with offerings that include pasta, barbecued chicken, soup, salad, and the best ice cream in Future World. Also available are coffee, espresso, beer, and wine. The Farmer's Market is a place to avoid between 11 AM and 2 PM, and between 5 and 7:30 PM, when it is mobbed with crowds. ☕️🍸

UNITED KINGDOM PAVILION IN THE WORLD SHOWCASE: *Rose & Crown Pub* — Several fine British ales are on tap in this busy and beloved hangout of World Showcase veterans. Along with beverages, pub snacks such as Stilton cheese and Scotch eggs are offered. Visitors who order snacks or drinks at the bar can carry them to the outdoor terrace adjacent to the Rose & Crown Dining Room. A traditional high tea is served at 4 PM; same-day reservations, made at the restaurant itself or at Earth Station, are required. ☕️🍸

MEXICO PAVILION IN THE WORLD SHOWCASE: *Cantina de San Angel* — This outdoor cafe overlooking the World Showcase Lagoon serves Mexican snacks such as burritos and tostadas as well as frozen Margaritas, beer, coffee, hot chocolate, and churros. ☕️🍸

❋

SERVICES

WORLDKEY INFORMATION SERVICE: This information and reservation system is headquartered in Earth Station, where visitors arrive early in the day to make restaurant reservations. There is also a WorldKey Information Service kiosk located at the Entrance Plaza to the World Showcase. The system's simple-to-use touch-screen computers offer detailed information about all of Epcot and schedules for the day's events and shows. Also, by touching the words *Call Attendant,* visitors can speak directly to a Guest Relations representative to make restaurant reservations.

TELEPHONES: Public telephones are located in the Entrance Plaza, near Spaceship Earth; on the far side of CommuniCore East; on the far side of CommuniCore West; outside and inside the Odyssey restaurant; and outside the Journey Into Imagination pavilion. For quieter, air-conditioned conversations, use the telephones at FutureCom in CommuniCore West, or slip into the Coral Reef Restaurant or the Land Grille Room, where phones are located in an alcove at the entrance.

REST ROOMS: Public rest rooms are located outside Epcot's main gate; in the Entrance Plaza, near Spaceship Earth; on the far side of CommuniCore East; on the far side of CommuniCore West; and outside the Journey Into Imagination pavilion. There are fairly deserted rest rooms in the World of Motion pavilion, which can be entered directly through TransCenter; in The Land pavilion next to the Land Grille Room, and in the entrance hall to the Coral Reef Restaurant. The rest rooms inside the Odyssey Restaurant are also generally pleasant and unfrequented.

MESSAGE CENTER: At Walt Disney World's computerized Message Center, located in Earth Station at the Guest Services Desk, visitors can leave and retrieve messages for one another. The Message Center is on a network also shared by the Magic Kingdom and Disney-MGM Studios, so visitors at one park can exchange messages with companions visiting elsewhere.

FILM AND TWO-HOUR EXPRESS DEVELOPING: Film is available at most of the shops in Future World. Drop-off points for express developing are at the Kodak Camera Center at Epcot's Entrance Plaza, and at the Cameras & Film shop in the Journey Into Imagination pavilion. Developed pictures can be picked up in the Kodak Camera Center or delivered to any WDW resort.

CAMERA RENTAL: Video cameras (and replacement batteries) and 35mm cameras are available in the Kodak Camera Center at Epcot's Entrance Plaza, and in Cameras & Film at Journey Into Imagination.

MAIL DROPS: There are mail drops at the following locations in Future World: Epcot's main entrance; the Guest Relations Window at Epcot's Entrance Plaza, near the Kodak Camera Center; Earth Station; CommuniCore East; CommuniCore West; and Odyssey Restaurant. There is a postage stamp machine near the lockers at Epcot's Entrance Plaza.

BANKING: Banking and foreign currency exchange services are available at Sun Bank, located at Epcot's Entrance Plaza. Personal checks up to $25 can be cashed at Earth Station, behind the Epcot geosphere. An American Express cash machine is located just outside Epcot's Entrance Plaza.

LOCKERS: Lockers are located at Epcot's Entrance Plaza, near the Kodak Camera Center, and at the Bus Information Center.

PACKAGE PICKUP: To avoid carrying purchases, visitors can forward them free of charge to the Guest Relations Window at Epcot's Entrance Plaza and pick them up as they leave the park. Allow two to three hours between purchase and pickup.

FIRST AID: The first-aid office is adjacent to the Odyssey Restaurant. Aspirin and other first-aid needs are dispensed free of charge. Over-the-counter medications are available at the Centorium in CommuniCore East and at the Stroller Shop in Epcot's Entrance Plaza. They are not on display and must be requested.

VISITORS WITH DISABILITIES: A complimentary guidebook for disabled guests is available at Earth Station, behind the Epcot geosphere. All attractions in Future World have wheelchair access except the following, where disabled visitors need to be able to leave their wheelchairs to board the ride vehicle: Spaceship Earth, Body Wars, Horizons, and Journey Into Imagination.

WHEELCHAIR RENTALS: Wheelchairs and motorized wheelchairs may be rented outside the main gate near the handicapped parking area, at Epcot's Entrance Plaza, and at the International Gateway. Motorized wheelchair replacements are available in the World Showcase at Glas und Porzellan in Germany and Lords and Ladies in the United Kingdom.

HEARING-IMPAIRED VISITORS: A written text of Epcot's attractions is available at Earth Station, behind the Epcot geosphere, as are personal translator unit (PTU) listening devices for some of the attractions. A telecommunications device for the deaf (TDD) is available at Earth Station and at FutureCom in CommuniCore West. Hearing aid–compatible and amplified telephones are located throughout Epcot.

F U T U R E   W O R L D

SIGHT-IMPAIRED VISITORS: Tape players and touring cassettes that describe the park are available at Earth Station, behind the Epcot geosphere.

FOREIGN LANGUAGE ASSISTANCE: Personal translator units (PTUs) that translate some attractions and presentations into French, Spanish, and German are available at Earth Station, behind the Epcot geosphere. Also available are park maps in French, Spanish, and German.

✷

COMING ATTRACTIONS

Walt Disney conceived of Future World as an exposition center that would be continually changing. As a result, new attractions are always in the works and are always subject to modifications and delays. At the time of publication, several new additions and the updating of many of the current attractions were scheduled for Future World.

MAGIC EYE THEATER: A new 3-D movie, perhaps based on the movie *Honey, I Shrunk the Kids,* is expected to dazzle visitors when it premieres in 1994 at the Journey Into Imagination pavilion. It will replace *Captain EO,* which may be moving to Tomorrowland at the Magic Kingdom.

JOURNEYS IN SPACE: This new attraction has been in the planning stages for some time and may replace the current Horizons attraction. High-tech systems and thrilling special effects will create the illusion of a journey through outer space and into distant galaxies.

THE LAND PAVILION: During the next two years, The Land pavilion will undergo a major updating and remodeling. Kitchen Kabaret will take on a nutritional rock and roll theme, and *Symbiosis* will be replaced by an updated attraction. The pavilion's restaurants also will be restructured.

✷

Half-Day Tours at Future World

The morning and evening half-day tours that follow are designed to allow first-time visitors to experience the best of Future World in four to six hours, including lunch or dinner. If possible, make your restaurant reservation in advance.

The Morning Nature and Technology Tour, below, is designed for low-attendance times: September through April, excluding holidays. (If you wish to visit Future World in the morning during the summer or during holiday periods, you will be better off joining the Guided Tour of Epcot, which leaves from the Tour Desk at 9:45 AM.) Be sure to enter Future World through Epcot's main entrance for the morning tour. The International Gateway entrance often opens one half hour later and is some distance from Future World. The IllumiNations Afternoon and Evening Tour may be used effectively year round, since attendance at Future World tends to drop dramatically after 5 PM.

To create your own custom vacation at Walt Disney World, you can combine one of the half-day Future World tours with a half-day tour from any other theme park. For example, combine a morning tour at Typhoon Lagoon with the IllumiNations Afternoon and Evening Tour. The theme parks are most crowded in the afternoons, which is an ideal time to take advantage of the resort amenities at Walt Disney World.

✦ *FUTURE WORLD* ✦

✦

MORNING NATURE AND TECHNOLOGY TOUR

Five to six hours — September through April — including lunch.
If possible, a day or two before this tour reserve a late lunch (1 PM or later)
at the Land Grille Room or the Coral Reef Restaurant.

✔ Eat a full breakfast before leaving your hotel.

✔ Arrive at Epcot's Entrance Plaza at least one half hour before the official opening time. While waiting for the rest of the park to open, ride **SPACESHIP EARTH,** which often opens about one half hour before the park. As you exit the ride in Earth Station, pick up an entertainment schedule at Guest Relations.

✔ If you do not have a lunch reservation: After you leave Spaceship Earth at Earth Station, step over to the WorldKey Information Service and make a lunch reservation for 1 PM or later at the Land Grille Room or the Coral Reef Restaurant. If reservations are not available or you prefer a light meal, plan to enjoy a late lunch at the Farmer's Market food court in The Land pavilion.

✔ When the park opens (between 8 and 9 AM), visit, in the order listed below, those attractions that interest you:

- Wonders of Life pavilion — **BODY WARS** and/or **CRANIUM COMMAND**
- Universe of Energy pavilion — **UNIVERSE OF ENERGY** (if there is a short wait)
- The Land pavilion — **LISTEN TO THE LAND** and **KITCHEN KABARET** (if time permits)
- The Living Seas pavilion — **CARIBBEAN CORAL REEF RIDE** (allow thirty minutes)
- If you still have a half hour or so before your lunch reservation, visit the exhibits in Communi-Core West, especially **FUTURECOM.**

✔ Plan to arrive at your lunch destination ten minutes early. If you are lunching at the Farmer's Market, arrive at your leisure, the later the better for avoiding crowds.

✔ If you wish to see a bit more of Future World after lunch, visit some of the following attractions:

- Journey Into Imagination pavilion — **MAGIC EYE THEATER** (if the line is reasonable)
- CommuniCore East — **BACKSTAGE MAGIC**
- Horizons pavilion — **HORIZONS**
- World of Motion pavilion — **IT'S FUN TO BE FREE.**

✦

ILLUMINATIONS AFTERNOON AND EVENING TOUR

Four to five hours — year round — including dinner, on nights when IllumiNations is at 9 PM or later.
If possible, make your dinner reservations a day or two before this tour.
If you prefer an early dinner (6 PM or before), select from the Land Grille Room
or the Coral Reef Restaurant in Future World.
If you prefer a late dinner, reserve a seating at the end of your tour no less than ninety minutes
before IllumiNations begins. Select from the Rose & Crown Dining Room
or the San Angel Inn Restaurante in the adjacent World Showcase.

F U T U R E   W O R L D

✔ Arrive at Epcot's Entrance Plaza at 4:30 PM. At the gate, pick up an entertainment schedule, which lists the show times for live performances and IllumiNations.

✔ If you do not have a dinner reservation: Proceed to Earth Station and use the WorldKey Information Service to make an early dinner reservation (6 PM or before) at the Land Grille Room or the Coral Reef Restaurant. Or, reserve a late dinner at the Rose & Crown Dining Room or the San Angel Inn Restaurante. (Let the reservationist know that you need to finish your meal before IllumiNations.) If no seatings are available or if you prefer a light meal, plan to enjoy dinner at the Farmer's Market food court in The Land pavilion or Le Cellier cafeteria in the Canada pavilion. Neither takes reservations.

✔ If you have reserved an early dinner at the Coral Reef Restaurant or the Land Grille Room or if you plan to eat at the Farmer's Market, visit, in the order listed below, those attractions that interest you. Your tour will be temporarily interrupted for dinner.
  - SPACESHIP EARTH
  - The Living Seas pavilion — CARIBBEAN CORAL REEF RIDE
  - The Land pavilion — LISTEN TO THE LAND
  - Universe of Energy pavilion — UNIVERSE OF ENERGY
  - Wonders of Life pavilion — BODY WARS (If the wait is more than fifteen minutes, you may want to skip it and see the CRANIUM COMMAND attraction instead.)
  - World of Motion pavilion — IT'S FUN TO BE FREE (If there is no wait and you have more than forty minutes before IllumiNations begins.)
  - One half hour before IllumiNations begins, proceed to the World Showcase.

✔ If you have reserved a late dinner in the World Showcase at the Rose & Crown Dining Room or the San Angel Inn Restaurante, or if you plan to eat at Le Cellier cafeteria, visit, in this order, those attractions that interest you:
  - SPACESHIP EARTH
  - The Living Seas pavilion — CARIBBEAN CORAL REEF RIDE
  - The Land pavilion — LISTEN TO THE LAND
  - Universe of Energy pavilion — UNIVERSE OF ENERGY
  - Wonders of Life pavilion — BODY WARS (If the wait is more than ten minutes, skip it and see the CRANIUM COMMAND attraction instead.)
  - World of Motion pavilion — IT'S FUN TO BE FREE (If there is no wait and you have more than thirty minutes before your dinner reservation.)
  - Plan to arrive at your dinner destination in the World Showcase about ten minutes early.

✔ About twenty minutes before ILLUMINATIONS is scheduled to begin, position yourself along the World Showcase promenade. Good views of IllumiNations can be found at the following locations:
  - Mexico (near Cantina de San Angel)
  - United Kingdom (on either side of the United Kingdom pavilion)
  - Along the promenade between Mexico and Norway
  - Along the promenade between the United Kingdom and France.

✔ After IllumiNations ends and while the crowds rush out, you may want to linger in the World Showcase. In time, a bus will stop for you anywhere along the promenade and give you a lift to your exit. ◆

THE WORLD SHOWCASE AT EPCOT

The World Showcase — occupying one half of Epcot Center — is designed as a permanent and ever-expanding world's fair. To date, eleven international pavilions encircle the forty-acre World Showcase Lagoon. Each pavilion features entertainment, restaurants, and shops, and each displays that country's architecture, clothing, horticulture, music, dance, crafts, and fine arts.

WHEN TO GO: Large crowds arrive here between lunch and dinner, but because the World Showcase is spread out over a very large area, it rarely feels overcrowded. The best time to visit is before noon, when most visitors are focusing on Epcot's Future World, and at night when the pavilions are strikingly lit. In the early evening, the World Showcase restaurants fill with diners, and crowds linger to wait for the IllumiNations fireworks show, which occurs at closing time. Opening and closing times vary throughout the year, so check ahead at Guest Services in your resort, or call 407 824-4321.

HOW TO GET THERE: The World Showcase is customarily entered by walking through Epcot's Future World from the main gate toward the World Showcase Lagoon. The large parking lot at Epcot is free to guests at WDW resorts (day visitors are charged a nominal fee). The parking lot is served by trams. WDW buses and monorails stop at Epcot's main entrance. The buses serve all WDW hotels. The monorail system services the Transportation and Ticket Center, the Magic Kingdom, and the following resorts: Contemporary, Polynesian, and Grand Floridian. Visitors can also enter the World Showcase directly through the International Gateway. Trams service the International Gateway from the following resorts: Dolphin, Swan, and Yacht Club. The Beach Club is within walking distance.

IN-PARK TRANSPORTATION: The promenade around the World Showcase Lagoon is 1¼ miles long. Three double-decker buses circle the promenade clockwise, stopping for passengers at bus stops located at Mexico, Canada, France, and Italy. Watercraft called FriendShips carry passengers back and forth across the lagoon, from Germany or Morocco to the World Showcase Entrance Plaza near Future World.

✳

ATTRACTIONS

✗✗✗ – Good entertainment. **✗✗** – Enjoyable if you have the time and interest. **✗** – Of limited appeal.

MEXICO: The Mexico pavilion is designed as a massive Mayan pyramid surrounded by lush tropical foliage. At the entrance is an exhibition of Mexican and pre-Columbian art. The interior of the pavilion is fashioned after an open-air market in a Mexican village at twilight. Handicrafts, jewelry, and clothing are offered in an array of colorful shops housed in the colonial-style façades that encircle the town square. At the rear of the pavilion, a restaurant overlooks an indoor river and a smoking volcano in the distance.

✦ *El Rio del Tiempo* — This charming Mexican travelogue by boat lacks the sophisticated special effects of many Disney attractions, but its simplicity is refreshing. It makes a relaxing interlude after lunch or dinner. Duration: 7 minutes. **✗✗**

NORWAY: As visitors enter this serene Old World pavilion, a fourteenth-century fortress and medieval church give way to the cobblestone courtyards and steep gabled rooftops of a traditional Norwegian town

WORLD SHOWCASE

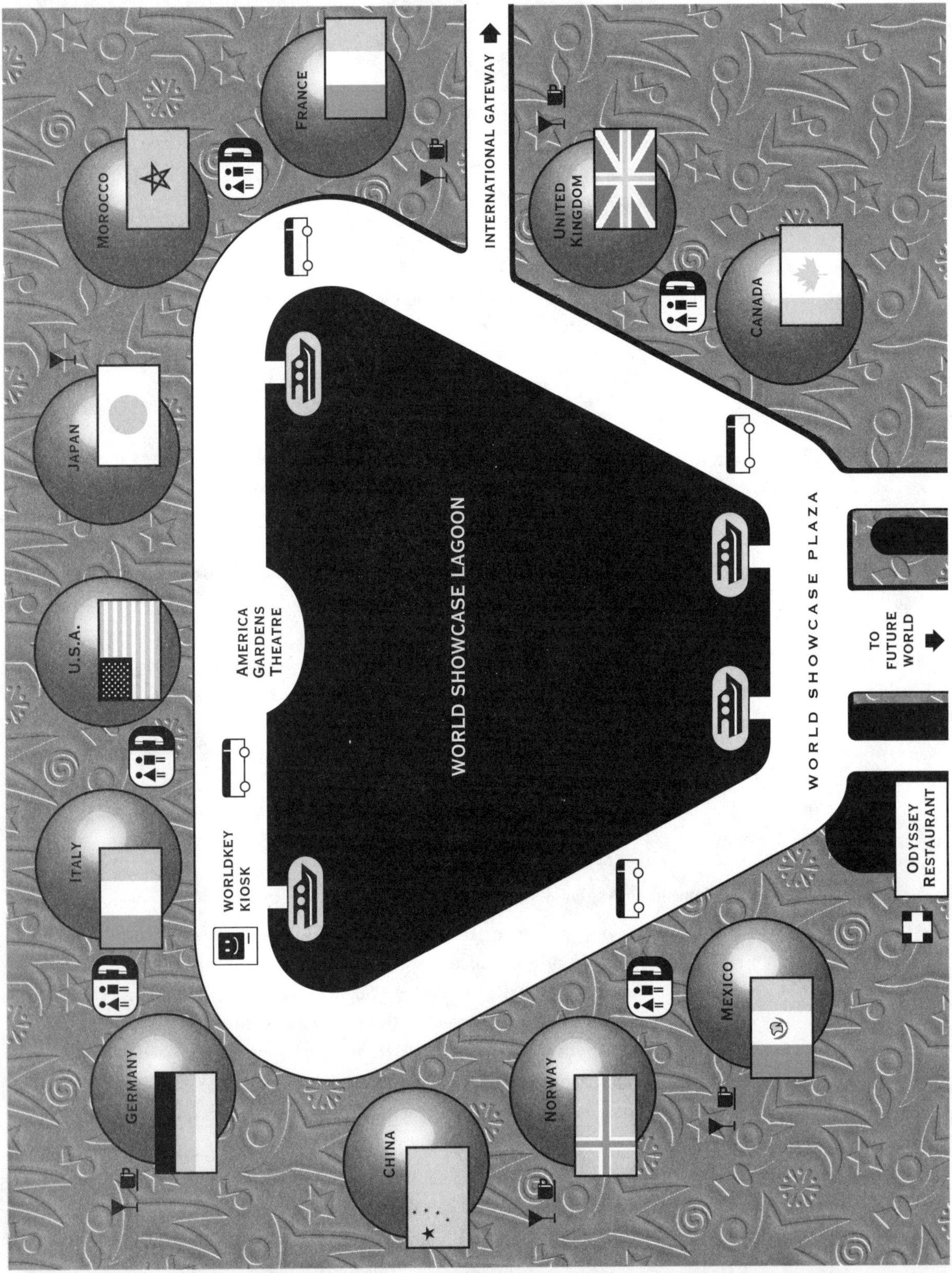

FRANCE

MOROCCO

INTERNATIONAL GATEWAY

UNITED KINGDOM

CANADA

JAPAN

U.S.A.

AMERICA GARDENS THEATRE

WORLD SHOWCASE LAGOON

WORLD SHOWCASE PLAZA

TO FUTURE WORLD

ITALY

WORLDKEY KIOSK

ODYSSEY RESTAURANT

GERMANY

CHINA

NORWAY

MEXICO

square. Shops housed in the fortress offer hand-knit woolens, Norwegian wood carvings, and metal and glass artifacts.

✦ *Maelstrom* — Clever special effects and Audio-Animatronics enliven this dramatic shipboard passage through the era of Viking sea exploration. But take care: Visitors in the front of the boat may get splashed. Following the ride, a short film showcases the spirit of Norway. Duration: 15 minutes. ✗✗

CHINA: A colorful half-scale model of the Temple of Heaven is the centerpiece of this exotic pavilion. Traditional Chinese music accompanies strollers through charming Oriental gardens filled with roses, mulberry trees, water oaks, and pomegranates and accented with landscaped reflecting pools. The large shopping gallery offers a multitude of Chinese gifts and goods, including furniture and fine arts. The exhibition of Chinese art at the House of the Whispering Willows gallery is particularly impressive.

✦ *Wonders of China* — This vivid, fast-paced Circle-Vision 360 film is a living essay on the people and culture of China narrated by a fancifully recreated Li Po, treasured poet of ancient China. Viewers, who stand within the large circular screen, are transported from the vast grasslands of Mongolia to modern-day Shanghai. No seating. Duration: 19 minutes. ✗✗✗

GERMANY: Fairy-tale Bavarian architecture surrounds the charming town square of the Germany pavilion. A statue of St. George and the dragon dominates the center of the square, which is ringed by a festive Biergarten restaurant and entertainment hall, plus several colorfully stocked shops offering wines, toys, glassware, and timepieces. At the rear of the square, a chiming glockenspiel rings the hour, and a strolling musician plays waltzes and polkas on the accordion.

ITALY: A scaled-down version of the Venetian Campanile and a faithful replica of the Doge's Palace dominate the piazza of the Italy pavilion. The fountain at the rear of the piazza is a lovely re-creation of the Fontana de Nettuno. Venetian bridges lead to a gondola landing at the edge of the World Showcase Lagoon. The popular Commedia di Bologna troupe performs spirited and amusing outdoor theater based on Italian folktales. Members of the audience are invited to play parts.

U.S.A.: The American Adventure pavilion is housed in a colonial-style plantation mansion. Inside, the Heritage Manor gift shop sells glassware, toys, and hand-painted porcelain. The colorful gardens surrounding the pavilion are dotted with sycamore and magnolia trees, and a carefully tended rose garden at the side of the pavilion blooms with specimens named after U.S. Presidents. At the edge of the World Showcase Lagoon, the America Gardens Theatre presents live entertainment throughout the day.

✦ *The American Adventure* — This recently updated Audio-Animatronic performance is an outstanding example of Disney technology. Mark Twain and Benjamin Franklin guide the audience on a patriotic multimedia trip through American historic events with contributions from Susan B. Anthony and Andrew Carnegie, to name a few. The Disney genius for detail shines in every vignette, from Will Rogers' spin on a lariat to Theodore Roosevelt's notoriously ruddy complexion. Duration: 29 minutes. ✗✗✗

JAPAN: In the garden of the Japanese pavilion, rocks, manicured trees, fish ponds, and wind chimes are carefully blended to create a mood of peaceful reflection. A scarlet *torii* gate, symbol of good luck, greets visitors arriving by way of the World Showcase Lagoon. The pavilion's prominent pagoda is a replica of the eighth-century Horyuji Temple of Nara. Throughout the day, classical Japanese music and dances are performed in the pavilion, and the Bijutsu-kan Gallery features traditional and modern Japanese art.

MOROCCO: This pavilion meticulously recreates the architecture and mystery of Islam. A replica of the Koutoubia Minaret of Marrakesh greets visitors at the entrance to a flower-filled courtyard, complete with a splashing fountain. The Bab Boujouloud gate leads into the Medina, a bazaar where rugs, jewelry, clothing, leather goods, pottery, and brasswares spill out of shops into the narrow passageways. The exquisitely tiled Gallery of Arts and History exhibits examples of fine Moroccan craftsmanship.

FRANCE: The Belle Epoque reigns once more in the Parisian streets and gardens of the French pavilion. Models of the Eiffel Tower and the Galerie des Halles are reproduced here alongside mansard roofs, poster-covered kiosks, and sidewalk cafes. Quaint shops along the street offer perfumes, leather goods, jewelry, and crystal. Strolling street musicians sing familiar French ballads, an acting troupe stages comic skits, and talented French artists render portraits of visitors along the waterfront. In the large park at the side of the pavilion, the sweeping lawn and Lombardy poplars are reminiscent of the Georges Seurat painting, *A Sunday Afternoon on the Island of La Grande Jatte.*

  ✦ *Impressions de France* — Shown in the Palais du Cinema, this wide-screen travel film immerses viewers in the culture and topography of France. The soundtrack highlights France's contributions to the world of classical music. Duration: 18 minutes. ✗✗

UNITED KINGDOM: In this pavilion, visitors stroll from an elegant British town square through English gardens and down a street filled with small Tudor, Georgian, and Victorian buildings. A replica of Anne Hathaway's thatched-roof cottage adds special charm. London plane trees and box hedges line the sidewalks, and visitors can use the classic red phone booths, once hallmarks of the United Kingdom. Several lovely shops offer toys, cashmere, china, crystal, and fine teas. Of special interest are the hedged herb and perennial gardens behind the Tea Caddy, and the formal garden courtyard and gazebo at the rear of the pavilion.

CANADA: Magnificent towering totem poles frame the Northwest Mercantile trading post at the entrance to the Canada pavilion. The natural beauty of the Canadian Rockies, complete with a waterfall and a rushing stream, is impressively captured here. The Northwest Mercantile sells Indian and Eskimo crafts and traditional trapper's clothing. The Caledonia Bagpipe Band can be heard by visitors walking under the birch, willow, maple, and plum trees in the pavilion's Victoria Gardens, where more than forty different flowering plants are always in bloom.

  ✦ *O Canada!* — This scenic film sweeps across Canada, from the Pacific Coast to the Rockies to the Arctic Ocean. Standing within the Circle-Vision 360 screen, visitors are surrounded by Canada's breathtaking natural wonders, along with scenes of its sporting events and urban and rural life. No seating. Duration: 18 minutes. ✗✗✗

EVENTS AND LIVE ENTERTAINMENT

Live entertainment is scheduled daily in each international pavilion. In addition, guest artisans from the individual nations demonstrate their crafts throughout the day. As you enter the park, pick up an entertainment schedule at Earth Station, behind the Epcot geosphere, or at the International Gateway near the France pavilion. Schedules are also available at most World Showcase shops.

AMERICA GARDENS THEATRE: This outdoor theater is located on the edge of the World Showcase Lagoon in front of the U.S.A. pavilion. Here, regularly scheduled performances of American folk dancing and music are featured throughout the day and evening. On weekends during the summer and on holidays, guest celebrities are featured. There is little shade here, so choose a time when the sun is not too hot and you are ready to sit down and relax. Duration: 25 minutes. ✘

ILLUMINATIONS: This spectacular fireworks, laser, music, and water show bursts into action over the World Showcase Lagoon nightly between 8 and 10 PM, depending on the time of year. Arrive at the World Showcase early for a good viewing position along the promenade. Some of the best viewing locations are the Cantina de San Angel in Mexico; lagoonside at the Rose & Crown Dining Room in the United Kingdom; along the promenade between China, Germany, and Italy; and along the promenade between France, the United Kingdom, and Canada. There are somewhat limited but dramatic views at the gondola landing in front of Italy and on the upper deck in front of the Matsu No Ma Lounge in Japan. Duration: 20 minutes. ✘✘✘

TOUR: *Hidden Treasures of the World Showcase* — This walking tour explores the architecture of the international pavilions and reveals many of the construction secrets that make the World Showcase a renowned panorama of design. The tour leaves on Sunday, Wednesday, and Friday at 9:30 AM, and places must be reserved in advance (407 354-1855); about $20. Duration: 3¹/₂ hours. ✘✘

TOUR: *Gardens of the World* — This walking tour explains the horticultural efforts that created the unique, often sensational landscaping in the World Showcase, much of which was imported from the various nations represented. The tour leaves on Monday, Tuesday, and Thursday at 9:30 AM, and places must be reserved in advance (407 354-1855); about $20. Duration: 3¹/₂ hours. ✘✘

TOUR: *Guided Tour of Epcot* — This tour covers both the World Showcase and Future World. The attractions often visited in Future World include Cranium Command, Horizons, and World of Motion, with a break for lunch at The Land, followed by the France and U.S.A. pavilions in the World Showcase. (Attractions visited may vary.) The tour is limited to twenty-five people and leaves from the Tour Desk at Epcot's Entrance Plaza at 9:45 AM. No reservations; about $5. Duration: 4 hours. ✘✘

FULL-SERVICE RESTAURANTS

Guests staying at WDW resorts may make restaurant reservations up to three days in advance. Same-day reservations should be made the moment the park opens, in Earth Station, or at a WorldKey Information Service kiosk, or at the restaurant itself. Smoking is not permitted in most of the World Showcase restaurants. See "Restaurants," page 167, for detailed restaurant reviews and reservation strategies.

MEXICO: *San Angel Inn Restaurante* — Mexican specialties are served at the edge of an indoor river under a cleverly simulated night sky, complete with a smoking volcano in the distance. The atmosphere is both romantic and entertaining. Beer (Dos Equis), wine, and spirits are served. Open for lunch and dinner; reservations necessary.

NORWAY: *Restaurant Akershus* — This Norwegian smorgasbord features a hot and cold buffet of fish, meats, salads, and cheeses. The interior is fashioned as a dining room in a medieval fortress. The service is all-you-can-eat buffet-style, and beer (Ringnes), wine, and spirits are available. Open for lunch and dinner; reservations recommended.

CHINA: *Nine Dragons Restaurant* — Dishes in the cooking styles of several different China provinces are served in a formal Oriental dining room. Entrees are served as individual meals, not family-style dishes. Beer (Tsing Tao), wine, and spirits are available. Open for lunch and dinner; reservations necessary.

GERMANY: *Biergarten* — Diners enjoy traditional German dishes at long communal tables in a huge Bavarian hall. German wines and beer (Beck's, in thirty-three-ounce steins) are served. During dinner, half-hour-long performances feature musicians, yodelers, and folk dancers. Open for lunch and dinner; reservations necessary.

ITALY: *L'Originale Alfredo di Roma Ristorante* — This popular restaurant features Italian dishes, including the house specialty, fettuccine Alfredo. Musicians sing Italian ballads during dinner. Beer, wine, and spirits are served. Open for lunch and dinner; reservations necessary.

JAPAN: *Teppanyaki Dining* — In this large second-floor restaurant above the Mitsukoshi Department Store, guests can enjoy *teppanyaki*-style cooking. Seating is at large communal dining tables, each with its own grill, where a stir-fry chef prepares the meal — a show in itself. The menu includes beef, chicken, or seafood, accompanied with stir-fry vegetables. Beer, wine, and spirits are served. Open for lunch and dinner; reservations necessary.

Tempura Kiku — In this small restaurant adjacent to Teppanyaki Dining, guests are seated at a U-shaped counter surrounding a tempura bar and grill, where they dine on batter-fried chicken, seafood, and vegetables. Beer, wine, and spirits are served. Open for lunch and dinner; no reservations.

MOROCCO: *Restaurant Marrakesh* — Traditional Moroccan cuisine is featured in this exotic dining room. Beef, lamb, fish, and chicken are prepared with couscous, pastries, and a variety of aromatic spices. Musicians and belly dancers entertain guests during lunch and dinner. Beer, wine, and spirits are served. Open for lunch and dinner; reservations recommended.

FRANCE: *Chefs de France* — Traditional French cuisine created by three of France's most celebrated chefs is served in a small, busy, French-style dining room. The menu incorporates fresh seafood from Florida. The wine list is classically French, and beer and spirits are also served. Open for lunch and dinner; reservations necessary.

Bistro de Paris — Located above the Chefs de France, this restaurant serves nouvelle French cuisine in a romantic and intimate setting. French wines, beer, and spirits are served. Open for dinner only (lunch may be offered during peak attendance times); reservations necessary.

Au Petit Café — Light French entrees, salads, and sandwiches are served in this pleasant canopied outdoor cafe, which faces the promenade and affords many excellent people-watching opportunities. Beer, wine, and spirits are served. The restaurant has a smoking section. Open all day; no reservations.

UNITED KINGDOM: *Rose & Crown Dining Room* — This handsome lagoonside restaurant serves steak and kidney pie, roast prime rib, and very good fish and chips. Guests may sit outside on the terrace overlooking the lagoon. Spirits, wine, and a selection of ales on tap are available. Open for lunch and dinner; reservations necessary.

✳ WORLD SHOWCASE ✳

CANADA: *Le Cellier* — In this large but cozy restaurant with its wine-cellar atmosphere, guests select from hearty Canadian dishes such as pork pie, chicken and meatball stew, and poached salmon. Cafeteria-style service with Canadian wine and beer (La Batt's). Open all day; no reservations.

✶

COCKTAIL LOUNGES AND CAFES

The international pavilions have refreshment stands that serve all-day snacks and fast-food meals. A few, listed below, are especially pleasant rest stops and also make ideal meeting spots for visitors who want to shop or tour separately and rendezvous at a later time. For before-dinner cocktails, try the restful Matsu No Ma Lounge in Japan or the lively Rose & Crown Pub in the United Kingdom.

MEXICO: *Cantina de San Angel* — This outdoor cafe, overlooking the World Showcase Lagoon, serves Mexican snacks such as burritos and tostadas, frozen Margaritas, beer, coffee, and hot chocolate. ☕️🍸

NORWAY: *Kringla Bakeri og Kafé* — This pleasant snack bar cafe offers open-faced sandwiches, pastries, and beer. Its shaded outdoor location is perfect for an afternoon or evening rest stop. ☕️🍸

GERMANY: *Sommerfest* — Cold German beers and wines, along with such traditional snacks as soft pretzels and bratwurst, are available at this outdoor cafe. ☕️🍸

    Weinkeller — There's a wine-tasting bar in this lively shop. On a warm day, it is an ideal place to cool off while sampling the wines of Germany. No seating. 🍸

JAPAN: *Matsu No Ma Lounge* — This comfortable and serene second-floor cocktail lounge affords an excellent view of the entire World Showcase and is a great place to cool off on a hot day. The full bar serves Japanese beer, hot sake, and cocktails, as well as sashimi, sushi, and green tea. All the while, soothing Japanese *koto* music is played softly in the background. 🍸

FRANCE: *Boulangerie Pâtisserie* — This popular shop bakes its pastry on the premises and serves strong French-roast coffee that guests can enjoy at outdoor tables. For those who enter the park at the International Gateway, this is a great place to start the morning or end the day. ☕️

    La Maison du Vin — Guests can sample and buy the fine wines of France in this handsome wine shop. No seating. 🍸

UNITED KINGDOM: *Rose & Crown Pub* — This busy public house, a beloved hangout for World Showcase veterans, serves several fine ales on tap. Guests who order snacks or drinks at the bar can carry them to the outdoor terrace adjacent to the Rose & Crown Dining Room. At 4 PM, the pub serves a traditional high tea. It is popular with insiders and must be reserved early. Same-day reservations can be made at Earth Station or at the restaurant itself. ☕️🍸

✶

SERVICES

WORLDKEY INFORMATION SERVICE: This innovative information and reservation computer system is headquartered in Earth Station, where visitors arrive early in the day to make restaurant reservations. There are also WorldKey Information Service kiosks located at the Entrance Plaza to the World Showcase and in front of the Germany pavilion. These simple-to-use touch-screen computers offer information

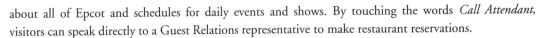

about all of Epcot and schedules for daily events and shows. By touching the words *Call Attendant,* visitors can speak directly to a Guest Relations representative to make restaurant reservations.

TELEPHONES: Outdoor public telephones are located near the rest rooms in Norway, Germany, U.S.A., Morocco, and the United Kingdom. Telephones are also located near the rest rooms in the cooler, quieter restaurants in Mexico, Japan, the United Kingdom, and Canada.

REST ROOMS: Public rest rooms are located in Norway, Germany, U.S.A., Morocco, the United Kingdom, and at the International Gateway. During busy times and for quieter accommodations, slip into the rest rooms at the Rose & Crown Pub (United Kingdom), the Matsu No Ma Lounge (Japan), or the San Angel Inn Restaurante (Mexico).

MESSAGE CENTER: Walt Disney World's computerized Message Center is located in Earth Station at Guest Relations. Here, visitors can leave and retrieve messages for one another. The Message Center is on a network also shared by the Magic Kingdom and Disney-MGM Studios, so visitors at one park can exchange messages with companions visiting elsewhere.

FILM AND TWO-HOUR EXPRESS DEVELOPING: Film is available in at least one shop in every World Showcase pavilion. Drop-off points for two-hour express developing include Mexico (Artesanías Mexicanas), U.S.A. (Heritage Manor Gifts), the International Gateway (World Traveler), and Canada (Northwest Mercantile). Developed pictures can be picked up in the Kodak Camera Center at Epcot's Entrance Plaza or delivered to any WDW resort.

CAMERA RENTAL: Video cameras (and replacement batteries) and 35mm cameras are available in World Traveler at the International Gateway and in the Kodak Camera Center at Epcot's Entrance Plaza. Replacement batteries for video cameras are also available at Die Weinachts Ecke in Germany.

MAIL DROPS: Mail drops are located at the following pavilions: Mexico, China, Germany, U.S.A., France, and the United Kingdom. A postage stamp machine is located near the lockers at Epcot's Entrance Plaza.

BANKING: There are no banking services available inside the World Showcase. The nearest bank and foreign currency exchange is Sun Bank, located at Epcot's Entrance Plaza. If the bank is closed, personal checks up to $25 may be cashed at Earth Station, behind the Epcot geosphere. An American Express cash machine is located just outside Epcot's Entrance Plaza.

LOCKERS: Lockers are located at the International Gateway; at Epcot's Entrance Plaza, just past the Kodak Camera Center; and at the Bus Information Center, just outside Epcot's Entrance Plaza.

PACKAGE PICKUP: To avoid carrying purchases, visitors can forward them free of charge to either Showcase Gifts at the International Gateway or the Guest Relations Window at Epcot's Entrance Plaza to be picked up as they leave. Allow two to three hours between purchase and pickup.

FIRST AID: The first-aid office is adjacent to the Odyssey Restaurant, located near the Mexico pavilion where Future World meets the World Showcase. Aspirin and other first-aid needs are dispensed free of charge. Over-the-counter medications are available at Disney Traders on the World Showcase Plaza. They are not displayed and must be requested at the counter.

VISITORS WITH DISABILITIES: A complimentary guidebook for disabled guests is available at Earth Station, behind the Epcot geosphere. Most attractions in the World Showcase accommodate wheelchairs; however, in Norway disabled visitors must leave their wheelchairs to ride the attraction.

WHEELCHAIR RENTALS: Wheelchairs and motorized wheelchairs may be rented outside Epcot's main gate near the handicapped parking area, at Epcot's Entrance Plaza, and at the International Gateway. Glas und Porzellan in the Germany pavilion and Lords and Ladies in the United Kingdom pavilion have motorized wheelchair replacements.

HEARING-IMPAIRED VISITORS: A written text of Epcot's attractions is available at Earth Station, behind the Epcot geosphere, as are personal translator unit (PTU) listening devices for some of the attractions. A telecommunications device for the deaf (TDD) is available at Earth Station and at FutureCom in CommuniCore West. Hearing aid–compatible and amplified telephones are located throughout Epcot.

SIGHT-IMPAIRED VISITORS: Complimentary touring cassettes that describe the park are available at Earth Station, behind the Epcot geosphere.

FOREIGN LANGUAGE ASSISTANCE: Personal translator units (PTUs) that translate some Epcot attractions and presentations into French, Spanish, and German are available at Earth Station, behind the Epcot geosphere. Also available are park maps in French, Spanish, and German.

✶

COMING ATTRACTIONS

Plans are always on the drawing board for new attractions throughout Walt Disney World. Until ground is actually broken, however, these plans have a way of changing or becoming delayed. At the time of publication, several World Showcase additions have been in the planning stage for some time.

SWITZERLAND: This new pavilion, which has recently lagged in development, is proposed to be built near Norway. The pavilion will include a chalet restaurant and a Matterhorn ride attraction.

RUSSIA: A Russian pavilion featuring an early version of Red Square, complete with onion-dome spires, and attractions and exhibits featuring Russian folktales has long been in the planning stages.

JAPAN: An expansion of the Japanese pavilion will give visitors a taste of modern Japan. In the works are the glitz and glamor of Tokyo's Ginza district and an exciting Mt. Fuji ride.

AFRICA: Plans for the Africa pavilion, located between China and Germany, are again being discussed. Possible attractions include a Congo River ride, perhaps similar to Jungle Cruise.

✶

Half-Day Tours at the World Showcase

The morning and evening half-day tours that follow are designed to allow first-time visitors to experience the best of the World Showcase in four to six hours, including lunch or dinner in one of the World Showcase restaurants. If possible, make your restaurant reservation in advance.

To create your own custom vacation at Walt Disney World, you can combine one of the half-day World

Showcase tours with a half-day tour from any other theme park. For example, combine the Morning Around the World Tour at the World Showcase with an evening tour at Future World. The theme parks are most crowded in the afternoons, which is an ideal time to relax or take advantage of the resort amenities at WDW.

MORNING AROUND THE WORLD TOUR

Four to six hours — year round — including lunch.
If possible, a day or two before this tour reserve a late lunch (1 PM or later) at a World Showcase restaurant.

✔ Eat a full breakfast before leaving your hotel.

✔ Arrive at Epcot's Entrance Plaza or at the International Gateway just before the official opening time. Pick up an entertainment schedule.

✔ When the park opens (between 8 and 9 AM), proceed to the World Showcase Lagoon.

✔ If you do not have a lunch reservation: When the park opens, walk quickly to Earth Station (if you enter the park through Epcot's Entrance Plaza), or to the WorldKey Information Service kiosk in the World Showcase Entrance Plaza (if you enter through the International Gateway). Make a lunch reservation for 1 PM or later at a World Showcase restaurant.

✔ Catch a double-decker bus at the nearest bus stop, either at Mexico, Canada, France, or Italy. Ride the bus around the lagoon once or twice to get a complete overview of the World Showcase.

✔ Get off at the bus stop nearest the pavilion where you will be having lunch, and begin your walking tour of the World Showcase.

✔ Tour the international pavilions in a clockwise direction. As you visit the international pavilions, try to take in some of the following highlights:
  • Mexico — shops and **EL RIO DEL TIEMPO** (if there is no line)
  • Norway — **MAELSTROM** (if the line there is short)
  • China — shops, architecture, and gardens
  • Germany — shops and wine tasting at the Weinkeller
  • Italy — street theater performance and architecture
  • U.S.A. — crafts exhibit and **THE AMERICAN ADVENTURE**
  • Japan — gardens, shops, and street musicians
  • Morocco — shops, architecture, and courtyard musicians
  • France — **IMPRESSIONS DE FRANCE** film presentation (if there is a short wait)
  • United Kingdom — shops, street theater, and Rose & Crown Pub for refreshments
  • Canada — Victoria Gardens and **O CANADA!** film presentation (if time permits).

✔ Plan to arrive at your lunch destination ten minutes early.

ILLUMINATIONS AFTERNOON AND EVENING TOUR

Four to five hours — year round — including dinner, on nights when IllumiNations is at 9 PM or later.
If possible, make a dinner reservation at one of the World Showcase restaurants before this tour.

If you prefer an early dinner, reserve a table at 6 PM or before.
If you prefer a late dinner, reserve a seating for the end of your tour,
no less than ninety minutes before IllumiNations begins (at 9 or 10 PM).

✔ Arrive at the World Showcase at 4:30 PM. Pick up an entertainment schedule, which lists the show times for live performances and IllumiNations.

✔ Catch a double-decker bus at the nearest bus stop, either at Mexico, Canada, France, or Italy.

✔ Ride the bus around the lagoon once or twice to get a complete overview of the World Showcase. If you have not already made an advance restaurant reservation, select an international restaurant where you would like to dine. (Restaurant Marrakesh in Morocco, Biergarten in Germany, and L'Originale Alfredo di Roma Ristorante in Italy all offer entertainment at dinner. The restaurants in Morocco, Germany, and Japan often have available seating, while Italy, France, and Mexico fill up quickly.)

✔ For your early dinner or to begin your tour, get off at the bus stop nearest your selected or reserved restaurant. If you do not have a reservation, request a seating — tables are most plentiful before 6 PM. If you cannot be seated or if you prefer a later dinner, proceed to a WorldKey Information Service kiosk, located in front of Germany or at the World Showcase Entrance Plaza. There, speak with an attendant via touch-screen computer. Tell the attendant that you want a seating that lets you finish your dinner before IllumiNations begins. (If you have difficulty making a reservation, Le Cellier in Canada has cafeteria-style service and Au Petit Café in France and Tempura Kiku in Japan do not take reservations.)

✔ After dinner, tour the World Showcase, walking in a clockwise direction. As you visit the international pavilions, try to take in some of the following highlights:
  • Mexico — shops and **EL RIO DEL TIEMPO** (if there is no line)
  • Norway — **MAELSTROM** (if the line there is short)
  • China — shops, architecture, and **WONDERS OF CHINA** film presentation (if time permits)
  • Germany — wine tasting at the Weinkeller
  • Italy — shops and street theater performance
  • U.S.A. — **THE AMERICAN ADVENTURE** or **AMERICA GARDENS THEATRE** (if time permits)
  • Japan — shops, art exhibit, and before-dinner refreshments at the Matsu No Ma Lounge
  • Morocco — shops and architecture
  • France — **IMPRESSIONS DE FRANCE** film presentation (if there is a short wait)
  • United Kingdom — shops, street theater, and Rose & Crown Pub for refreshments
  • Canada — Victoria Gardens (if there is still daylight).

✔ One half hour before **ILLUMINATIONS** is scheduled to begin, find a viewing spot at the edge of the World Showcase Lagoon. The following locations offer some of the best views:
  • Mexico (at Cantina de San Angel)
  • United Kingdom (on either side of the pavilion)
  • Along the promenade between China, Germany, and Italy
  • Along the promenade between France and the United Kingdom

✔ After IllumiNations, you may want to linger and browse while the crowds rush out. In time, a bus will stop for you anywhere along the promenade and give you a lift to your exit. ◆

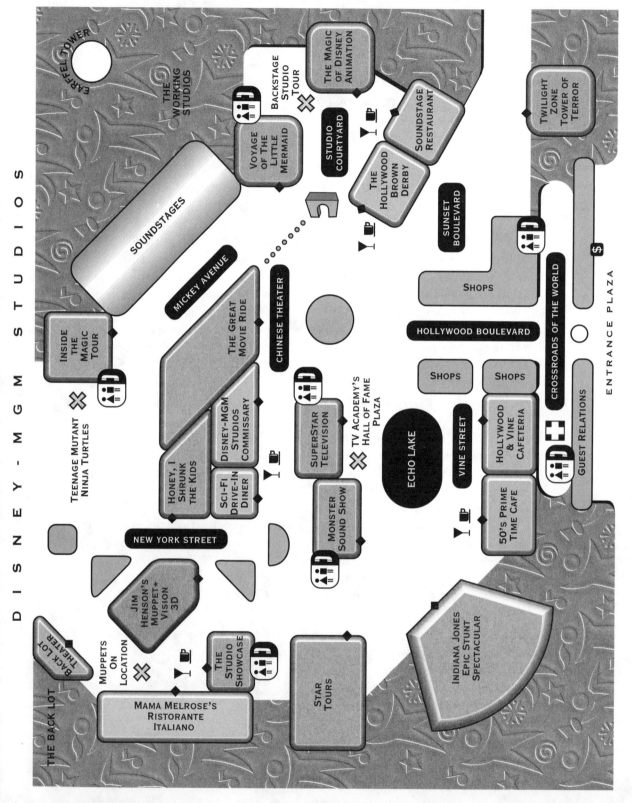

DISNEY-MGM STUDIOS

EARFFEL TOWER

THE WORKING STUDIOS

BACKSTAGE STUDIO TOUR

THE MAGIC OF DISNEY ANIMATION

TWILIGHT ZONE TOWER OF TERROR

VOYAGE OF THE LITTLE MERMAID

STUDIO COURTYARD

SOUNDSTAGE RESTAURANT

THE HOLLYWOOD BROWN DERBY

SOUNDSTAGES

SUNSET BOULEVARD

SHOPS

MICKEY AVENUE

THE GREAT MOVIE RIDE

CHINESE THEATER

HOLLYWOOD BOULEVARD

CROSSROADS OF THE WORLD

$

INSIDE THE MAGIC TOUR

TEENAGE MUTANT NINJA TURTLES

DISNEY-MGM STUDIOS COMMISSARY

SUPERSTAR TELEVISION

TV ACADEMY'S HALL OF FAME PLAZA

SHOPS

SHOPS

ENTRANCE PLAZA

HONEY, I SHRUNK THE KIDS

SCI-FI DRIVE-IN DINER

ECHO LAKE

VINE STREET

HOLLYWOOD & VINE CAFETERIA

GUEST RELATIONS

NEW YORK STREET

MONSTER SOUND SHOW

50'S PRIME TIME CAFE

JIM HENSON'S MUPPET*VISION 3D

BACK LOT THEATER

MUPPETS ON LOCATION

THE STUDIO SHOWCASE

STAR TOURS

INDIANA JONES EPIC STUNT SPECTACULAR

THE BACK LOT

MAMA MELROSE'S RISTORANTE ITALIANO

DISNEY-MGM STUDIOS

Disney-MGM Studios offers visitors an opportunity to experience the nuts-and-bolts aspects of film and television production while steeping themselves in the aura and ambience of Hollywood's most glamorous era. From its active soundstages to its elaborately reproduced, full-scale replica of Hollywood's Chinese Theater (complete with handprints of stars in the cement of the forecourt), the park combines working film and television production studios with rides, live entertainment, exhibits, shops, and restaurants that reflect the world of motion picture entertainment.

WHEN TO GO: The best times to visit Disney-MGM Studios are just as the park opens in the morning or at about 4 PM, when parents push a stroller brigade down Hollywood Boulevard in a mass exodus from the park. Some attractions, such as the Great Movie Ride and Star Tours, often open about one half hour before the official opening. The Sorcery in the Sky fireworks performance is presented only on Saturday nights during the off-peak seasons, and the television shows and movies made in the studios are in production only during weekdays. Opening, closing, and event times vary throughout the year, so check ahead at Guest Services in your resort, or call 407 824-4321.

Visitors who would like to view work on a film production or join the audience of a television show (or even appear as guests) should check at the Production Information Window or Guest Relations, both located near the Entrance Plaza, or call ahead for show times and admission information (407 560-7299). A Guest Information Board, located on Hollywood Boulevard near the Hollywood Brown Derby, keeps visitors informed on attraction wait times and other special events. Be sure to pick up an entertainment schedule at the Crossroads of the World kiosk as you enter the park.

HOW TO GET THERE: The parking lot at Disney-MGM Studios is free to WDW resort guests (day visitors are charged a nominal fee). The parking lot is serviced by trams. WDW buses travel between Disney-MGM Studios and all WDW resorts, theme parks, and the Transportation and Ticket Center. Water launches service the following resorts: Dolphin, Swan, Yacht Club, and Beach Club.

ATTRACTIONS

✘✘✘ – Good entertainment. **✘✘** – Enjoyable if you have time and interest. **✘** – Of limited appeal.

THE GREAT MOVIE RIDE: Tucked into the Chinese Theater, this ride takes visitors on a multimedia journey through the history of the movies. Even waiting to board the ride is a fascinating experience, since the line goes through a superbly reproduced theater lobby and a display of well-known film artifacts, including a carousel horse from *Mary Poppins* and one of the three pairs of ruby slippers made for *The Wizard of Oz*. The ride itself combines live talent, Audio-Animatronics, spectacular sets, and convincing special effects to re-create scenes in remarkable detail from such popular films as *Mary Poppins*, *The Wizard of Oz*, *Public Enemy*, *Alien*, and *Raiders of the Lost Ark*. The ride culminates in a grand finale of clips from Academy Award–winning films. Duration: 20 minutes. **✘✘✘**

SUPERSTAR TELEVISION: In this audience-participation show, selected visitors are given the chance to play roles from famous television shows. They perform on a stage with a special blue backdrop that allows a video editor to "key" them in as characters in popular shows such as "I Love Lucy," "Cheers,"

"The Golden Girls," and "General Hospital." The results, shown on huge overhead monitors, can be hilarious. Participants are selected in the preshow area. Duration: 30 minutes. **✗✗✗**

MONSTER SOUND SHOW: Sound effects — the work of "Foley" artists — are the focus of this audience-participation show. After a brief preshow video featuring David Letterman, selected visitors are put to work as sound technicians on a short film starring Martin Short and Chevy Chase. The film is shown once with its original soundtrack, and then a second time to give the "technicians" a chance to put in their designated sound effects. Finally, the film is shown once more with its new sound track, and the results can be highly amusing. After the show, visitors can try their skills in Soundworks, a not-to-be-missed hands-on sound-effects gallery, which can also be entered directly through the exit doors to the right of the Monster Sound Show entrance. Duration: 15 minutes. **✗✗**

STAR TOURS: Visitors enter a somewhat alien, futuristic building, into a large hangar where intergalactic craft are being serviced. *Star Wars* robots R2D2 and C3PO are there, working for the travel agency that owns the spacecraft and booking visitors on a tour to the Moon of Endor. Visitors board the spacecraft, which is actually a modified flight simulator that moves, tilts, and bucks dramatically during the show. Through special effects and spectacular imagery, visitors are hurtled through space at the speed of light in a ship run amok, risking collisions with giant ice crystals and destruction by laser-wielding fighter ships. The seat belts provided are definitely required for this ride, which will not disappoint thrill seekers of all ages but is definitely not for those prone to motion sickness. Duration: 6 minutes. **✗✗✗**

JIM HENSON'S MUPPET✱VISION 3D: This brilliantly conceived attraction is one of those most-often recommended by both visitors and employees at Disney-MGM Studios. Muppet✱Vision 3D, billed as "3D taken to the next dimension," is a multimedia presentation (the audience is given special glasses to wear) that revolves around the escapades in the Muppet Lab when Waldo, a new character symbolizing 3-D, is unleashed. The show combines amusing 3-D film with live characters from the Muppets, pyrotechnics, bubbles, and a number of other effects designed to evoke a "you-are-there" feeling. The special effects in this attraction seem to appeal to both young people and adults. Duration: 20 minutes. **✗✗**

HONEY, I SHRUNK THE KIDS MOVIE SET ADVENTURE: This elaborate playground, based on the film *Honey, I Shrunk the Kids*, combines slides, rope ladders, and other equipment in a set that resembles a gigantic backyard filled with huge blades of grass and monstrously large ants. While the oversized props are quite interesting because of their scale, this playground was really designed for the children who pack the place. Duration: No time limit. **✗**

THE STUDIO SHOWCASE: A pleasant break from standing in lines or feeling rushed, the Studio Showcase is actually a two-story gallery displaying some of the actual props, models, miniatures, and costumes used in many popular feature films. **✗✗**

TV ACADEMY HALL OF FAME PLAZA: This outdoor exhibit, located adjacent to SuperStar Television, is a replica of the original American Academy of Television Arts and Sciences Hall of Fame in North Hollywood. The busts of inductees include Johnny Carson, Walter Cronkite, Lucille Ball, Bill Cosby, Dinah Shore, Ted Turner, Jack Benny, Jim Henson and, of course, Walt Disney. **✗**

LIVE SHOWS AND SPECIAL EVENTS

Live entertainment events and extemporaneous happenings occur daily throughout Disney-MGM Studios. Along Hollywood Boulevard, visitors encounter zany Hollywood characters who involve them in antics surrounding the making of movies and, on certain afternoons, a Star Motorcade carries one of Hollywood's current greats down the Boulevard to the Chinese Theater for a Handprint Ceremony and Star Interview. Visitors can pick up entertainment schedules at Crossroads of the World or at Guest Relations near the Entrance Plaza. Schedules are also available at most of the shops.

INDIANA JONES EPIC STUNT SPECTACULAR: This dramatic, live-action attraction showcases the work of stunt designers and performers. Designed around scenes from the Indiana Jones movies, the show features professional performers staging hair-raising stunts and selected audience members who act as "extras." The stunt performers fall from buildings and dodge threatening boulders, fiery explosions, and out-of-control trucks. The fascinating demonstrations of the secrets behind the stunts do not seem to reduce the excitement and sense of realism of the stunts themselves. For the best view, arrive at least twenty minutes early and find a seat in the upper center. Shows are scheduled continuously throughout the day, but may be abbreviated if the weather looks threatening. Duration: 30 minutes. ✗✗

BACKLOT THEATER: This outdoor theater temporarily replaced Theater of the Stars, and may be the future appearance site for Muppets on Location and Teenage Mutant Ninja Turtles. Here, talented singers and dancers, top-flight choreography and stage direction, elaborate sets, and imaginative costumes are combined to create memorable productions that adults as well as children enjoy. The shows change periodically and are based on the latest Disney film releases. The best time to see the show is late in the day, when the crowds have thinned and the sun is not directly overhead. Several shows are scheduled throughout the day. Duration: 25 minutes. ✗✗✗

JIM HENSON'S MUPPETS ON LOCATION: This is a very funny live performance of Muppets characters, who are ostensibly taking a break from filming their latest musical. Visitors can collect autographs and have their photos taken with their favorite Muppets. This is a chance to pick up a one-of-a-kind gift for a pint-sized fan. Appearances are scheduled several times daily. Duration: 18 minutes. ✗

VOYAGE OF THE LITTLE MERMAID: This is a live performance of scenes from the film of the same name. One of the many theatrical effects simulates rippling water overhead, conveying the sense of being under the sea. Visitors unfamiliar with the Disney movie might want to ignore the plot and enjoy the show as a series of song-and-dance vignettes primarily featuring bright and cheerful denizens of the sea. Families with young children find this a delightful attraction. Adults could find it tiresome, although it's a nice place to sit down and cool off — in fact, the audience is misted occasionally, in keeping with the watery theme. Shows are scheduled continuously throughout the day. Duration: 15 minutes. ✗

ALADDIN'S ROYAL CARAVAN: This daily parade presents Aladdin in his triumphant role as Prince Ali, with the Genie who made it all possible transformed into a twenty-six-foot-high giant. Humorous re-creations from the animated film feature make up the prince's wacky entourage, including the mischievous monkey Abu, turbaned palace guards, acrobats, snake charmers, harem girls, a brass band, and golden camels (who spit water at unwary onlookers). The parade features some not-to-be-missed new technologies such as massive inflatable costumes, but the musical theme can be annoyingly repetitive, so it's best viewed at the beginning of Hollywood Boulevard where it starts. Parades are scheduled once or twice daily. Duration: Approximately 20 minutes. ✗✗

TEENAGE MUTANT NINJA TURTLES: The Teenage Mutant Ninja Turtles drive up in a colorful van and put on a performance of singing, dancing, and martial arts. Each turtle then enters his own booth to pose for photographs and stamp out autographs. The attraction appeals to young fans, who eagerly flock to the scene. Appearances are scheduled several times daily. Duration: Approximately 20 minutes. ✗

SORCERY IN THE SKY: Perhaps the most dramatic display of pyrotechnics at Walt Disney World, this show is well worth seeing. Designed around Mickey Mouse's role as the Sorcerer's Apprentice in *Fantasia,* the musical fireworks show lights the sky over the Chinese Theater. Multicolored overhead bursts, silver and gold comets, and dramatic fountains of glittering sparks create a dazzling vision that, coupled with the appearance of a fifty-foot-high inflatable Mickey, leaves visitors cheering for more. The best viewing spot is at the end of Hollywood Boulevard, near the Hollywood Brown Derby. Sorcery in the Sky is presented nightly at about 9 or 10 PM during the summer months, and on Saturday nights during holiday seasons. Duration: 10 minutes. ✗✗✗

TOURS

BACKSTAGE STUDIO TOUR FEATURING CATASTROPHE CANYON: This tram ride takes visitors through costume and scenic shops, lighting and camera departments, and residential street sets used in films and television shows — a truly informative behind-the-scenes look at motion picture production. The highlight of the tour is Catastrophe Canyon, where visitors feel the searing heat from an exploding tanker truck and, if they are sitting on the left side, find themselves drenched by the waters of a flash flood. Tours are continuous. Duration: 25 minutes. ✗✗✗

INSIDE THE MAGIC — SPECIAL EFFECTS AND PRODUCTION TOUR: This walking tour, which presents no real opportunity to sit down, is an optional continuation of the Backstage Studio Tour and appeals to visitors who want a more in-depth view of movie making. The tour introduces several types of special effects, and visitors learn how sea battles and storm sequences are created in a special-effects water tank. In the prop room, a giant bee is used to demonstrate "blue screen" techniques that allow filmmakers to drop actors into already existing background scenes. While touring the soundstages, visitors are shown a short film featuring Bette Midler. Afterward, a narration explains how Midler's antics were filmed, and visitors enter the set to look over the actual props and effects used in making the film. This show is most interesting by far when productions are actually underway on the soundstages, so before committing to this tour, visitors should check at the Production Information Window or Guest Relations. Tours are continuous. Duration: Approximately 45 minutes. ✗

THE MAGIC OF DISNEY ANIMATION: A mostly self-guided walking tour, this popular attraction begins in the waiting area, where animation fans can view both classic and current animation cels on display. Visitors then enter a theater for a highly entertaining and educational film about animation starring Robin Williams and Walter Cronkite. After the film, visitors tour Disney's working animation studio, where actual animation projects are underway. The various activities going on are explained on overhead monitors. In the Disney Classics Theater, all the parts of the tour come together, and visitors see the techniques they witnessed employed in classic Disney animation sequences. Tours are continuous. Duration: Approximately 30 minutes. ✗✗✗

✳

FULL-SERVICE RESTAURANTS

WDW resort guests can make restaurant reservations up to three days in advance. Same-day reservations can be made at the Restaurant Desk near the Hollywood Brown Derby on Hollywood Boulevard. Smoking is not permitted in the restaurants. See "Restaurants," page 167, for detailed restaurant reviews and reservation strategies.

THE HOLLYWOOD BROWN DERBY: Caricatures of famous personalities line the walls of this elegant, bustling restaurant. Steaks, seafood, pasta, and salads, including the house specialty, Cobb salad, are featured, along with a selection of specialty desserts. Beer, wine, and spirits are served, as are espresso and cappuccino. Open for lunch and dinner; reservations necessary.

SCI-FI DRIVE-IN DINER: Under a twinkling night sky, rows of booths shaped like vintage convertibles create a drive-in movie ambience, complete with car-side speakers, and classic science fiction and horror film clips shown on the big screen. The restaurant is popular with families with young children. Burgers and specialty dishes such as The Red Planet — linguini topped with sautéed vegetables — are the order of the day, along with the perfect movie appetizer, popcorn. Beer and wine are served. Open for lunch and dinner; reservations necessary.

50'S PRIME TIME CAFE: Decorated with fifties-style kitchens, black and white televisions, and dinette tables of the period, this restaurant airs sitcoms from the fifties and serves such delectables as Aunt Selma's Chicken Salad, Magnificent Meat Loaf, and a French Fry Feast. Soda fountain treats are also featured. Beer, wine, and spirits are served. Open for lunch and dinner; reservations necessary.

HOLLYWOOD & VINE CAFETERIA: Located next door to the 50's Prime Time Cafe, this cafeteria-style restaurant's design is a chromium blend of Art Deco and Diner Classic. Featured entrees include baby back ribs, chicken cooked on a rotisserie, and a variety of salads. Beer and wine are available. Open for breakfast, lunch, and dinner; no reservations.

MAMA MELROSE'S RISTORANTE ITALIANO: Red-checked tablecloths and loud good humor create an offbeat trattoria ambience in this restaurant, which serves Italian cuisine including gourmet pizza baked in brick ovens. Beer, wine, and spirits are served, as are espresso and cappuccino. Open for lunch and dinner; reservations necessary.

✳

COCKTAIL LOUNGES AND CAFES

Refreshment stands that serve all-day snacks and fast-food meals are located throughout Disney-MGM Studios. A few, listed below, are especially pleasant and also make ideal meeting spots for visitors who want to tour separately and rendezvous at a later time. For before-dinner cocktails, try the Catwalk Bar in the Soundstage Restaurant or the lively and surreal Tune In Lounge adjacent to the 50's Prime Time Cafe.

SOUNDSTAGE RESTAURANT: This food court is designed as a massive production studio, and employs props from the latest Disney feature films. Available at the counter are snacks such as pizza, sandwiches, soup, and salad, as well as coffee, beer, and wine.

THE CATWALK BAR: Filled with props, lights, production equipment, and an old wooden phone booth, this pleasant secluded bar serves a limited selection of appetizers, along with beer, wine, and spirits. It is located in the Soundstage Restaurant, in the scaffolding above.

TUNE IN LOUNGE: Located adjacent to the 50's Prime Time Cafe, this bar serves up beer, wine, and spirits, along with sitcoms, in a classic fifties environment complete with black-and-white TVs and Naugahyde couches.

DISNEY-MGM STUDIOS COMMISSARY: Located next to the Chinese Theater, this large counter-service eatery has a streamlined contemporary decor. Snacks and fast-food meals including vegetarian chili are available here, as are beer and coffee.

S E R V I C E S

REST ROOMS: Public rest rooms are located throughout Disney-MGM Studios. The rest rooms located upstairs at the Catwalk Bar are very nice and usually deserted. Visitors can also find cool and quiet rest rooms at the Hollywood Brown Derby, Mama Melrose's Ristorante Italiano, the Disney-MGM Studio Commissary, and the Tune In Lounge.

TELEPHONES: Public telephones are located throughout Disney-MGM Studios, usually near the rest rooms. The most private outdoor phones are those near the first-aid offices in the Entrance Plaza. Those located upstairs at the Catwalk Bar are private and pleasant, and those at Mama Melrose's Ristorante Italiano and the Disney-MGM Studio Commissary are also quiet and air-conditioned.

MESSAGE CENTER: At Walt Disney World's computerized Message Center, located at Guest Relations, visitors can leave and retrieve messages for each other. The Message Center is on a network also shared by Epcot Center and the Magic Kingdom, so visitors at one park can exchange messages with companions visiting elsewhere.

FILM AND TWO-HOUR EXPRESS DEVELOPING: Film is available at most shops throughout Disney-MGM Studios. Drop-off points for express developing are at the Darkroom, on Hollywood Boulevard; at the Disney Studio Store, next to Voyage of the Little Mermaid; and at the Loony Bin, at the far end of Mickey Avenue. Developed film may be picked up at the Darkroom or delivered to any WDW resort. The Darkroom also offers one-hour developing for visitors in a hurry.

CAMERA RENTAL: Video cameras (and replacement batteries) and 35mm cameras are available at the Darkroom, on Hollywood Boulevard.

MAIL DROPS: The mail-drop location at Disney-MGM Studios is just outside the Entrance Plaza. A stamp machine is located next to Oscar's Classic Car Souvenirs on Hollywood Boulevard.

BANKING: An automated teller machine (ATM) is located outside the Entrance Plaza, near the Production Information Window.

LOCKERS: Lockers are located at Oscar's Classic Car Souvenirs on Hollywood Boulevard.

FIRST AID: The first-aid office is located at Disney-MGM Studios' Entrance Plaza, next to Guest Relations. Aspirin and other first-aid needs are dispensed free of charge. Over-the-counter medications are available at Golden Age Souvenirs, located near SuperStar Television. They are not on display and must be requested at the counter.

VISITORS WITH DISABILITIES: A guidebook for disabled guests is available free of charge at Guest Relations, at Disney-MGM Studios' Entrance Plaza. All attractions at Disney-MGM Studios except Star Tours have wheelchair access.

WHEELCHAIR RENTALS: Wheelchairs (but not motorized wheelchairs) may be rented at Oscar's Classic Car Souvenirs on Hollywood Boulevard, just inside the Main Gate.

HEARING-IMPAIRED VISITORS: A written text of Disney-MGM Studios' attractions is available at Guest Relations at Disney-MGM Studios' Entrance Plaza. PAL units (personal audio listening units) are available at Muppet*Vision 3D and Sci-Fi Drive-In Diner. A telecommunications device for the deaf (TDD) is available at Guest Relations, at Disney-MGM Studios' Entrance Plaza. Hearing aid–compatible and amplified telephones are available throughout the park.

SIGHT-IMPAIRED VISITORS: Tape players and touring cassettes that describe the park are available at Guest Relations, at Disney-MGM Studios' Entrance Plaza.

FOREIGN LANGUAGE ASSISTANCE: Park maps in French, Spanish, and German are available at Guest Relations, at Disney-MGM Studios' Entrance Plaza.

✴

COMING ATTRACTIONS

Plans are always on the drawing board for new attractions throughout Walt Disney World. Until construction actually begins, however, these plans have a way of changing or becoming delayed. At the time of publication, a major expansion was underway at Disney-MGM Studios.

SUNSET BOULEVARD EXPANSION: Sunset Boulevard, adjacent to Hollywood Boulevard, features shops, attractions, restaurants, and entertainment events in the style of the 1930s, with vintage streetcars carrying visitors up and down the long street. Sunset Boulevard is scheduled for completion during 1994 and 1995.

THE TWILIGHT ZONE TOWER OF TERROR: Opening in 1994 on Sunset Boulevard, this thrill ride is actually an exploration of a deserted and spooky Hollywood hotel haunted by the ghosts of tinsel-town past and filled with supernatural events. The climax of the ride is a thirteen-story free-fall.

ROGER RABBIT'S HOLLYWOOD: This group of attractions, also called Toontown, reproduces the "cartoon reality" that was made famous in the movie *Who Framed Roger Rabbit?* It is still in the planning stage, but included among the proposed rides are Toontown Transit, a wacky journey aboard a flight simulator through the cartoon perils of Toontown, and Baby Herman's Runaway Baby Buggy Ride — based on the Roger Rabbit short feature, *Tummy Trouble* — which puts visitors in the buggy seat as they careen through the Toontown Hospital.

Half-Day Tours at Disney-MGM Studios

The morning and evening half-day tours that follow are designed to allow first-time visitors to experience the best of Disney-MGM Studios in four to six hours, including a lunch or dinner in one of the park's restaurants. If possible, make your restaurant reservation in advance.

To create your own custom vacation at Walt Disney World, you can combine one of the half-day Disney-MGM Studios tours with a half-day tour from any other theme park. For example, combine the Morning Movieland Tour at Disney-MGM Studios with an evening tour at the World Showcase. The theme parks are most crowded in the afternoons, which is an ideal time to relax or take advantage of the resort amenities at Walt Disney World.

MORNING MOVIELAND TOUR

Four to six hours — year round — including lunch.
If possible, a day or two before this tour reserve a late lunch (after 1 PM)
at one of the Disney-MGM Studios restaurants.

✔ Eat a full breakfast before leaving your hotel.

✔ Arrive at Disney-MGM Studios' Entrance Plaza at least one half hour before the scheduled opening time (between 8 and 9 AM).

✔ When the park opens, proceed to the Crossroads of the World kiosk and pick up an entertainment schedule.

✔ If you do not have a lunch reservation: Walk quickly to the Restaurant Desk at the end of Hollywood Boulevard and make a lunch reservation for 1 PM or later. (If you have difficulty making reservations, or would prefer a light meal, plan on eating at Disney-MGM Studios Commissary or Hollywood & Vine Cafeteria, which do not require reservations.)

✔ Your tour begins on the left side of the park, behind Echo Lake. Visit the following attractions that interest you in this order:
- STAR TOURS (if you like thrill rides)
- THE GREAT MOVIE RIDE
- SUPERSTAR TELEVISION (See Aladdin's Royal Caravan first, if it is about to start.)
- ALADDIN'S ROYAL CARAVAN (Check the entertainment schedule for parade times.)
- BACKSTAGE STUDIO TOUR FEATURING CATASTROPHE CANYON (tram portion only)
- If you still have an hour or so before your lunch reservation, see THE MAGIC OF DISNEY ANIMATION, or continue on the walking portion of the Backstage Tour, INSIDE THE MAGIC.

✔ Plan to arrive at your lunch destination ten minutes early.

✔ If you wish to continue touring after lunch, take in the stage show at BACKLOT THEATER or see INDIANA JONES EPIC STUNT SPECTACULAR.

DISNEY-MGM STUDIOS

SORCERY IN THE SKY AFTERNOON AND EVENING TOUR

Five to six hours — May through August (and Saturdays during holidays) — including dinner.
If possible, make your dinner reservations a day or two before this tour.
If you prefer an early dinner, reserve a table at 6 PM or before.
If you prefer a late dinner, reserve a seating toward the end of your tour,
but no later than ninety minutes before Sorcery in the Sky
is scheduled to begin (at about 9 or 10 PM).

✔ Arrive at Disney-MGM Studios' Entrance Plaza about 4 PM.

✔ Pick up an entertainment schedule at the Crossroads of the World kiosk, which lists the show times for live performances and Sorcery in the Sky.

✔ If you do not have a dinner reservation: Proceed to the Restaurant Desk at the end of Hollywood Boulevard and make a reservation for either an early dinner or a late dinner. Be sure to let the reservationist know that you want a seating that lets you finish your meal before Sorcery in the Sky starts. (If you have difficulty making reservations, or would prefer a light meal, plan on eating at the Disney-MGM Studios Commissary, which does not require reservations.)

✔ Visit, in the order listed below, those attractions that interest you (your tour will be temporarily interrupted if you have an early dinner reservation):

- THE TWILIGHT ZONE TOWER OF TERROR
- THE GREAT MOVIE RIDE
- BACKSTAGE STUDIO TOUR FEATURING CATASTROPHE CANYON (tram portion only)
- THE MAGIC OF DISNEY ANIMATION
- INDIANA JONES EPIC STUNT SPECTACULAR
- STAR TOURS (if you like thrill rides and the line is short)
- STUDIO SHOWCASE (for a quick tour while you're in the neighborhood).

✔ Pause your tour in order to arrive at your dinner destination ten minutes early.

✔ After dinner, resume your tour. If you still have time before Sorcery in the Sky begins, check the entertainment schedule for special events or visit attractions you may have missed earlier. Some of the more entertaining attractions include:

- SUPERSTAR TELEVISION
- MONSTER SOUND SHOW (especially Soundworks, which you can enter at the exit)
- MUPPET*VISION 3D.

✔ About fifteen minutes before SORCERY IN THE SKY is scheduled to begin, find a viewing spot anywhere at the end of Hollywood Boulevard. One of the best views is by the popcorn cart near the Guest Information Board.

✔ After Sorcery in the Sky, you may wish to stroll along the shores of Echo Lake, browse through the shops along Hollywood Boulevard (they stay open late), or find an empty bench and people-watch while the crowds rush out. ◆

DISNEY-MGM STUDIOS

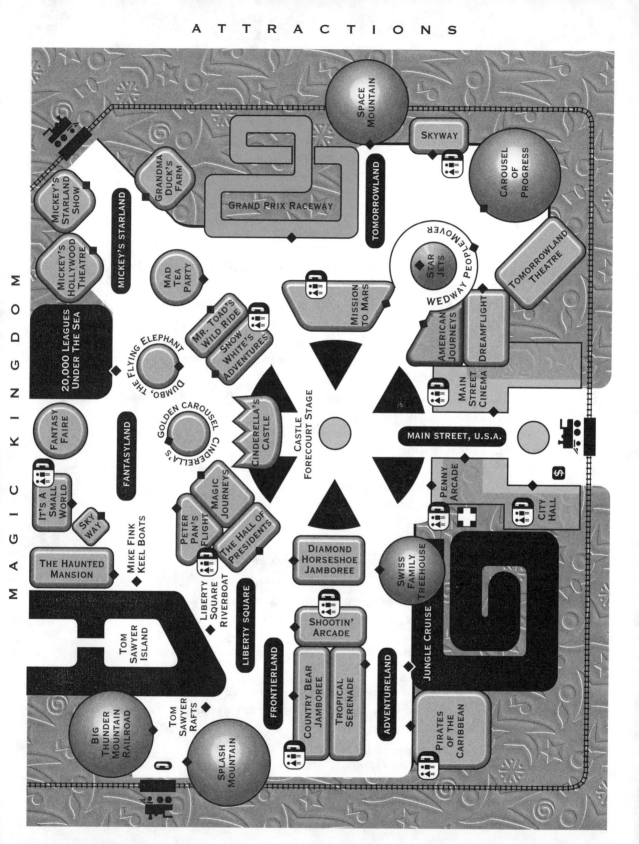

MAGIC KINGDOM

The Magic Kingdom, a fraternal twin of Disneyland in Anaheim, California, was the first theme park built at Walt Disney World. Covering about one hundred acres, (twenty acres larger than Disneyland), the park opened in 1971 with six theme lands: Adventureland, Frontierland, Liberty Square, Fantasyland, Tomorrowland, and Main Street, U.S.A. In 1988, a seventh theme land, Mickey's Starland, was added. The Magic Kingdom has most of the same attractions as Disneyland plus a number of additional attractions, and whereas Sleeping Beauty's Castle is the focal point of Disneyland, Cinderella's Castle is the centerpiece of the Magic Kingdom. Designed to captivate the wonder of children, the Magic Kingdom has a way of triggering childhood nostalgia in adults, especially serious Disney fans and those who visited Disneyland in their youth.

WHEN TO GO: The best time to visit the Magic Kingdom is at times when school is in session, certainly not during the summer months or holiday periods. Even during off-peak seasons, it's a good idea to arrive at the gates in the early morning, at least one half hour before the official opening time. It's even better to begin touring after 4:30 PM, when floods of parents are herding their exhausted children toward the exit. Visitors should try to go on an evening when the SpectroMagic parade and/or Fantasy in the Sky fireworks are scheduled. Opening, closing, and event times vary throughout the year, so check ahead at Guest Services in your resort, or call 407 824-4321.

HOW TO GET THERE: The vast parking lot at the Magic Kingdom is free to guests at WDW resorts (day visitors are charged a nominal fee). The parking lot is serviced by trams, which carry visitors to the Transportation and Ticket Center (TTC), the hub for all WDW transportation. Water launches and monorails transport visitors from the TTC to the park entrance. Water launches also service the Magic Kingdom from Discovery Island, River Country, and the following resorts: Fort Wilderness, Polynesian, and Grand Floridian. Monorails, with nearly fourteen miles of track, connect the Magic Kingdom and the TTC to Epcot Center and the following resorts: Contemporary, Polynesian, and Grand Floridian. (Visitors who want to make the most of the futuristic monorail ride should ask the driver if there is room in front, where the view is great.) WDW buses travel between the Magic Kingdom and all Walt Disney World resorts and theme parks, and drop passengers at the park entrance.

IN-PARK TRANSPORTATION: Several transportation options are available in each part of the Magic Kingdom. Visitors can travel down Main Street in plowhorse-drawn trolleys, jitneys, colorful double-decker buses, bell-clanging fire trucks, or smoothly purring antique cars. Between Fantasyland and Tomorrowland, visitors can ride the Skyway, an aerial gondola that provides a sweeping view of the Magic Kingdom. The Walt Disney World Railroad, with four authentic steam engine–powered trains, circles the park continuously, with stations at Main Street, U.S.A., Frontierland, and Mickey's Starland.

✳

ATTRACTIONS

✗✗✗ – Solid Disney entertainment. ✗✗ – Good fun if you're in the mood. ✗ – For the very young at heart.
👫 – Strictly for small fry.

MAIN STREET, U.S.A.: From its train station entryway to its view of Cinderella's Castle in the distance, Main Street, U.S.A., is the first environment visitors encounter as they enter the Magic Kingdom.

It is a picture-perfect turn-of-the-century town. Visitors can take care of banking needs in a traditional setting; drop by City Hall for entertainment schedules; browse through a wide variety of specialty shops (including the Chapeau, featuring the monogrammed mouse ears made famous by the Mouseketeers); ride horse-drawn trolleys, double-decker buses, jitneys, and antique cars; peer into the old-time Harmony Barber Shop or even get a haircut (call 407 824-6550 for an appointment); and take a break to people-watch in the Town Square, a pleasant plaza with benches, shade, and periodic live band concerts.

✦ *City Hall Information Center* — One of the first stops visitors should make on arriving at the Magic Kingdom, City Hall is located at the beginning of Main Street. A helpful staff provides maps and entertainment schedules; operates a Message Center for visitors; and makes resort, guided tour, and dinner show reservations (except for the Diamond Horseshoe Jamboree, which must be reserved immediately on arrival, at the podium in front of Disneyana Collectibles, just across Town Square). City Hall is also a good rendezvous point for visitors traveling in groups.

✦ *Main Street Cinema* — In this old-fashioned (and air-conditioned) movie house, visitors can watch classic short films and cartoons, including silent screen performances by Charlie Chaplin, and see *Steamboat Willie,* the historic cartoon that introduced Mickey Mouse to the world (and was the first animated film to use sound). The theater has no seats and usually airs several films simultaneously, since they are mostly silent. Duration: Films run continuously. Good for about 5 minutes. ✗

✦ *Penny Arcade* — A mix of contemporary electronic games and vintage arcade games, this attraction gives adult visitors the opportunity to experience the Kiss-O-Meter and gaze at early moving pictures produced by rapidly flipping cards while stepping cautiously around entranced youngsters. The Penny Arcade is worth a few minutes of time in the very early morning, just after arrival and before the rest of the park opens. Like the Frontierland Shootin' Gallery, the Penny Arcade requires some spending money in the form of small change. Duration: Good for about 10 minutes. ✗

✦ *Walt Disney World Railroad, Main Street Station* — Four open-air trains, pulled by whistle-blowing steam-puffing engines, travel the Walt Disney World Railroad on a mile-and-a-half tour of the park. Visitors expecting to see the Grand Canyon and dinosaur diorama that the Anaheim Disneyland train is noted for will be disappointed, since it is absent here, but this leisurely trip through the lush foliage lining the track, coupled with views of most of the theme lands, is still worth the ride. Visitors can board and disembark at the Main Street, Frontierland, and Mickey's Starland stations. The trains run every four to seven minutes. Duration: Approximately 20 minutes for the entire circuit. ✗✗

ADVENTURELAND: At the end of Main Street, off to the left, Adventureland welcomes visitors into a tropical fantasy that is a blend of Africa, the Caribbean, the South Seas, and a bit of New Orleans. The dense foliage and the rustles, squawks, and cries of mysterious creatures lend an exotic air.

✦ *Jungle Cruise* — A lighthearted reminder of the Bogart-Hepburn classic film *The African Queen,* this attraction takes visitors on a steamy adventure cruise down some of the world's great rivers — the Nile, Congo, and Amazon — with a detour past a mysterious Asian temple. The guide provides a witty narration on the rivers and their denizens, all the while protecting visitors from the clearly fake but entertaining local hostiles and wild animals along the riverbank. Exotic jungle plants, cascading waterfalls, Audio-Animatronic figures, and delightful special effects all add up to an ambience of adventure. There are always long lines, and repeat visitors consider the attraction overrated. Duration: 9 minutes. ✗✗✗

◆ *Pirates of the Caribbean* — In the underground catacombs of a mysterious stone fortress, visitors board boats for a ride through a coastal settlement under attack by a band of raucous, rum-sotted pirates. After floating through dimly lit passages with unexpected drops, visitors are treated to humorous and, at times, disturbing vignettes of attacking ships with shots exploding overhead, high-spirited drunken debauchery, buildings on fire, and treasure rooms heaped with jewels and gold. While not nearly as riveting as the same attraction at Disneyland, the elaborate sets, rich costuming, and sophisticated Audio-Animatronics still make this a must-see special-effects attraction. Duration: 9 minutes. ✘✘✘

◆ *Swiss Family Treehouse* — This walkthrough attraction invites visitors to tour the home of the famous shipwrecked family. Built into a replica of a banyan tree about ninety feet in diameter, the multi-level home is the ultimate treehouse, with everything from cozy bedrooms to an intricate plumbing system — running water in every room! Visitors should be aware that there are several sets of stairs and lots of kids enthusiastically exploring the novel rustic abode. Duration: Approximately 15 to 20 minutes. ✘

◆ *Tropical Serenade* — Singing birds and flowers, chanting totem poles, and a tropical storm await guests in the lodge of the Enchanted Tiki Birds. At one point, the birds sing their national anthem "Let's All Sing Like the Birdies Sing," inviting guests to sing along. It's a good place to relax and cool off, although the recently renovated sound system isn't what it should be. Duration: 25 minutes. ✘

FRONTIERLAND: Adjacent to Adventureland, visitors enter the American frontier of the nineteenth century, the world of Davy Crockett, Mark Twain, and the miners of the Gold Rush. Stone, clapboard, and split-log structures evoke the distinct frontier atmospheres of the East, the Midwest, and the Southwest. The Frontierland attractions have a rough-and-tumble quality to them, and two of the three roller coaster rides at the Magic Kingdom are located here.

◆ *Big Thunder Mountain Railroad* — On this roller coaster ride, visitors take a trip through a Gold Rush–era mountain mining town on what soon becomes a runaway train. As roller coasters go, this one relies on side-to-side, rather than up-and-down, motion, but it's fast nonetheless and its special effects and scenery are great as they flash by. Crashing rocks, rushing waterfalls, flapping bats, braying donkeys, and a flooded mining town make for a lively experience. Many visitors feel this ride is more fun and enchanting at night. Duration: 4 minutes. ✘✘✘

◆ *Country Bear Jamboree* — The lively antics of almost two dozen whimsical Audio-Animatronic bears amuse visitors who attend the performance in Grizzly Hall. Headed by Big Al, the bears tell tall tales, crack corny jokes, and perform musical numbers. The show and decor are changed throughout the year to reflect seasonal holidays. Duration: 15 minutes. ✘

◆ *Frontierland Shootin' Arcade* — The traditional carnival shooting gallery gets an electronic spin in this attraction. Visitors use real buffalo rifles (fitted with infrared beams instead of bullets) to shoot at frontier-motif targets in a Tombstone Territory setting. Through the magic of special effects, targets that are "hit" do not just fall — they twist, leap, howl, or even trigger another, secondary humorous effect. The Nintendo-style effects are clearly oriented to kids, who flock to this arcade. Like the Penny Arcade on Main Street, this attraction requires loose change. Duration: 5 shots for 25 cents. 👫

◆ *Splash Mountain* — The theme of this water-chute roller coaster, the newest attraction in Frontierland, is from the Disney classic, *Song of the South*. Amidst the antics of Brer Rabbit, Brer Fox, Brer Bear, and their friends, visitors are swept along in log boats on a half-mile journey through bayous, gardens, swamps, and caves. Sudden unexpected drops and slow, lazy drifts alternately startle and lull visitors until they confront Brer Fox, in a quandary about throwing Brer Rabbit into the Briar Patch. From there, the ride goes downhill, literally, plunging almost five stories to splash into the giant briar patch below. The Audio-Animatronics and sets in this attraction, as well as the pacing and soundtrack, are outstanding examples of Disney wizardry at its most creative. Visitors should expect to get fairly soaked in the plunge (take along a plastic poncho or large garbage bag). Duration: 11 minutes. ✗✗✗

◆ *Tom Sawyer Island* — This attraction, reached by raft, evokes the adventuresome Missouri frontier of Mark Twain's famed character, and it appeals to youngsters with plenty of energy to burn. Ferried back and forth to the island on rafts, visitors can spelunk in a spooky cave, wobble across a barrel bridge, walk along mysterious winding paths, see a working windmill and waterwheel, and explore the stockade architecture of Fort Sam Clemens. Although the island can be a pleasant interlude for adults, it is overrun with free-wheeling children all day and closes at sundown. Duration: 30 to 40 minutes. 🏃‍♂️

◆ *Walt Disney World Railroad, Frontierland Station* — With its open, airy boarding platform and large wooden water tank, this Old West railroad station captures the mood of train travel in the nineteenth century. Of the three stops on the Walt Disney World Railroad, this one is the busiest. Duration: Approximately 20 minutes for the entire circuit. ✗✗

LIBERTY SQUARE: Merging seamlessly with Frontierland, Liberty Square captures the ambience of a town square during the time of the American Revolution. The buildings are accurate in their architectural styling and detail, complete with shutters that hang slightly askew on their hinges of leather. An excellent reproduction of the Liberty Bell, with its signature crack, hangs in the square, and the huge one-hundred-year-old live oak nearby is hung with thirteen metal lanterns representing the light of freedom in each of the original thirteen colonies.

◆ *Liberty Square Riverboat* — Visitors board this steam-powered stern-wheeler that actually rides on an underwater rail for a slow-moving journey around Tom Sawyer Island. On the river, visitors pass by a burning log cabin, Fort Sam Clemens, and a number of other props and wilderness settings along the banks. The boat leaves on the hour and the half hour. Duration: 15 minutes. ✗

◆ *Mike Fink Keel Boats* — The small, squat boats on this water ride evoke a backwoods mood. Like the Liberty Square Riverboat, the keel boats circle Tom Sawyer Island. Visitors glide by various riverbank sights, including a burning log cabin and Fort Sam Clemens. The attraction closes at sundown. Duration: 10 minutes. ✗

◆ *The Hall of Presidents* — The U.S. Constitution and selected highlights of American history are showcased in this attraction. It opens with a 70mm film featuring dramatic paintings in the artistic styles of the times they represent. As the film ends, a curtain rises to reveal an incredibly lifelike Audio-Animatronic tableau of all the U.S. Presidents, from George Washington to Bill Clinton. When the roll call begins, each figure responds to his name, while the others nod, shift in their seats, turn to look, rustle, cough, and generally persuade the audience of their reality. The tone of this attraction is distinctly more serious and educational than that of most in the Magic Kingdom. The presidential roll call (plus the sit-down air-conditioned theater) makes this attraction truly worthwhile. Duration: 24 minutes. ✗✗

◆ *The Haunted Mansion* — This mysterious red-brick mansion, from which eerie sounds emanate, is Liberty Square's most popular attraction. Visitors pass by a town graveyard, with its wretchedly punned tombstone epitaphs, to be welcomed into the eighteenth-century house by a creepy, supercilious butler and led into a waiting area decorated with some very unusual family portraits. Visitors then board ride vehicles that carry them off on a dark and spooky tour of the mansion. Rattles, rustles, and screams permeate the air, and the ongoing narration has a quirky, ghastly humor. The clever sets, props, and visual effects make The Haunted Mansion especially enjoyable for adults. Duration: 9 minutes. ✖✖✖

FANTASYLAND: The theme land that best reflects the light-hearted side of Walt Disney's imagination, Fantasyland is a potpourri of glittering carousel horses, colorful banners, wacky rides, and fairy-tale encounters. The appealing Alpine-village setting, with its half-timbered buildings and striped tentlike structures, spreads out behind Cinderella's Castle, the truly beautiful signature icon of the Magic Kingdom. Although most of the attractions are really designed for children, adults will certainly enjoy taking in the sights, perhaps even indulging in a few moments of nostalgia about a world that never was.

✦ *Cinderella's Golden Carousel* — Sparkling with mirrors, gilded decorations, painted scenes from *Cinderella,* and beautifully detailed horses, this elegant merry-go-round is a true classic. Its riders are carried back in time in leisurely, pleasant circles. No two horses are alike, and the carousel is especially pretty and evocative at twilight. Duration: 2 minutes. 👫

✦ *Dumbo, the Flying Elephant* — Appealing primarily to very young children, this kiddie carnival attraction takes visitors in gondolas shaped like the famed Dumbo, complete with big ears, on a slow, circular ride with occasional gentle lifts and drops. Adults can bypass this attraction without missing out on anything special. Duration: 2 minutes. 👫

✦ *It's A Small World* — Visitors board boats for this whimsical water journey through a world populated by dolls representing children of every nationality. The dolls, dressed in elaborately detailed folk costumes, sing the verses to "It's A Small World" in the language of the culture they represent. Although the tune is difficult to shake off, visitors seem to come away feeling happy, or perhaps mesmerized by the repetitive expressions of the designers' good intentions. On a hot day, this air-conditioned ride can be a godsend. Duration: 11 minutes. ✖✖

✦ *Mad Tea Party* — Drawing from the classic film *Alice in Wonderland,* this attraction features giant, pastel-painted, madly spinning teacups on a whirling ride that is not for the weak of stomach. The Mad Tea Party is really a fairly typical carnival ride that has been dressed up Disney style. Little children are its greatest fans. Duration: 2 minutes. 👫

✦ *Magic Journeys* — This 70mm film was originally shown at the Journey Into Imagination pavilion at Epcot. Visitors don special viewing glasses to watch the creative flights of fantasy of a group of children. The 3-D effects are so well done that visitors often involuntarily dodge hurtling objects or duck lightning bolts. Some adult viewers mention that they actually prefer this film, with its beautiful scenes from nature, to the flashier *Captain EO* that replaced it at Future World. Duration: 18 minutes. ✖✖

✦ *Mr. Toad's Wild Ride* — This wacky drive takes visitors through barn doors, chicken coops, a fireplace, and on a collision course with an oncoming train. Adults who expect the word *wild* to have a meaning other than "silly" will be disappointed, although the ride has its fans. Duration: 3 minutes. 👫

✦ *Peter Pan's Flight* — Set in Never-Never Land, this attraction takes visitors for a ride in a miniature version of Captain Hook's pirate ship. The ship flies above the rooftops of London, dipping down from time to time through some memorable scenes from *Peter Pan*. Although designed with children in mind, Peter Pan's Flight is actually a surprisingly delightful journey through the night sky that seems to leave adults with a happy glow. Duration: 4 minutes. ✖✖

◆ *Skyway to Tomorrowland* — Located across from Peter Pan's Flight, this Alpine chalet is home to an overhead cable car ride to the futuristic Skyway station in Tomorrowland. Sitting in the open-air gondola, visitors get a spectacular bird's-eye view of the Magic Kingdom and its surroundings. Since each car only holds a few people and there is no specific scenario demanding viewer attention, visitors who are comfortable with heights will find this ride an excellent opportunity to just sit back, relax, and enjoy the view. Duration: 5 minutes. ✖✖

◆ *Snow White's Adventures* — Focusing on the down side of the fairy tale, this ride takes visitors in wooden mining cars on a mildly spooky trip through a dark forest, with menacing witches and threatening trees. Most adult visitors will find little to enchant them in this attraction. Duration: 3 minutes. 👫

◆ *20,000 Leagues Under the Sea* — In this attraction, based on underwater scenes from the movie of the same name, visitors voyage in a submarine past sunken ships and coral reefs aswim with brightly colored fish, under a polar ice cap, and into an encounter with a giant attacking squid. The ride vehicles are designed with strange cramped seating and small portholes, and visitors may be disappointed (or perhaps amused) by the clearly fake scenery they pass. Duration: 9 minutes. ✖

MICKEY'S STARLAND: Mickey's Starland, the newest Magic Kingdom theme land, was originally Mickey's Birthdayland, a tribute to Mickey Mouse's sixtieth birthday in 1988. Its picture-perfect, brightly colored kid-sized buildings look as though they were taken right out of a cartoon and set in the small model country town called Duckburg. It boasts a farm animal petting zoo, a live theater, Mickey's personal residence, and a large population of Disney characters. Mickey's Starland appeals primarily to small children and devoted Disney character fans.

◆ *Grandma Duck's Farm* — In this barnyard petting zoo, complete with windmill and water tower, visitors have a chance to encounter Minnie Moo the cow and her many animal friends, including ponies, ducks, rabbits, pigs, sheep, and roof-climbing goats. (Watch for the natural Mickey Mouse markings on the cow, pigs, and other animals.) This attraction is rarely crowded, and animal lovers of all ages can enjoy it at any time of day. Duration: No time limitation. ✖

◆ *Mickey's Hollywood Theatre* — This large, round, tentlike structure houses Mickey's dressing room, fitted with lighted mirrors and racks of costumes. Here, Mickey Mouse fans have a chance to collect autographs and photographs when they meet Mickey backstage between his many public appearances. Duration: No time limitation. ✖

◆ *Mickey's House and Starland Show* — Mickey's bright yellow house, decorated with furnishings and props familiar to Disney cartoon lovers, is always open. When visitors exit the house at the rear, they pass the residences of other Disney characters, including Donald Duck's houseboat and Goofy's sloppy bachelor pad, as they head for the yellow-and-white striped tent. Inside, Mickey Mouse and other Disney characters perform energetic live skits. Duration: Approximately 35 minutes. 👫

◆ *Walt Disney World Railroad, Mickey's Starland Station* — The vividly painted train station at Mickey's Starland sets the cartoon-fantasy tone of the small, cheerful town of Duckburg. Disney characters can often be seen at the station greeting or seeing off their visitors. Duration: Approximately 20 minutes for the entire circuit. ✗✗

TOMORROWLAND: Tomorrowland is distinguished from the rest of the Magic Kingdom's theme lands by large expanses of cement walkways, trees trimmed into futuristic shapes, and the huge UFO-like building that houses Space Mountain. Although some of the attractions have been recently updated, much of what was once a high-tech vision for the future now seems dated and campy. (A major revamping is planned over the next few years.) Surprisingly, though, this quality can add an unexpected twist, as visitors will find yesterday's visions of the future an entertainment in itself.

◆ *American Journeys* — This Circle-Vision 360 film, shown in a stand-up theater, takes visitors through some of America's spectacular landscapes. Despite the highly patriotic overtones of the film's narration, visitors from all over the world can't help but enjoy the trip as they fly over the stark beauty of Alaska, view Mt. St. Helens two days after its eruption, swim through Florida's underwater wonderlands, and watch a huge fireworks display at the Statue of Liberty. In 1995, this attraction will be updated as a multi-media film-in-the-round adventure. The theater accommodates more than three thousand visitors each hour, so this attraction can be enjoyed at almost any time. Duration: 20 minutes. ✗✗

◆ *Carousel of Progress* — This attraction examines the lifestyles of the American family as it has been changed, and will further change, through technological progress. Visitors seated on a revolving turntable watch while Audio-Animatronic figures depict lifestyles of the future in authentically detailed settings. The original show was quite dated, but Carousel of Progress will be updated in 1994 to reflect a more modern version of the future. Duration: 25 minutes. ✗✗

◆ *Dreamflight* — This cheerful and informative attraction, although somewhat dated technically, is a journey through the history of modern aviation. The ride, which uses giant pop-up books as opening and closing motifs, mixes three-dimensional sets and props with 70mm film footage, video imagery, computer graphics, and special "you-are-there" effects. Duration: 6 minutes. ✗✗

◆ *Grand Prix Raceway* — Visitors drive miniature gasoline-powered cars along one of four parallel tracks, each half a mile long. The cars were designed for children and roar along noisily at a top speed of seven miles per hour. Adults will probably be disappointed, unless they have entered their second childhood. Duration: Approximately 5 minutes, depending on driving speed. 👫

◆ *Mission to Mars* — In this attraction, visitors take a simulated rocket voyage, complete with shaking seats and deafening engine roars, to the Red Planet. During the journey, views of outer space appear in a theater-in-the-round format, followed by a brief fly-over look at the surface of Mars and the largest known volcano in the solar system. While many of these images are actual pictures from NASA's space exploration archives, the overall presentation is rather dull and dated. Duration: 17 minutes. ✗

◆ *Skyway to Fantasyland* — This overhead cable car ride transports visitors from Tomorrowland to Fantasyland. Sitting in an open-air gondola, visitors get a spectacular view of the Magic Kingdom. Since each car only holds a few people and there is no specific scenario demanding viewer attention, visitors will find this ride an excellent opportunity to relax and enjoy the view. Duration: 5 minutes. ✗✗

◆ *Space Mountain* — Housed in a huge spired and domed structure visible throughout the Magic Kingdom and beyond, Space Mountain takes visitors on a wild roller coaster ride through the cosmos.

From the moment they enter the spaceport, with its sleek, futuristic decor and atmosphere, visitors are caught up in the excitement. Once on board, they are hurtled through mostly dark space, illuminated occasionally by flashing comets, colorful bursts, and whirling galaxies. Distinctive special effects, the creative use of darkness, and two roller coasters running concurrently make this attraction a must-try experience. The thrill can be taxing, however, and health restrictions apply. Duration: Preshow and post-show 20 minutes; ride 3 minutes. ✗✗✗

✦ *StarJets* — This attraction features miniature space shuttles that spin, dip, and lift in circles. Most adult visitors will find StarJets a disappointment, despite the memories of those who thrilled to it as children. Duration: 2 minutes. 🚶

✦ *WEDway PeopleMover* — On this attraction, visitors see an experiential sampler of the many attractions at Tomorrowland as they ride on a pollution-free, elevated-track tram. Basically a pleasant and informative orientation tour, the WEDway PeopleMover wends its way above, alongside, or through almost every attraction, including Space Mountain, traveling at a top speed of ten miles per hour. First-time visitors will find this ride especially helpful in orienting themselves. Duration: 10 minutes. ✗✗

SPECIAL EVENTS AND LIVE ENTERTAINMENT

Live entertainment events are scheduled throughout the day at numerous locations in the Magic Kingdom. As you enter the park, pick up an entertainment schedule at City Hall, on Main Street.

DIAMOND HORSESHOE JAMBOREE: Visitors of all ages are entertained here with a selection of songs and dances from the Gay Nineties. Staged in an Old West saloon in Frontierland, the lively production includes rollicking tunes, comic vignettes, and skilled performances of can-can dancing, as well as some delightfully provocative moments. A limited selection of sandwiches and snacks is available for purchase before the show starts. The Diamond Horseshoe Jamboree is an extremely popular attraction that usually plays to a full house. Visitors who plan to attend this show should make reservations as soon as they arrive at the Magic Kingdom at the podium in front of Disneyana Collectibles on Main Street. Visitors unable to get a confirmed reservation can show up at the saloon about forty-five minutes before the scheduled show time and talk to the hostess, who will seat them on a first-come, first-served basis if an empty table is available. (See "Dinner Shows," page 209.) Duration: 1 hour and 15 minutes. ✗✗

AFTERNOON PARADE: This large-scale extravaganza, sometimes called "Surprise Celebration Parade," gives visitors to the Magic Kingdom a taste of Mardi Gras every afternoon at 3 PM. Elaborate floats, dancers and stilt-walkers in flashy costumes, and giant inflatables of Disney characters over three stories high are just some of the features of this grand parade. It is best watched from Frontierland or Liberty Square, where crowds are thinner than on Main Street. Duration: Approximately 15 minutes. ✗✗

SpectroMagic: At selected times throughout the year, SpectroMagic, a magical nighttime parade of elaborate, twinkling floats, combines high-tech lighting and sound sophistry, fantastic set designs, and live performers to re-create scenes from a number of Disney films, including *Fantasia* and *The Little Mermaid*. Check the entertainment schedule for show times. SpectroMagic attracts huge crowds, especially along Main Street, where viewers gather as much as an hour before the parade begins. A handy tip: Those who want to watch the parade on Main Street should try to find a spot by a trash container — there will rarely be someone standing in front of it, and the top is a convenient place to set packages, beverages, and other items. Otherwise, SpectroMagic is best watched from Frontierland or Liberty Square, where the crowds are thinner. Duration: Approximately 20 minutes. ✘✘✘

FANTASY IN THE SKY FIREWORKS: At selected times, when Magic Kingdom hours are extended to 10 PM or later, visitors can enjoy this fantasy fireworks show above Cinderella's Castle. The show begins with Tinkerbell's dramatic flight from a high castle tower across the sky to Tomorrowland. Check the entertainment schedule for show times and dates. Duration: Approximately 15 minutes. ✘✘✘

CASTLE FORECOURT STAGE: At this outdoor gathering spot in front of Cinderella's Castle (the Main Street side), visitors can enjoy a variety of musical stage performances featuring Disney characters from recent film releases. Check the entertainment schedule for show times. ✘✘

FANTASY FAIRE: Various musical and theatrical performances by guest artists and Disney characters are staged daily in this giant, fairy-tale tent located across from Cinderella's Golden Carousel in Fantasyland. Check the entertainment schedule for events and show times. ✘

TOMORROWLAND THEATRE: Live music and dance performances by visiting bands or musical groups are staged in this large, open-air theater located in Tomorrowland. Check the entertainment schedule for events and show times. ✘

TOUR: *Guided Tour of the Magic Kingdom* — Departing daily at 10:30 AM from City Hall, this walking tour is an informative, hassle-free way for visitors to see the highlights of the Magic Kingdom and learn about the history of Walt Disney World. Often included in the tour are Dreamflight, It's A Small World, The Haunted Mansion, Diamond Horseshoe Jamboree (for lunch), Pirates of the Caribbean, and Jungle Cruise. (Attractions visited on the tour may vary with the seasons.) Same-day reservations only, made at City Hall; about $5 excluding food. Duration: Approximately 3 to 4 hours. ✘✘

✳

FULL-SERVICE RESTAURANTS

Guests staying at WDW resorts can make restaurant reservations up to three days in advance for the Liberty Tree Tavern and King Stefan's Banquet Hall. Same-day reservations must be made in person at the restaurant itself. Tony's Town Square Restaurant accepts reservations only on the same day. There are no alcoholic beverages served in the Magic Kingdom. Smoking is not permitted in the restaurants. See "Restaurants," page 167, for detailed restaurant reviews and reservation strategies.

MAIN STREET, U.S.A.: *Tony's Town Square Restaurant* — Diners in this Victorian-style restaurant, with its elaborately painted woodwork and spacious interior, enjoy meals in a pleasant *Lady and the Tramp* setting. The menu features waffles, eggs, and pancakes in the morning, and pasta, pizza, and other Italian dishes throughout the day. Espresso and cappuccino are served. Open for breakfast, lunch, and dinner; same-day reservations only, taken at the door. Reservations suggested.

The Plaza Restaurant — This light and airy restaurant has a pleasant, fanciful Art Nouveau ambience. The menu features a selection of hot entrees, sandwiches, hamburgers, and salads. Espresso, cappuccino, and café mocha are served. Open for lunch and dinner; no reservations.

The Crystal Palace — This replica of a Victorian-era conservatory has a circular atrium and skylights throughout and offers cafeteria-style service in a spacious plant-filled environment. The menu features a full breakfast menu in the morning, and prime rib, roast chicken, seafood, and sandwiches during the day. Open for breakfast, lunch, and dinner. No reservations.

LIBERTY SQUARE: *Liberty Tree Tavern* — With its low lighting, plank floors, and giant fireplace, this restaurant provides friendly service in a comfortable colonial setting. The menu features New England clam chowder all day long, with large salads and sandwiches served throughout the day and prime rib, fresh seafood, and chicken dishes in the evening. Open for lunch and dinner; reservations required.

FANTASYLAND: *King Stefan's Banquet Hall* — High up in Cinderella's Castle, majestic carved doors, stained-glass windows, and costumed servers give this restaurant a medieval elegance. Cinderella herself makes an occasional appearance here. The menu features salads, sandwiches, roast beef, seafood, and chicken dishes. Open for lunch and dinner; reservations required.

CAFES

There are refreshment stands that serve snacks and fast-food meals throughout the Magic Kingdom. A few, listed below, are especially pleasant rest stops and meeting spots for visitors who want to tour separately and rendezvous at a later time. No alcohol is served in the Magic Kingdom.

MAIN STREET, U.S.A.: *Main Street Bake Shop* — Freshly baked cookies, cakes, tarts, and other pastries are available to eat at small, cozy tables tucked into a turn-of-the-century tearoom. 🍴

ADVENTURELAND: *Adventureland Veranda* — Teriyaki-type sandwiches and snacks, as well as a limited selection of desserts, are served in this spacious, tropical-style fast-food eatery. 🍴

LIBERTY SQUARE: *Columbia Harbour House* — This cozy, antique-filled restaurant serves clam chowder, sandwiches, and seafood dishes in a nautical colonial atmosphere. 🍴

FANTASYLAND: *Pinocchio Village Haus* — This two-story Bavarian-styled fast-food restaurant serves bratwurst, turkey sandwiches, and pasta salads. 🍴

TOMORROWLAND: *Plaza Pavilion* — Large open rooms decorated in bright contemporary colors and an outdoor terrace overlooking nearby gardens provide a comfortable place to take a break and enjoy pizza, pasta, and other fast-food fare. 🍴

SERVICES

REST ROOMS: Public rest rooms are numerous throughout the Magic Kingdom. On Main Street, the rest rooms to the right of City Hall, although crowded in the morning and evening, are relatively free of people in the afternoon. Despite large crowds, rest rooms located across from the Swiss Family Treehouse, in the breezeway between Adventureland and Frontierland, rarely have waits. In Fantasyland, the rest rooms behind the Enchanted Grove (near Mr. Toad's Wild Ride) usually do not attract large crowds. In Tomorrowland, the least crowded rest rooms are those by the Skyway to Fantasyland. For quieter accommodations, King Stefan's Banquet Hall in Cinderella's Castle has rest rooms halfway up the stairs, although most restaurant rest rooms are crowded during mealtimes.

TELEPHONES: Public telephones are located throughout the Magic Kingdom. The least busy are those located near the Crystal Palace restaurant at the end of Main Street; at the exit to Pirates of the Caribbean in Adventureland; behind the Enchanted Grove (near Mr. Toad's Wild Ride) in Fantasyland; near the Skyway to Fantasyland in Tomorrowland; and at the Frontierland Railroad Station. For air-conditioned calls, slip into a full-service restaurant, where telephones are located near the rest rooms.

MESSAGE CENTER: At Walt Disney World's computerized Message Center, located at Guest Relations in City Hall on Main Street, visitors can leave and retrieve messages for one another. The Message Center is on a network also shared by Epcot Center and Disney-MGM Studios, so visitors at one park can exchange messages with companions visiting elsewhere.

FILM AND TWO-HOUR EXPRESS DEVELOPING: Film is available at many shops throughout the Magic Kingdom. Drop-off points for express developing are at the Kodak Camera Center on Main Street; at the Crow's Nest in Adventureland; at the Kodak Kiosk in Fantasyland, across from Cinderella's Golden Carousel; and at the Skyway Station Shop in Tomorrowland. Developed pictures may be picked up at the Kodak Camera Center on Main Street or delivered to any WDW resort.

CAMERA RENTAL: Video cameras (and replacement batteries) and 35mm cameras are available at the Kodak Camera Center on Main Street. Film is available at shops and kiosks throughout the park.

MAIL DROPS: Mail-drop locations are scattered throughout the Magic Kingdom. Mail drops are located at the Guest Relations Window in the Entrance Plaza, in front of City Hall and Tony's Town Square Restaurant, and here and there on both sides of Main Street (look for the olive-colored boxes); in Adventureland across from the Swiss Family Treehouse and across from the Pirates of the Caribbean; in Frontierland across from the Country Bear Jamboree; in Fantasyland near Tinkerbell Toy Shop across from Cinderella's Castle; and in Tomorrowland across from the Grand Prix Raceway. Stamps may be purchased at City Hall, the Emporium, and the Penny Arcade, all located on Main Street.

BANKING: The Sun Bank, with full banking services and a foreign currency exchange, is located on Main Street, near the park entrance. An automated teller machine (ATM) can be found nearby.

LOCKERS: Lockers are located on the lower level of the Main Street Railroad Station. Oversized packages may be left at City Hall, on Main Street.

PACKAGE PICKUP: To avoid carrying purchases, visitors can forward them free of charge to the Guest Relations Window in the Magic Kingdom's Entrance Plaza and pick them up as they leave the park. Allow two to three hours between purchase and pick up.

FIRST AID: The first-aid station is near the Crystal Palace restaurant, just to the left off Main Street. Aspirin and other first-aid needs are dispensed free of charge. Over-the-counter medications are available at the Emporium on Main Street. They are not on display and must be requested at the counter.

VISITORS WITH DISABILITIES: A complimentary guidebook for disabled guests is available at the Guest Relations Window in the Entrance Plaza and at City Hall, on Main Street. Visitors with disabilities should note that the monorail stop at the Contemporary resort is not accessible to wheelchairs. Most attractions within the Magic Kingdom have direct, uncomplicated wheelchair access, but there are a number of exceptions. For many of the these attractions, however, special arrangements can be made to transfer visitors from wheelchairs into the ride vehicle. Ask at City Hall. Special areas along the Magic Kingdom parade route are designated for visitors who depend on wheelchairs. Ask at City Hall for these locations, available on a first-come, first-served basis.

WHEELCHAIR RENTALS: Wheelchairs can be rented at the Stroller Shop, just inside the park's main entrance. Motorized wheelchair replacements are available at the Briar Patch in Frontierland, the Tinker-bell Toy Shop in Fantasyland, and the Space Port in Tomorrowland.

HEARING-IMPAIRED VISITORS: A written description of the Magic Kingdom attractions is available at City Hall, on Main Street. Hearing aid–compatible and amplified telephones can be found throughout the Magic Kingdom.

SIGHT-IMPAIRED VISITORS: Complimentary touring cassettes that describe the park are available at City Hall, located on Main Street. Also available is a Braille text describing sights and attractions.

FOREIGN LANGUAGE ASSISTANCE: Park maps in French, Spanish, and German are available at City Hall, located on Main Street.

✦

COMING ATTRACTIONS

Plans are always on the drawing board for new attractions throughout Walt Disney World, but until construction actually begins, these plans have a way of changing or becoming delayed. At the time of publication, several new attractions and a major revamping of Tomorrowland were planned for the Magic Kingdom. The Tomorrowland remodeling is currently scheduled for completion in 1995.

TOMORROWLAND: *New Circle-Vision 360 Attraction* — This film-in-the-round adventure will replace the current offering, *American Journeys.* The new show will be a multimedia production combining Audio-Animatronic figures with film, and presenting visitors with an overview of Western civilization and culture. (We'll have to wait and see what that means.)

TOMORROWLAND: *One Man's Dream* — This stage show, currently a big draw at Tokyo's Disneyland, is scheduled to debut at Tomorrowland Theatre in the near future. The show highlights the musical films created by Disney over the past sixty-five years.

TOMORROWLAND: *Tomorrowland Remodeling* — By 1995, all of Tomorrowland is scheduled to be completely remodeled. Its current sterile appearance will take on an elaborate science fiction ambience, a high-tech cross between Buck Rogers and the Jetsons. Mission to Mars will become Alien Encounter, involving a scary teleporting error that brings a terrifying alien being into visitors' midst. Other proposed attractions include Plectu's Fantastic Galactic Revue, a musical show set in outer space, with Audio-Animatronic alien performers. Also planned is an attraction featuring time travel, and StarJets will be updated to soar through the solar system. Carousel of Progress will reopen in 1994, redesigned to reflect a broader version of the past and future, accompanied by a revised theme song.

Half-Day Tours at the Magic Kingdom

The morning and evening half-day tours that follow are designed to allow first-time visitors to experience the best of the Magic Kingdom in four to five hours, including a lunch or dinner in one of Magic Kingdom restaurants. If you wish to eat at King Stefan's Banquet Hall or Liberty Tree Tavern, make your restaurant reservation in advance, if possible. Otherwise, you will need to make same-day reservations in person at the restaurant's door, as there is no central reservations facility in the Magic Kingdom.

The Magic Kingdom Morning Tour, below, is designed for low-attendance times — September through March, excluding holidays. If you want to visit the Magic Kingdom in the morning during a crowded time, hurry first thing in the morning to some of the popular attractions that are not included on the Guided Tour of the Magic Kingdom, then join the Guided Tour, which leaves City Hall at 10:30 AM. The Guided Tour is not always offered in the summer. Check ahead for the attractions that will be visited (407 824-4521).

The SpectroMagic Afternoon and Evening Tour, however, *is* designed for peak-attendance times when the Magic Kingdom is open late and the SpectroMagic parade and Fantasy in the Sky fireworks are scheduled: May through August, during holiday periods, and on Saturday nights throughout the year.

To create your own custom vacation at Walt Disney World, you can combine one of these half-day Magic Kingdom tours with a half-day tour from any other theme park. For example, combine the Magic Kingdom Morning Tour with an evening tour at Future World. The theme parks are most crowded in the afternoons, which is an ideal time to relax or take advantage of the resort amenities at Walt Disney World.

✳

MAGIC KINGDOM MORNING TOUR

Four to five hours — September through March (except holiday periods) — including lunch.
If possible, a day or two before this tour reserve a late lunch (1 PM or later)
at King Stefan's Banquet Hall or Liberty Tree Tavern,
or plan to have lunch at Tony's Town Square Restaurant or at your resort.

✔ Eat a full breakfast before leaving your hotel.

✔ Arrive at the Magic Kingdom Entrance Plaza one half hour before the scheduled opening time.

✔ Take in the sights along Main Street, which opens one half hour before the rest of the park. If you do not have restaurant reservations, you may want to stop at Tony's Town Square Restaurant at the beginning of Main Street, and make lunch reservations for 1 PM or later. Time your Main Street tour so you arrive at the entrance to Adventureland when the park opens (between 8 and 9 AM).

✔ Beginning in Adventureland, visit, in the order listed below, the following attractions that interest you:
  - Adventureland — **JUNGLE CRUISE** and **PIRATES OF THE CARIBBEAN**
  - Frontierland — **SPLASH MOUNTAIN** and **BIG THUNDER MOUNTAIN RAILROAD** (if you like roller coasters)
  - Liberty Square — **THE HAUNTED MANSION** and **THE HALL OF PRESIDENTS** (if U.S. history interests you)
  - Fantasyland — **PETER PAN'S FLIGHT** (if you're feeling young at heart) and **IT'S A SMALL WORLD** (ditto)

- Mickey's Starland — take a stroll through Duckburg (Do not spend more than fifteen minutes.)
- Tomorrowland — **SPACE MOUNTAIN** (if you like roller coasters and the wait is not too long) and **WEDWAY PEOPLEMOVER** and **DREAMFLIGHT** (if time and energy permit).

✔ Plan to arrive at your lunch destination ten minutes early. If you did not have enough time to visit all the attractions you wanted to see, return in the evening when the crowds are smaller.

✳

SPECTROMAGIC AFTERNOON AND EVENING TOUR

Four to six hours — May through August (plus holidays and Saturday nights) — including dinner.
If possible, a day or two before this tour reserve an early dinner
at King Stefan's Banquet Hall or Liberty Tree Tavern.
If you prefer a late dinner, be sure to let the reservationist know that you want to see SpectroMagic and
would like to finish dinner before the first parade begins (usually at 9 PM).

✔ Arrive at the Magic Kingdom Entrance Plaza at 4 PM. Pick up an entertainment schedule, which lists the show times for live performances and SpectroMagic.

✔ If you do not have a dinner reservation and would like to eat at King Stefan's Banquet Hall or Liberty Tree Tavern, go directly to the restaurant to make a reservation. Or, if you wish, stop at Tony's Town Square Restaurant at the beginning of Main Street and make a reservation there for later.

✔ As you make your way toward Adventureland, take in the sights along Main Street.

✔ Beginning in Adventureland, visit, in the order listed below, the following attractions that interest you (your tour will be interrupted at times for dinner and for SpectroMagic):
  - Adventureland — **JUNGLE CRUISE** and **PIRATES OF THE CARIBBEAN**
  - Frontierland — **SPLASH MOUNTAIN** and **BIG THUNDER MOUNTAIN RAILROAD** (if you like roller coasters)
  - Liberty Square — **THE HAUNTED MANSION** and **THE HALL OF PRESIDENTS** (if U.S. history interests you)
  - Frontierland — for a ride on the **WALT DISNEY WORLD RAILROAD** to Mickey's Starland
  - Mickey's Starland — for a stroll through Duckburg on your way to Fantasyland
  - Fantasyland — **PETER PAN'S FLIGHT** and **IT'S A SMALL WORLD** (for the young at heart)
  - Tomorrowland — **SPACE MOUNTAIN** (if you like roller coasters and the wait is not too long) and **WEDWAY PEOPLEMOVER** and **DREAMFLIGHT**.

✔ Pause in your tour for your dinner reservation, then continue your tour where you left off.

✔ Within one half hour of **SPECTROMAGIC**, secure a viewing spot along the parade route. Liberty Square and Frontierland are usually less crowded than Main Street.

✔ After SpectroMagic passes your viewing spot, return to Tomorrowland (if you did not yet get there or wish to see more), where the lines will now be shorter.

✔ On nights when the park stays open late, be sure to stay for the **FANTASY IN THE SKY** fireworks show, which is scheduled about one hour after SpectroMagic. A good viewing location is from the walkway between Tomorrowland and Main Street, U.S.A. ◆

PLEASURE ISLAND

Pleasure Island was designed exclusively for adult visitors to Walt Disney World — its six acres comprise a fantasy of upbeat, sophisticated entertainments. During the day, visitors can shop the main street for trendy attire and contemporary gifts, enjoy lunch, or catch a matinee at the Island's ten-screen theater complex. At night, Pleasure Island is transformed: Limousines line up at the entrance, the streets fill with party goers, the nightclubs open for business and pleasure, and the outdoor stage comes alive with music and dance performances, culminating with a splashy, every-night New Year's Eve celebration and fireworks show.

WHEN TO GO: Pleasure Island's clubs are open from between 7 and 8 PM until 2 AM, the shops are open from 10 AM until 1 AM, and the AMC Theatres screen films from 10 AM until 10:30 PM (and until 12:30 AM on weekends). The Island's legendary nightlife begins at 7 PM, when the ticket booths open and admission is charged. The most crowded nights are Thursday (when WDW Cast Members receive discounts) and Friday and Saturday, when local residents join WDW visitors' ranks. To sample the entertainment offerings at all the clubs, which are running full speed as early as 7:45 PM, it is best to arrive early and plan to stay late. Entertainment events in Pleasure Island's clubs change frequently, as does the time of the nightly New Year's Eve countdown. The day you go, you may want to check the time of the New Year's Eve show (934-7781) and plan accordingly. For performance schedules for the various clubs, pick up an entertainment schedule as you enter Pleasure Island. For information on featured films and show times at the AMC Pleasure Island 10 Theatres, call 827-1300.

HOW TO GET THERE: Pleasure Island is located in the Disney Village Resorts Area. Free parking is available in the large lot at Pleasure Island and at the nearby Disney Village Marketplace and AMC Theatres. Starting at 5:30 PM, valet parking is offered. WDW buses travel at night between all WDW resorts and theme parks and Pleasure Island. Water launches service the following resorts: Vacation Club, Dixie Landings, Port Orleans, and Village Resort. Taxi service is available.

ADMISSIONS AND RESTRICTIONS: From 10 AM until 7 PM, admission to Pleasure Island is free and there are no age restrictions. After 7 PM, admission is about $16 for the evening, which includes admission to all clubs and entertainment. Admission to Pleasure Island is included with some multiday passes. Movie-Island combo tickets are also available.

After 7 PM, no one under the age of eighteen is permitted on Pleasure Island or in the clubs without an accompanying adult, and one club, Mannequins, prohibits those under twenty-one. Even visitors over 18 should be sure to bring along a picture ID (valid passport, U.S. driver's license, or foreign driver's license with a back-up ID). Florida law prohibits serving alcohol to anyone under twenty-one. Alcoholic beverages may be consumed anywhere on Pleasure Island as long as they are carried in plastic cups, which are conveniently placed at the exits of all the clubs. Smoking is not permitted inside the clubs.

✳

NIGHTCLUBS

XXX – Solid entertainment. **XX** – Good fun if it meets your special interests. **X** – Worth a quick walkthrough.

MANNEQUINS DANCE PALACE: Featuring mannequins that are dressed and posed to reflect myriad aspects of dance, dazzling light and sound shows, and live on-stage dance performances, this club is rated,

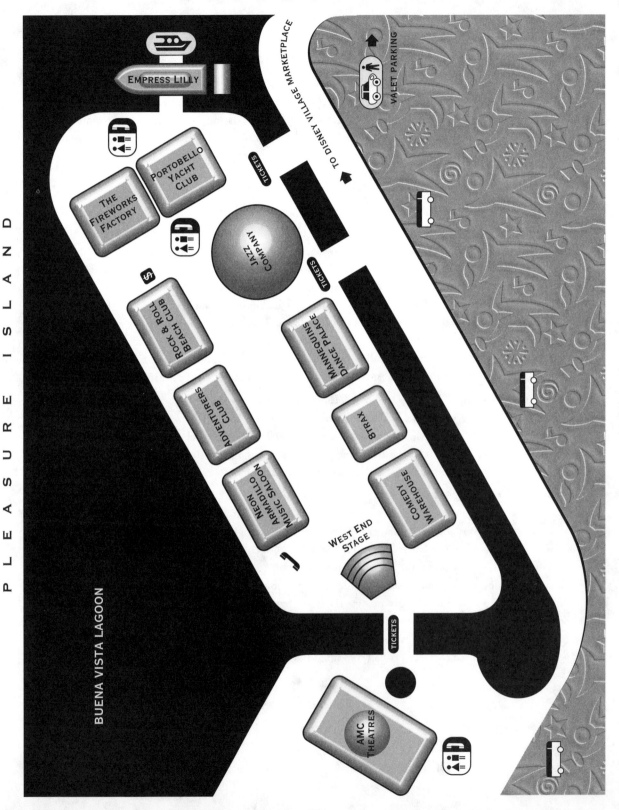

PLEASURE ISLAND

BUENA VISTA LAGOON

EMPRESS LILLY

THE FIREWORKS FACTORY

PORTOBELLO YACHT CLUB

JAZZ COMPANY

ROCK & ROLL BEACH CLUB

ADVENTURERS CLUB

NEON ARMADILLO MUSIC SALOON

MANNEQUINS DANCE PALACE

8TRAX

COMEDY WAREHOUSE

WEST END STAGE

AMC THEATRES

TO DISNEY VILLAGE MARKETPLACE

VALET PARKING

TICKETS

deservedly, as the No. 1 dance club in the Southeast. The dance floor is a giant moving turntable that fills quickly as professional DJs work with high-tech sound equipment to spin contemporary pop tunes. Mannequins is the most popular gathering spot on Pleasure Island, and weekend lines start to form at the club door around 8:30 PM. Beer, wine, and spirits are served. A selection of champagnes, including Dom Perignon, is offered, as are specialty drinks. Mannequins opens at 8 PM. No one under the age of twenty-one may enter. A special-effects sound, laser, and dance performance is scheduled twice nightly, and it's well worth the effort to catch it. Check the entertainment schedule for show times. ✘✘✘

8TRAX: This club has gone through several transformations, and in its latest version it revives the music of the late sixties and early seventies. The black cagelike scaffolding of its predecessor remains, but the decor has been enhanced with lava lamps, tie-dyed fabrics, and a giant peace symbol wall hanging. The video monitors scattered about show psychedelic light-show footage, while the club's superior sound system pumps out the Village People, Led Zeppelin, the Bee Gees, and early Michael Jackson the way they were meant to sound. 8trax picks up speed later in the evening, when cages holding go-go dancers in hot pants drop from the ceiling. Visitors perch on stools tucked into intimate alcoves or overlooking the dance floor, below. Beer, wine, and spirits are served, including specialty drinks with names like Running on Empty and Brady Bunch Punch. Light snacks are also available. ✘✘

COMEDY WAREHOUSE: Each night, Pleasure Island visitors crowd into this large multilevel room decorated with movie props and settle onto one of its stools for some solid comedy entertainment. The five talented comedians, accompanied by their musician sidekick, are experts at improvising hilarious skits and routines that play heavily off audience participation — and the audience loves every minute of it. Guest comedians also make appearances on selected nights. Beer, wine, and spirits are served, including specialty drinks. Lines form at the door up to an hour before the shows on busy nights. The first show is easiest to get into and, on weekends, the third show is timed to get guests back out on the street for the New Year's Eve show. The thirty-five-minute shows begin around 7:40 PM. Check the entertainment schedule for show times. ✘✘

NEON ARMADILLO MUSIC SALOON: This high-energy country-western club features a large dance floor, a startlingly different chandelier in the shape of a spur, and live shows by well-known country-western performers. Free dance classes, where visitors can learn two step, country swing, and line dances like the Tush Push, are offered on some evenings, beginning at 7 PM. Beer, wine, and spirits are served, including specialty drinks such as Cactus Coolaid — a blend of cactus juice, Triple Sec, and vodka — and the Bloody Bullet, a throat-searing, sinus-clearing Cajun martini. The Neon Armadillo offers quesadillas, hamburgers, and fajitas, along with finger foods such as onion rings and Cow Chips (potato skins). The club opens at 7 PM, with forty-five-minute sets of live music starting at around 8 PM, although visitors can come and go as they please. Check the entertainment schedule for show times. ✘✘✘

ADVENTURERS CLUB: Visitors enter this take-off on a 1930s British explorers club from an octagonal balcony overlooking the room below. The balcony, which houses a small bar in the back and comfortable chairs to sink into, is filled with books, photos, and memorabilia from faraway and exotic places, including a curio cabinet in the shape of a large zebra. The main room, downstairs, is furnished with sofas and love seats and a larger bar with barstools that rise and lower unexpectedly at the whim of the bartender.

The regular club members, a slightly eccentric and delightfully self-centered group of actors, mingle with the merely visiting, embroiling them in altercations, lectures, and a number of curious and inexplicable events that seem to happen every half hour or so. Beer, wine, and spirits are served, including specialty drinks such as the Kungaloosh, a frozen blend of fruit juices laced with rum and blackberry brandy. The Adventurers Club opens at 7 PM, with periodic shows presented in the adjacent library, complete with haunted organ. Check the entertainment schedule for show times. ✗✗

ROCK & ROLL BEACH CLUB: Visitors follow the surfboards lining the handrails up three flights of stairs and enter this dance club on the third level before descending through two levels of bars, pool tables, and video games to the stage and dance floor below. Live bands perform Top 40 and classic rock numbers, and DJs pick up the slack between sets. The atmosphere is relaxed and casual, and caters to the tastes of a younger crowd, which means the music is very loud. (There is a small alcove with seating on the second level, by the elevator, where guests can get away from the noise, have a conversation, and look out over the street in front of the club.) Beer, wine, and spirits are served, and New York–style pizza is sold by the slice. The Rock & Roll Beach Club opens at 7 PM, with forty-five-minute sets of live music starting at about 8 PM. Check the entertainment schedule for show times. ✗

JAZZ COMPANY: The Jazz Company offers a sophisticated atmosphere where visitors can hold conversations as they enjoy live jazz, blues, and classic jam sessions by local, national, and international performers. Beer, wine, and spirits are served, with a special focus on wines and champagnes by the glass. Snacks and appetizers are available, and the Jazz Company features a tapas bar with an assortment of appetizers for light meals. The Jazz Company opens at 7:30 PM, with sets of live music starting at about 8 PM. Check the entertainment schedule for show times. ✗✗✗

EVENTS AND ENTERTAINMENT

AMC PLEASURE ISLAND 10 THEATRES: The Pleasure Island movie theaters are open to all WDW visitors. In the evenings, Pleasure Island guests can cross the bridge behind the West End Stage to reach the theaters, which are housed in a large industrial-style building with a soaring glass and steel atrium. Ten screens show first-run movies, and all have Dolby stereo digital Surround Sound (four have THX sound). Just as one would expect from Disney, all the modern comforts are present and accounted for, from the nifty decor to the comfortable seats with armrest drink holders. Furthermore, the theaters are an achievement in spotlessness. WDW resort guests receive a discount with their resort ID. Low-attendance times are before 4 PM. Visitors can avoid lines by charging their tickets by phone just before they leave for the show (827-1308). Call 827-1300 for movie listings and show times. ✗✗

WEST END STAGE: This huge outdoor performance platform, framed by shiny, high-tech lighting trusses and massive speakers, presents live rock that gets guests moving and keeps them jumping all night long, culminating with the spectacular New Year's Eve Street Party. Talented local bands or guest artists appear in concert nightly, with shows beginning around 7:30 PM. Check the entertainment schedule for show times and events. To avoid the dense crowd near the stage, visitors can view the performances on the Video Stage, an outdoor wall of twenty-five video monitors located near Mannequins. ✗✗

✦ PLEASURE ISLAND ✦

NEW YEAR'S EVE STREET PARTY: The New Year's Eve blast that you have always dreamed about materializes every night at Pleasure Island. At the West End Stage, professional dancers in sexy, eye-popping costumes work up a sweat as they power through slick, complex, and fabulously choreographed routines. As the countdown to the New Year begins, around 10:45 PM (11:45 PM on Fridays and Saturdays), visitors join in from the street, creating a revelry that erupts — along with fireworks, confetti, and a sound and light show — into a frenetic, ecstatic dance party. Check the entertainment schedule for show times. ✖✖✖

✦

FULL-SERVICE RESTAURANTS

The Fireworks Factory and the restaurants on board the Empress Lilly *riverboat accept reservations, which can be made up to thirty days in advance. Smoking is not permitted in the* Empress Lilly *restaurants. See "Restaurants," page 167, for detailed restaurant reviews and reservation strategies.*

EMPRESS ROOM ON BOARD THE *EMPRESS LILLY:* This is one of the the most elegant (and expensive) of the restaurants at Walt Disney World. It features sophisticated Continental cuisine in an ambience reminiscent of the days of Mme. de Pompadour, with secluded tables, etched-glass partitions, gold-leaf detailing, and a sparkling crystal chandelier. Beer, wine, and spirits are served. Men must wear jackets. Open for dinner only; reservations are required.

STEERMAN'S QUARTERS ON BOARD THE *EMPRESS LILLY:* Prime rib, steaks, and a limited selection of seafood are served in this cozy dining room, with its red-upholstered and dark mahogany furnishings, and windows overlooking the riverboat's revolving paddle wheel. Beer, wine, and spirits are served. Open for dinner only; reservations recommended.

FISHERMAN'S DECK ON BOARD THE *EMPRESS LILLY:* Fresh seafood and salads are featured in this delicate, comfortable salon, which is dominated by a large curved window overlooking Buena Vista Lagoon. Beer, wine, and spirits are served. Open for lunch and dinner; reservations are recommended.

THE FIREWORKS FACTORY: "Dynamite" barbecued ribs and other applewood-smoked specialties are served in this lively open dining room decorated with pyrotechnic paraphernalia and powder burns. Free souvenir postcards are available — ask your Factory Worker. Beer, wine, and spirits are served. The restaurant has a smoking section. Open all day until 3 AM; reservations are recommended.

PORTOBELLO YACHT CLUB: Guests can enjoy Italian specialties, fresh seafood, and a variety of oven-fired thin-crust pizzas on the outdoor terrace, or indoors in one of several spacious dining areas featuring yachting trophies, photographs, and other maritime mementos. Beer, wine, and spirits are served, as are excellent espresso and cappuccino. The restaurant has a smoking section. Open all day until 1:30 AM; no reservations.

✦

COCKTAIL LOUNGES AND CAFES

A number of refreshment stands and shops scattered around Pleasure Island serve fast-food meals and snacks. The lounges listed below are the most pleasant for a sit-down respite from the clubs. They can also serve as rendezvous spots for visitors who want to club-hop separately and meet up later. For before-dinner cocktails, drop into the friendly Fireworks Factory bar during happy hour.

THE FIREWORKS FACTORY BAR: This busy bar features more than forty-five domestic and imported beers, including ales and stouts. "Explosive" specialty drinks are also offered, including the Summer Sparkler (pink lemonade laced with citron-flavored vodka) and the Bangmaster (a spicy martini designed to blow your socks off). Appetizers include Sizzling Catfish, Super Smokehouse Wings, Fireworks Cheddar Cheese Fries, and BBQ Baby Back Ribs. Drinks are served at reduced prices on weekday afternoons, from 3 PM until 7 PM. ☕️🍸

PORTOBELLO YACHT CLUB BAR: Warm, dark mahogany wall panels coupled with polished brass fixtures give this bar a pleasant, clubby atmosphere. The full bar features an extensive array of grappas and good Italian wines. Appetizers include Quattro Fromaggi Pizza, Antipasto Assortito, Calamaretti Fritta, and Carpaccio, consisting of thinly sliced raw sirloin with artichoke hearts and Parmigiano cheese, chives, and balsamic vinaigrette. WDW's most potent espresso and cappuccino can be found here. ☕️🍸

BATON ROUGE LOUNGE: With its large open room, dark wood paneling, cozy tables, and comfortable bar, this lounge has a showboat ambience that makes it an appealing stop on an evening out. The bar serves such specialty drinks as the Tom Sawyer, a frozen blend of rum and fruit juice, and the Paddlewheeler, concocted from vodka, peach schnapps, and cranberry juice. Appetizers include Bayou Chips (homemade potato chips) and Crescent City Wings. Light music and comedy entertainment are presented in the evenings from the stage above the horseshoe-shaped bar. ☕️🍸

D-ZERTZ: This small snack shop is in the thick of the action at Pleasure Island. It features pastries, candy, and ice cream as well as coffee, espresso, and cappuccino. There is a small indoor seating area. ☕️

SERVICES

REST ROOMS: All restaurants and clubs have several rest rooms on the premises. An uncrowded public rest room is located between the Fireworks Factory and the Portobello Yacht Club. The Fireworks Factory has quiet and uncrowded rest rooms at the top of the stairs. The rest rooms on the *Empress Lilly* riverboat are very private and well appointed, especially those on the second deck, just outside the Empress Room restaurant.

TELEPHONES: Outdoor public telephones are located near the rest rooms between the Fireworks Factory and Portobello Yacht Club. There are telephones near the rest rooms in all restaurants and clubs, but the quietest phones are those at the Neon Armadillo, or upstairs at the Fireworks Factory. For the most privacy, use the phones on the *Empress Lilly* riverboat. Those on the second deck outside the Empress Room restaurant have plush, private sit-down cubicles.

BANKING: An automatic teller machine (ATM) and a change machine are located under the stairs leading up to the Rock & Roll Beach Club.

LOCKERS: Outdoor lockers are located near the rest rooms between the Fireworks Factory and the Portobello Yacht Club and around the corner from the Rock & Roll Beach Club. At 8trax there are lockers on the ground level near the rest room. Lockers at the Rock & Roll Beach Club are on the second level, near the elevator. At Mannequins Dance Palace, lockers are near the rest rooms on the ground level, inside the rest rooms, and next to the exit.

VISITORS WITH DISABILITIES: All areas of Pleasure Island are wheelchair accessible, and all clubs have elevators.

✳

Evening Tour at Pleasure Island

Five to six hours — year round — including dinner.
Make an early dinner reservation (about 6:30 PM)
at one of the Empress Lilly *riverboat restaurants or at the Fireworks Factory,*
or drop into the Portobello Yacht Club, where seating is usually available before 7 PM.

This tour is designed to allow first-time visitors to experience the best of Pleasure Island in a single evening. To create your own custom vacation at Walt Disney World, combine this tour with a morning tour at any other theme park. For example, combine the Evening Tour at Pleasure Island with a morning tour and lunch at Disney-MGM Studios. Use the afternoon to relax and enjoy the resort amenities at WDW.

✔ Enter Pleasure Island at 6 PM for a quick overview tour of the shops and attractions. At the entrance gate, pick up an entertainment schedule listing the evening's show times and events, and buy an admission ticket for later, if the ticket booths are open and you need one.

✔ Proceed to your selected restaurant for your 6:30 PM dinner.

✔ After dinner, stroll through the Fireworks Factory restaurant to the bar, where there is a back entrance to Pleasure Island. There, your ticket and/or ID will be checked.

✔ As you plan your early tour of the clubs, include some of the following entertainment events:
  • **COMEDY WAREHOUSE** — for an improvisational comedy performance (The first show starts around 7:30 PM.)
  • **MANNEQUINS DANCE PALACE** — for the terrific light, sound, and dance show that begins around 9:30 PM (Settle in upstairs with the stage platform clearly in view.)
  • **ADVENTURERS CLUB** — to eavesdrop on the club members' altercations or catch one of the bizarre performances in the adjacent library
  • **NEON ARMADILLO MUSIC SALOON** — for live and lively country-western music and dancing.

✔ At about 10:30 PM (11:30 PM on Fridays and Saturdays), begin to work your way toward the West End Stage and find a place in the crowd where you can enjoy the **NEW YEAR'S EVE STREET PARTY**.

✔ If you plan to party on, resume your late tour with some of the following attractions:
  • **8TRAX** — for dancing and music seventies-style
  • **JAZZ COMPANY** — to catch a set of live jazz by featured performers
  • **ROCK & ROLL BEACH CLUB** — to dance to R&R hits performed by a live band
  • **BATON ROUGE LOUNGE** — for a late-night music and comedy performance on board the *Empress Lilly* in a plush, low-key lounge setting
  • **AMC PLEASURE ISLAND 10 THEATRES** — for a late-night first-run feature. ◆

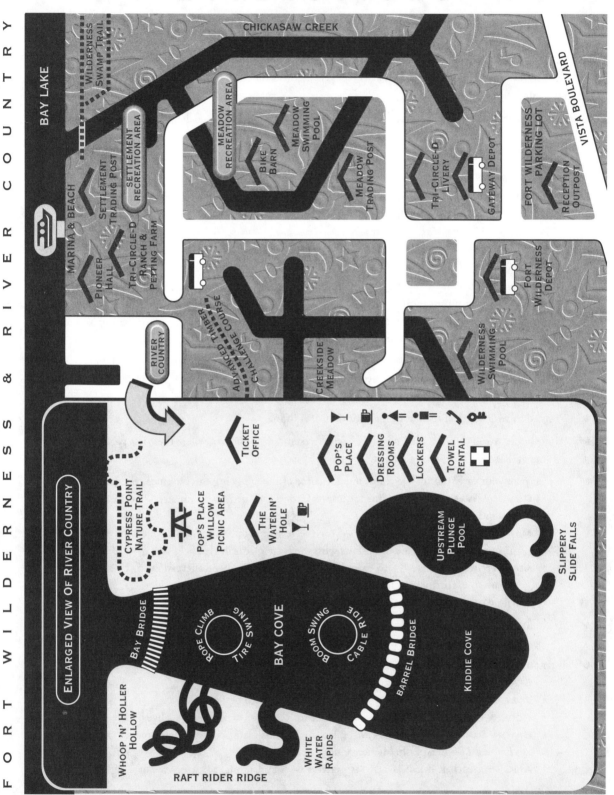

FORT WILDERNESS & RIVER COUNTRY

CHICKASAW CREEK

BAY LAKE

WILDERNESS SWAMP TRAIL

SETTLEMENT TRADING POST

SETTLEMENT RECREATION AREA

MEADOW RECREATION AREA

BIKE BARN

MEADOW SWIMMING POOL

MEADOW TRADING POST

TRI-CIRCLE-D LIVERY

GATEWAY DEPOT

FORT WILDERNESS PARKING LOT

VISTA BOULEVARD

RECEPTION OUTPOST

MARINA & BEACH

PIONEER HALL

TRI-CIRCLE-D RANCH & PETTING FARM

FORT WILDERNESS DEPOT

RIVER COUNTRY

ADVANCED TIMBER CHALLENGE COURSE

CREEKSIDE MEADOW

WILDERNESS SWIMMING POOL

ENLARGED VIEW OF RIVER COUNTRY

TICKET OFFICE

CYPRESS POINT NATURE TRAIL

POP'S PLACE WILLOW PICNIC AREA

THE WATERIN' HOLE

POP'S PLACE

DRESSING ROOMS

LOCKERS

TOWEL RENTAL

UPSTREAM PLUNGE POOL

SLIPPERY SLIDE FALLS

BAY BRIDGE

ROPE CLIMB

TIRE SWING

BAY COVE

BOOM SWING

CABLE RIDE

BARREL BRIDGE

KIDDIE COVE

WHOOP 'N' HOLLER HOLLOW

WHITE WATER RAPIDS

RAFT RIDER RIDGE

FORT WILDERNESS & RIVER COUNTRY

At Fort Wilderness, a 740-acre cypress- and pine-wooded recreation area and campground, visitors can experience an old-fashioned country vacation: swimming, boating, picnicking, hiking, horseback riding, fishing, and just kicking back. This carefully preserved wilderness area is also one of the Walt Disney World resorts where guests can camp in tents, hook up RVs, or vacation in one of the resort's permanent trailer homes (see "Hotels," page 143). It is not unusual to spot native white-tailed deer, raccoons, opossums, and armadillos, and the wetlands are home to numerous waterfowl.

Fort Wilderness consists of three main recreation complexes: MEADOW RECREATION AREA in the center of the park, where meandering canals attract both canoers and fishers and where bike paths lead off in every direction; SETTLEMENT RECREATION AREA at the edge of Bay Lake, with its busy marina and white sand beach, nature trails, working ranch, and restaurants; and RIVER COUNTRY at Bay Lake, a Disney-designed version of an old-fashioned swimming hole, complete with water slides and raft rides. Throughout Fort Wilderness, visitors will find swimming pools, nature walks, volleyball nets, shuffleboard and tennis courts, fishing, waterskiing, horseback-riding excursions, and live entertainment in the evenings.

WHEN TO GO: Fort Wilderness is open year round, and there are activities, attractions, and entertainment suitable to every type of weather. At the Fort Wilderness Marina, boats may be rented from 10 AM until sundown. At the Bike Barn, recreational equipment may be rented or borrowed from 8 AM until sundown. Closing times vary with the seasons.

River Country is open year round, except for the first three weeks in December, when it is closed for refurbishing. During holidays and peak attendance months (March through September), the park fills early with families and children, but during low-attendance periods (October through February), River Country can be a welcome escape for adults seeking a breather from the intense pace of the theme parks. Opening and closing times at River Country vary throughout the year, so check ahead at Guest Services in your resort or call River Country Information (824-2760). River Country may close on very cold days or during lightning storms. If the weather looks uncertain, call Disney Weather (824-4104) for details.

HOW TO GET THERE: Fort Wilderness is in the Magic Kingdom Resorts Area, adjacent to Bonnet Creek Golf Club, and extends from Vista Boulevard to the shores of Bay Lake. The Fort Wilderness Marina is serviced by ferry from the Magic Kingdom, Discovery Island, and the Contemporary resort. WDW shuttle buses service Fort Wilderness from the Magic Kingdom, Disney-MGM Studios, Epcot Center, and the Transportation and Ticket Center. Visitors who are driving can reach the Fort Wilderness Guest Parking Lot by following the signs to the Magic Kingdom Resorts Area and then to Fort Wilderness, or they can enter by way of Vista Boulevard, a shortcut. Parking at Fort Wilderness is free for guests at WDW resorts (day visitors are charged a nominal fee).

IN-PARK TRANSPORTATION: The roads within Fort Wilderness are reserved for the Fort Wilderness internal bus transportation system, which operates daily from 7:30 AM until 2 AM. Bus routes are posted at all bus stops. (Passenger cars are allowed on the roads only to reach campsites, and there is no parking at the Fort Wilderness attractions.) After parking, visitors should proceed to one of the two bus stops in the Fort Wilderness Guest Parking Lot, depending on their destination: The bus terminal marked "Gateway Depot" is the stop for the express bus (orange-flag bus) to River Country. The smaller bus terminal marked "Fort Wilderness Depot" is the stop for buses to the Settlement Recreation Area and the Meadow Recreation Area (brown- and silver-flag buses), as well as to River Country (orange-flag bus). Guests who want to get around Fort Wilderness at their own pace can rent bicycles or electric carts at the Bike Barn, located in the Meadow Recreation Area. The electric carts hold up to four passengers and plug in for continuous recharging at scores of outlets throughout Fort Wilderness.

ADMISSION: Fort Wilderness is free to all visitors at Walt Disney World. Admission to River Country water park is about $16 for adults (about $13 for children). Admission to River Country is included with some multiday passes.

✳

SETTLEMENT RECREATION AREA

✗✗✗ – A worthwhile adventure. **✗✗** – Good fun if you're in the mood. **✗** – Strictly for the young at heart.

The Settlement Recreation Area is nestled at the far end of Fort Wilderness, where it borders Bay Lake. The area itself encompasses the Fort Wilderness Marina and beach; Pioneer Hall, where the nightly Hoop-Dee-Doo Musical Revue dinner show is held; the Tri-Circle-D Ranch exhibits; and the Settlement Trading Post and Delicatessen, where visitors can buy groceries and sandwiches, beverages including beer and wine, and gifts and sundries, or simply cool off with a game of checkers. River Country is a short walk away.

FORT WILDERNESS MARINA: The Marina is situated in the center of Fort Wilderness' long, lovely white sand beach. At the Marina, guests can rent motorboats and sailboats or join waterskiing or fishing excursions. (See "Sporting Activities," page 217.) At the beach, guests can swim or simply relax in lounge chairs under umbrellas or in the shade of the nearby trees. Lockers are available nearby for storing belongings, and the Beach Shack provides refreshments and cold beer. The Fort Wilderness Marina is open every day from 10 AM until sundown. **✗✗**

WILDERNESS SWAMP TRAIL: The 2.2-mile-long Wilderness Swamp Trail offers a beautiful nature hike highlighting the local flora and fauna. Only the sounds of nature break the silence along the trail, which begins behind the Settlement Trading Post. The trail meanders into the forest, crosses the sun-drenched grassy banks of the Fort Wilderness waterways, and skirts the wetlands — populated by egrets, herons, and other native waterfowl — before plunging back into the deep shade of the overgrown forest canopy. The array of swamp ferns, saw palmetto, vine-covered cypress hung with Spanish moss, and rainbow-hued berries and flowers creates a semitropical paradise for nature-lovers. **✗✗✗**

ADVANCED TIMBER CHALLENGE COURSE: This two-mile asphalt exercise course begins across from the Tri-Circle-D Ranch. Self-guiding exercise stations along the way cue fitness enthusiasts in the sit-ups, stretches, chin-ups, and other activities that form a serious workout. The course winds through a deeply shaded pine forest, lush with ferns and palmettos. Twittering birds, shy marsh rabbits, deep shadows, and silence convey a soothing sense of isolation and privacy. **✗✗**

TRI-CIRCLE-D RANCH: This working ranch consists of the stables that house the horses used in Walt Disney World parades and the Blacksmith Shop where their hooves are tended. Inside the Horse Barn, a small museum displays photographs of Walt Disney and his beloved horses. Outside, the horses are bathed and groomed, much to their pleasure. Horse enthusiasts will enjoy close-up views of the beautiful

Percherons that pull the trolleys along Main Street in the Magic Kingdom, and the elegant steeds with elaborately braided manes that are featured in the parades. At the Blacksmith Shop, visitors can watch the horses being shoed and their hooves being cared for. ✗✗

PETTING FARM: The Petting Farm corral at the Tri-Circle-D Ranch is filled with turkeys, rabbits, goats, ducks, and some very beautiful and well-cared-for ponies. A purebred white Brahma bull is also in residence, and is much smaller and more approachable than the interbred American Brahma variety. Interestingly, the Petting Farm, with its hand-on opportunities, attracts as many adults as children. ✗✗

MEADOW RECREATION AREA

The Meadow Recreation Area lies in the center of Fort Wilderness and offers access to the Fort Wilderness Waterways and bicycle trails. This area encompasses the Bike Barn, where visitors can rent bicycles, canoes, electric carts, fishing gear, and tennis equipment; and the Meadow Recreation Complex, which offers swimming, tennis, volleyball, and shuffleboard. (See "Sporting Activities," page 217.) The Meadow Trading Post and Delicatessen sells groceries, sandwiches, beverages including beer and wine, and gifts and sundries. On hot days, visitors can go into the Trading Post to cool off and play a game of checkers. Out back, a flock of congenial ducks paddle on the pond, and tree-shaded tables beckon to picnickers.

CANOEING: The grassy banks and tree-canopied waterways of Fort Wilderness are home to a variety of native waterfowl and fish. Visitors may tour the waterways by canoe or pedal boat and are welcome to fish for the bass or bream that live there. The Bike Barn rents canoes from 8 AM until sundown. Canoers are given a map of the waterway system and can bring along a picnic lunch on their adventure. ✗✗

BICYCLING: There are eight miles of roads and trails throughout Fort Wilderness that are ideal for bicycles. Bikers must contend with occasional buses and cars on the paved roads, but the extensive trail system was designed with bicycles in mind. The trails meander along waterways, past beaches and wetlands, through shady forests, and across bridges and boardwalks. The Bike Barn rents bicycles and tandem bikes from 8 AM until sundown and provides maps of the bike trails and roads of Fort Wilderness. ✗✗

CANAL FISHING: Fishing in the scenic waterways of Fort Wilderness is one of the hidden pleasures at Walt Disney World. Fishers may walk along the shores or canoe to any fishing spot that appeals to them. The Meadow Trading Post sells bait, and visitors who do not have their own fishing gear can rent cane poles at the Bike Barn. Unless guests have their own kitchens, the fishing rule is catch-and-release. ✗✗

RIVER COUNTRY ATTRACTIONS

River Country water park, located just a short walk from the Settlement Recreation Area, was designed as the kind of old-fashioned swimming hole that Huck Finn might have enjoyed. Visitors pay admission at the gate and, once inside, they can rent lockers and towels and settle into lounge chairs around the pool or along the sandy beach. There are two snack bars in River Country: Pop's Place, located near the pool, offers hamburgers, hot dogs, salads, beer, and wine; the Waterin' Hole, located near the beach, is a smaller version of Pop's Place, with a more limited selection. Generally, River Country is filled with kids, but it happens to be one of the best people-watching respites at Fort Wilderness.

BAY COVE: Bay Cove is actually an inlet of Bay Lake, which is bordered on one side by a large beach. Bay Cove is the home of old-fashioned water play at River Country and features the Boom Swing, Rope Climb, Tire Swing, and Cable Ride. Two rickety bridges, Barrel Bridge and Bay Bridge, span Bay Cove and lead swimmers to the water play equipment and beyond to Raft Rider Ridge. ✘

WHOOP 'N' HOLLER HOLLOW: Across Bay Cove from the beach, swimmers will find Whoop 'n' Holler Hollow, where they can climb to two thrilling, corkscrewing flume rides. One is longer than the other, but both are fast, and they twist and turn and wind around each other, depositing riders, with a splash, into Bay Cove. This attraction is big with the kids. ✘

WHITE WATER RAPIDS: Despite its name, this is actually a slow raft ride among gentle currents and calm pools. Riders cross Barrel Bridge and plop onto inner tubes atop Raft Rider Ridge. They meander down a 330-foot-long contoured chute, sometimes revolving in a slow whirlpool, before being gently washed into Bay Cove. ✘✘

UPSTREAM PLUNGE POOL: This 330,000-gallon swimming pool is one of the largest in the state of Florida. The crystal-clear pool is heated in winter and surrounded by lounge chairs, where most of the adults can be found at River Country. At the back of the pool, Slippery Slide Falls offers two spine-tingling water slides for the very adventurous. The slides are steeply angled and cleverly hide from view the seven-foot, free-fall splash landing at the bottom. ✘✘

CYPRESS POINT NATURE TRAIL: On this short but beautiful nature walk, visitors stroll on a wooden boardwalk through the natural wetlands at the edge of Bay Lake. Old-growth bald cypress provide shade and egrets fish among the water reeds. Aviaries tucked into the moss-hung bayous house rehabilitated birds, including a red-tailed hawk, who are no longer able to survive in the wild. ✘✘✘

✳

EXCURSIONS AND TOURS

WATERSKIING EXCURSION: Waterskiers will enjoy ideal conditions on the smooth surface of Bay Lake. Skiers can bring their own equipment or use the skis, Surfers, or Hydraslides provided. Excursion boats carry up to five skiers and leave from the Fort Wilderness Marina throughout the day. Guides will also pick up skiers from other Magic Kingdom resorts. Waterskiing excursions must be booked in advance and cost about $70 per hour. (See "Waterskiing Excursions," page 247.) ✘✘

FORT WILDERNESS TRAIL RIDE: The Tri-Circle-D Livery maintains a well-trained herd of quarter-horses, paints, and Appaloosas for trail rides. Groups of up to twenty take this gentle ride-at-a-walk through the shady pine forest. The Tri-Circle-D Livery is adjacent to the Fort Wilderness Guest Parking Lot. The trail ride leaves four times daily, and reservations are recommended. The excursion costs about $14 for forty-five minutes. (See "Horseback Riding," page 233.) ✘✘

FISHING EXCURSION: Anglers can try their luck reeling in largemouth bass, bluegill, and other fish from Bay Lake. The Fort Wilderness Marina offers two-hour fishing excursions three times daily. Fishers can use their own equipment or that provided on the boat, but only guests with kitchens are permitted to keep their fish. No fishing license is required. Excursions must be booked in advance and cost about $120 for two hours. (See "Fishing Excursions," page 224.) ✘✘

EVENTS AND LIVE ENTERTAINMENT

A variety of entertainment events are offered at Fort Wilderness. Some of the activities, including hayrides, Disney movies, and camp fires, are designed with younger guests in mind. The selected events described below are intended also to appeal to adults.

ELECTRICAL WATER PAGEANT: This shimmering light show appears on Seven Seas Lagoon and Bay Lake every night. A thousand-foot-long string of barges transports an intricate and dynamic light and music show past the Polynesian, Grand Floridian, Contemporary, and Fort Wilderness resorts. King Neptune presides over the dancing images of sea life that come alive in animated lights and are reflected across the black waters of the lake. The show is brief, approximately seven minutes, but spectacular nonetheless. The Electrical Water Pageant reaches Fort Wilderness at about 9:45 PM. The best viewing location is at the Fort Wilderness Marina and beach. ✗✗✗

HOOP-DEE-DOO MUSICAL REVUE: This popular dinner show is held three times nightly in the boisterous, family steakhouse atmosphere of Pioneer Hall. Colorfully dressed entertainers rely heavily on audience participation in a song-and-dance vaudeville performance laced with puns, broad humor, and groan-inducing punch lines. Reservations are difficult to get, so visitors who wish to see the show should book well in advance of their visit. (See "Dinner Shows," page 209). Same-day reservations are sometimes available during off-peak seasons (824-2748). ✗

RESTAURANTS

Refreshment stands throughout Fort Wilderness serve all-day snacks and fast-food meals. The restaurants below are located at Pioneer Hall in the Settlement Recreation Area. Also at Pioneer Hall, three hoe-down-style dinner shows are presented nightly at the Hoop-Dee-Doo Musical Revue, which must be reserved in advance (see "Events and Live Entertainment," above). Smoking is not permitted in the restaurants.

TRAIL'S END BUFFETERIA: Fried chicken, pizza, casseroles, soups, and a salad and fruit bar are the typical fare in this cafeteria-style restaurant. The daily buffet breakfast, lunch, and dinner are dished up in a casual country setting. Saturday night is Italian Night, featuring a variety of pasta dishes. There is entertainment nightly, and beer and wine are served. Open for breakfast, lunch, and dinner; no reservations.

CROCKETT'S TAVERN: Frontier-style dinners are served in this log cabin bedecked with Davy Crockett memorabilia. Guests waiting for tables can sit in comfortable rockers on the large wraparound porch outside, or perch at the long saloon-style bar. The menu features chicken, prime rib, seafood, Mexican food and, interestingly enough, buffalo burgers. Beer, wine, and spirits are served. Open for dinner; no reservations.

SERVICES

REST ROOMS: Rest rooms are located at the Meadow Trading Post, Settlement Trading Post, Pioneer Hall, and at the Reception Outpost in the Fort Wilderness Guest Parking Lot. Air-conditioned comfort stations, complete with rest rooms, laundromats, showers, ice dispensers, and telephones, are located near all bus stops throughout the Fort Wilderness campsite locations.

ELECTRIC CART RENTALS: Visitors can rent electric carts by the day or hour for use in Fort Wilderness. The carts carry up to four passengers and cost about $25 per day. They run up to an hour (depending on the number of passengers) before a recharge is required at one of the numerous plug-in recharging posts located throughout Fort Wilderness. Carts can be rented at the Bike Barn in the Meadow Recreation Area, which is open from 8 AM until sundown.

LOCKERS: Lockers are located at the Fort Wilderness Marina, River Country, Meadow Recreation Area, and at the Gateway Depot bus stop in the Fort Wilderness Guest Parking Lot.

VISITORS WITH DISABILITIES: Wheelchairs are available at the Reception Outpost in the Fort Wilderness Guest Parking Lot, but must be reserved in advance through Guest Services at Fort Wilderness (824-2900). Guests can also rent electric carts at the Bike Barn for use in Fort Wilderness.

Getaway Tours at Fort Wilderness

The half-day and full-day tours that follow are designed to allow first-time visitors to experience the best of Fort Wilderness in four to seven hours, including lunch or dinner in one of the Fort Wilderness restaurants. To create your own custom vacation at Walt Disney World, you can combine a Fort Wilderness tour with a half-day tour from any other theme park. For example, combine a morning tour at Disney-MGM Studios with the Late Afternoon and Evening Wilderness Tour, or combine the Surf and Turf Day at Fort Wilderness with an evening tour at Pleasure Island.

LATE AFTERNOON AND EVENING WILDERNESS TOUR

Four to five hours — year round — including the Hoop-Dee-Doo Musical Revue dinner show.
Well in advance of this tour, make reservations for the 7:15 PM Hoop-Dee-Doo Musical Revue dinner show.
If you are touring during peak attendance times, make your dinner show reservation
at the time you book your hotel. (See "Dinner Shows," page 209.)

✔ Park at the Contemporary resort and take the ferry to the Fort Wilderness Marina at about 3:30 PM.

✔ Rent a Water Sprite, sailboat, or canopy boat at the Fort Wilderness Marina for a relaxing hour-long boat tour of Bay Lake and Seven Seas Lagoon. Dock at any theme resorts that interest you for a quick tour.

✔ Return your boat to the Fort Wilderness Marina and stroll to the **TRI-CIRCLE-D RANCH.** Tour the small museum in the Horse Barn, the Blacksmith Shop, and the Petting Farm.

✔ If you have time and would enjoy a nature walk, follow the **WILDERNESS SWAMP TRAIL** behind the Settlement Trading Post. Or if you prefer, drop into Crockett's Tavern for a before-dinner cocktail or beverage. (Some visitors consider this a must to prepare for the entertainment that follows.)

✔ Plan to arrive about fifteen minutes early at Pioneer Hall for the 7:15 PM **HOOP-DEE-DOO MUSICAL REVUE** dinner show.

✔ After dinner, if you wish to linger, you can catch the **ELECTRICAL WATER PAGEANT,** which cruises past the Fort Wilderness beach about 9:45 PM. The last ferry leaves Fort Wilderness at 10 PM.

❋

SURF AND TURF DAY AT FORT WILDERNESS

Five to seven hours — October through March — includes picnic lunch or lunch at Trail's End Buffeteria and (optional) the Hoop-Dee-Doo Musical Revue dinner show.
Well in advance of this tour, make reservations for the 5 PM Hoop-Dee-Doo Musical Revue dinner show, if you plan to attend. (See "Dinner Shows," page 209.)
If you are taking the Fort Wilderness Trail Ride, make advance reservations for the 2 PM ride. (Same-day reservations can be made during off-peak seasons. See "Horseback Riding," page 233.)

✔ Arrive at either the Fort Wilderness Guest Parking Lot or Fort Wilderness Marina at about 10 AM. Take a shuttle (silver- or brown-flag bus) to the Bike Barn at the Meadow Recreation Area and rent an electric cart for the day.

✔ Drive your cart through Fort Wilderness, exploring the paths on your way to the **TRI-CIRCLE-D RANCH** in the Settlement Recreation Area. Find an electric hitching post for your cart (short posts with electrical outlets are located throughout Fort Wilderness). Plug the cart in before you tour the ranch. Drop into the Blacksmith Shop, the Petting Farm, and the small museum in the Horse Barn.

✔ If you are planning a picnic lunch, purchase picnic supplies at the Settlement Trading Post. Otherwise, head over to the Trail's End Buffeteria, nearby, for lunch. (Trail's End can also prepare food to go.)

✔ If you're picnicking, hike the **WILDERNESS SWAMP TRAIL,** which begins behind the Settlement Trading Post. There is a shady picnic spot near the bridge over Chickasaw Creek where the Wilderness Swamp Trail meets Bay Lake. If you're eating at Trail's End Buffeteria, take your nature walk on the Wilderness Swamp Trail after lunch.

✔ After your hike, choose between a boat tour of Bay Lake and Seven Seas Lagoon or a horseback trail ride through the forest.

    If you select the **BOAT TOUR,** walk to the Fort Wilderness Marina, nearby, and rent the boat of your choice for your outing. Explore the far reaches of Bay Lake and the adjacent wetlands, or dock at the themed resorts at Seven Seas Lagoon for quick tours.

    If you have reserved the 2 PM **FORT WILDERNESS TRAIL RIDE,** drive your cart to the Tri-Circle-D Livery, adjacent to the Fort Wilderness Guest Parking Lot. Be sure to plug your cart in when you get there. The trail ride wanders through the forest and lasts about forty-five minutes.

✔ When you've finished your afternoon outing, take a final spin in your electric cart, touring the campsites and vacation trailers at Fort Wilderness, then return it to the Bike Barn. If you are not attending the Hoop-Dee-Doo Musical Revue dinner show, you can linger at the Meadow Recreation Area for a swim, tennis, shuffleboard, fishing, or any number of playful options before returning to your hotel.

    If you have reserved the 5 PM **HOOP-DEE-DOO MUSICAL REVUE** dinner show, take the shuttle bus back to Pioneer Hall. If you have time before the show, you may want to drop into Crockett's Tavern and prepare yourself with a before-dinner cocktail or beverage.

✔ Arrive about fifteen minutes early for the dinner show. ◆

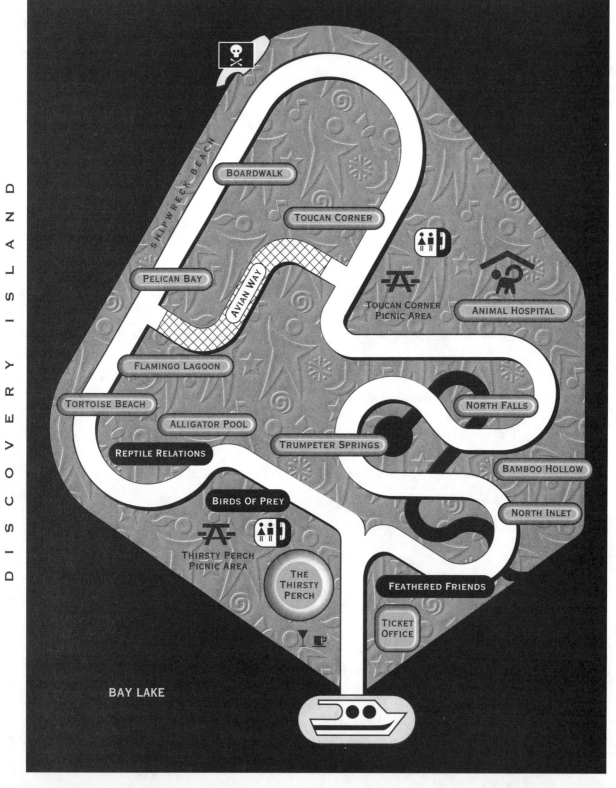

DISCOVERY ISLAND

BAY LAKE

Boardwalk

Toucan Corner

Shipwreck Beach

Pelican Bay

Avian Way

Toucan Corner Picnic Area

Animal Hospital

Flamingo Lagoon

Tortoise Beach

North Falls

Alligator Pool

Reptile Relations

Trumpeter Springs

Bamboo Hollow

North Inlet

Birds Of Prey

Thirsty Perch Picnic Area

The Thirsty Perch

Feathered Friends

Ticket Office

DISCOVERY ISLAND

Discovery Island is an idyllic escape into nature from the more structured entertainments at Walt Disney World. This natural eleven-acre island, in the middle of Bay Lake, was originally planned by Disney as a *Treasure Island* adventure. To create a lush forest environment, the island was landscaped with native trees, palms, and bamboo, along with hundreds of tropical specimen plants from around the world. A white sand beach was added, and a wrecked wooden sailing ship was transported from the Florida coast to lend atmosphere. Aviaries were built and stocked with a wide variety of exotic birds, from elegant demoiselle cranes to flashy scarlet ibises. As the island ecology evolved and more wildlife arrived and thrived — both imported species and local volunteers — the *Treasure Island* concept was dropped and Discovery Island blossomed into a nature park. In 1979, it was accredited by the American Association of Zoological Parks and Aquariums, and it regularly exchanges animals with zoos throughout the world. Today, Discovery Island is a sanctuary and home to more than 250 species of birds, reptiles, and mammals, including endangered species and disabled wildlife such as Galapagos tortoises, brown pelicans, and the American bald eagle.

At Discovery Island, visitors are invited to stroll along a winding three-quarter-mile path through lush tropical foliage, picnic on the white sand beach, pause beside a stream with gurgling cascades, and come face-to-face with a variety of birds and animals at almost every turn. Peacocks and rabbitlike Patagonian cavies, along with visiting waterfowl native to the area, are among the many animals that roam freely on Discovery Island. Almost an acre of the island is enclosed in nearly invisible fine green netting, creating one of the largest walkthrough aviaries in the United States. The aviary is so large, in fact, that its boundaries disappear, and often visitors do not realize they are in an enclosure. There are only a few places to sit down along the shady paths, so visitors should be comfortable with walking the three-quarter-mile distance.

WHEN TO GO: Discovery Island opens every day at 10 AM and closes between 5 PM and 7 PM depending on the season. It is a delightful place to visit at any time of day. The best month to visit is November, before Thanksgiving when the weather is cool and the island is virtually deserted. Discovery Island, however, is seldom crowded at any time. Nesting season lasts from February through September, and from about mid-February to mid-March, the island is closed for refurbishing (and perhaps to give the wildlife a people vacation). For up-to-the-minute information, call Walt Disney World Information (407 824-4321) or Discovery Island Information (407 824-2875). If the weather looks uncertain, call Disney Weather (824-4104) for details.

HOW TO GET THERE: The only way to reach Discovery Island is by ferries that depart every twenty minutes from the Magic Kingdom Dock, the Fort Wilderness Marina, and the Contemporary Resort Marina. The last ferries depart for Discovery Island at about 4 PM, although ferries do stop to pick up Discovery Island visitors until the park closes. Ferry times vary with the season, so check ahead. Before boarding the ferries, hats should be held firmly or tied on, as the breezes can blow them overboard. Visitors are not permitted to dock their rental boats at Discovery Island.

ADMISSION: Adult admission to Discovery Island is about $10 (about $6 for children). Discovery Island admission is included with some multiday passes. Tickets may be purchased at Guest Services in any WDW resort or at the Discovery Island ticket office. Ferries to Discovery Island are complimentary for guests staying at WDW resorts (day visitors must purchase a transportation ticket).

LIVE EXHIBITS

While signs scattered around Discovery Island inform visitors about the specific kinds of animals they might see, most signs do not include pictures, which makes identification difficult. Discovery Island changes from day to day as plants grow and flower and birds and animals mature, breed, and give birth. Many of its residents are tucked away in intimate nooks in the foliage, and visitors can find one of the animal residents at almost every turn. At the Discovery Island ticket office, be sure to pick up a current brochure, which includes descriptions of some of the birds and animals and a schedule of the animal shows. Follow the path to the right after you leave the Discovery Island Dock.

DISCOVERY ISLAND PATH: The three-quarter-mile Discovery Island path directs visitors in a roughly counter-clockwise direction through the island. The path first enters an area known as Parrots Perch, where the Feathered Friends bird show is staged. This is the home of brightly plumaged macaws, cockatoos, and other colorful birds that perform in the show. The large trees that grow here shade the path and provide nesting homes during mating season.

NORTH INLET: At the approach to North Inlet, visitors pass a wrinkled hornbill from Southeast Asia and palm cockatoos from New Guinea. The path crosses a flowing island stream where it empties into Bay Lake, then turns to enter a dense forest of tropical plants, palms, and flowering hibiscus. The path winds back and forth across a series of footbridges, passing many specimen plants along the way including a stand of Senegal date palms. North Inlet is home to the laughing kookaburras, kingfishers from Australia that pipe their signature laugh at sundown, when visitors are departing.

TRUMPETER SPRINGS: This area is home to a pair of beautiful black neck swans, as well as the large, white trumpeter swans, with their distinctive call. These fairy-tale birds, the largest of the swans, have been nearly hunted out of existence. Discovery Island is hoping that the trumpeter swans will breed successfully, so they can supply other zoos. During the spring, great white egrets nest in the treetops at Trumpeter Springs. The purple flowering princess shrub, a native to Brazil, is among the plants that flourish here.

NORTH FALLS: At North Falls, visitors can enjoy the cascading waterfalls and spot a variety of waterfowl fishing in the pools below. The natural-looking flowing waterways on Discovery Island are actually a man-made water system that is engineered to keep the water fresh and aerated. Water is pumped to a high level at North Falls, then drained through the lagoons and wetlands across the island, which are home to many species of waterfowl. Graceful Chilean flamingos occupy the lagoon at North Falls. They are lighter in color than the familiar bright orange Caribbean flamingos. Also nearby are yellow-billed hornbills from Ethiopia, who seem to spend the entire day grooming themselves.

BAMBOO HOLLOW: This lovely grove combines almost a dozen varieties of bamboo from many parts of the world, including vivid green golden bamboo, and is filled with fragrant flowering ginger. Bamboo Hollow is the home to beautiful golden conures from Brazil and offers safe haven to a number of small mammals, including the endangered ring-tailed lemur from Madagascar, with its foxlike face and monkeylike body. Also in residence here are the tree-dwelling, yellow-furred golden lion tamarins from the American tropics.

✳ DISCOVERY ISLAND ✳

ANIMAL HOSPITAL: A recent addition to Discovery Island, the colorful, wood-shingled Animal Hospital has walk-up windows where visitors can catch a glimpse into the various animal-care facilities. In the nursery, animals orphaned in the wild are kept and cared for around the clock until they can be released back into the wild or incorporated into exhibits. Another window looks into the operating room, where animals undergo surgery for traumatic injuries. Visitors can also watch the goings-on in the lab, where blood samples are studied to help diagnose animal diseases. The lab also houses an X-ray machine for diagnosing internal organ problems and bone fractures. The powerful X-ray machine on Discovery Island is capable of X-raying their five-hundred-pound Galapagos tortoises. (You probably don't want to stand too close to the window when one of those guys steps onto the table.)

TOUCAN CORNER: Easily identified by their large beaks and distinctive squawking sounds, the colorful toucans that live here are native to the Western Hemisphere. The beautiful toto toucans reside in the large circular centerpiece aviary. Down the path leading to the beach, visitors will see the colorful keel-billed toucans from southern Mexico. In the other direction, a spacious aviary is home to the small, shy muntjac deer from Southeast Asia, who live companionably close to a flock of delicate demoiselle cranes. White-crested hornbills can also be found here, a species threatened by the destruction of their rain forests; and nearby are federally protected sandhill cranes with distinct red streaks above their eyes.

AVIAN WAY: Just beyond Toucan Corner, visitors can enter Avian Way, which is devoted to South American birds and waterfowl. Covering almost an acre, this huge walkthrough aviary is home to a colorful population, including one of the largest U.S. breeding colonies of the scarlet ibis. These distinctively plumaged birds, almost Day Glo in color from a diet high in carotenes, were described by the early Spanish explorers as being covered in blood. Visitors pass through the aviary on elevated walkways high above the lagoons and nesting areas of the waterfowl. Tall trees reach through the top of the enclosure, creating the remarkable illusion of open sky. The aviary exits at the beach.

PELICAN BAY: The brown pelican is the state bird of Florida, and those that are sheltered here are among the permanently disabled birds on Discovery Island, unable to survive in the wild. Once threatened with extinction due to the effects of the pesticide DDT, the brown pelican is now protected by federal law and is slowly recovering its population. In the late afternoon, about 4 PM, animal-caretakers feed the pelicans, which is an entertainment event in itself.

BOARDWALK: The Boardwalk skirts a lush tropical forest as it follows the island's white sand beach. Here, visitors have a chance to see many of the birds in the wild that are native to the area, including herring gulls, American coots, herons, egrets, and large turkey vultures. At the far end of the island the *Hispaniola* is beached. This wrecked single-masted schooner was salvaged from the Florida Keys and offers a vivid example of the shipmaking craft of the eighteenth century. The waters of Bay Lake lap on the beach, and visitors may leave the path, if they wish, to lounge on the sand or walk barefoot at the water's edge to cool off.

FLAMINGO LAGOON: This shady lagoon, across from the beach, is home to a breeding colony of Caribbean flamingos, with their distinctive bright pink plumage and awkward grace. The flamingos have adapted to the presence of humans, unlike their cousins, the Florida flamingos, which have not been seen in the wild since about 1920.

TORTOISE BEACH: Along the sandy beach of Discovery Island, Galapagos tortoises from the islands off the coast of Ecuador have found a new resort. These great lumbering beasts, weighing up to five hundred pounds and with lifespans of up to 150 years, are now rare and endangered as a species.

ALLIGATOR POOL: Remodeled in 1992, this picturesque grotto is home to a number of American alligators. These Florida natives, once declining in number because of the dictates of fashion and encroaching development, are successfully increasing their population. The rare broadnose caiman, virtually extinct in the wild, also can be found at Alligator Pool.

EDUTAINMENT

✗✗✗ – A do-not-miss for animal-lovers.   **✗✗** – An interesting diversion if you come upon it.   **✗** – Of limited appeal.

Animal shows are scheduled several times daily at Discovery Island. Pick up an entertainment schedule at the Discovery Island ticket office for exact show times. Shows may be cancelled due to inclement weather.

FEATHERED FRIENDS: Visitors sit on shaded benches to watch this pleasant, often funny show featuring the antics of tame macaws, cockatoos, parrots, and other exotic, colorful birds. The parrot wranglers also describe the special care and captive breeding programs for many of the birds on Discovery Island. Four shows daily. Duration: Approximately 30 minutes. **✗✗✗**

BIRDS OF PREY: A red-tailed hawk, a large owl, and a king vulture are the featured performers in this show, which gives visitors a chance to see these remarkable birds up close and learn about their feeding and mating habits. Visitors are seated on benches for the show and can ask questions about the birds while learning more about the wildlife rehabilitation and protection programs at Discovery Island. Four shows daily. Duration: Approximately 30 minutes. **✗✗✗**

REPTILE RELATIONS: This informative reptile show is staged at Alligator Pool. Visitors stand for the show, while an animal handler introduces them to a number of interesting reptiles and amphibians, including a small but toothy American alligator, a vivid green iguana from the treetops of the rain forest, and a gopher tortoise who burrows as deep as thirty feet underground. Other performers include an indigo snake and a friendly Burmese python that literally hangs out with the crowd. Four shows daily. Duration: Approximately 20 minutes. **✗✗**

REFRESHMENTS AND PICNIC AREAS

Discovery Island has a number of picnic areas for those who have brought their own food and one refreshment stand that offers light meals and snacks. The picnic spots are also pleasant rest stops and meeting points for visitors who prefer to tour separately.

THE THIRSTY PERCH: The only snack bar on Discovery Island, the Thirsty Perch offers sandwiches, snacks, soft drinks, coffee, and beer, as well as a selection of nature-oriented publications and souvenirs. It is located near the Discovery Island Dock. Visitors may purchase food and beverages at the Thirsty Perch and consume it anywhere on the island, provided they do not litter or offer it to any of the animals or birds. ⬛🍸

THIRSTY PERCH PICNIC AREA: Located on the beach just beyond the Thirsty Perch, this area is studded with a dozen or so picnic tables. To one side, a thick grove of bamboo provides shelter, and picnickers can watch the ferries dock as they eat. Egrets, cranes, peahens, and peacocks mingle with picnickers and provide entertainment. Don't miss the majestic American bald eagle behind the Thirsty Perch. Trash containers and rest rooms are nearby.

TOUCAN CORNER PICNIC AREA: Just across the path from Toucan Corner, this picnic area is tucked into a secluded glade. Three picnic tables are set on thick grass under the shade of tall palms. Toucan Corner Picnic Area is located in the center of the island and is filled with the sounds of the birds in the area. Trash containers and rest rooms are nearby.

BOARDWALK AND SHIPWRECK BEACH: Visitors who bring along a towel or ground cloth will find the white sands of Shipwreck Beach a fine spot for a beach picnic. Although swimming is not permitted, visitors may take off their shoes and walk along the water's edge. In the forest, across from the shipwrecked *Hispaniola,* a hidden shelter and shady bench provide lovely views of Bay Lake and the resorts beyond. Trash containers are nearby; the nearest rest rooms are at Toucan Corner and the Thirsty Perch.

✳

SERVICES

REST ROOMS: Public rest rooms are located behind the Thirsty Perch and across from Toucan Corner in the Toucan Corner Picnic Area.

TELEPHONES: Public telephones are located behind the Thirsty Perch and adjacent to the Toucan Corner Picnic Area.

FILM: A wide variety of film is available at the Thirsty Perch.

VISITORS WITH DISABILITIES: All of Discovery Island is wheelchair accessible, and wheelchairs are available free of charge at the dock. Some, but not all of the ferries have wheelchair access, so guests needing assistance must wait for the properly outfitted ferry.

✳

ADULT TOURING TIPS

✦ Visitors are cautioned to watch where they step, as many of the animal residents of Discovery Island wander freely along the pathways. They are also in the trees overhead, so expect the obvious.

✦ It is not a good idea to let any of the roaming birds or animals eat from your hands. They are not tame.

✦ The animal caretakers on Discovery Island are very knowledgeable and friendly. Ask questions when you spot caretakers feeding the animals or tending cages; you will learn a wealth of fascinating facts about Discovery Island and its residents. If you are on the island at around 3:30 PM, head over to Pelican Bay for feeding time.

✳

Getaway Tours at Discovery Island

The tours that follow are designed to allow first-time visitors to experience the best of Discovery Island in two to three hours, including a picnic lunch on one of the tours. To create your own custom vacation at Walt Disney World, you can combine the Mid-Morning Nature Walk and Picnic with an afternoon and evening tour from one of the theme parks. Or, you can use the Afternoon Nature-Break Tour for a midday getaway.

AFTERNOON NATURE-BREAK TOUR

Two to three hours — year round — does not include lunch.

✔ After lunch, catch the ferry to Discovery Island. Try to schedule your arrival no later than 1:15 PM. (Discovery Island ferries depart every twenty minutes from the Magic Kingdom Dock, the Fort Wilderness Marina, and the Contemporary Marina.)

✔ On arriving at Discovery Island, pick up an entertainment schedule at the ticket office.

✔ If it is before 1:20 PM, stop by the Thirsty Perch, just ahead, and purchase a beverage to take along on your tour if you wish. Step over to the path and bear to the left (clockwise), walking to the pleasant outdoor area where the Birds of Prey show is staged.

✔ Catch the 1:30 PM performance of the **BIRDS OF PREY** show, where you will learn about the wildlife rehabilitation and protection programs on Discovery Island.

✔ After the performance, continue down the path to **ALLIGATOR POOL**, for an up-close, but quite safe view of its residents. If the 2 PM **REPTILE RELATIONS** show is underway, you may want to linger.

✔ Continue down the path to **TORTOISE BEACH** for a look at the huge, slow-moving Galapagos tortoises, then walk past **FLAMINGO LAGOON** on your right. Enjoy the distant view of Shipwreck Beach and the *Hispaniola*. Disney brought the wrecked sailing ship to the island when it was known as Treasure Island, after the Robert Louis Stevenson pirate novel.

✔ When you arrive at **PELICAN BAY**, turn right and enter the enormous aviary at **AVIAN WAY**. Stroll through and view the South American waterfowl far below the walkway. Exit at Toucan Corner.

✔ Explore the toucan aviaries at **TOUCAN CORNER**, then continue along the path toward the **ANIMAL HOSPITAL**. Take a brief tour of the facility, especially the nursery, before returning to the path.

✔ Continue down the path and enjoy the many sights and sounds as you walk past **BAMBOO HOLLOW**, **NORTH FALLS**, and **TRUMPETER SPRINGS**. As you stroll, keep an eye out for the many fascinating plants in the area. It is here that Discovery Island shows off its colorful flowers and lovely scents.

✔ Arrive at the **FEATHERED FRIENDS** bird show in time for the 3:15 PM performance, and experience the antics of these beautiful trained birds.

✔ After the show, return to the Discovery Island Dock for your ferry back.

MID-MORNING NATURE WALK AND PICNIC

Three hours — year round — including a picnic lunch.

✔ If you are planning to bring your own picnic lunch, ask your hotel coffee shop to pack one for you. You can buy beverages at Discovery Island. If you would like to picnic on the beach, you may want to bring along towels or a ground cloth.

✔ Catch the ferry at about 11 AM to Discovery Island. (Ferries depart every twenty minutes from the Magic Kingdom Dock, the Fort Wilderness Marina, and the Contemporary Resort Marina.)

✔ On arriving at Discovery Island, pick up an entertainment schedule at the ticket office.

✔ If it is before 11:20 AM, stop by the Thirsty Perch, just ahead, and purchase beverages for your picnic (and food if you did not bring your own). Step over to the path and bear to the right (counter-clockwise). Follow the path to the Feathered Friends bird show staging area.

✔ Catch the 11:30 AM performance of **FEATHERED FRIENDS** and experience the antics of these beautiful trained birds.

✔ When the show ends, continue down the path toward **NORTH INLET**. Enjoy the sights and sounds as you walk along past **TRUMPETER SPRINGS**, **NORTH FALLS**, and **BAMBOO HOLLOW**. As you stroll, notice the many fascinating species of trees and shrubs and tropical flowers.

✔ Stop at the **ANIMAL HOSPITAL** on your right and peek into the nursery and examining rooms.

✔ Just ahead on the path is **AVIAN WAY**. Enter the large enclosed aviary and stroll all the way through on the elevated walkways. Below you will see a variety of graceful South American waterfowl.

✔ Exit the aviary and turn right. Pass **PELICAN BAY** and walk along the **BOARDWALK**, which follows the sandy beach toward the *Hispaniola*, a wrecked sailing ship that was brought to the island when it was known as Treasure Island, after the Robert Louis Stevenson pirate novel.

✔ If you're planning to picnic at the beach, choose a sunny spot on the sand or look for the hidden shelter with its shady bench in the forest across from the *Hispaniola*. If you prefer to picnic at shaded tables, continue on.

✔ As you continue along the Boardwalk, past the *Hispaniola*, the path turns right, leading you back toward the center of the island. Just ahead is **TOUCAN CORNER**. If you would like to picnic at a table in a secluded grassy glade, stop at the Toucan Corner Picnic Area for lunch.

✔ Reenter **AVIAN WAY** and stroll through again. (There's a lot to see here!) When you arrive at the exit, follow the path to the left this time.

✔ Walk past **FLAMINGO LAGOON** and over to **TORTOISE BEACH**, on your right, for a look at the huge, slow-moving Galapagos tortoises. Some weigh as much as five hundred pounds.

✔ Continue on to **ALLIGATOR POOL**, where you can have an up-close, but quite safe view of its residents. If the **REPTILE RELATIONS** show is underway, you may want to linger.

✔ Stroll down the path to the rustic benches on your right for the 1:30 PM **BIRDS OF PREY** show.

✔ After the show, return to the Discovery Island Dock for your ferry back. ◆

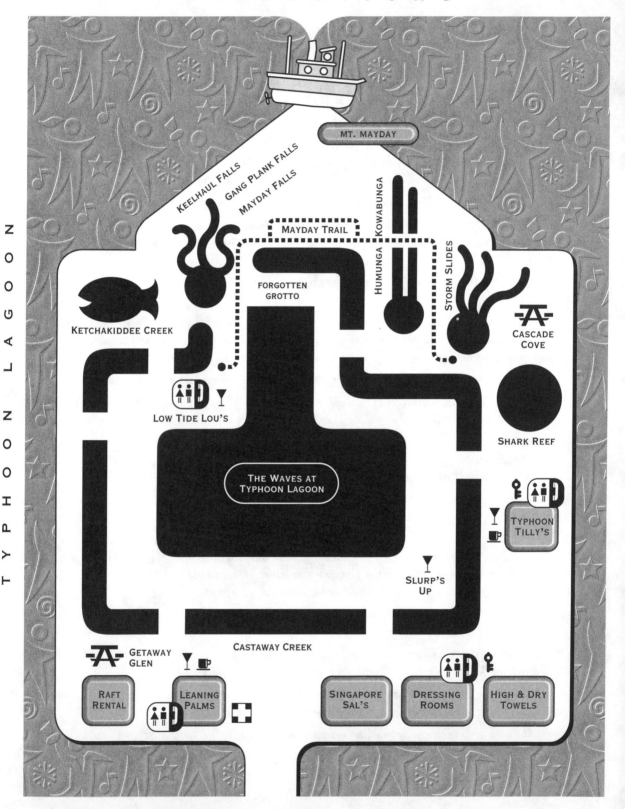

TYPHOON LAGOON

MT. MAYDAY

KEELHAUL FALLS
GANG PLANK FALLS
MAYDAY FALLS

MAYDAY TRAIL

HUMUNGA KOWABUNGA

STORM SLIDES

FORGOTTEN GROTTO

KETCHAKIDDEE CREEK

CASCADE COVE

LOW TIDE LOU'S

SHARK REEF

THE WAVES AT TYPHOON LAGOON

TYPHOON TILLY'S

SLURP'S UP

CASTAWAY CREEK

GETAWAY GLEN

RAFT RENTAL

LEANING PALMS

SINGAPORE SAL'S

DRESSING ROOMS

HIGH & DRY TOWELS

TYPHOON LAGOON

Typhoon Lagoon is an imaginatively designed fifty-six-acre theme park devoted to an array of water activities including snorkeling, white-water rafting, water slides, body surfing atop the largest machine-made waves in the world, and a long, lazy float down the meandering creek encircling the park. Depending on where their adventures take them, visitors can enjoy white sand beaches, shady coves, misty rain forests, and plunging waterfalls. According to Disney legend, the Lagoon was once the site of a peaceful fishing village that was devastated by a raging typhoon. A fishing boat called the *Miss Tilly* was neatly deposited on top of Mt. Mayday, the Placid Palms restaurant became the Leaning Palms, and the steamship at Shark Reef was permanently overturned. Part of the fun of Typhoon Lagoon is finding other telltale signs of the storm, which blend in cleverly with the rest of the scenery.

WHEN TO GO: Typhoon Lagoon is open all year, except from January to mid-February when it is closed for refurbishing. Operating hours vary throughout the year, so check ahead at Guest Services in your resort or call Typhoon Lagoon Information (407 560-4141). During peak-attendance times, from March through September, it is essential to arrive at Typhoon Lagoon before it opens, since the park fills to capacity by about 10:30 AM and is closed to new arrivals until mid afternoon. During low-attendance times (October through February), mornings can be cool, so plan your visit in the afternoon, when Typhoon Lagoon provides a welcome contrast to the frenzied stimulation in the theme parks. Florida experiences brief tropical rain showers in the summer months, usually in the late afternoon. During storms, swimmers are chased from the water to wait it out, and many simply leave for the day — especially families with children. Once the storm passes, the park has emptied significantly, making a post-storm visit highly desirable. If the weather looks uncertain, call Disney Weather (824-4104) for details.

HOW TO GET THERE: Typhoon Lagoon is in the Disney Village Resorts Area not far from the Disney Village Marketplace. Free parking is available in the Typhoon Lagoon parking lot. WDW buses service Typhoon Lagoon from Epcot Center, the Disney Village Marketplace, the Epcot Resorts, Disney Village Resorts, and the Transportation and Ticket Center.

ADMISSION: Adult admission is about $25 per day (about $20 for children). Admission to Typhoon Lagoon is included with some multiday passes.

✳

ATTRACTIONS

✘✘✘ – A must for water-lovers.   ✘✘ – Enjoyable if you're in the mood.   ✘ – Of limited appeal.

THE WAVES AT TYPHOON LAGOON: The centerpiece of the park is the 2½-acre lagoon and its famous wave maker, which creates impressive six-foot surfing waves. The machine also produces gentle bobbing waves perfect for floating on the inner tubes available for rent. The two types of waves alternate for an hour at a time all day long; surfing waves usually start on the even hours. Near the Lagoon, a blackboard with the surf report gives information on the water temperature, weather, and alternating surf conditions. The *Miss Tilly,* a shrimp boat perched atop Mt. Mayday, gives a hoot and sprays a fifty-foot plume of water in the air every half hour, so visitors who are waiting for that first big curl can keep track of the time while experiencing other attractions. ✘✘✘

CASTAWAY CREEK: Giant turquoise inner tubes draped with relaxed swimmers are swept along in the currents of Castaway Creek for a lazy thirty-minute float around the perimeter of the theme park. Visitors can simply swim with the currents of the creek if they wish. At the five entrances at different points along the fifteen-foot-wide creek, swimmers can wait for an empty tube to float by or grab one of the tubes stacked nearby for the taking. The currents are strong enough to keep floaters moving, and lifeguards along the way keep an eye on things. Rafters struggling to dodge flotsam and jetsam create laughing and bumping logjams. Where Castaway Creek passes through a misty rain forest, the going is slow enough to permit floaters-by to read the labels on the tropical trees and shrubs. A waterfall soaks all who pass under Mt. Mayday, so floaters should leave hats and cameras behind. ✘✘✘

SHARK REEF: Before entering the Reef, be sure to visit the underwater viewing station. Fashioned as the boiler room of a half-sunken, overturned steamship, its windows reveal snorkelers swimming among the fish in the water above. The water in Shark Reef is salty and unheated to accommodate the Caribbean sea life. Those who wish to swim with the fish get life vests, snorkels and masks, and a five-minute lesson in using them. Then it's off for a shower and a brief swim across the lagoon, which contains two islands, loads of interesting fish, and several small sharks. Since Shark Reef is kept at a cooler temperature than the rest of the Lagoon, it's a great place to really cool down on hot days. ✘✘

HUMUNGA KOWABUNGA: Thrill-seeking water-slide enthusiasts will be thoroughly satisfied by this terrifyingly steep and fast descent — about a fifty-foot drop. Clothing with rivets or buckles is not allowed and one-piece bathing suits are advised for women; sliding in thong-style suits may result in friction burns. Riders hit the water hard at the bottom, so nose plugs are also a good idea. The steepness of the slide is hidden from those in line by cleverly planted bushes. There are two slides, with viewing bleachers at the bottom. Only physically fit people are allowed on the ride, which is over in less than thirty seconds. ✘✘

STORM SLIDES: The three body slides at Storm Slides are tamer than those at Humunga Kowabunga, but they are still pretty exciting. Riders can choose from the Stern Burner, Jib Jammer, and Rudder Buster, all of which deliver more or less the same ride. Instead of a straight downward descent, these slides take riders on a circuitous corkscrew route through caves and waterfalls. The pool at the bottom is just deep enough to cushion landings. Note: Wearing two-piece bathing suits on these slides can lead to immodest exposure. There are viewing bleachers at the bottom. ✘✘

MAYDAY FALLS: Mayday Falls offers a twisty, bumps-and-ridges tube ride with a very speedy descent. The tubes are for single riders only, and riders are timed at the top and urged out at the bottom by lifeguards. Mayday Falls is slightly faster than Keelhaul Falls. ✘✘

GANG PLANK FALLS: Extra-large tubes that hold up to four people zip along speedily down the chute. Although this is the tamest of the three raft rides, in the process of shoving them off, the lifeguards duck every raft under a nearby waterfall, thoroughly soaking the occupants. ✘✘

KEELHAUL FALLS: The tube ride down Keelhaul Falls is slower than the one down Mayday Falls, but it takes riders through a pitch-black tunnel about halfway down. This is a real thrill and completely unexpected, since riders are hurtling along with no clue as to what's coming next. Riders end up safely at the common landing pool, where they quickly exit. ✘✘

KETCHAKIDDEE CREEK: This kids-only area is specially designed for small fry and their parents. An assortment of scaled-down water rides similar to those found throughout the park are offered here, along with floating toys and a little waterfall. It's a happy but noisy area, so those seeking relaxation should be sure to camp some distance away. ✗

REFRESHMENT STANDS AND PICNIC AREAS

The refreshment stands at Typhoon Lagoon serve snacks and fast-food meals all day, although the lines can be quite long. Beverage carts throughout the park sell beer and soft drinks, and guests may bring food and beverages into the park. However, guests may not carry in glass containers and alcoholic beverages, and there are no cooking facilities available. Visitors who wish to eat in a full-service restaurant can drive or catch a WDW bus to nearby Disney Village Marketplace.

LEANING PALMS: The largest refreshment stand, Leaning Palms, is to the left of the main entrance. Pizza, hamburgers, and chicken and tuna sandwiches are sold here along with soft drinks, beer, and coffee. Several large eating areas with shaded tables are nearby. ▪Ɣ

TYPHOON TILLY'S GALLEY & GROG: Located on the far right side of the Lagoon, this refreshment stand is divided into two separate walk-up counters. Both sides offer snacks, beverages, and ice cream, but the left counter, which opens earlier in the day, serves hot dogs and sandwiches as well as beer and coffee. There are tables nearby, or diners can picnic on the sand at Cascade Cove. ▪Ɣ

SLURP'S UP: This thatched-roofed beach shack serves a limited supply of snacks as well as frozen fruit drinks, wine coolers, and beer. The snack bar is located at the shoreline on the right side of Typhoon Lagoon. Ɣ

LOW TIDE LOU'S: This small beach shack near the entrance to Gang Plank Falls sells the usual beach snacks plus soft drinks, wine coolers, and draft beer, which can be enjoyed in the quaint shelter nearby. Low Tide Lou's is near Ketchakiddee Creek, so the noise and activity level can be fairly high. Ɣ

GETAWAY GLEN PICNIC AREA: This picnic area with many tables and play areas is located on the left side of the Lagoon near Leaning Palms. A volleyball net is permanently installed, but there is plenty of room for both playing and eating. Overhanging shelters provide a shady break from the sun, and mists from the rain forest cool diners on windy days.

CASCADE COVE PICNIC AREA: Cascade Cove is located between Shark Reef and Castaway Creek on the right side of the Lagoon. Chaise lounges, wooden tables, and shady overhangs create a welcome picnic spot. Cascade Cove is larger than Getaway Glen but fills up rapidly because of its proximity to Typhoon Tilly's.

SERVICES

REST ROOMS: Public rest rooms are located near Typhoon Tilly's snack bar and the Leaning Palms snack bar, and at the base of Gang Plank Falls, close to Low Tide Lou's snack bar. All the rest rooms can get quite crowded in the afternoons. The rest rooms at the Dressing Rooms are the largest and least crowded.

TELEPHONES: Public telephones are located outside the Dressing Rooms next to Singapore Sal's and near all the rest rooms. The phones inside the Dressing Rooms offer a quiet spot for making calls. Those at Typhoon Tilly's are generally available.

TOWELS: Towels can be rented at High & Dry Towels, located to the right of the entrance walkway.

DRESSING ROOMS: The Dressing Rooms are located next to Singapore Sal's. Since all rest rooms in the park have showers, visitors may also use them to change from wet to dry, and most are less crowded than those at the Dressing Rooms.

LOCKERS: Keys to the day lockers near the Dressing Rooms can be rented in front of High & Dry Towels. Coin lockers are located at the rest rooms near Typhoon Tilly's snack bar.

WATERTOYS: Life vests can be rented at High & Dry Towels. Tubes for the bobbing waves in Typhoon Lagoon can be rented at Raft Rentals. During busy times, tubes are also rented on the beach. Visitors are not permitted to bring their own equipment.

FIRST AID: The first-aid station is located to the left of the main entrance, near Leaning Palms snack bar. Aspirin and other first-aid needs are dispensed free of charge.

VISITORS WITH DISABILITIES: Wheelchairs may be rented just inside the entrance gate to Typhoon Lagoon, although only a limited number are available. All pathways are wheelchair accessible, and there is a ramp to the viewing station in Shark Reef. Most of the thrill rides are off-limits to people with serious physical disabilities, but Castaway Creek and the bobbing waves in Typhoon Lagoon can be ideal.

TOURING TIPS FOR ADULTS

✦ During high-attendance times, there is always a long line for rental towels and locker keys. If you are planning a visit on a crowded day, bring your own towel and a handful of quarters. Bypass the lockers at the main entrance and use the coin-operated lockers near Typhoon Tilly's instead.

✦ Establish a base of operations by claiming a lounge chair and leaving your towels and belongings on top. At Typhoon Lagoon, this signals to all that the chairs are occupied. Try to choose a site in the shade or under a shelter, which will keep your belongings dry in a sudden downpour and protect you against overexposure to the sun. If you want to work on your tan, you can always find a place in the sun.

✦ During the summer months, Typhoon Lagoon is a tempting destination, but the crowds can make it difficult. The smart time to visit is after 4 PM, when parents are taking their tired kids back to their hotels and others are leaving to pursue dinner plans. Late afternoon is an enchanting time at Typhoon Lagoon, which often stays open until 8 PM. The park takes on a tropical remoteness, and lines to the attractions are short or nonexistent, so you can frolic to your heart's content or simply plop down in a lounge chair under the swaying palms with a Mai Tai in hand.

✦ Many of the coffee shops in the WDW resorts will prepare a boxed lunch for you to take into the park. This way, you can eat well and avoid the long lines at the refreshment stands. You can purchase your beverages at one of the beverage carts scattered around Typhoon Lagoon.

Half-Day Tour at Typhoon Lagoon

The half-day tour that follows is designed to allow first-time visitors to experience the best of Typhoon Lagoon in three to four hours. Depending on the time of year, this tour works best either in the early morning during warm months or the afternoon during winter months, and does not include meals. If you are visiting in the morning, you can buy a fast-food lunch inside the park, bring a boxed lunch from the coffee shop in your hotel, or plan a late lunch (1 PM or later) at your hotel or a restaurant in nearby Disney Village Marketplace. If you are touring in the afternoon, you may wish to eat lunch before you arrive.

MORNING OR AFTERNOON LAGOON TOUR

Three to four hours.
Morning tour — March through September — does not include lunch.
Afternoon tour— October through February — does not include lunch.

✔ Pack a tote bag with sunblock, a hat or visor, and quarters for the lockers. Wear your bathing suit under your clothes. If you have a towel, you might want to bring it rather than waste time in the towel line.

✔ If you are on the morning tour, arrive at the entrance to Typhoon Lagoon ten to fifteen minutes before the park officially opens. Call 560-4141 or check Guest Services in your resort for opening times, which vary with the season.

✔ When you enter the park, rent towels if you need them at High & Dry Towels but bypass the lockers at the main entrance and proceed to the coin-operated lockers near Typhoon Tilly's snack bar. Leave your valuables, except any money you will need for refreshments, in the locker.

✔ Set up camp in one of the sheltered coves beyond Typhoon Tilly's.

✔ Proceed to **CASTAWAY CREEK**. There is an entrance close to Typhoon Tilly's. Grab one of the extra tubes stacked here or look for an empty one floating by. Use the Water Tower as your exit landmark and take off down the Creek for a revolution or two around the park.

✔ After you leave Castaway Creek, walk over to the **SHARK REEF** viewing station for an underwater view. Then, go topside to get your snorkeling gear and join the snorkeling tour of Shark Reef.

✔ When you're done at Shark Reef, walk toward Mt. Mayday. Climb the stairs to Humunga Kowabunga, and turn off halfway up on **MAYDAY TRAIL**. Follow the trail across Mt. Mayday and behind Forgotten Grotto for a bird's-eye view of Typhoon Lagoon. Mayday Trail ends near **KEELHAUL FALLS**, where you can catch a white-water raft ride (or grab a beverage at Low Tide Lou's).

✔ If Keelhaul Falls whets your appetite for thrills, backtrack to **STORM SLIDES** for a ride down one of the spiraling water chutes. This should prepare you for another optional water thrill, the terrifying plunge at **HUMUNGA KOWABUNGA**.

✔ Spend the rest of your visit riding the bobbing waves or body surfing in **TYPHOON LAGOON**. Be sure to check the wave schedule in front of the Lagoon. While you're waiting for the wave of your choice, take the opportunity to browse at Singapore Sal's Saleable Salvage or work on your tan at the beach. The eruption of Mt. Mayday on the half hour will tell you when surf's up. ◆

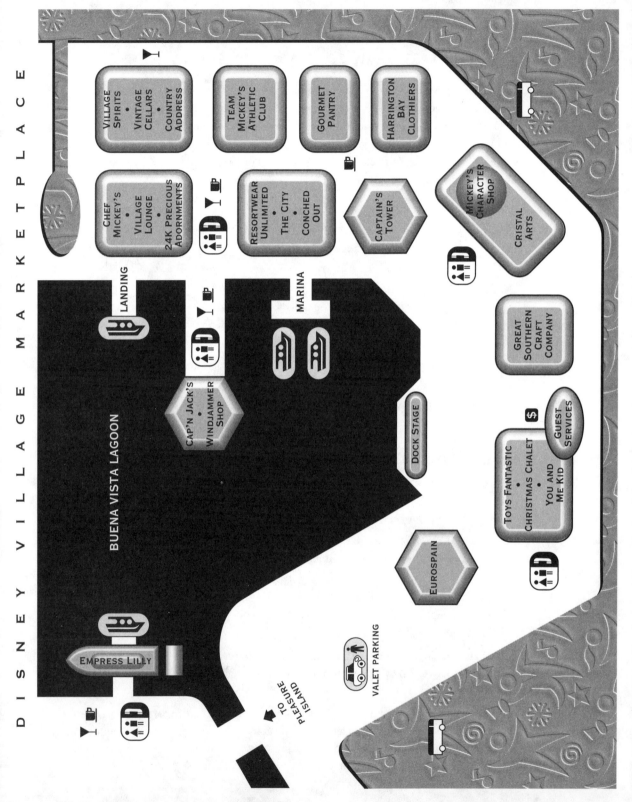

DISNEY VILLAGE MARKETPLACE

VILLAGE SPIRITS • VINTAGE CELLARS • COUNTRY ADDRESS

TEAM MICKEY'S ATHLETIC CLUB

GOURMET PANTRY

HARRINGTON BAY CLOTHIERS

CHEF MICKEY'S • VILLAGE LOUNGE • 24K PRECIOUS ADORNMENTS

RESORTWEAR UNLIMITED • THE CITY • CONCHED OUT

CAPTAIN'S TOWER

MICKEY'S CHARACTER SHOP • CRISTAL ARTS

GREAT SOUTHERN CRAFT COMPANY

LANDING

MARINA

CAP'N JACK'S WINDJAMMER SHOP

BUENA VISTA LAGOON

DOCK STAGE

TOYS FANTASTIC • CHRISTMAS CHALET • YOU AND ME KID

GUEST SERVICES

EUROSPAIN

EMPRESS LILLY

TO PLEASURE ISLAND

VALET PARKING

DISNEY VILLAGE MARKETPLACE

Disney Village Marketplace is a picturesque shopping and entertainment complex resembling a small water-front town. It is situated alongside Pleasure Island on the edge of Buena Vista Lagoon. Here, visitors can stroll along the boardwalk, duck into shops, or relax in one of several restaurants or lounges. The many shops and boutiques in the Marketplace offer name-brand clothing, gourmet foods, special-interest gifts, and Disney collectibles. Disney Village Marketplace is also the site of outdoor entertainment, crafts demonstrations, and seasonal celebrations, and has a large marina where watercraft can be rented.

WHEN TO GO: Disney Village Marketplace and its shops are open every day of the year from 9:30 AM until 10 PM. Unless you are going for a specific entertainment event, plan a visit first thing in the morning or in the evening after dinner, when crowds are smaller and parking places more abundant. For information on special events, call Disney Village Marketplace Guest Services (407 828-3058).

HOW TO GET THERE: Disney Village Marketplace is in the Disney Village Resorts Area. Free parking is available in the large parking lot. The Marketplace is within walking distance of Disney's Village Resort and most of the Hotel Plaza resorts. WDW buses travel between all resorts and theme parks and the Village Marketplace. Water launches service the following resorts: Dixie Landings, Port Orleans, Vacation Club, and Village Resort. Starting at 5:30 PM, valet parking is offered.

✳

SHOPS

EUROSPAIN: Eurospain offers a vast array of collectibles from all over the world, all displayed in uniquely designed showcases. The shop stocks delicate floral ceramics from Italy, Austrian and Italian crystal, Goebbels miniatures, ceramic masks, music boxes, porcelain figurines, and a variety of crystal and enameled jewelry. Crafts demonstrations include figurine painting and gold filigree work.

TOYS FANTASTIC: Toys Fantastic is a Disney-Mattel collaboration that has, perhaps, the most complete selection of Barbie dolls and Barbie doll paraphernalia in the Western Hemisphere. The latest Disney character collectibles — such as Aladdin and Beauty and the Beast dolls, and Sleeping Beauty and Cinderella dolls (which look very much like Barbie clones) — appear here first. Mattel's Bigfoot truck is also featured along with truckloads of accessories and, for new arrivals, there's a Disney Infant Department.

CHRISTMAS CHALET: The Christmas Chalet is the most popular shop year round at Disney Village Marketplace. One-of-a-kind Christmas ornaments, nativity scenes, recordings of Christmas music, garlands, wreaths, and almost anything else required for the Christmas season is available here. Also offered are Mickey Christmas sweatshirts — a popular pick even in the middle of summer.

YOU AND ME KID: The interior of this shop is designed to suggest a brightly colored toy box, and it's filled to the brim with toys, games, electric trains, stuffed animals, and children's clothing. In the store's several annexes, youngsters can get their pictures taken with Disney characters, adults can buy stationery and books including bestsellers, and small children can play in an area designed especially for them.

GREAT SOUTHERN CRAFT COMPANY: In the outdoor area at the entrance to this shop, artisans demonstrate their craftmaking skills throughout the day. Inside, American crafts are featured, with a vast profusion of folk art, folk toys, handmade belts, quilts, dolls, stuffed animals, stained glass, ceramics, decoys, hand puppets, birdhouses, and baskets. Also on display are hand-dipped candles, scented oils and soaps, and Caswell-Massey toiletries. At the Lilly Langtry Photo Studio, tucked into an alcove, visitors can have themselves photographed in period costumes (some weigh as much as seventy-five pounds!). An expert stylist is on hand to outfit individuals or groups from a large rack of reproduction costumes.

CRISTAL ARTS: This shop is hung with magnificent crystal chandeliers and, as its name implies, it carries a large and sparkling selection of crystal jewelry, ornaments, vases, lamps, glasses, and bowls in all colors from all over the world. Also on view is a distinguished collection of Czechoslovakian crystal goblets, bowls, and decanters. Throughout the day, glassblowers demonstrate their skills, creating tiny glass figurines for visitors, and custom crystal engraving is done on site.

MICKEY'S CHARACTER SHOP: This store is an emporium for all Disney merchandise — watches, clothing, books, videos, music, collectible statuary, stuffed animals, stickers, notebooks, candy, gift wrap, cards, and clothing. The centerpiece at Mickey's Character Shop is the Robomat, a spray-painting robot that customizes Mickey character tee-shirts with the purchaser's name. With the ongoing demonstrations and the enormous collection of Disney character merchandise for sale here, this shop is always crowded.

HARRINGTON BAY CLOTHIERS: This store sports a pleasant masculine decor and provides a peaceful oasis for the shopping-weary. Men's casual and dress fashions are offered, including such brand names as Polo by Ralph Lauren, Boston Traders, and Calvin Klein. Also on display are accessories, tote bags, windbreakers, ties, and golf wear.

GOURMET PANTRY: On one side of this store, shoppers will find a kitchenware collectors' paradise — a dizzying variety of gourmet cookware, utensils, cookbooks, and culinary gifts. The other half of the store houses a delicatessen stocked with cheese, salami, cold meats, quiches, salads, and Italian sandwiches sold by the inch. A large bakery sells muffins, pastries, and cookies, and brews several gourmet coffees strong enough to get shoppers back on their feet. The grocery department carries an interesting selection of regional condiments and stocks frozen foods, fresh fruit, beer, and California wines. Shaded tables are scattered about outside the shop.

CONCHED OUT: Murals, mobiles, kaleidoscopes, and wind chimes decorate this pleasant natural wonders shop. Shoppers browse while listening to samples of nature-inspired New Age CDs. Garden-lovers will find bonsai trees, seeds and bulbs, birdhouses, gardening books and tools, straw sun hats, pith helmets and, of course, Birkenstock sandals. Also available are a large selection of exotic stuffed animals including giraffes, gorillas, lion cubs, and frogs.

THE CITY: Catering to a young adult crowd, this shop carries tee-shirts, miniskirts, decorated blue jeans, sharply tailored jackets, leather jackets, men's jeans, and a few flashy outfits suitable for the nightclub scene on nearby Pleasure Island. Also offered are sunglasses, belts, handbags, hats, and earrings — all in the trendy category. Designers include Nicole Miller and Perry Ellis.

RESORTWEAR UNLIMITED: In the summer months, this is the place to find women's casual wear, sun hats, sandals, sunglasses, and one of the largest selections of swimwear at Walt Disney World. During the winter months, jackets, slacks, and sweaters are also featured. Designers include Platinum, Liz Claiborne, and Peter Popovich. The shop carries Keds sneakers, low-heeled dress shoes, and costume jewelry that includes Rolex-style Minnie and Mickey Mouse watches.

WINDJAMMER DOCK SHOP: Located in the lobby of Cap'n Jack's Oyster Bar, Windjammer offers duffel bags, postcards, books, nautical gifts, and travel guides. Appealing to vacationing sailors, the Cap'n Jack logo appears on sweatshirts, windbreakers, caps, and glassware.

24K PRECIOUS ADORNMENTS: Here shoppers can peruse fine gold jewelry and decorative gifts. The Mickey Mouse watches in this shop are designed by famous watchmakers, and some sport diamonds. In fact, many of the finest pieces, including exquisite cameos, incorporate Disney characters.

COUNTRY ADDRESS: Tastefully decorated and arranged, this up-scale shop features women's clothing and accessories. Styles range from classically tailored suits to evening wear and everything in between and underneath — slacks, sweaters, leather skirts and jackets, sequined dresses, and lingerie. Brand names include Carole Little, Liz Claiborne, and Adrienne Vittadini. Also on display are Lancôme cosmetics.

VILLAGE SPIRITS: The most outstanding feature at Village Spirits is its incredible selection of miniature liquors (which some visitors consider quite handy at the Magic Kingdom). Souvenir hunters on the lookout for exotic miniature liquors will be able to augment their collections here. Also available is an interesting array of grappa and Scotch, as well as mixers, bar accessories, and cigarettes and cigars.

VINTAGE CELLARS: This wine shop adjoins Village Spirits, and here shoppers can inspect popular American varietal wines as well as rare European vintages. Wine tastings are held daily at the handsome mahogany wine bar, and membership in Disney's Food and Wine Society may be obtained here.

TEAM MICKEY'S ATHLETIC CLUB: This popular shop offers a huge selection of special-interest sportswear (most festooned with the Disney insignia) including bowling shirts and bags, baseball jerseys and jackets, golfing sweaters and bags, bicycling gear, rugby and polo shirts, aerobics outfits, and warm-up suits. Here, collectors and gift hunters will find college- and professional-team-logo sweatshirts plus baseball caps for every major and minor team in the United States. In the athletic shoe department, a set of bleachers faces one wall of the store, where a display of sixteen video monitors broadcast sporting events all day. It's a great place to park shopping-weary companions who enjoy spectator sports.

CAPTAIN'S TOWER: This octagonal shop, in a building that is open on all sides, is the site of special events and seasonal activities at Disney Village Marketplace, such as the Festival of the Masters art show. During those times, the Captain's Tower becomes a merchandising outlet for the featured event. The shop has several complete merchandise overhauls annually. At times, the store is dedicated exclusively to Reebok athletic shoes and sportswear. In the summer, fun-in-the-sun merchandise is featured.

✳

ACTIVITIES, EVENTS, AND LIVE ENTERTAINMENT

Live entertainment and seasonal events are scheduled throughout the year at the Marketplace. These include a classic car show in June, a boat show in October, the Festival of the Masters art show in November, and a Nativity pageant at Christmas. Many of the shops feature daily demonstrations by guest artisans. Check with Disney Village Marketplace Guest Services for current entertainment schedules (407 828-3058).

DOCK STAGE: The Dock Stage is located on an open plaza at the edge of Buena Vista Lagoon. Throughout the year, it it the site of such diverse live entertainments as country clogging, Nativity scenes, Disney film festivals, jazz concerts, and high school band competitions.

DISNEY VILLAGE MARKETPLACE MARINA: This busy and beautiful marina rents canopy boats, pontoon boats, and zippy little two-seater Water Sprites for taking a spin on Buena Vista Lagoon, exploring the bayoulike waterways, or touring the theme resorts in the Disney Village Resorts Area. Fishing excursions on Buena Vista Lagoon can also be arranged here. (See "Boating & Marinas," page 220, and "Fishing Excursions," page 224.) The marina is open every day from 10 AM until sundown.

FULL-SERVICE RESTAURANTS

All WDW visitors can make restaurant reservations up to thirty days in advance at Disney Village Marketplace restaurants. Same-day reservations can be made at the restaurant itself or at Guest Services. Smoking is not permitted in the restaurants. See "Restaurants," page 167, for detailed restaurant reviews and reservation strategies.

CHEF MICKEY'S VILLAGE RESTAURANT: This spacious, sunlight-filled, family-oriented restaurant offers an American-style menu, featuring Florida seafood, steak, and pasta dishes. Chef Mickey wanders through every evening during dinner, which thrills the small fry. Beer, wine, and spirits are served. Open for breakfast, lunch, and dinner; reservations suggested.

CAP'N JACK'S OYSTER BAR: This octagonal restaurant is perched on a pier out in the lagoon, and is the ultimate oasis for harried shoppers and theme-park escapees. The unusual architecture offers diners a great view from any table, and the restaurant attracts a lively crowd for clams and oysters on the half-shell, shrimp cocktails, crab cakes, lobster, and pasta. Beer, wine, and spirits are served. Open all day; no reservations. Visitors who just want to snack can seat themselves at the bar.

EMPRESS ROOM ON BOARD THE *EMPRESS LILLY:* This elegant (and expensive) restaurant features sophisticated Continental cuisine served in an intimate setting, with secluded tables, etched-glass table partitions, and a sparkling crystal and brass chandelier. The menu is seasonal and changes frequently. Beer, wine, and spirits are served. Jackets and ties are recommended for men. Open for dinner only; reservations are required.

STEERMAN'S QUARTERS ON BOARD THE *EMPRESS LILLY:* Prime rib and steaks are served in this cozy dining room, with its red upholstery and dark mahogany furnishings, and windows overlooking the riverboat's huge paddle wheel. Beer, wine, and spirits are served. Open for dinner only; reservations recommended.

FISHERMAN'S DECK ON BOARD THE *EMPRESS LILLY:* Seafood, salads, and a delicious chicken potpie are featured in this delicate, comfortable salon, which is dominated by a large curved window overlooking Buena Vista Lagoon. Beer, wine, and spirits are served. Open for lunch and dinner; reservations recommended.

✦ DISNEY VILLAGE MARKETPLACE ✦

CAFES AND LOUNGES

Several counter-service restaurants at Disney Village Marketplace serve all-day snacks and fast-food meals. Those listed below are especially pleasant rest stops and also make ideal meeting spots for visitors who want to shop and tour separately and rendezvous later.

VILLAGE LOUNGE: Adjacent to Chef Mickey's Village Restaurant, this large, comfortable lounge has low tables and armchairs that offer "slouch-with-a-sigh" comfort. The lounge also features two wide-screen TVs — the one at the bar generally broadcasts sports events. No snacks are served. ☕Y

CAP'N JACK'S OYSTER BAR: The circular copper bar in this lively restaurant is known for its frozen strawberry Margaritas. This convivial bar is a great place for a quick pick-me-up or for a long, relaxing view of the sunset over Buena Vista Lagoon. Coffee and espresso are available as well. ☕Y

VINTAGE CELLARS: Wine tastings are held throughout the day in this handsome wood-paneled wine shop. No seating. Y

GOURMET PANTRY: Step up to the bakery counter and check out the selection of freshly brewed gourmet coffees along the back wall. There are shaded tables outside the shop. ☕

BATON ROUGE LOUNGE ON BOARD THE *EMPRESS LILLY*: With its dark wood paneling, cozy tables, and windows overlooking the lagoon, this lounge has a vintage riverboat feel. It opens at 5 PM on weekdays and at noon on weekends. ☕Y

✦

SERVICES

REST ROOMS: Public rest rooms are located throughout Disney Village Marketplace. The cooler, quieter rest rooms can be found in Chef Mickey's Village Restaurant and Cap'n Jack's Oyster Bar. The rest rooms on the *Empress Lilly* riverboat are very private and well appointed, especially those on the second deck outside the Empress Room restaurant.

TELEPHONES: Outdoor public telephones can be found throughout Disney Village Marketplace, usually adjacent to the rest rooms. To make calls in air-conditioned comfort, slip into Chef Mickey's Village Restaurant or Cap'n Jack's Oyster Bar. There are private, plush sit-down phone cubicles on the second deck of the *Empress Lilly* riverboat, just outside the Empress Room restaurant.

GIFT WRAPPING: Gift wrapping is available at Guest Services; prices start at about $4.

FILM AND TWO-HOUR EXPRESS DEVELOPING: A wide range of film may be purchased at Guest Services. Two-hour film processing is available at Guest Services, and developed film can be picked up there or delivered to any WDW resort.

BANKING: A branch of Sun Bank is located across the street from Disney Village Marketplace. There is an automatic teller machine (ATM) just outside of the Guest Services building.

MAIL DROP: A mail box is located just outside the Guest Services building. Stamps are available inside.

LOCKERS: Coin lockers, useful for storing purchases, are located at the Village Marketplace Marina.

WHEELCHAIR RENTALS: Wheelchairs are available for rent at Guest Services. ◆

VACATION ITINERARIES

Visitors who have vacationed at Walt Disney World know how difficult and stressful it can be to try to see everything they would like to during a limited time period. Many rely on serendipity and their instincts to accomplish their vacation goals, and most are not aware of all the options available to them and how many entertainment choices they have. The Vacation Itineraries are designed to help both first-time and repeat visitors focus on their special interests while streamlining planning and simplifying logistics after arrival. If you are an experienced WDW visitor, you will immediately recognize the efficacy of the Vacation Itineraries, which can be easily modified to meet your current interests and past experiences.

SELECTING A VACATION ITINERARY

Each Vacation Itinerary covers four days beginning the afternoon of arrival, although the planning begins months earlier. On the day of arrival, the preplanning will be complete, decisions and reservations will be made, and your most difficult task will be showing up at each event. Some of the itineraries are designed for low-attendance periods, although careful planning and eliminating some of the rides make it possible to use the itineraries effectively during peak seasons as well. Afternoons are generally spent engaged in optional activities or simply relaxing and enjoying the resort life.

The Vacation Itineraries work best when you have your own car or a rental car. WDW transportation can also be used, but you may not be able to travel as easily to some of the recreation areas unless you rely on taxis. If you are not planning to drive, it is especially important to choose a WDW resort that offers many transportation options, preferably one in the Epcot Resorts Area or the Magic Kingdom Resorts Area (see "Hotels," page 143). The Vacation Itineraries are designed with the assumption that you will stay at a WDW resort. The reservation and transportation privileges available to WDW resort guests are essential to the advance planning and logistics involved. Although a stay at Walt Disney World is not inexpensive, there are a number of budget options built into the itineraries, so additional savings are possible (see "Discount Travel Clubs," page 250).

Each Vacation Itinerary is eight pages long. The first four pages describe the experience you will have on the itinerary; the second four pages describe the schedule you need to follow. The schedules can be copied, and there are spaces to jot your travel dates, which comes in handy when making reservations. On the first page of each itinerary, note the suggested arrival days, which are timed to make the schedules work smoothly.

EXPANDING A VACATION ITINERARY

If you are planning to stay longer than four days, there are a number of options available to you, depending on your interests and the time of year. You may want to return to some of the parks you've seen to explore them further or to pursue optional activities that you missed earlier. The activities listed below can be used to expand your selected Vacation Itinerary. Add these activities at the end of your four-day tour, but remember to make any necessary advance reservations for those you select:

EDUCATION AND DISCOVERY EXPEDITION: *Additional Days for the Intellectually Curious* — ❶ Join the studio audience for a television production at Disney-MGM Studios and spend the evening at the Magic Kingdom for SpectroMagic and the Fantasy in the Sky fireworks show (call 407 560-7299 for Disney-MGM production information). ❷ Drop by the Casting Center to see how potential Disney Cast Members learn about Walt Disney World, and tour the unique Team Disney building and gardens. In the evening, take in the MurderWatch Mystery Dinner Theater (see "Dinner Shows," page 209). ❸ Spend the day touring the themed architecture, art, landscaping, and entertainment at the Walt Disney World resorts, or call Walt Disney World Information (407 824-4321) for a schedule of featured events and shows that may be happening during your stay.

SPORTING LIFE VACATION: *Additional Days for Active Visitors* — ❶ Take the Guided Tour of the Magic Kingdom in the morning; in the evening, attend the Polynesian Luau dinner show (see "Dinner Shows," page 209). ❷ Follow the Surf and Turf Day at Fort Wilderness tour and take in the Hoop-Dee-Doo Musical Revue in the evening (see "Fort Wilderness & River Country," page 68, and "Dinner Shows," page 209). ❸ Spend the day at Typhoon Lagoon, then catch a first-run movie at the AMC Pleasure Island 10 Theatres (for movie schedules call 827-1300).

DAY-AND-NIGHT ROMANTIC FANTASY: *Additional Days for Couples* — ❶ Follow the Surf and Turf Day at Fort Wilderness tour and take in the Hoop-Dee-Doo Musical Revue in the evening (see "Fort Wilderness & River Country," page 68, and "Dinner Shows," page 209). ❷ Join the studio audience for a television production at Disney-MGM Studios, then catch a first-run movie at the AMC Pleasure Island 10 Theatres (call 560-7299 for Disney-MGM production information; for movie schedules, call 827-1300). ❸ Enjoy an active day — bicycling, golfing, playing tennis, waterskiing, fishing — then see the MurderWatch Mystery Dinner Theater and spend the late evening touring the Hotel Plaza dance clubs (see "Sporting Activities," page 217, and "Dinner Shows," page 209).

GARDENS AND NATURAL WONDERS TOUR: *Additional Days for Nature Lovers* — ❶ Enjoy an active day — golfing, tennis, waterskiing, fishing — and dine in the early evening at Portobello Yacht Club and take in a movie at AMC Pleasure Island 10 Theatres (see "Sporting Activities," page 217; for movie schedules call 827-1300). ❷ Spend the day touring the gardens and landscaping at Walt Disney World's themed resorts, then return to the World Showcase at night to see the beautiful lighting at the international pavilions. ❸ Bicycle through the Village Resorts Area on the Country Club and Old Key West Ride, then take the Late Afternoon and Evening Wilderness Tour at Fort Wilderness and catch the Hoop-Dee-Doo Musical Revue dinner show (see "Bicycle Paths," page 218, and "Dinner Shows," page 209).

WILD KINGDOM: *Additional Days for Singles and the Young at Heart* — ❶ Join the Hidden Treasures of the World Showcase tour, then spend the afternoon at Typhoon Lagoon or catch a first-run movie at the AMC Pleasure Island 10 Theatres (to reserve the tour, call 407 354-1855 well in advance; for movie schedules call 827-1300). ❷ Follow the Surf and Turf Day at Fort Wilderness tour and take in the Hoop-Dee-Doo Musical Revue dinner show (see "Fort Wilderness & River Country," page 68, and "Dinner Shows," page 209). ❸ Join the studio audience for a television production at Disney-MGM Studios; spend the evening club-hopping at Hotel Plaza (call 560-7299 for Disney-MGM production information; for information on the Hotel Plaza dance clubs, see "Dinner Shows," page 209). ◆

EDUCATION AND DISCOVERY EXPEDITION

A Holiday Adventure in Art and Architecture, Technology and Nature,
International Cultures, and Special-Effects Entertainment

BEST TIME OF YEAR FOR THIS ITINERARY
All year round

LEAST CROWDED TIMES FOR THIS ITINERARY
September through March and the month of May (except holidays)

BEST ARRIVAL DAY FOR THIS ITINERARY
Monday, Wednesday, or Friday — preferably Friday

BEST BUDGET HOTELS FOR THIS ITINERARY
Disney's Dixie Landings Resort (river view)
Disney's Port Orleans Resort (river view)
Grosvenor Resort (garden view, upper floor)

BEST MODERATE HOTELS FOR THIS ITINERARY
Buena Vista Palace (Disney view)
Disney's Polynesian Resort (garden view)

BEST DELUXE HOTELS FOR THIS ITINERARY
Disney's Grand Floridian Beach Resort (courtyard view)
Walt Disney World Swan (Epcot view)
Walt Disney World Dolphin (Epcot view)

ULTIMATE HOTEL EXPERIENCE FOR THIS ITINERARY
Walt Disney World Swan (Royal Beach Club)

LOCAL TRANSPORTATION
For this itinerary, it is best to rent a car or use your own.

PACKING
Much of this itinerary is spent outside, so winter travelers should bring warm
clothing (it can get very cold in Orlando). Summer travelers will need umbrellas.

TIPS
Grosvenor Resort and Buena Vista Palace offer good-value vacation packages.

Day One

EVENING AT THE WORLD SHOWCASE: Your expedition begins as you tour the extraordinary Swan and Dolphin hotels, splendid examples of post-modern entertainment architecture designed by noted architect Michael Graves. The Swan hotel sports a fanciful seashore motif with detailing on a grand scale. Across the waterfront promenade is the pyramid-shaped Dolphin. You pass under a multitiered fountain of giant clamshells to enter the hotel, where a soaring striped circus tent fills the lobby.

The tram to the World Showcase leaves from the promenade, and your tour begins in CANADA, with its bloom-filled Victoria Gardens and the spectacular 360-degree film, O CANADA! At the UNITED KINGDOM pavilion nearby, the streets are lined with charming Tudor, Georgian, and Victorian buildings, and the Old Globe Players embroil visitors in comedic Shakespearian skits. In FRANCE, a bustling Parisian neighborhood is re-created, and the film IMPRESSIONS DE FRANCE introduces visitors to the people, music, and landscapes of France. Farther on, through MOROCCO'S Bab Boujouloud gate, an intricate and mysterious shopping medina spills over with North African handicrafts. Your dinner destination is the exotic RESTAURANT MARRAKESH, which features belly-dancing performances during dinner.

After dinner, you tour JAPAN, with its pagoda, rustic country-inn architecture, and serene Japanese gardens. At the U.S.A. pavilion, THE AMERICAN ADVENTURE presents Audio-Animatronic hosts Mark Twain and Benjamin Franklin, who narrate a journey through the highlights of American history. Farther on, in ITALY, is a replica of Venice's Doge's Palace, where actors stage Italian folktale comedies.

Just before ILLUMINATIONS begins, the entire World Showcase dims and, one by one, each nation is celebrated in music and light. Suddenly, the night sky is brilliant with fireworks, and colorful fountains of water shoot up from the lagoon. In the distance, laser projections (which are bounced off the windows of the Dolphin hotel) transform Epcot's giant silver geosphere into a radiant, spinning planet earth.

Day Two

MORNING AT THE MAGIC KINGDOM: This morning, you join the GUIDED TOUR OF THE MAGIC KINGDOM to learn about the background of Walt Disney World, from the personal dreams of its founder to the engineering required to build on swampland. Your tour begins on MAIN STREET, U.S.A., with its quaint shops and small-town ambience. In TOMORROWLAND, the multimedia ride DREAMFLIGHT transports you through the history of aviation, from early flight experiments to jaunts in outer space. In FANTASYLAND, you're surrounded by attractions based on classic children's stories. You tour IT'S A SMALL WORLD, with its ethnic costumes and diverse languages. At THE HAUNTED MANSION in LIBERTY SQUARE, you become part of a masterful special-effects haunting, with a narration incorporating the works of Edgar Allan Poe. In FRONTIERLAND, lunch is served at the DIAMOND HORSESHOE JAMBOREE, accompanied by a lively Gay Nineties dance hall show; and in ADVENTURELAND, a PIRATES OF THE CARIBBEAN watercraft carries you underground to an island settlement where a pirate raid is underway. Your tour ends at JUNGLE CRUISE, where an explorer boat journeys down the world's great rivers.

OPTIONAL AFTERNOON TEA: After the guided tour ends, you board the monorail, sitting in the front for a sweeping overview of the landscape. The final stop is Disney's elegant Grand Floridian Beach Resort, designed after the grand Victorian-style seaside resorts from the turn of the century. Live music plays in the spacious stained glass–domed lobby, and in the Garden View Lounge, overlooking the resort's central courtyard, high tea is served in the traditional British fashion.

EVENING AT DISNEY-MGM STUDIOS: This evening, the focus is on the illusions and wonder of Hollywood at Disney-MGM Studios. On the BACKSTAGE STUDIO TOUR, you're carried by tram past the scenics shop, costume room, and a number of sets used for film locations, including a not-to-be-missed disaster in Catastrophe Canyon. At INSIDE THE MAGIC, you explore the production techniques used to create special-effects scenes in the movies. Then it's on to the impeccably reproduced Chinese Theater, where THE GREAT MOVIE RIDE travels through the history of classic films. Live performers and Audio-Animatronic figures re-create great moments from the movies. At JIM HENSON'S MUPPET*VISION 3D, a variety of advanced special effects, puppetry, and animation techniques are combined to create a striking entertainment event. If you have time, the INDIANA JONES EPIC STUNT SPECTACULAR is an educational foray into the careful orchestration, safety features, props, and effects used to produce adventure scenes in films. Your dinner destination is the 50's PRIME TIME CAFE, a time capsule of fifties-style kitchenette tables and black and white televisions playing sitcoms of the era.

After dinner, if SORCERY IN THE SKY is scheduled, you'll want to position yourself at the end of Hollywood Boulevard for the best view. This fireworks light-and-sound extravaganza, based on the movie *Fantasia*, opens with the flickering light of a movie projector aimed at the Chinese Theater before the night sky is illuminated with lasers, strobes, fireworks, and fountains of silver and gold sparks.

Day Three

MORNING AT FUTURE WORLD AND THE WORLD SHOWCASE: The HIDDEN TREASURES OF THE WORLD SHOWCASE tour leaves from Earth Station, behind Epcot Center's dazzling eighteen-story geosphere. If you have time beforehand, CommuniCore East presents entertaining hands-on exhibits demonstrating how computers are used for design, engineering, and information management.

During your World Showcase tour, a well-informed guide leads you through each pavilion's gardens and buildings, and describes the behind-the-scenes techniques used to create the architectural effects, landscaping, and attractions. When the tour ends, it's time for lunch at the congenial ROSE & CROWN DINING ROOM at the UNITED KINGDOM pavilion.

OPTIONAL AFTERNOON WATER ADVENTURE: After lunch, you're off for a boating adventure through the bayoulike DISNEY VILLAGE WATERWAYS. Your first stop is DIXIE LANDINGS, a resort featuring the architecture and landscaping of the plantation mansions and bayou lodges of the Old South. Here, you'll rent a canopy boat at the Dixie Levee marina for a tour of the themed resorts along the waterways. You enter the Sassagoula River and cruise past PORT ORLEANS, with its French Quarter–style waterfront and maze of charming city streets being prepared for Mardi Gras. You take a side trip through the Trumbo Canal to take a look at Old Key West at the VACATION CLUB, then continue on to Buena Vista Lagoon, where the *Empress Lilly* is docked. This nineteenth-century replica stern-wheeler was inspired by the tales of Mark Twain. If you're in the mood, you can dock at DISNEY VILLAGE MARKETPLACE to browse through the specialty shops and boutiques.

EVENING ON PLEASURE ISLAND: Your dinner destination this evening is aboard the *Empress Lilly*. The cozy STEERMAN'S QUARTERS is tucked in the stern, on the main deck, and as you dine, the riverboat's giant red paddle wheel turns slowly outside the window.

The nightlife is now in full swing on **PLEASURE ISLAND**, where you'll explore all of the clubs, beginning with the opening show at **MANNEQUINS**. The **ADVENTURERS CLUB** offers amusing encounters with a group of eccentric actors who mingle with the crowd telling preposterous stories of their explorations. At the **JAZZ COMPANY**, **8TRAX**, and **NEON ARMADILLO**, contrasting musical styles can be sampled, and at the **COMEDY WAREHOUSE** performances are staged hourly. Back outside at the **NEW YEAR'S EVE STREET PARTY**, Pleasure Island erupts in celebration as confetti falls and fireworks explode overhead.

Day Four

MORNING AT DISCOVERY ISLAND: With a picnic lunch in hand, you ferry across Bay Lake for a morning tour of eleven-acre **DISCOVERY ISLAND**, an internationally recognized zoo and sanctuary for disabled and endangered birds, reptiles, and small mammals. The animal caretakers tell fascinating stories about the residents of Discovery Island, including the Galapagos tortoises, and at the entertaining **FEATHERED FRIENDS**, **BIRDS OF PREY**, and **REPTILE RELATIONS** shows, you can learn even more. You'll picnic at Toucan Corner, a shady glade filled with the squawks and calls of the island's inhabitants.

AFTERNOON AT FUTURE WORLD: In the Epcot geosphere, an impeccably researched journey through the world of communications past, present, and future is presented aboard **SPACESHIP EARTH**. Nearby, the **UNIVERSE OF ENERGY** pavilion houses a solar-powered theater that travels through the eerie, primeval twilight of the time when fossil fuels began. Giant dinosaurs loom in an ancient forest, and you can actually feel the clammy warm air of the swamp and smell the sulfur from erupting volcanoes in the distance. The golden-domed **WONDERS OF LIFE** pavilion, nearby, features three attractions dealing with the human body: **BODY WARS**, **CRANIUM COMMAND**, and **THE MAKING OF ME**. Then it's on to **JOURNEY INTO IMAGINATION**, a ride through the world of imagination and ideas. At **THE LAND** pavilion, on the **LISTEN TO THE LAND** tour, you travel by boat through desert, prairie, and rain forest biomes and view experimental greenhouses, hydroponic gardens, and aquaculture facilities. Afterward, at **THE LIVING SEAS** pavilion, the **CARIBBEAN CORAL REEF RIDE** travels along the ocean floor to Sea Base Alpha, a six-million-gallon tropical saltwater aquarium. Although the coral is fake (live coral is too toxic for the enclosed environment), the sea life is genuine. The manatees at the Marine Mammal Center are worth a close inspection, and a marine biologist is on hand to answer questions. In CommuniCore West, **EPCOT OUTREACH** provides information about all Epcot Center attractions. If you have time, CommuniCore East features **BACKSTAGE MAGIC**, which describes the evolution of the microcomputer and offers an eye-opening, behind-the-scenes look at Walt Disney World's computer operations center. Three Disney-owned space satellites are accessed here, that control the entertainment events throughout WDW.

EVENING IN POLYNESIA: The torchlit grounds of the Polynesian resort are landscaped with exquisite tropical foliage. Behind the resort, at Seven Seas Lagoon, you catch the animated lights and music of the **ELECTRICAL WATER PAGEANT**. (Yes, this show, too, is controlled by satellite.) At Luau Cove, nearby, the **POLYNESIAN LUAU** dinner show is about to begin. In this tropical grotto, under the night sky, you are served a luau-style feast and entertained with the exotic music and dance of the South Sea Islands. ➤

Expedition Schedule

The next four pages show the schedule you will follow and the arrangements and reservations you must make to organize the Education and Discovery Expedition. You may want to copy these pages and carry them with you.

BEFORE YOU GO

AT THE TIME YOU MAKE YOUR HOTEL RESERVATIONS: Call the Disney Learning Program (407 354-1855) and make reservations for DAY THREE for the Hidden Treasures of the World Showcase tour, which usually occurs on Wednesday, Friday, and Sunday. (Try to schedule your stay so that DAY THREE of your itinerary falls on one of these days, preferably Sunday. If this is not possible, switch DAY THREE with DAY TWO and be sure that DAY TWO falls on a Wednesday, Friday, or Sunday.) Make reservations for the 9:30 PM Polynesian Luau dinner show for DAY FOUR (407 934-7639).

THREE DAYS BEFORE YOU LEAVE: Call Theme Park Restaurant Reservations (407 824-8800) and make 7:30 PM dinner reservations for DAY ONE at Restaurant Marrakesh in the Morocco pavilion at the World Showcase. (If you prefer another restaurant, choose one in Japan, France, or Italy.) Be sure your seating is no later than ninety minutes before IllumiNations is scheduled to begin. Call Village Restaurant Reservations (407 828-3900) and make 7:30 PM dinner reservations for DAY THREE in Steerman's Quarters aboard the *Empress Lilly* riverboat at Pleasure Island. (If you prefer another restaurant, consider Fisherman's Deck.)

TWO DAYS BEFORE YOU LEAVE: Call Theme Park Restaurant Reservations (407 824-8800) and make 7:30 PM dinner reservations for DAY TWO at the 50's Prime Time Cafe at Disney-MGM Studios. (If you prefer another restaurant, consider the Hollywood Brown Derby or Mama Melrose's.)

ONE DAY BEFORE YOU LEAVE: Call Theme Park Restaurant Reservations (407 824-8800) and make 1:45 PM lunch reservations for DAY THREE at the Rose & Crown Dining Room in the United Kingdom pavilion at the World Showcase. (If you prefer another restaurant, consider one in Mexico or China.)

DAY ONE: THE EVENING OF ARRIVAL

DAY / DATE

AFTER YOU CHECK INTO YOUR HOTEL: Stop at Guest Services, and if you do not have park admission tickets, consider buying a multiday pass that includes Discovery Island and Pleasure Island. Also at Guest Services, purchase your tickets for the 9:30 PM Polynesian Luau dinner show for DAY FOUR and ask for a *Times and Information* pamphlet showing the operating schedules at the Magic Kingdom, Epcot Center, and Disney-MGM Studios. Your reservations are now complete for the remainder of your vacation.

5 PM: Drive or taxi to the Walt Disney World Swan. Walk through the hotel's lobby for a look at the fanciful architectural and decorative details, then stroll to the Walt Disney World Dolphin for a look at a different but complementary style of post-modern entertainment architecture.

5:45 PM: Tram from the Dolphin and Swan promenade to the WORLD SHOWCASE. Tour the pavilions of CANADA, the UNITED KINGDOM, and FRANCE and catch the films O CANADA! and IMPRESSIONS DE FRANCE. Step over to the MOROCCO pavilion and explore the shopping bazaar.

7:30 PM DINNER: Restaurant Marrakesh is located in the Morocco pavilion at the World Showcase.

AFTER DINNER: If ILLUMINATIONS begins at 10 PM tonight, continue your tour of the architecture and gardens at the JAPAN pavilion, catch a performance of THE AMERICAN ADVENTURE in the U.S.A. pavilion, and enjoy the street theater at the ITALY pavilion. If IllumiNations begins at 9 PM, find a viewing spot at the edge of the lagoon. There are good views along the promenade at France and on the bridges in front of Italy.

BEFORE YOU RETIRE: Leave a wake-up call and perhaps order a room-service breakfast tonight to be delivered early in the morning. You'll leave for the Magic Kingdom one half hour before it opens.

DAY TWO

DAY / DATE

ONE HALF HOUR BEFORE THE MAGIC KINGDOM OPENS: Drive or take WDW transportation to the MAGIC KINGDOM. If you are driving, park at the Grand Floridian resort and take the monorail from there to the Magic Kingdom. Enter the park (Main Street generally opens early) and step into City Hall. Make reservations for the 10:30 AM Guided Tour of the Magic Kingdom and pick up an entertainment schedule. Stroll down Main Street, taking note of the turn-of-the-century architectural features, window signs, and horse-drawn vehicles. If you have time, catch a vintage Disney cartoon at the MAIN STREET CINEMA, then return to City Hall for the guided tour.

10:30 AM: The GUIDED TOUR OF THE MAGIC KINGDOM lasts about $3^1/_2$ hours and takes you on the following attractions: DREAMFLIGHT; IT'S A SMALL WORLD; THE HAUNTED MANSION; DIAMOND HORSESHOE JAMBOREE (for lunch); PIRATES OF THE CARIBBEAN; and JUNGLE CRUISE. (Attractions visited on the tour may vary.) An informative guide will answer your questions, call your attention to a number of interesting details in the Magic Kingdom, and provide tidbits of history about Walt Disney World.

OPTIONAL AFTERNOON TEA: When the guided tour ends, you can continue touring the Magic Kingdom, return to your resort to relax, or continue to the Optional Afternoon Tea. Exit the park and monorail to the Grand Floridian. Tour the Victorian gardens and common areas of this premier theme resort. Be seated in the Garden View Lounge about fifteen minutes early for the 3 PM high tea.

5 PM: Drive or take WDW transportation to DISNEY-MGM STUDIOS. Stop at Guest Relations as you enter and inquire about movies or television shows in production while you are touring this evening. Stroll to the end of Hollywood Boulevard and visit the following attractions in this order: ❶ BACKSTAGE STUDIO TOUR (the tram portion); ❷ INSIDE THE MAGIC (if there is no production scheduled, you may want to skip this); ❸ THE GREAT MOVIE RIDE; ❹ JIM HENSON'S MUPPET*VISION 3D; and, if you have time before dinner, ❺ INDIANA JONES EPIC STUNT SPECTACULAR.

7:30 PM DINNER: The 50's Prime Time Cafe is located off Hollywood Boulevard, across from Echo Lake. (If the park closes early on the evening of your visit, return to your hotel for dinner.)

AFTER DINNER: If Disney-MGM Studios is open late, continue your tour until it is time for the **SORCERY IN THE SKY** fireworks show at 9 or 10 PM (if scheduled). Ten minutes before the show begins, position yourself at the end of Hollywood Boulevard for the best view.

BEFORE YOU RETIRE: You may again wish to order a wake-up call and breakfast for tomorrow morning. You'll be leaving your hotel one half hour before Epcot opens.

DAY THREE

DAY / DATE

BEFORE YOU LEAVE YOUR HOTEL: Start with a full breakfast, as you'll be eating a late lunch.

ONE HALF HOUR BEFORE EPCOT OPENS: Drive or take WDW transportation to **FUTURE WORLD** at Epcot. Proceed to Earth Station, located behind the Epcot geosphere. There, check in with Guest Relations for the Hidden Treasures of the World Showcase tour, and pick up an entertainment schedule. If you have time while you're waiting for the tour to begin, take a quick tour of CommuniCore East.

9:30 AM: The **HIDDEN TREASURES OF THE WORLD SHOWCASE** tour lasts about $3^1/_2$ hours and explores the architectural features and special design techniques used to create the international pavilions. The tour ends back at Earth Station. Drop out of the tour before it returns to Future World and proceed to the United Kingdom pavilion. If you have time before lunch, tour the shops and gardens at the pavilion.

1:30 PM LUNCH: The Rose & Crown Dining Room is on the edge of the World Showcase Lagoon across from the United Kingdom pavilion. (Light eaters and budget diners can try Le Cellier cafeteria in the Canada pavilion, or Cantina de San Angel in the Mexico pavilion.)

OPTIONAL AFTERNOON WATER ADVENTURE: After lunch, you can return to your hotel to relax and enjoy the resort amenities, or proceed on the Optional Afternoon Water Adventure. Drive or bus to Dixie Landings resort. At the Dixie Levee marina, rent a canopy boat. Cruise the tree-lined **DISNEY VILLAGE WATERWAYS** and visit the following theme resorts (dock at any resorts you would like to tour): ❶ Follow the Sassagoula River through **DIXIE LANDINGS** for a look at the grand plantation mansions and rustic bayou lodges of the Old South. ❷ At **PORT ORLEANS**, view the streets of New Orleans' French Quarter as it prepares for Mardi Gras. ❸ Follow the winding Trumbo Canal through Old Key West at the **VACATION CLUB**. ❹ Backtrack to the Buena Vista Lagoon, where you'll see the *Empress Lilly* riverboat, a replica of a nineteenth-century stern-wheeler. If you're in the mood to shop, dock at **DISNEY VILLAGE MARKETPLACE** and explore its many stores and boutiques. When you've had enough, return your boat to Dixie Landings and head back to your hotel to rest up for the late-night festivities ahead.

7 PM: Drive, bus, or taxi to Pleasure Island.

7:30 PM DINNER: Steerman's Quarters is on the main deck of the *Empress Lilly* riverboat, docked at the entrance to Pleasure Island.

AFTER DINNER: Enter PLEASURE ISLAND and tour as many nightclubs as you can this evening. Start with MANNEQUINS for the not-to-be-missed light show and dance performance that begins about 9:30 PM; then drop into the ADVENTURERS CLUB, the JAZZ COMPANY, the NEON ARMADILLO, and 8TRAX, and catch a performance at the COMEDY WAREHOUSE, if you have time. At 10:45 PM (11:45 PM on weekends), be sure to be back outside at the West End Stage for Pleasure Island's spectacular NEW YEAR'S EVE STREET PARTY, complete with music, dance, fireworks, and confetti.

BEFORE YOU RETIRE: Arrange for your hotel coffee shop to prepare a picnic lunch to take along tomorrow. Go ahead and sleep in; you won't leave for Discovery Island until 10 AM.

DAY FOUR

DAY / DATE

BEFORE YOU LEAVE YOUR HOTEL: Take along a hat or visor, and don't forget your picnic lunch!

10 AM: Drive or monorail to the Contemporary resort. Take the short ferry ride across Bay Lake from the Contemporary Marina to DISCOVERY ISLAND. Follow the path through the zoological park, talk to the animal caretakers, visit the ANIMAL HOSPITAL, and try to catch the FEATHERED FRIENDS, BIRDS OF PREY, and REPTILE RELATIONS shows. Head over to the Toucan Corner Picnic Area to set up your picnic lunch. When you are ready to leave Discovery Island, ferry back to the Contemporary Marina and return to your hotel to take advantage of its resort amenities, take in a movie, or relax before the busy afternoon and evening ahead.

4 PM: Drive or take WDW transportation to FUTURE WORLD at Epcot Center. Visit the following attractions in this order: ❶ SPACESHIP EARTH; ❷ UNIVERSE OF ENERGY; ❸ Wonders of Life pavilion — BODY WARS (and, if the lines are not too long, CRANIUM COMMAND and THE MAKING OF ME); ❹ JOURNEY INTO IMAGINATION; ❺ The Land pavilion — LISTEN TO THE LAND; and ❻ The Living Seas pavilion — CARIBBEAN CORAL REEF RIDE. If you'd like more information about the exhibits you've toured, stop at EPCOT OUTREACH, in CommuniCore West, for printed materials. If you have time, cross the courtyard to CommuniCore East and proceed to Epcot Computer Central for BACKSTAGE MAGIC.

8 PM: Drive, monorail, or bus from Future World to the Polynesian resort. Explore the resort's South Pacific architecture and enjoy the blooming orchids and live parrots in the resort's indoor jungle atrium. Then stroll through the torchlit outdoor tropical gardens, where the specimen plants are marked.

9 PM: On the beach at Seven Seas Lagoon, catch the shimmering lights of the ELECTRICAL WATER PAGEANT barges that float by nightly. If you prefer, you can see them from the windows of the hotel's Tambu Lounge. Here, you can enjoy Polynesian-style cocktails, appetizers, and music until just before show time.

9:30 DINNER SHOW: Arrive at Luau Cove about fifteen minutes early for the POLYNESIAN LUAU dinner show. Under the stars, on your final evening, you will be served a luau-style meal and entertained late into the night with performances of South Seas Islands music and dancing . ◆

SPORTING LIFE VACATION

An Active-Life Holiday of Sporting Pursuits, Outdoor Adventures,
Theme Land Expeditions, and Evening Entertainments

BEST TIME OF YEAR FOR THIS ITINERARY
All year round

LEAST CROWDED TIMES FOR THIS ITINERARY
September through April (except holidays)

BEST ARRIVAL DAY FOR THIS ITINERARY
Friday

BEST BUDGET HOTELS FOR THIS ITINERARY
Disney's Fort Wilderness Resort and Campground (campsite)
Disney's Dixie Landings Resort (river view)

BEST MODERATE HOTELS FOR THIS ITINERARY
Disney's Village Resort (Clubhouse Suite)
Disney Vacation Club (studio, upper-floor fairway view)
The Disney Inn (fairway view)

BEST DELUXE HOTELS FOR THIS ITINERARY
Disney's Contemporary Resort (tower room)
Disney's Wilderness Lodge (lake view)
Disney's Grand Floridian Beach Resort (courtyard view)

ULTIMATE HOTEL EXPERIENCE FOR THIS ITINERARY
Disney Vacation Club (one bedroom, upper floor)

LOCAL TRANSPORTATION
For this itinerary, it is best to rent a car or use your own.

PACKING
Bring dress clothing and sports equipment (if you want to use your own).

TIPS
Golfers should inquire about WDW's golf vacation packages when making reservations.

Day One

EVENING AT THE WORLD SHOWCASE: Your tour begins at Disney's Beach Club Resort, fashioned after the classic seaside resorts of New England. You stroll along the waterfront toward the International Gateway to the World Showcase, and emerge at **FRANCE**, into the sights and sounds of a bustling Parisian neighborhood. Just beyond France is **MOROCCO**, with its intricate bazaar filled with shops spilling over with the exotic handicrafts of North Africa. In nearby **JAPAN**, the rustic country-inn architecture and serene gardens create a soothing atmosphere. Farther on, street actors stage elaborate comedies in **ITALY**,

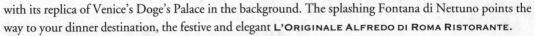
with its replica of Venice's Doge's Palace in the background. The splashing Fontana di Nettuno points the way to your dinner destination, the festive and elegant L'ORIGINALE ALFREDO DI ROMA RISTORANTE.

After dinner, you continue to the fairytale-like town square of GERMANY and on to CHINA, with its water gardens and exotic architecture. In NORWAY, an ancient fortress houses MAELSTROM, a thrilling Viking adventure ride, and in the distance is the massive Mayan pyramid that houses MEXICO and EL RIO DEL TIEMPO, a charming, relaxing boat ride that takes you on an instant Mexican vacation. If you have time before ILLUMINATIONS, you can stroll past the FriendShip docks to CANADA, with its magnificent totem poles and bloom-filled Victoria Gardens. The UNITED KINGDOM, nearby, is designed as a quaint English village, with shops tucked into small Tudor, Georgian, and Victorian buildings.

As show time approaches, you wander to the edge of the World Showcase Lagoon for ILLUMINATIONS. One by one, each international pavilion comes alive with lights as each country in turn is celebrated in music. The night sky is brilliant with fireworks and laser effects, and colorful fountains shoot up from the lagoon. In the distance, Epcot's giant silver geosphere is transformed into a spinning globe.

Day Two

SPORTING MORNING AT THE DISNEY VILLAGE RESORTS AREA: This morning, you'll engage in your favorite outdoor activity in the Disney Village Resorts Area. Here, fishers can angle for largemouth bass, bluegill, and catfish on the BUENA VISTA LAGOON FISHING EXCURSION. Golfers will enjoy the beautiful LAKE BUENA VISTA GOLF COURSE, with mature greens lined with pines, oaks, and magnolias. At Lake Buena Vista Clubhouse, tennis buffs can play on courts that offer a panoramic view of the Disney Village Waterways, and the Village Resorts Area offers miles of bicycle paths that meander past fairways and waterways, and through shady forests and winding, cottage-lined streets. The Disney Village Waterways are ideal for boaters who would like to navigate past the many themed resorts along the shore. Afterward, you'll lunch at LAKE BUENA VISTA RESTAURANT, with its unhurried country-club ambience and spectacular water views.

AFTERNOON AND EVENING AT DISNEY-MGM STUDIOS: At Disney-MGM Studios, you stroll down Hollywood Boulevard toward STAR TOURS, where you lift off on a special-effects sci-fi trip into deep space. Nearby, at INDIANA JONES EPIC STUNT SPECTACULAR, the secrets of professional stunt performers are revealed as boulders crash down and fiery explosions fill the air. JIM HENSON'S MUPPET*VISION 3D combines special effects, puppetry, and animation wizardry to create a thoroughly entertaining spectacle. In the Chinese Theater, THE GREAT MOVIE RIDE presents classic movie moments using both live actors and Disney's remarkable Audio-Animatronics. The BACKSTAGE STUDIO TOUR carries you by tram through the working sets that serve as actual film locations and to the not-to-be-missed disaster in Catastrophe Canyon. At the MONSTER SOUND SHOW, selected visitors are put to work as sound technicians on a short film with unexpected and amusing results.

Your dinner destination this evening is the HOLLYWOOD BROWN DERBY, a replica of the renowned eating and meeting place. Afterward, you're back on Hollywood Boulevard for SORCERY IN THE SKY, which opens with the flickering light of a movie projector aimed at the Chinese Theater, followed by a

light-and-sound extravaganza, with brilliant laser effects, fireworks, and fountains of silver and gold sparks.

If your dinner destination is the **Portobello Yacht Club** on Pleasure Island, you'll be immersed in its nautical decor, which includes an extensive collection of yachting trophies and maritime mementos.

Optional Late-Night "Workout": After dinner, it's club-hopping time at **Pleasure Island**, where the night life is now in full swing. To find the perfect nightclub for your "workout," you begin with the dance clubs **Mannequins** and **8Trax**, before checking out the live entertainment at **Neon Armadillo**, **Comedy Warehouse**, **Adventurers Club**, and the **Jazz Company**. At the stroke of "midnight" Pleasure Island throws a spectacular **New Year's Eve Street Party**, an island-wide celebration with eye-popping music and dance performances, and exploding fireworks overhead.

Day Three

Sporting Morning in the Magic Kingdom Resorts Area: This morning, your sporting activities are centered in the Magic Kingdom Resorts Area. Bay Lake and Seven Seas Lagoon together make up the largest body of water at Walt Disney World, and offer an array of watercraft rentals for boating enthusiasts. Golfers can choose from the Magnolia or Palm golf courses, made famous by the Walt Disney World/Oldsmobile Golf Classic, and longtime favorites of professional golfers worldwide. The **Magnolia Golf Course**, planted with more than fifteen hundred magnolia trees, is notorious for its sand traps, especially the Mickey-shaped "mousetrap" on the sixth hole. The nearby **Palm Golf Course** features numerous water hazards and difficult doglegs, and it is not unusual to see deer and other wildlife strolling on its tree-lined terrain. Tennis fans will play at the **Racquet Club** at the Contemporary resort, with its professionally appointed courts overlooking Bay Lake.

If you've been golfing, your lunch destination is the pleasant **Garden Gallery** at the Disney Inn; if you've been boating or playing tennis, you'll lunch at the Contemporary resort's **Concourse Grille**, with its American Southwest theme and overhead view of the monorail as it passes through the building.

Optional Afternoon Trek on Discovery Island: After lunch, you ferry across Bay Lake to Discovery Island. Shady paths meander through the beautifully landscaped island, which is recognized throughout the world as a sanctuary for disabled and endangered birds, tortoises, reptiles, and small mammals. The animal caretakers have fascinating stories to share about the island's residents. You'll also want to catch the **Feathered Friends**, **Birds of Prey**, or **Reptile Relations** shows, if you can.

Afternoon and Evening at Future World: Your tour of Future World begins inside Epcot's immense eighteen-story geosphere, where **Spaceship Earth** travels through the history and future of human communications. At the angular, mirrored **Universe of Energy** pavilion, you enter a prehistoric twilight where dinosaurs loom in an ancient forest and the warm swamp air carries the smell of sulfur from erupting volcanoes. The golden-domed **Wonders of Life** pavilion features **Body Wars**, a microscopic race against time through the human body, and **Cranium Command**, a hilarious and harrowing perspective on the mind and body of a twelve-year-old boy. The **World of Motion** pavilion

presents IT's Fun to be Free, a whimsical excursion through the history of transportation. At The Land pavilion, the Listen to The Land boat ride travels through desert, prairie, and rain forest environments, as well as through experimental greenhouses and hydroponic gardens. At The Living Seas pavilion, the Caribbean Coral Reef Ride moves along the ocean floor to Sea Base Alpha, a six-million-gallon tropical-reef aquarium alive with thousands of fish and sea mammals.

You return to The Land pavilion for dinner at the Land Grille Room, which revolves slowly past the environments you visited earlier.

Day Four

Sporting Morning at Fort Wilderness: Your final sporting morning is in Fort Wilderness, a 740-acre cypress- and pine-wooded recreation area and campground. Bay Lake provides the perfect surface for waterskiers. Both novice and advanced skiers can pick up tips and techniques under the instruction of certified professionals. The Bay Lake waters are also the fishing grounds for hefty large-mouth bass on the Fort Wilderness Fishing Excursion. Pine forests bank three sides of the Fort Wilderness tennis courts, providing a quiet country setting for a morning game, and the eight miles of bike paths throughout Fort Wilderness meander along waterways, past beaches, through shady forests, and over bridges and boardwalks. Nearby, at the Bonnet Creek Golf Club, the Osprey Ridge and Eagle Pines golf courses are designed to challenge. Osprey Ridge Golf Course, considered the toughest of the five PGA courses at Walt Disney World, is an extra-long course with plenty of berms and mounds and some excellent par-3s. Eagle Pines Golf Course calls for strategic play. Its undulating terrain features water hazards on sixteen holes, and the fairways are lined with pine needles and sand.

You return to your resort for lunch and spend time soaking up the resort life or indulging in a massage at the health club. If you still have energy to burn, you can head over to Typhoon Lagoon to brave the water thrill attractions featured there.

Evening at the Top of the World: Your evening entertainment begins at the sophisticated Broadway at the Top dinner show on the top floor of the Contemporary resort. The four-course dinner is accompanied by a panoramic view before the lights go down and a jazzy quintet strikes up. Women in sequined gowns and men in white dinner jackets sing and dance an energetic medley of show tunes from Broadway hits. Between the cabaret-style acts, diners can take to the dance floor for a spin of their own.

Optional Late-Night Out: If the Magic Kingdom is open late after dinner, you may want to monorail over for the spectacular Fantasy in the Sky fireworks show. Afterward, the enchanting SpectroMagic parade appears, with its elaborate twinkling floats that combine high-tech lighting and sound as live performers re-create memorable scenes from Disney classics.

If the Magic Kingdom closes early, you head for Buena Vista Palace's panoramic Palace Lounge or the vibrant dance club Laughing Kookaburra. To the music of live bands or the club's professional DJs, you dance and carouse with a mix of local residents, Disney Cast Members on their time off, and travelers from all over the world — an exhilarating finish to your Sporting Life Vacation. ➜

Sporting Schedule

The next four pages show the schedule you will follow and the arrangements and reservations you must make to organize the Sporting Life Vacation. You may want to copy these pages and carry them with you.

BEFORE YOU GO

AT THE TIME YOU MAKE YOUR HOTEL RESERVATIONS: Make reservations for the 6 PM Broadway at the Top dinner show for **DAY FOUR** (407 934-7639). If Broadway at the Top is not playing, reserve the 6:45 PM Polynesian Luau dinner show, instead.

TWENTY-SIX DAYS BEFORE YOU LEAVE: If you plan to golf during your vacation, call the Walt Disney World Master Starter (407 824-2270) to reserve early morning tee times. Reserve the Lake Buena Vista Golf Course for **DAY TWO**. Reserve either the Palm Golf Course or the Magnolia Golf Course for **DAY THREE**, and reserve either the Osprey Ridge Golf Course or the Eagle Pines Golf Course for **DAY FOUR**. Schedule your games so you will be finished by about 12:30 PM.

TEN DAYS BEFORE YOU LEAVE: If fishing is your preferred activity, make reservations for the early morning Buena Vista Lagoon Fishing Excursion for **DAY TWO** (407 828-2204) and/or make reservations for the early morning Fort Wilderness Fishing Excursion for **DAY FOUR** (407 824-2757). If you plan to waterski at Fort Wilderness, make reservations for a morning excursion for **DAY FOUR** (407 824-2621).

THREE DAYS BEFORE YOU LEAVE: Call Theme Park Restaurant Reservations (407 824-8800) and make 6:30 PM dinner reservations for **DAY ONE** at L'Originale Alfredo di Roma Ristorante in the Italy pavilion at the World Showcase. (If you prefer another restaurant, consider one in Germany or Norway.)

TWO DAYS BEFORE YOU LEAVE: Call Theme Park Restaurant Reservations (407 824-8800) and make 7:30 PM dinner reservations for **DAY TWO** at the Hollywood Brown Derby. If the Disney-MGM Studios Theme Park closes early that night, plan to dine on Pleasure Island at the Portobello Yacht Club (which does not accept reservations).

ONE DAY BEFORE YOU LEAVE: Call Theme Park Restaurant Reservations (407 824-8800) and make 7:30 PM dinner reservations for **DAY THREE** at the Land Grille Room in The Land pavilion in Future World at Epcot. (If you prefer another restaurant, consider the Coral Reef Restaurant.)

DAY ONE: THE EVENING OF ARRIVAL

DAY / DATE

AFTER YOU CHECK INTO YOUR HOTEL: Stop at Guest Services and make the following arrangements: If you do not have park admission tickets, consider purchasing a multiday pass that includes Typhoon Lagoon, Discovery Island, and Pleasure Island. If you plan to play tennis on **DAY THREE**, make morning court reservations at the Racquet Club at the Contemporary resort. If you do not have a car, inquire about transportation to the golf courses you will be playing. Ask also for a *Times and Information*

SPORTING LIFE VACATION

pamphlet showing the operating schedules at the Magic Kingdom, Epcot Center, and Disney-MGM Studios. Your reservations are now complete for the remainder of your vacation.

5 PM: Drive or taxi to Disney's Beach Club Resort. Walk through the hotel to the waterfront and stroll toward the International Gateway to the WORLD SHOWCASE. Tour the pavilions of FRANCE, MOROCCO, JAPAN, and ITALY, and catch the attractions and live entertainment until it is time for dinner.

6:30 PM DINNER: L'Originale Alfredo di Roma Ristorante is located in the Italy pavilion at the World Showcase.

AFTER DINNER: Continue your tour of the World Showcase, including GERMANY, CHINA, NORWAY, and MEXICO. If you have time before IllumiNations, ride MAELSTROM in Norway and EL RIO DEL TIEMPO in Mexico. If ILLUMINATIONS begins at 9 PM, find a viewing spot at the edge of the lagoon. If Illumi-Nations begins at 10 PM, continue your counter-clockwise tour in CANADA and the UNITED KINGDOM and watch IllumiNations from the United Kingdom. After the show, exit at the International Gateway.

DAY TWO

DAY / DATE

SPORTING MORNING AT THE DISNEY VILLAGE RESORTS AREA: Drive or take WDW transportation to your sporting destination.

• For TENNIS or GOLF on the Lake Buena Vista Golf Course, proceed to the Lake Buena Vista Clubhouse at Disney's Village Resort. Check in at the Pro Shop and rent any equipment that you need.

• For BICYCLING, proceed to the Reception Center at Disney's Village Resort. Rent a bicycle at the bell stand, ask for a map showing the bike paths at the Village Resort and the Vacation Club, and follow the COUNTRY CLUB AND OLD KEY WEST RIDE (see "Bicycle Paths," page 218).

• For FISHING, proceed to the Disney Village Marketplace Marina and join the BUENA VISTA LAGOON FISHING EXCURSION. After your excursion and before lunch, you may wish to browse through the shops and boutiques of the Disney Village Marketplace.

• For BOATING, proceed to the Disney Village Marketplace Marina, rent the watercraft of your choice, cruise the Buena Vista Lagoon, and enter the Disney Village Waterways. Follow the tree-lined Sassagoula River first to PORT ORLEANS and then on to DIXIE LANDINGS. Dock if you wish for a quick tour of either theme resort. Cruise back to the Trumbo Canal and follow it to the VACATION CLUB. If it's a hot day, pull up at the dock near the red lighthouse for a refreshing poolside beverage or swim. When you've had enough, return your boat to the Disney Village Marketplace Marina.

1 PM LUNCH: Lake Buena Vista Restaurant is located in the Lake Buena Vista Clubhouse at Disney's Village Resort. (If you're at Disney Village Marketplace, you can try Cap'n Jack's Oyster Bar, or stroll, bus, or drive to the Lake Buena Vista Clubhouse.)

AFTER LUNCH: Return to your hotel to enjoy the resort amenities and rest up for the late night ahead.

4 PM: Drive or take WDW transportation to DISNEY-MGM STUDIOS. Stroll down Hollywood Boulevard and visit the following attractions in this order until dinner time: ❶ STAR TOURS (if you like thrill rides

and the lines are not too long); ❷ INDIANA JONES EPIC STUNT SPECTACULAR; ❸ JIM HENSON'S MUPPET*VISION 3D; ❹ THE GREAT MOVIE RIDE; ❺ BACKSTAGE STUDIO TOUR (the tram portion only); and ❻ MONSTER SOUND SHOW (especially the Soundworks exhibit, which can be entered directly).

7:30 PM DINNER AT DISNEY-MGM STUDIOS: If Disney-MGM is open late tonight, dine at the Hollywood Brown Derby, located at the end of Hollywood Boulevard. After dinner, stay for the SORCERY IN THE SKY fireworks show. If Disney-MGM closes early, proceed to Pleasure Island for dinner.

7:30 PM DINNER AT PLEASURE ISLAND: Portobello Yacht Club is located on Pleasure Island, adjacent to the Disney Village Marketplace and the *Empress Lilly* riverboat.

OPTIONAL LATE-NIGHT "WORKOUT": After dinner, enter PLEASURE ISLAND and visit the nightclubs. Start with MANNEQUINS for the sensational light show and dance performance, at about 9:30 PM, to get you charged up, then club-hop as you will. Just be back outside at the West End Stage at 10:45 PM (11:45 PM on weekends) for Pleasure Island's spectacular NEW YEAR'S EVE STREET PARTY.

DAY THREE

DAY / DATE

SPORTING MORNING IN THE MAGIC KINGDOM RESORTS AREA: Drive or taxi to your sporting destination in the Magic Kingdom Resorts Area.

• For GOLF on the Magnolia or Palm golf courses, proceed to the Disney Inn. Check in at the Pro Shop and rent any equipment that you need.

• For TENNIS, proceed to the Racquet Club at Disney's Contemporary Resort. Check in at the Pro Shop and rent any equipment that you need.

• For BOATING, proceed to the marina at Disney's Contemporary Resort, rent the sailboat of your choice and catch the breezes on the waters of Bay Lake, then sail over the water bridge to enjoy the sights at Seven Seas Lagoon. (If you prefer a speedboat, rent a Water Sprite.) Dock and take a quick tour of any of the theme resorts that interest you.

1 PM LUNCH FOR GOLFERS: The Garden Gallery is located above the Pro Shop at the Disney Inn.

12 PM LUNCH FOR TENNIS PLAYERS AND BOATERS: The Concourse Grille is located on the fourth-floor at the Concourse level in Disney's Contemporary Resort.

OPTIONAL AFTERNOON TREK ON DISCOVERY ISLAND: After lunch, return to your hotel to relax and enjoy the resort amenities, or proceed on the Optional Afternoon Trek. From the Contemporary Marina, take the short ferry ride across Bay Lake to Discovery Island. Explore the zoological park, talk to the caretakers, visit the ANIMAL HOSPITAL, and catch the FEATHERED FRIENDS, BIRDS OF PREY, or REPTILE RELATIONS shows, if you can. When you're ready to leave, ferry back to the Contemporary Marina.

4 PM: Drive or take WDW transportation to FUTURE WORLD at Epcot. Visit as many of the following attractions as you can before dinner (skip any with long lines or waits): ❶ SPACESHIP EARTH; ❷ UNIVERSE OF ENERGY; ❸ Wonders of Life pavilion — BODY WARS and CRANIUM COMMAND;

SPORTING LIFE VACATION

❹ World of Motion pavilion — IT's FUN TO BE FREE; ❺ The Land pavilion — LISTEN TO THE LAND; and ❻ The Living Seas pavilion — CARIBBEAN CORAL REEF RIDE.

7:30 PM DINNER: The Land Grille Room is located in The Land pavilion at Future World.

AFTER DINNER: Continue your tour of the attractions where you left off. As the crowds head for the nightly performance of IllumiNations at the World Showcase, you should have no problem with lines at any popular attractions you skipped earlier.

DAY FOUR

DAY / DATE

SPORTING MORNING AT FORT WILDERNESS: Drive or taxi to your sporting destination (do not use WDW public transportation today).

• For GOLF, proceed to the Bonnet Creek Golf Club. Check in at the Pro Shop and rent any equipment that you need.

• For TENNIS, proceed to the Fort Wilderness Guest Parking Lot. Take a gray- or brown-flag bus from the Fort Wilderness Depot to the Meadow Recreation Area. At the Bike Barn, rent any equipment that you need, then stroll toward the Meadow Tennis Courts for tennis in a quiet country setting.

• For BICYCLING, proceed to the Fort Wilderness Guest Parking Lot. Take a gray- or brown-flag bus from the Fort Wilderness Depot to the Meadow Recreation Area. Rent a bicycle at the Bike Barn, request a map, and take the WILDERNESS RIDE (see "Bicycle Paths," page 218).

• For FISHING, proceed to the Fort Wilderness Guest Parking Lot. Take an orange-flag bus from the Gateway Depot to the Settlement Recreation Area. At the marina, nearby, join the FORT WILDERNESS FISHING EXCURSION. (Guests at the Contemporary resort can ferry to Fort Wilderness.)

• For WATERSKIING, proceed to the Fort Wilderness Guest Parking Lot. Take an orange-flag bus from the Gateway Depot to the Settlement Recreation Area. At the marina, board the FORT WILDERNESS WATERSKIING EXCURSION speedboat. (Guests at the Contemporary resort can ferry to Fort Wilderness.)

1 PM LUNCH: Return to your resort for lunch at the restaurant of your choice.

AFTER LUNCH: Relax and enjoy the resort amenities or drop into your resort's spa or health club for a massage or workout. Or, if you would like to spend an hour or two in some serious water play, head over to TYPHOON LAGOON and brave the incredible surfing waves or try the thrilling body slides.

5 PM: Drive, taxi, or monorail to Disney's Contemporary Resort for the 6 PM BROADWAY AT THE TOP dinner show. (Or leave at 5:50 PM for the Polynesian resort if you've booked the Polynesian Luau, instead.)

OPTIONAL LATE-NIGHT OUT: If the Magic Kingdom is open late after dinner, monorail from the Contemporary resort to the MAGIC KINGDOM for FANTASY IN THE SKY fireworks at 10 PM and the SpectroMagic parade at 11 PM (if scheduled). Or, if you would like to go dancing, drive or taxi to the Buena Vista Palace and drop into the panoramic PALACE LOUNGE or the subterranean LAUGHING KOOKA-BURRA dance club, where live bands and DJs take turns entertaining local residents, Disney Cast Members (on their time off), and visitors from all over the world — *the* place to burn off that last bit of energy. ◆

DAY-AND-NIGHT ROMANTIC ADVENTURE

*An Around-the-World Honeymoon Tour of International Cultures,
Outdoor Adventures, and Luxury Dining*

BEST TIME OF YEAR FOR THIS ITINERARY
April through October

LEAST CROWDED TIMES FOR THIS ITINERARY
April, May, September, and October (except holidays)

BEST ARRIVAL DAY FOR THIS ITINERARY
Tuesday or Wednesday

BEST BUDGET HOTELS FOR THIS ITINERARY
*Disney's Dixie Landings Resort (river view)
Disney's Port Orleans Resort (river view)*

BEST MODERATE HOTELS FOR THIS ITINERARY
*Disney's Village Resort (Clubhouse Suite, lagoon view)
Buena Vista Palace (Palace Suites)
Disney's Yacht Club Resort (standard room)*

BEST DELUXE HOTELS FOR THIS ITINERARY
*Disney Vacation Club (one bedroom)
Disney's Beach Club Resort (forest view)
Disney's Grand Floridian Beach Resort (lagoon view)*

ULTIMATE HOTEL EXPERIENCE FOR THIS ITINERARY
Disney's Grand Floridian Beach Resort (concierge room)

LOCAL TRANSPORTATION
For this itinerary, it is best to rent a car or use your own.

PACKING
*Bring dress clothing, spa clothing and, for the visit to Disney-MGM Studios,
optional costume dress.*

TIPS
When making reservations, ask if the hotel has a honeymoon package.

Day One

EVENING IN POLYNESIA: Your tour begins on the evening you arrive with the **POLYNESIAN LUAU** dinner show. A shell lei is slipped over your head at Luau Cove, and tropical drinks and a luau-style meal are served. In a tropical grotto under the night sky, you enjoy the compelling music and lovely dances of the South Sea Islands. After dinner, you walk the torchlit paths to the edge of the Seven Seas Lagoon to see the **ELECTRICAL WATER PAGEANT** as it enters the dark lagoon. The sparkling, animated lights of the floating vessels are reflected in the water, and the music and sound effects drift across the lagoon.

Day Two

MORNING AT THE MAGIC KINGDOM: This morning at the Magic Kingdom, you will time-travel through Africa, the Caribbean, and turn-of-the-century America. The tour begins on **MAIN STREET, U.S.A.**, with its quaint shops and small-town ambience. You pass under the exotic totems leading to **ADVENTURE-LAND**, and enter a tropical fantasy. Dense foliage and the rustles, squawks, and cries of mysterious creatures lend an exotic note to the surroundings. At the **JUNGLE CRUISE** just ahead, you climb aboard one of the explorer boats for an adventurous cruise down the world's great rivers. At Caribbean Plaza, you board a **PIRATES OF THE CARIBBEAN** watercraft and travel underground to an island settlement, where a pirate raid is underway. In **FRONTIERLAND**, the background sounds change along with the architecture in this replica of the Old West. If you enjoy thrill rides, **BIG THUNDER MOUNTAIN RAILROAD** offers an exhilarating race on a runaway train and **SPLASH MOUNTAIN** features a water-flume ride with a wild and wet finish. In colonial America at **LIBERTY SQUARE**, you see the steep gables of **THE HAUNTED MANSION** in the distance, where you become part of a special-effects haunting. Your lunch destination is in nearby **FANTASYLAND**, where high in a turret of Cinderella's Castle, you'll dine in the medieval ambience of **KING STEFAN'S BANQUET HALL**.

OPTIONAL AFTERNOON SAFARI: After lunch, you ferry across Bay Lake and disembark at **DISCOVERY ISLAND**. You follow the shady paths through the beautifully landscaped island, which is recognized throughout the world as a sanctuary for disabled, endangered, and nearly extinct birds, tortoises, and small wildlife. The animal caretakers have fascinating stories to share about the island's residents; and you'll want to keep an eye out for the huge Galapagos tortoises and try to catch the **FEATHERED FRIENDS**, **REPTILE RELATIONS**, or **BIRDS OF PREY** shows, if you can.

EVENING AT THE WORLD SHOWCASE: As evening approaches, you arrive at Disney's Beach Club Resort. Here, you pass through a New England–style seaside resort and stroll along the waterfront to the World Showcase. Entering through the International Gateway, you emerge at **FRANCE** and into the sights and sounds of a bustling Parisian neighborhood. **MOROCCO** lies a little farther on, with its lively, intricate bazaar. The narrow passageways are filled with small shops spilling over with the exotic handicrafts of North Africa. You stroll along the World Showcase Lagoon to **JAPAN**, to be soothed by the rustic country-inn architecture and serene Japanese gardens, while *koto* music plays softly in the background. In **ITALY**, you find yourself in a festive piazza, with a replica of Venice's Doge's Palace. As dinner approaches, you retrace your steps to France and the romantic **BISTRO DE PARIS**.

After dinner, you wander to the edge of the World Showcase Lagoon for the **ILLUMINATIONS** sky show. One by one, the international pavilions come alive with lights as each country in turn is celebrated in music. The night sky is brilliant with fireworks and laser effects, and colorful fountains of water shoot up from the lagoon. Laser projections transform Epcot's giant silver geosphere into a radiant globe spinning in the distance.

❤

Day Three

MORNING AT DISNEY-MGM STUDIOS: This morning your tour takes you to Disney-MGM Studios and the glamor of early- and present-day Hollywood. You might enjoy dressing for the part — there are plenty of movie "extras" floating around, so you'll feel right at home draped in sequins, or wearing a Great Gatsby linen suit, a Stetson hat, or sparkling sunglasses.

You stroll down Hollywood Boulevard on your way to **STAR TOURS**, where you lift off on a special-effects sci-fi trip into deep space. In the Chinese Theater you board **THE GREAT MOVIE RIDE**, a re-creation of classic movie moments using both live actors and Disney's remarkable Audio-Animatronics. At the Disney-MGM working studios, the **BACKSTAGE STUDIO TOUR** carries you by tram through the working sets that serve as actual film locations, and a not-to-be-missed disaster in Catastrophe Canyon. Your theatrical garb can really pay off during lunch at the **HOLLYWOOD BROWN DERBY**, a replica of the famous eating spot and meeting place. You might not quite believe that the people at the next table are high-powered agents, but if you've decided to go costumed, they may mistake you for a celebrity. The Hollywood Brown Derby is a favorite with real stars in production at Disney-MGM Studios.

OPTIONAL AFTERNOON WATER ADVENTURE: After lunch, you're off to your afternoon water adventure, either taking the plunge at Typhoon Lagoon or boating through the bayoulike waterways of the Disney Village Resorts Area.

If you select **TYPHOON LAGOON**, you'll explore the attractions at this water park, which has been inventively designed as a funky island resort just moments after a devastating typhoon has struck. At **CASTAWAY CREEK**, you drape yourself across a giant inner-tube and float slowly around the meandering "creek" that encircles the park. Then it's off to **SHARK REEF** to don snorkeling gear for a swim among the Caribbean undersea life in a saltwater lagoon, complete with a sunken, overturned steamer. If you're a thrill seeker, you'll brave the white-water rapids at **GANG PLANK FALLS** and **THE WAVES AT TYPHOON LAGOON** before plopping into your lounge chair to soak up the sun.

If you decide to explore the **DISNEY VILLAGE WATERWAYS**, you'll rent a canopy boat at Disney Village Marketplace Marina and cruise out of Buena Vista Lagoon and into the tree-canopied waterways on your way to visit some of the themed resorts along the shores. First stop is the Old South at **DIXIE LANDINGS**, where you cruise past antebellum mansions and rustic bayou lodges. Then, it's on to **PORT ORLEANS** and its French Quarter–styled waterfront. Last stop is the **VACATION CLUB**, fashioned after Key West, where you can dock at the lighthouse for a quick tour or a leisurely poolside beverage.

EVENING AT FUTURE WORLD AND THE WORLD SHOWCASE: The trademark icon of Epcot Center, an eighteen-story geosphere, towers high above Epcot's Entrance Plaza. Standing in the gardens beyond is the angular, mirrored building that houses the **UNIVERSE OF ENERGY**. Inside, you enter the prehistoric twilight of an eerie primeval world. Mighty dinosaurs loom in an ancient forest, and you can actually feel the warm swamp air and smell the sulfur of erupting volcanoes. The golden-domed **WONDERS OF LIFE** pavilion, nearby, features **BODY WARS**, a microscopic race against time through the human body; and at **HORIZONS**, nearby, you are carried forward in time to witness the imagined lifestyles of the twenty-first century. Afterward, you cross the bridge that spans a secluded lagoon, home to a flock of graceful pink flamingos, to enter the WORLD SHOWCASE.

MEXICO is just ahead. Its pavilion is enclosed in a massive Mayan pyramid, where guests emerge into the nighttime scene of a bustling plaza filled with shops, street merchants, and festive *mariachi* music. SAN ANGEL INN RESTAURANTE is perched on the edge of an indoor river, where you dine under make-believe stars. Across the river, far in the distance, an active volcano sends up its smoky plumes.

After dinner, the charming and uncomplicated boat ride EL RIO DEL TIEMPO takes you down the river and into an instant Mexican vacation. Emerging from the pavilion, you cross the promenade to the Cantina de San Angel at the edge of the World Showcase Lagoon for a very different view of tonight's ILLUMINATIONS spectacular. If you have time before IllumiNations, you can stroll down the promenade to NORWAY with its cobblestoned village streets, to CHINA with its ornate architecture and extensive shopping gallery, and to the fairytale-like town square of GERMANY.

Day Four

MORNING AT EPCOT'S FUTURE WORLD: You return to Epcot Center this morning to explore the land, the sea, and the world of ideas. When the park opens, you enter the Epcot geosphere and SPACESHIP EARTH, a ride that explores the history and future of communications. At the large wave-shaped building that houses THE LIVING SEAS pavilion, you take the CARIBBEAN CORAL REEF RIDE along the ocean floor to Sea Base Alpha, a six-million-gallon tropical reef aquarium alive with thousands of fish and sea mammals. At THE LAND pavilion, LISTEN TO THE LAND transports you by boat through desert, prairie, and rain forest environments, as well as through experimental greenhouses and hydroponic gardens. Your lunch destination is the LAND GRILLE ROOM, a restaurant on the upper level of the pavilion that revolves slowly past the environments you've just visited.

You're free to luxuriate at your resort in the afternoon. If you decide to continue your tour after lunch, however, you'll enter the WORLD SHOWCASE at CANADA, with its flowering Victoria Gardens set against dramatic rock formations that represent the rugged Canadian Rockies. Further on, the UNITED KINGDOM pavilion re-creates a quaint English village, with shops inside the small Tudor, Georgian, and Victorian buildings, and tiny formal gardens tucked behind them. In the bustling Parisian neighborhood setting of nearby FRANCE, you can see the beautiful travel film IMPRESSIONS DE FRANCE.

EVENING ON PLEASURE ISLAND: The *Empress Lilly*, docked in Buena Vista Lagoon, looks like a nineteenth-century riverboat about to launch itself down the Mississippi. On the upper deck is the elegant EMPRESS ROOM restaurant, your dinner destination. The small, romantic dining room is softly lit by a crystal chandelier, and etched-glass and gold-leafed partitions provide an intimate setting for dinner.

After dinner, it's club-hopping time at Pleasure Island, where the nightlife is now in full swing. You begin with MANNEQUINS' sensational opening show, then move on to the COMEDY WAREHOUSE, ADVENTURERS CLUB, JAZZ COMPANY, and NEON ARMADILLO. Toward midnight Pleasure Island erupts into a joyous NEW YEAR'S EVE STREET PARTY — musicians and dancers entertain on the outdoor stage as confetti rains down and fireworks explode overhead — a fitting finale to your Romantic Adventure. ➤

Adventure Schedule

The next four pages show the schedule you will follow and the arrangements and reservations you must make to organize the Day-and-Night Romantic Adventure. You may want to copy these pages and carry them with you.

♥

BEFORE YOU GO

AT THE TIME YOU MAKE YOUR HOTEL RESERVATIONS: Make reservations for the 6:45 PM Polynesian Luau dinner show for **DAY ONE** (407 934-7639). Travelers arriving in Orlando after 4 PM should reserve the 9:30 PM show.

TWENTY-SIX DAYS BEFORE YOU LEAVE: Call Village Restaurant Reservations (407 828-3900) and make 7:30 PM dinner reservations for **DAY FOUR** in the Empress Room aboard the *Empress Lilly* riverboat. (If you prefer another restaurant, consider Steerman's Quarters or Fisherman's Deck.)

TWO DAYS BEFORE YOU LEAVE: Call Theme Park Restaurant Reservations (407 824-8800) and make 12 PM lunch reservations for **DAY TWO** at King Stefan's Banquet Hall in the Magic Kingdom. Make 7:30 PM dinner reservations for **DAY TWO** at Bistro de Paris in the France pavilion at the World Showcase. (If you prefer another restaurant, consider one in Japan, Morocco, or Italy.) Be sure your seating is no later than ninety minutes before IllumiNations is scheduled to begin.

ONE DAY BEFORE YOU LEAVE: Call Theme Park Restaurant Reservations (407 824-8800) and make 12:30 PM lunch reservations for **DAY THREE** at the Hollywood Brown Derby at Disney-MGM Studios, and make 7:30 PM dinner reservations for **DAY THREE** at San Angel Inn Restaurante in the Mexico pavilion at the World Showcase. (If you prefer another restaurant, consider one in China, Norway, or Germany. Be sure your seating is no later than ninety minutes before IllumiNations is scheduled to begin.)

♥

DAY ONE: THE EVENING OF ARRIVAL

DAY / DATE

AFTER YOU CHECK INTO YOUR HOTEL: Stop at Guest Services, and if you do not have admission tickets, purchase a multiday pass that includes Typhoon Lagoon, Discovery Island, and Pleasure Island. Also at Guest Services, purchase your tickets for the Polynesian Luau dinner show this evening, and make 12:30 PM lunch reservations for **DAY FOUR** at the Land Grille Room in Future World at Epcot (if you prefer another restaurant, consider the Coral Reef Restaurant). Ask also for a *Times and Information* pamphlet showing the operating schedules at the Magic Kingdom, Epcot Center, and Disney-MGM Studios. Your reservations are now complete for the remainder of your vacation.

6 PM: Drive, monorail, or taxi to the Polynesian resort for the **POLYNESIAN LUAU** dinner show at 6:45 PM. Be in line at Luau Cove about fifteen minutes before show time. If you have booked the 9:30 PM show and have time on your hands, hop the monorail from the Polynesian resort to the Magic Kingdom (if the park is open late) to explore the shops and live entertainment along Main Street until

about 9 PM. Or, if you prefer, enjoy Polynesian-style cocktails and music at the hotel's Tambu Lounge until just before show time. (From the Tambu Lounge windows you can see the Electrical Water Pageant at 9 PM.)

AFTER DINNER: The 6:45 PM show will end at about 9 PM. If you leave a bit early and walk to the Seven Seas Lagoon beach behind Luau Cove, you can catch the **ELECTRICAL WATER PAGEANT**, which cruises by at about 9 PM. The 9:30 PM show of the Polynesian Luau ends at about 11:30 PM.

BEFORE YOU RETIRE: You may want to leave a wake-up call tonight and order a room-service breakfast for tomorrow morning. You'll leave your hotel one hour before the Magic Kingdom opens.

DAY TWO

DAY / DATE

ONE HOUR BEFORE THE MAGIC KINGDOM OPENS: Drive or take WDW transportation to the Magic Kingdom. If you are driving, park at the Contemporary resort and take the monorail from there to the Magic Kingdom. Enter the park (Main Street generally opens early) and walk to the end of Main Street to Adventureland. When the ropes are dropped, proceed immediately the following attractions in this order: ❶ **JUNGLE CRUISE;** ❷ **PIRATES OF THE CARIBBEAN;** and ❸ **THE HAUNTED MANSION** in Liberty Square. (If you like fast thrill rides and the lines are not too long, visit **SPLASH MOUNTAIN** and **BIG THUNDER MOUNTAIN RAILROAD** in Frontierland on your way to The Haunted Mansion.) If you have time before lunch, explore the shops at Liberty Square and drop into **THE HALL OF PRESIDENTS**.

12:30 PM LUNCH: King Stefan's Banquet Hall is located in Cinderella's Castle in Fantasyland at the center of the Magic Kingdom. (Light eaters and budget diners should try the Crystal Palace restaurant on the other side of the castle, at the end of Main Street.)

OPTIONAL AFTERNOON SAFARI ON DISCOVERY ISLAND: After lunch, you can continue touring the Magic Kingdom, return to your resort to relax, or go on the Optional Afternoon Safari. Exit the Magic Kingdom and hop the monorail to the Contemporary resort. Take the short ferry ride across Bay Lake from the Contemporary Marina to Discovery Island. Tour the zoological park, talk to the animal caretakers, visit the **ANIMAL HOSPITAL**, and catch the **FEATHERED FRIENDS, REPTILE RELATIONS,** or **BIRDS OF PREY** shows, if you can. When you're ready to leave, ferry back to the Contemporary resort.

5:30 PM: Drive or taxi to the Beach Club resort. Walk through the hotel to the waterfront, stroll to the International Gateway, and enter the **WORLD SHOWCASE**. Explore the pavilions at **MOROCCO, JAPAN, U.S.A.,** and **ITALY,** and catch the live entertainment and attractions until it is time for dinner. If you wish, stop for cocktails and a great view of the World Showcase at the Matsu No Ma Lounge in Japan.

7:30 PM DINNER: Backtrack to Bistro de Paris, located in the France pavilion at the World Showcase.

AFTER DINNER: If **ILLUMINATIONS** begins at 10 PM tonight, continue your tour of **FRANCE,** the **UNITED KINGDOM,** and **CANADA**. If IllumiNations begins at 9 PM, find a viewing spot at the edge of the lagoon. There are good views along the promenade from France to both sides of the United Kingdom. After the show, exit at the International Gateway.

BEFORE YOU RETIRE: You may again wish to order a wake-up call and breakfast for tomorrow morning. You'll leave your hotel forty-five minutes before Disney-MGM Studios opens.

❤

DAY THREE

DAY / DATE

BEFORE YOU LEAVE YOUR HOTEL: Pack your tote bag with optional bathing suits and sunblock.

FORTY-FIVE MINUTES BEFORE DISNEY-MGM STUDIOS OPENS: Drive or take WDW transportation to Disney-MGM Studios. As you enter, pick up an entertainment schedule at the Crossroads of the World kiosk. Stroll down Hollywood Boulevard (which generally opens early) and visit the following attractions in this order: ❶ STAR TOURS (if you like thrill rides); ❷ THE GREAT MOVIE RIDE; and ❸ BACKSTAGE STUDIO TOUR (the tram portion only). If you have time before lunch, try to catch ALADDIN'S ROYAL CARAVAN, which parades up Hollywood Boulevard about noon. Or take in VOYAGE OF THE LITTLE MERMAID, browse through the shops along Hollywood Boulevard, or sample the fine California wines at the Catwalk Bar, upstairs from the Hollywood Brown Derby.

12:30 PM LUNCH: The Hollywood Brown Derby is located at the end of Hollywood Boulevard. (Light eaters and budget diners should try the Disney-MGM Studios Commissary, next to the Chinese Theater.)

OPTIONAL AFTERNOON WATER ADVENTURE: After lunch, you can continue touring Disney-MGM Studios, return to your resort to relax, or proceed on to the Optional Water Adventure. Choose from an active and wet Typhoon Lagoon expedition or a boat cruise through the Disney Village Waterways.

If you select **TYPHOON LAGOON**, get there by car or WDW bus. Rent towels at the entrance and set up camp in the shade on the beach across the creek from Typhoon Tilly's or at Cascade Cove, nearby. Use the changing rooms and lockers at Typhoon Tilly's. Include the following attractions in your adventure: ❶ CASTAWAY CREEK, for a long, lazy inner-tube journey around the park; ❷ SHARK REEF, for a snorkeling experience among Caribbean undersea life; ❸ GANG PLANK FALLS, for a wild white-water raft ride (if you enjoy water thrills); and ❹ THE WAVES AT TYPHOON LAGOON.

If you decide to cruise the **DISNEY VILLAGE WATERWAYS**, proceed to Disney Village Marketplace by car or WDW bus. Rent a canopy boat at the Village Marketplace Marina and cruise the tree-lined waterways to the following themed resorts: ❶ Follow the Sassagoula River to DIXIE LANDINGS for a look at the grand plantation mansions and rustic bayou lodges of the Old South. ❷ Dock at PORT ORLEANS and tour the streets of New Orleans' French Quarter as it prepares for Mardi Gras. Check out the decor and snacks at the Sassagoula Floatworks and Food Factory. ❸ Follow the winding waterways to Old Key West at the VACATION CLUB and, if it's a hot day, pull up at the dock and cool off with a relaxing poolside beverage.

5 PM: Drive or take WDW transportation to **FUTURE WORLD** at Epcot. Enjoy the following attractions in this order: ❶ UNIVERSE OF ENERGY; ❷ Wonders of Life pavilion — BODY WARS (if the line is not too long) and THE MAKING OF ME; ❸ HORIZONS; and, if you have thirty minutes or so before dinner,

❹ World of Motion pavilion — **IT'S FUN TO BE FREE**. Shortcut to the World Showcase by walking past the Odyssey Restaurant, which will put you near the entrance to the Mexico pavilion.

7:30 PM DINNER: San Angel Inn Restaurante is located inside the Mexico pavilion at the World Showcase. If you arrive early, there is a small lounge adjacent to the restaurant.

AFTER DINNER: If you have time, take the short **EL RIO DEL TIEMPO** boat ride through Mexico, which can be a fun and romantic finish to dinner. If **ILLUMINATIONS** begins at 9 PM tonight, view it from the Cantina de San Angel on the edge of the lagoon, just outside the Mexico pavilion. You may wish to accompany the experience with frozen Margaritas or *chocolate caliente* and *churros* (hot chocolate and Mexican pastry). If IllumiNations begins at 10 PM, continue your tour, exploring **NORWAY** (and the **MAELSTROM** attraction), **CHINA**, and **GERMANY**. About 9:45 PM, position yourself on one of the bridges in front of **ITALY** for IllumiNations.

BEFORE YOU RETIRE: You may want to leave a wake-up call and order breakfast tonight. You'll leave your hotel forty-five minutes before Epcot Center opens tomorrow.

♥

DAY FOUR

DAY / DATE

FORTY-FIVE MINUTES BEFORE EPCOT OPENS: Drive or take WDW transportation to **FUTURE WORLD** at Epcot. When the park opens, visit the following attractions in this order: ❶ **SPACESHIP EARTH** (which generally opens early); ❷ The Living Seas pavilion — **CARIBBEAN CORAL REEF RIDE**; ❸ The Land pavilion — **LISTEN TO THE LAND**; and ❹ Journey Into Imagination pavilion — **MAGIC EYE THEATER** (if you have forty minutes or so before lunch).

12:30 PM LUNCH: The Land Grille Room is located in The Land pavilion at Future World. (Light eaters and budget diners should try the Farmer's Market at The Land pavilion.)

AFTER LUNCH: You can continue your tour of any attractions you may have missed, especially **O CANADA!** and **IMPRESSIONS DE FRANCE** in the World Showcase (take the shortcut just beyond the Journey Into Imagination pavilion). Or, you can return to your hotel to rest up for the late night ahead and enjoy the resort amenities at the health club, on the courts, or at the beach or pool.

7 PM: Drive or taxi to Pleasure Island. This evening you'll want to dress up for dinner. At the romantic Empress Room, jackets are required for men.

7:30 PM DINNER: The Empress Room is on the upper deck of the *Empress Lilly* riverboat, which is docked in Buena Vista Lagoon at Pleasure Island.

AFTER DINNER: Enter **PLEASURE ISLAND** for your evening of club hopping. Start with **MANNEQUINS** for the dazzling dance performance that begins at about 9:30 PM, then drop into the **ADVENTURERS CLUB**, the **JAZZ COMPANY**, and the **NEON ARMADILLO**, or catch a performance at the **COMEDY WAREHOUSE**. Be sure to be back outside at the West End Stage about 10:45 PM (11:45 PM on weekends), when Pleasure Island celebrates a spectacular **NEW YEAR'S EVE STREET PARTY**, complete with fireworks and confetti. It's guaranteed to make the final evening of your Romantic Adventure a night to remember. ◆

GARDENS AND NATURAL WONDERS TOUR

*A Vacation Trek Among Tropical Wilderness and Wetlands, International Gardens,
High-Tech Horticulture, and Native Waterfowl and Endangered Wildlife*

BEST TIME OF YEAR FOR THIS ITINERARY
All year round

LEAST CROWDED TIMES FOR THIS ITINERARY
February through May, and September through November (except holidays)

BEST ARRIVAL DAY FOR THIS ITINERARY
Sunday, Monday, or Wednesday — preferably Wednesday

BEST BUDGET HOTELS FOR THIS ITINERARY
Disney's Fort Wilderness Resort and Campground (campsite)
Disney's Dixie Landings Resort (river view)

BEST MODERATE HOTELS FOR THIS ITINERARY
Disney Vacation Club (studio, quiet-pool view)
Disney's Fort Wilderness Resort and Campground (Wilderness Home)
Disney's Polynesian Resort (garden view)

BEST DELUXE HOTELS FOR THIS ITINERARY
Disney's Grand Floridian Beach Resort (lagoon view)
Disney's Yacht Club Resort (garden view)
Disney's Wilderness Lodge (lake view)

ULTIMATE HOTEL EXPERIENCE FOR THIS ITINERARY
Disney's Polynesian Resort (Royal Polynesian concierge suite)

LOCAL TRANSPORTATION
For this itinerary, it is best to rent a car or use your own.

PACKING
*Much of this itinerary is spent outside, so winter travelers should bring warm
clothing (it can get very cold in Orlando). Summer travelers will need umbrellas.*

TIPS
The Disney gardens are in bloom year round, so travel at your convenience.

✳

Day One

EVENING IN POLYNESIA: Your tour begins on the evening you arrive, with the **POLYNESIAN LUAU** dinner show. Exotic tropical drinks and a luau-style feast under the night sky create an enchanting backdrop for the music and dances of the South Sea Islands. After dinner, a stroll along torchlit paths through tropical gardens takes you to the edge of the Seven Seas Lagoon. From an inlet, the **ELECTRICAL WATER PAGEANT** enters the lagoon, where the dark waters reflect the animated lights of the floating sets, and the music and sound effects drift across the lagoon.

Day Two

MORNING AT FUTURE WORLD AND THE WORLD SHOWCASE: Flower gardens and Mexican fan palms welcome you to Epcot's Entrance Plaza. The giant silver geosphere houses **SPACESHIP EARTH**, a ride through the history and future of communications. The attraction exits in Earth Station, where you join the **GARDENS OF THE WORLD** tour. A horticulture professional leads a behind-the-scenes tour of the techniques used to create the international gardens at the World Showcase. As the tour returns to Future World, you proceed to your lunch destination, the lively **ROSE & CROWN DINING ROOM** in the **UNITED KINGDOM**. Afterward, you pass through the Victoria Gardens at **CANADA** to see the spectacular travel film **O CANADA!**, then explore **FRANCE** and the scenic film **IMPRESSIONS DE FRANCE**.

OPTIONAL AFTERNOON TEA: This afternoon, you step back in time to the Victorian era at the elegant Grand Floridian resort. Live music plays in the spacious lobby, light-filled and reminiscent of a turn-of-the-century conservatory, complete with pots of ornamental palms and Chinese evergreens and enormous vases of fresh-cut flowers. The Garden View Lounge offers the pleasures of high tea, served in the traditional British fashion. A stroll through the hotel's lovely gardens is a refreshing after-tea delight.

EARLY EVENING AT THE MAGIC KINGDOM: From the Grand Floridian, you board the monorail to the Magic Kingdom and sit in the front for a sweeping overview of the landscape. A skillful arrangement of plants and flowers greets disembarking passengers on their way to the bustling small-town ambience of **MAIN STREET, U.S.A.**, where he tree-shaded plazas, hanging pots of blooming plants, and clusters of flowering gardens provide pleasant, colorful accents. In **ADVENTURELAND**, a lush jungle of palms, orchids, and ferns surrounds the **SWISS FAMILY TREEHOUSE**, an impeccably reproduced giant banyan made of concrete and vinyl and draped in real Spanish moss. Nearby, a **JUNGLE CRUISE** explorer boat takes you on an imaginative adventure along the world's great rivers. Farther on, the tropical greenery evolves into the dry desert and mesa landscape of the Old West in **FRONTIERLAND**. Here, the **SPLASH MOUNTAIN** water-flume ride delivers a wild and wet finish in a gargantuan briar patch, and **BIG THUNDER MOUNTAIN RAILROAD** provides an exhilarating race on a runaway train. Colonial America is the focus at **LIBERTY SQUARE**, complete with its Liberty Tree, a lantern-hung live oak that is over one hundred years old. The sweeping, parterre-decorated lawns and steep gables of **THE HAUNTED MANSION** belie the masterful special-effects haunting that awaits you in its dark interior. In **FANTASYLAND**, Cinderella's Castle is the backdrop for whimsical topiaries and ornate flower beds. On the **SKYWAY TO TOMORROWLAND**, you get a bird's-eye view of Old World gardens and undersea reefs with imaginative phosphorescent growths on you way toward the automotive jungle, where the stark urban asphalt is softened with splashes of multicolored blooms. Angularly pruned Japanese yews, bright coleus, and strange-limbed ligustrums accent the landscaping at **TOMORROWLAND**, and a giant but friendly topiary serpent guards the bridge to the regal All-America Rose Selection Display Garden. Here, award-winning specimens of roses from around the nation are displayed in a garden that has flourished for over two decades.

Your dinner destination tonight is **NARCOOSSEE'S**, at Disney's Grand Floridian Beach Resort. The airy, octagon-shaped restaurant, perched on a pier over Seven Seas Lagoon, features seafood specialties and an excellent view of the fireworks above the Magic Kingdom.

Day Three

MORNING AT DISCOVERY ISLAND: A ferry from the Contemporary resort takes you across Bay Lake for a morning tour of richly landscaped eleven-acre Discovery Island. A spectacular variety of trees, shrubs, vines, and flowers line the shady paths of this internationally recognized sanctuary for disabled and endangered birds, reptiles, and small mammals. The **FEATHERED FRIENDS, BIRDS OF PREY**, and **REPTILE RELATIONS** shows tell you more about the island's inhabitants, and the animal caretakers will relate fascinating stories about the island's residents to anyone who asks.

AFTERNOON WILDERNESS WALK: You continue by ferry to your lunch destination at **TRAIL'S END BUFFETERIA** in Fort Wilderness, or you can purchase picnic supplies at the Settlement Trading Post to take along on your nature walk. The **WILDERNESS SWAMP TRAIL**, nearby, meanders through two miles of serenity and untamed nature, through wild wetlands and an old-growth cypress forest. Palmettos and vines flourish along the shady trail, bald cypresses and cattails sprout from the wetlands where the water-fowl live, and butterflies, lizards, and other wildlife give movement to this wilderness conservation area.

AFTERNOON AND EVENING AT EPCOT'S FUTURE WORLD AND WORLD SHOWCASE: You return to Epcot to explore the horticulture of the future, the present, and the primeval past. At **THE LAND** pavilion, the **LISTEN TO THE LAND** boats travel through desert, prairie, and rain forest biomes, and **KITCHEN KABARET** features whimsical Audio-Animatronic characters in an entertaining overview of nutrition. On the **HARVEST TOUR**, agriculture professionals lead you through experimental greenhouses, hydroponic gardens, and aquaculture facilities, and explain the ongoing NASA experiments designed to provide food and life support systems in space stations and outer space colonies.

At **THE LIVING SEAS** pavilion, the **CARIBBEAN CORAL REEF RIDE** takes you to Sea Base Alpha, a six-million-gallon tropical saltwater aquarium alive with fish and marine mammals. You visit the **JOURNEY INTO IMAGINATION** pavilion to see the delightful leaping fountains before returning to The Land pavilion and your dinner destination, the **LAND GRILLE ROOM**. The restaurant offers specialties grown grown in the pavilion's greenhouses and the dining room revolves slowly past the biomes you visited earlier.

Afterward, at the **UNIVERSE OF ENERGY** pavilion, you enter the eerie twilight of prehistory, where mighty dinosaurs loom in an ancient forest and the warm swamp air carries the smell of sulfur from erupting volcanoes. The golden-domed **WONDERS OF LIFE** pavilion features **BODY WARS**, a microscopic race against time through the human body; and the **HORIZONS** pavilion, nearby, offers a look at the life-styles of the twenty-first century, complete with undersea farms. At the **WORLD OF MOTION** pavilion, **IT'S FUN TO BE FREE** is an excursion through the history and future of transportation.

Just past the the World of Motion, you enter the World Showcase and stroll along the promenade toward **MEXICO**. Here, a massive Mayan pyramid encloses a nighttime scene of a festive plaza, and **EL RIO DEL TIEMPO** takes you on a charming boat ride and instant Mexican vacation. As the crowds gather for **ILLUMINATIONS**, you position yourself on the promenade. The entire World Showcase dims and, one by one, each nation is celebrated in music and light. Suddenly, the night sky is illuminated with fireworks and laser effects, and colorful fountains shoot up from the lagoon. In the distance, laser projections transform Epcot's immense geosphere into a radiant planet earth.

Day Four

MORNING CRUISE THROUGH THE OLD SOUTH: This morning, you're off for a pleasant cruise through the DISNEY VILLAGE WATERWAYS. Your first stop is the Disney Village Marketplace Marina, where you rent a canopy boat for a tour of the themed resorts along the shores, docking wherever you wish to take a closer look. You cruise out of Buena Vista Lagoon, past the *Empress Lilly*, a nineteenth-century replica riverboat, and enter the narrow, tree-canopied waterways. Traveling along the Sassagoula River, you pass by PORT ORLEANS, with its French Quarter–styled waterfront, charming city gardens, and maze of streets being prepared for Mardi Gras. Then, it's on to DIXIE LANDINGS, with its antebellum mansions set on wide green lawns with weeping willows, and its rustic lodges in an untamed bayou landscape. You enter the Trumbo Canal and cruise through the VACATION CLUB, where the tall palms and the Florida-style landscaping is reminiscent of Old Key West. You return your boat to Disney Village Marketplace, then browse through the shops and stop for lunch at CAP'N JACK'S OYSTER BAR.

OPTIONAL AFTERNOON WATER ADVENTURE: After lunch, you're off to explore TYPHOON LAGOON, a water park inventively designed as a funky island resort just moments after a devastating typhoon has struck. As you walk along, you'll find a wide variety of tropical plants and trees, many labeled for easy identification. In CASTAWAY CREEK, a giant inner-tube takes you on a lazy float around the park, and at SHARK REEF, you don snorkeling gear to swim among Caribbean undersea life in a saltwater lagoon, complete with a sunken steamer. If you're a thrill seeker, you'll also brave GANG PLANK FALLS before plopping into a lounge chair to soak up the atmosphere.

AFTERNOON AND EVENING AT DISNEY-MGM STUDIOS: This evening you experience the excitement and wonder of Hollywood at Disney-MGM Studios. At the far end of Hollywood Boulevard, you enter the working studios to join the BACKSTAGE STUDIO TOUR of the scenics shop, numerous sets used for film locations, and the not-to-be-missed disaster in Catastrophe Canyon. At the impeccably reproduced Chinese Theater, THE GREAT MOVIE RIDE presents live performers and Audio-Animatronic figures reenacting classic movie moments. In the magical undersea world at VOYAGE OF THE LITTLE MERMAID, live performers in imaginative costumes sing and dance popular favorites from the movie of the same name. Afterwards, the HONEY, I SHRUNK THE KIDS MOVIE SET ADVENTURE will give you a new, and quite different perspective on your backyard garden. If the SORCERY IN THE SKY fireworks show is scheduled this evening, your dinner destination will be the HOLLYWOOD BROWN DERBY, a replica of the famous eating and meeting place. If not, you'll head for the bright lights and lively action at PLEASURE ISLAND. There, you board the *Empress Lilly* riverboat for dinner at FISHERMAN'S DECK, overlooking Buena Vista Lagoon.

OPTIONAL LATE-NIGHT "HOTHOUSE" TOUR: After dinner, the lively nightlife is in full swing at PLEASURE ISLAND, where the ADVENTURERS CLUB features outrageous decor and performers who involve guests in preposterous tales. The NEON ARMADILLO and the JAZZ COMPANY present live entertainment and contrasting musical styles; and the COMEDY WAREHOUSE offers amusement hourly. At "midnight" you're back outside for the NEW YEAR'S EVE STREET PARTY, when Pleasure Island hosts its notorious celebration. As musicians and dancers entertain on the outdoor stage, confetti rains from the sky and fireworks bloom overhead, creating an exhilarating finale to the Gardens and Natural Wonders tour. ➡

Natural Wonders Schedule

The next four pages show the schedule you will follow and the arrangements and reservations you must make to organize the Gardens and Natural Wonders Tour. You may want to copy these pages and carry them with you.

BEFORE YOU GO

AT THE TIME YOU MAKE YOUR HOTEL RESERVATIONS: Call the Disney Learning Program (407 354-1855) and make reservations for DAY TWO for the Gardens of the World tour, which usually occurs on Monday, Tuesday, and Thursday. (Try to schedule your stay so that DAY TWO falls on one of these days, preferably Thursday. If this is not possible, switch DAY TWO with DAY THREE and be sure that DAY THREE falls on a tour day.) Make reservations for the 6:45 PM Polynesian Luau dinner show for DAY ONE (407 934-7639). Travelers arriving in Orlando after 4 PM should reserve the 9:30 PM show.

TWENTY-SIX DAYS BEFORE YOU LEAVE: Call the WDW Switchboard (407 824-2222) and make 8:30 PM dinner reservations for DAY TWO at Narcoossee's at Disney's Grand Floridian Beach Resort.

TWO DAYS BEFORE YOU LEAVE: Call Theme Park Restaurant Reservations (407 824-8800) and make 1:30 PM lunch reservations for DAY TWO at the Rose & Crown Dining Room in the United Kingdom pavilion at the World Showcase. (If you prefer another restaurant, consider one in Mexico or Canada.)

ONE DAY BEFORE YOU LEAVE: Call Theme Park Restaurant Reservations (407 824-8800) and make 6:30 PM dinner reservations for DAY THREE at the Land Grille Room at The Land pavilion in Future World. (If you prefer another restaurant, consider the Coral Reef Restaurant.)

DAY ONE: THE EVENING OF ARRIVAL

DAY / DATE

AFTER YOU CHECK INTO YOUR HOTEL: Stop at Guest Services and, if you do not have park admission tickets, purchase a multiday pass that includes Typhoon Lagoon, Discovery Island, and Pleasure Island. Also at Guest Services, purchase your tickets for the Polynesian Luau dinner show this evening and make 7:30 PM dinner reservations for DAY FOUR at the Hollywood Brown Derby at Disney-MGM Studios. Be sure your seating is no later than ninety minutes before Sorcery in the Sky is scheduled to begin. (If Disney-MGM Studios closes early on DAY FOUR, make 7:30 dinner reservations at Fisherman's Deck on board the *Empress Lilly* riverboat at Pleasure Island. If you prefer another restaurant, choose from the Steerman's Quarters or the Fireworks Factory.) Ask also for a *Times and Information* pamphlet showing the operating schedules at the Magic Kingdom, Epcot Center, and Disney-MGM Studios. Your reservations are now complete for the remainder of your vacation.

6 PM: Drive, taxi, or monorail to the Polynesian resort for the 6:45 PM **POLYNESIAN LUAU** dinner show. If you have booked the 9:30 PM show, proceed to the Polynesian resort at your leisure. If you have time on your hands, enjoy the one hundred blooming orchid plants in the resort's atrium jungle garden, then

tour the resort's torchlit paths and outdoor tropical gardens. At Seven Seas Lagoon, behind the hotel, catch the shimmering lights of the **ELECTRICAL WATER PAGEANT**, which floats by at 9 PM.

AFTER DINNER: The 6:45 PM show of the Polynesian Luau will end about 9 PM. If you leave a bit early and walk to the Seven Seas Lagoon beach behind Luau Cove, you will see the Electrical Water Pageant. The 9:30 PM show of the Polynesian Luau ends at about 11:30 PM.

BEFORE YOU RETIRE: Leave a wake-up call and perhaps order a room-service breakfast to be delivered early in the morning. Plan to leave your hotel at least forty-five minutes before Epcot opens.

DAY TWO

DAY / DATE

FORTY-FIVE MINUTES BEFORE EPCOT OPENS: Drive or take WDW transportation to **FUTURE WORLD** at Epcot. Ride **SPACESHIP EARTH**, which generally opens early. The ride exits in Earth Station, where you can check in at Guest Relations for the Gardens of the World tour. Check in by 9:15 AM.

9:30 AM: The **GARDENS OF THE WORLD** tour explores the horticultural achievements at the World Showcase. It lasts about 3½ hours and ends back at Earth Station. Drop out of the tour before it returns and proceed to the **UNITED KINGDOM** pavilion. If you have time before lunch, tour the pavilion's gardens.

1:30 PM LUNCH: The Rose & Crown Dining Room is on the edge of the World Showcase Lagoon across from the United Kingdom pavilion. (Light eaters and budget diners should try Le Cellier restaurant in the Canada pavilion or Cantina de San Angel in the Mexico pavilion.)

AFTER LUNCH: Continue touring the World Showcase as far as **FRANCE**, and try to see the film presentations O CANADA! and **IMPRESSIONS DE FRANCE** before returning to your resort to relax for the evening ahead. Or, if you wish, proceed to the Optional Afternoon Tea.

OPTIONAL AFTERNOON TEA: Drive, monorail, or bus to Disney's Grand Floridian Beach Resort at about 3:30 PM. Be seated at the Garden View Lounge for high tea, which is served from 3 to 5 PM. After tea, tour the resort's Victorian gardens and take in its turn-of-the-century architecture and details.

5 PM: If you are at the Grand Floridian, continue to the **MAGIC KINGDOM** by monorail. Otherwise, drive or take WDW transportation from your resort. (If you are driving, park at the Grand Floridian and continue by monorail.) Stroll down Main Street to Adventureland and take in the following attractions in this order: ❶ **SWISS FAMILY TREEHOUSE**; ❷ **JUNGLE CRUISE**; ❸ **SPLASH MOUNTAIN** (if you like thrill rides and the lines are not too long); ❹ **BIG THUNDER MOUNTAIN RAILROAD** (ditto); and ❺ **THE HAUNTED MANSION** in Liberty Square. (Look for the one-hundred-year-old Liberty Tree that was planted in Liberty Square.) At Fantasyland, take **SKYWAY TO TOMORROWLAND** and tour the unusual topiaries displayed there. As you walk over the bridge from Tomorrowland to Main Street, the serpent topiary, on your right, points the way to the All-America Rose Selection Display Garden.

8 PM: Exit the park and monorail back to the Grand Floridian Beach resort. On your way to dinner, stop at the lobby to hear the live music before continuing outside toward the waterfront.

8:30 PM DINNER: Narcoossee's is located on the waterfront behind the resort, overlooking Seven Seas Lagoon. Watch for the Magic Kingdom fireworks show as you leave, which goes off at about 10 PM.

DAY THREE

DAY / DATE

9:30 AM: Drive, taxi, or monorail to the Contemporary resort. Take the ferry across Bay Lake from the Contemporary Marina to DISCOVERY ISLAND. Explore the many plant specimens and intricate landscaping at the zoological park, talk to the animal caretakers, and catch the FEATHERED FRIENDS, REPTILE RELATIONS, and BIRDS OF PREY shows, if you can. When you're ready for lunch, continue by ferry across Bay Lake to FORT WILDERNESS.

11:30 PM LUNCH: The Trail's End Buffeteria, across from the Fort Wilderness Marina, has a salad bar and a variety of lunch entrees. If you would like to picnic, you can buy supplies at the Settlement Trading Post, nearby, to take along on your nature hike. (Trail's End can also prepare food to go.)

AFTER LUNCH: The WILDERNESS SWAMP TRAIL begins behind the Settlement Trading Post and meanders through two miles of forests, wetlands, beaches, and meadows. If you brought along a picnic lunch, you'll find a shady spot to eat near the bridge over Chickasaw Creek, where the Wilderness Swamp Trail meets Bay Lake. After your hike, ferry back to the Contemporary Marina and relax at your resort for the afternoon and evening ahead.

3 PM: Drive or take WDW transportation to FUTURE WORLD at Epcot. Proceed directly to The Land pavilion and make reservations for the next HARVEST TOUR, which explores the pavilion's futuristic agricultural techniques (the tour leaves every half hour). While at The Land, take in LISTEN TO THE LAND, browse through the pavilion's gardener's gift shop, and catch KITCHEN KABARET.

After the Harvest Tour, proceed to The Living Seas pavilion for the CARIBBEAN CORAL REEF RIDE to Sea Base Alpha, to tour the huge saltwater aquarium and kelp gardens. If you have time before dinner, stroll over to the Journey Into Imagination pavilion for a glimpse of the unusual fountains surrounding it.

6 PM DINNER: The Land Grille Room is located on the entry level of The Land pavilion. Much of the produce and fish served here is actually grown in the pavilion's greenhouses and aquaculture facilities.

AFTER DINNER: Proceed to CommuniCore West and EPCOT OUTREACH, where you can request specific information about the exhibits you have toured. Then continue your tour of Future World, visiting the following attractions: ❶ UNIVERSE OF ENERGY; ❷ The Wonders of Life pavilion to see the exhibit hall and BODY WARS (if the line is short and you like thrill rides); ❸ HORIZONS; and ❹ IT'S FUN TO BE FREE in the World of Motion pavilion (if you have forty minutes or so before IllumiNations begins).

Shortcut to the WORLD SHOWCASE by walking past the Odyssey Restaurant and stroll the World Showcase promenade, which is enchantingly lit at night. About twenty minutes before ILLUMINATIONS begins, find a viewing spot at the edge of the lagoon. There are good views along the promenade from Mexico to Norway, and on the bridges in front of Italy. (If IllumiNations begins at 10 PM tonight, you may have time to ride EL RIO DEL TIEMPO in MEXICO and the MAELSTROM attraction in NORWAY.)

❋ GARDENS AND NATURAL WONDERS TOUR ❋

DAY FOUR

_____

DAY / DATE

9:30 AM: Drive or take WDW transportation to Disney Village Marketplace. Rent a canopy boat at the Village Marketplace Marina for a cruise through the **DISNEY VILLAGE WATERWAYS.** You may dock wherever you wish on your voyage. Guide your boat through Buena Vista Lagoon, past the *Empress Lilly* riverboat, a replica of a nineteenth-century stern-wheeler. Enter the tree-lined waterways and visit some of the following theme resorts: ❶ Follow the Sassagoula River to **PORT ORLEANS,** where the streets and buildings of New Orleans' French Quarter have been fancifully re-created, complete with tiny city gardens. ❷ Continue upstream to **DIXIE LANDINGS** for a look at the landscaping of the Old South, from the elegant grassy banks and weeping willows bordering the plantation mansions to the untamed palmettos and pine forest surrounding the rustic bayou lodges. ❸ Follow the Trumbo Canal to Old Key West at the **VACATION CLUB** for a look at landscaping South Florida–style. ❹ Return your boat to the Village Marketplace Marina and, if you're in the mood to shop, don't miss Conched Out, which carries a variety of gardening accessories. When you're ready for lunch, try Cap'n Jack's Oyster Bar or Chef Mickey's Village Restaurant, which both overlook the Buena Vista Lagoon.

OPTIONAL AFTERNOON WATER ADVENTURE: After lunch, continue shopping, return to your resort to relax, or go on the Optional Water Adventure. Drive or bus to nearby **TYPHOON LAGOON.** Rent towels at the entrance, set up camp in the shade near Typhoon Tilly's, and use the changing rooms and lockers there. The landscapers at Typhoon Lagoon have incorporated a great variety of tropical specimens in the park, and many are labeled for easy identification. Begin your tour with the following attractions: ❶ **CASTAWAY CREEK,** for a long, lazy inner-tube float around the park; ❷ **SHARK REEF,** for a snorkeling tour of Caribbean undersea life; and ❸ **GANG PLANK FALLS,** for a wild tube ride (if you enjoy water thrills). When you've had enough sun and fun, head back to your resort to change for dinner.

4 PM: Drive or take WDW transportation to **DISNEY-MGM STUDIOS.** Stroll down Hollywood Boulevard and see as many of the following attractions as you can: ❶ **BACKSTAGE STUDIO TOUR;** ❷ **INSIDE THE MAGIC;** ❸ **THE GREAT MOVIE RIDE;** and ❹ **VOYAGE OF THE LITTLE MERMAID.** Check out the larger-than-life backyard props at **HONEY, I SHRUNK THE KIDS MOVIE SET ADVENTURE.** If Disney-MGM Studios is open late tonight, continue touring until dinner time, then stay on for the **SORCERY IN THE SKY** fireworks show. If the park closes early, proceed to your dinner destination at Pleasure Island.

7:30 PM DINNER AT DISNEY-MGM STUDIOS: The Hollywood Brown Derby is located at the end of Hollywood Boulevard, across from the Chinese Theater.

7:30 PM DINNER AT PLEASURE ISLAND: The Fishermen's Deck is located on the *Empress Lilly* riverboat, docked at the entrance to Pleasure Island.

OPTIONAL LATE-NIGHT "HOTHOUSE" TOUR: Drive, bus, or taxi to **PLEASURE ISLAND** for an evening of nightclub adventures. Check out the scene at the **ADVENTURERS CLUB,** take in some live entertainment at **NEON ARMADILLO** and the **JAZZ COMPANY,** and catch a set at the **COMEDY WAREHOUSE.** Be back outside at 11:45 PM (10:45 PM on weekdays), for Pleasure Island's renowned **NEW YEAR'S EVE STREET PARTY** — a splashy finish to your Natural Wonders tour. ◆

WILD KINGDOM

An International Safari of Sophisticated Playgrounds, Cosmopolitan Club-Hopping, and Sporting Adventures for Single Travelers and the Young at Heart

BEST TIME OF YEAR FOR THIS ITINERARY
April through August

LEAST CROWDED TIMES FOR THIS ITINERARY
April and May (except holidays)

BEST ARRIVAL DAY FOR THIS ITINERARY
Wednesday or Thursday

BEST BUDGET HOTEL FOR THIS ITINERARY
Disney's Port Orleans Resort (river view)

BEST MODERATE HOTELS FOR THIS ITINERARY
Buena Vista Palace (pool view)
The Hilton Resort (standard room)

BEST DELUXE HOTELS FOR THIS ITINERARY
Walt Disney World Swan (pool view)
Disney's Contemporary Resort (tower room)
Disney's Grand Floridian Beach Resort (pool view)

ULTIMATE HOTEL EXPERIENCE FOR THIS ITINERARY
Buena Vista Palace (concierge floor)

LOCAL TRANSPORTATION
For this itinerary, it is best to rent a car or use your own.

PACKING
Bring club-hopping clothes and sports equipment (if you plan to use your own).

TIPS
Buena Vista Palace offers a vacation package that includes accommodations, park admission, and rental car. Disney Cast Members frequent Pleasure Island on Thursdays.

★

Day One

EVENING AT DISNEY VILLAGE MARKETPLACE AND PLEASURE ISLAND: Your safari begins at Disney Village Marketplace, where the shops offer everything from casual attire to trendy clothing and specialty gifts. At the Gourmet Pantry you can stock up on room snacks and beverages, and at Village Spirits, you'll find a wide selection of miniature liquors, which some visitors claim are useful for surviving the touring rigors of the Magic Kingdom. You might join the friendly crowd seated at the circular bar at Cap'n Jack's Oyster Bar, or walk on to your dinner destination at the **FIREWORKS FACTORY** on Pleasure Island. Here, you can launch your evening at its popular happy hour event.

After dinner, it's club-hopping time at PLEASURE ISLAND, where the nightlife is in full swing. You begin with the sensational opening show at MANNEQUINS, the top-rated dance club in the Southeast. Then, it's on to the ADVENTURERS CLUB, where the outrageous decor and crowd-mingling actors draw everyone into preposterous discussions. NEON ARMADILLO and 8TRAX present contrasting music and dance styles, and the COMEDY WAREHOUSE and JAZZ COMPANY stage performances throughout the night. Back outside, at "midnight," Pleasure Island throws a NEW YEAR'S EVE STREET PARTY: Confetti falls from the sky, fireworks explode overhead, and perfect strangers toast one another as newfound friends.

★

Day Two

MORNING AT THE MAGIC KINGDOM: This morning, travelers from around the world gather for the GUIDED TOUR OF THE MAGIC KINGDOM, which begins in the small-town ambience of MAIN STREET, U.S.A. In TOMORROWLAND, the multimedia ride DREAMFLIGHT explores the history of aviation, from early flight to outer space jaunts. In FANTASYLAND, you embark on a musical cruise past the ethnic costumes and diverse languages of IT'S A SMALL WORLD, then become part of a masterful special-effects haunting at THE HAUNTED MANSION in LIBERTY SQUARE. In FRONTIERLAND, at the DIAMOND HORSE-SHOE JAMBOREE, a slightly risqué Gay Nineties dance hall show accompanies lunch. In ADVENTURE-LAND, a PIRATES OF THE CARIBBEAN watercraft carries you through an island settlement where a pirate raid is underway. The tour ends at JUNGLE CRUISE, a whimsical exploration of the world's great rivers.

OPTIONAL AFTERNOON COOL-DOWN AT THE CONTEMPORARY RESORT: At the ultra-modern Contemporary resort, the monorail disembarks *inside* the hotel. The resort's beach is the perfect spot for sunbathing and mingling with visitors, and the ongoing volleyball games at the beach always welcome new players. A rented Water Sprite provides an exhilarating race across the waters of Bay Lake and Seven Seas Lagoon, and the Olympiad Health Club offers massages, tanning beds, and workout equipment. Or, perhaps you prefer to relax and cool off with a matinee at Pleasure Island's ten-screen movie theater.

EVENING AT THE MAGIC KINGDOM: Your dinner destination is NARCOOSSEE'S, at Disney's Grand Floridian Beach Resort. The octagon-shaped restaurant offers seafood specialties and a great view of the animated lights and music of the ELECTRICAL WATER PAGEANT as it floats by. After dinner, you board the monorail for the evening action at the Magic Kingdom. MAIN STREET buzzes with excited crowds, faces upturned to watch Tinkerbell's dramatic flight across the sky from a tower high in Cinderella's Castle, followed by the multicolored bursts of the FANTASY IN THE SKY fireworks. In the Old West of FRONTIERLAND, SPLASH MOUNTAIN features a water-flume ride with a wild and wet finish, and BIG THUNDER MOUNTAIN RAILROAD offers an exhilarating race on a runaway train. By now crowds will have gathered for SPECTROMAGIC, a high-tech parade of elaborately lit floats that re-create scenes from Disney films. In FANTASYLAND, PETER PAN'S FLIGHT takes you over London's rooftops aboard a miniature version of Captain Hook's ship. In TOMORROWLAND, you hurtle through the voids of space on futuristic SPACE MOUNTAIN, then enlist for the MISSION TO MARS, a more sedate extraterrestrial experience. You might also enjoy the live entertainment (and the audience it attracts) at the TOMORROWLAND THEATRE.

Day Three

ACTIVE MORNING: The day starts with your selected sporting activity at Typhoon Lagoon or Fort Wilderness. At **TYPHOON LAGOON**, you can explore the attractions at this inventively designed water park, including **CASTAWAY CREEK**, where giant inner-tubes take swimmers on a lazy float around the park. Then it's off to **SHARK REEF** to don snorkeling gear for a swim with the fishes of the Caribbean in a saltwater lagoon. Thrill seekers will brave **GANG PLANK FALLS**, **STORM SLIDES**, and **THE WAVES AT TYPHOON LAGOON** before plopping into a lounge chair to soak up the sun or indulge in people-watching.

At Fort Wilderness recreation area, the **FORT WILDERNESS WATERSKIING EXCURSION** offers skiers a breathtaking morning skimming the waters of Bay Lake, while the knowledgeable guide offers tips to beginners and tells experienced skiers the secrets of making that splashy turn smoothly. The **FORT WILDERNESS TRAIL RIDE** takes a group of trailmates for a leisurely horseback ride through a shady natural wonderland. On the two-hour **FORT WILDERNESS FISHING EXCURSION**, participants socialize and swap fishing stories as they attempt to entice largemouth bass from Bay Lake. The **WILDERNESS RIDE** is a biker's dream come true: eight miles of bike paths that meander along waterways, past beaches, into forests, and through the wetlands along bridges and boardwalks.

AFTERNOON AND EVENING AT DISNEY-MGM STUDIOS: The focus here is the glamor and excitement of Hollywood at Disney-MGM Studios. You stroll down Hollywood Boulevard toward **STAR TOURS**, where you lift off on a special-effects sci-fi trip into deep space. At the **INDIANA JONES EPIC STUNT SPECTACULAR**, the secrets of motion picture professionals are revealed as boulders crash down, trucks careen out of control, and fiery explosions fill the air. At **JIM HENSON'S MUPPET*VISION 3D**, a variety of advanced special effects, puppetry, and animation techniques are combined to create a striking entertainment event. The **MONSTER SOUND SHOW** enlists audience members to act as sound technicians for a short, funny film. In the Chinese Theater, **THE GREAT MOVIE RIDE** re-creates classic movie moments using both live actors and Disney's remarkable Audio-Animatronics. The **BACKSTAGE STUDIO TOUR** carries you by tram through the working sets that serve as actual film locations, and the not-to-be-missed disaster in Catastrophe Canyon; and at the **INSIDE THE MAGIC** walking tour, you're behind the scenes at Disney's working soundstages and production facilities. Your dinner destination tonight is the **HOLLYWOOD BROWN DERBY**, a replica of the renowned eating and meeting place, and a favorite with stars in production at Disney-MGM Studios.

After dinner, at **SUPERSTAR TELEVISION**, audience members are put to work as actors in familiar television roles, and on Sunset Boulevard, you enter the **TWILIGHT ZONE TOWER OF TERROR**, a hair-raising supernatural experience that takes place in a creepy deserted hotel. Then, you're back on Hollywood Boulevard for **SORCERY IN THE SKY**, a light-and-sound extravaganza of lasers, strobes, fireworks, and soaring fountains of silver and gold sparks.

OPTIONAL NIGHT OWL EVENT: Your leisurely afternoon pays off! With energy to burn, you set out for the **LAUGHING KOOKABURRA**, the vibrant dance club at the Buena Vista Palace. To the music of live bands and the club's professional DJs, you dance and carouse with a mix of local residents, business travelers, Disney Cast Members, and visitors from around the world.

Day Four

MORNING AT THE WORLD SHOWCASE: Your World Showcase tour starts at Disney's Beach Club Resort, a re-creation of a grand New England seaside hotel. You stroll along the waterfront to the International Gateway and emerge at FRANCE into the sights and sounds of a bustling Parisian neighborhood. MOROCCO is just beyond, with its lively, intricate bazaar of shops spilling over with the exotic handicrafts of North Africa. JAPAN, with its striking pagoda, serene gardens, and rustic country-inn architecture, is farther down the promenade. The U.S.A. pavilion features THE AMERICAN ADVENTURE with Audio-Animatronic hosts Mark Twain and Benjamin Franklin narrating a journey through the highlights of American history. In the ITALY pavilion, street actors stage Italian folktale comedies, tapping members of the audience to play parts. Beyond is the fairytale-like town square of GERMANY and the ornate architecture and extensive shopping gallery of CHINA, where the beautiful film, WONDERS OF CHINA, is featured. At NORWAY, an ancient fortress houses MAELSTROM, a thrilling Viking adventure ride, and beyond is the massive Mayan pyramid that houses MEXICO, with its nighttime scene of a festive shopping plaza. The carved totem poles and bloom-filled Victoria Gardens at CANADA welcome visitors to the Circle-Vision 360 film O CANADA! Your lunch destination is in the UNITED KINGDOM at the lively ROSE & CROWN DINING ROOM. The adjacent Pub bar is one of the most congenial spots in the World Showcase.

After lunch, you return to the Beach Club to relax before the evening ahead by soaking up the pleasant resort atmosphere, sunning at the beach, boating on the lake, browsing the shops at the Beach Club and the adjoining Yacht Club, or dropping into the Crews Cup Lounge to take in a televised sports event.

EVENING AT FUTURE WORLD AND ILLUMINATIONS: The land, the sea, and the world of ideas is this evening's theme at Future World. You return to the International Gateway and head for the glass pyramids and leaping fountains of the JOURNEY INTO IMAGINATION pavilion. In the MAGIC EYE THEATER, you can catch Disney's latest 3-D film extravaganza before continuing on to THE LAND pavilion for LISTEN TO THE LAND, a boat ride through three environmental biomes: desert, prairie, and rain forest. At THE LIVING SEAS pavilion, the CARIBBEAN CORAL REEF RIDE moves along the ocean floor to Sea Base Alpha, a six-million-gallon tropical-reef aquarium alive with thousands of fish and sea mammals. Inside Epcot's dazzling eighteen-story geosphere, the spectacular SPACESHIP EARTH ride explores the history and future of human communications. Beyond, at the UNIVERSE OF ENERGY pavilion, you enter the prehistoric twilight of a primeval world, where dinosaurs loom in an ancient forest and the balmy swamp air carries a whiff of sulfur from erupting volcanoes. The WONDERS OF LIFE pavilion features BODY WARS, a microscopic race against time through the human body, and CRANIUM COMMAND, a hilarious and harrowing perspective on the mind and body of a twelve-year-old boy. At the WORLD OF MOTION pavilion, IT'S FUN TO BE FREE takes you on a whimsical ride through the history of transportation. Your dinner destination tonight is the LAND GRILLE ROOM at The Land pavilion, which revolves slowly past the biomes you visited earlier.

After dinner, you return to the World Showcase for ILLUMINATIONS. The entire World Showcase is dimmed and, one by one, each nation is celebrated in music and light. Suddenly, fireworks and lasers light the night sky and colorful fountains shoot up from the lagoon. Far in the distance, Epcot's enormous silver geosphere is transformed into a glimmering, turning globe. ➤

Wild Kingdom Schedule

The next four pages show the schedule you will follow and the arrangements and reservations you must make to organize the Wild Kingdom, a peak attendance–time tour. You may want to copy these pages and carry them with you.

★

BEFORE YOU GO

AT THE TIME YOU MAKE YOUR HOTEL RESERVATIONS: Try to schedule your stay so that DAY ONE of your itinerary falls on a Wednesday or Thursday, to take advantage of the weekend activities.

TEN DAYS BEFORE YOU LEAVE: Call the Walt Disney World Switchboard (407 824-2222) and make 7:30 PM dinner reservations for DAY TWO at Narcoossee's at Disney's Grand Floridian Beach Resort. For the Active Morning on DAY THREE, make any morning reservations you will need: Fort Wilderness Fishing Excursion (407 824-2757); Waterskiing Excursion at Fort Wilderness (407 824-2621); Fort Wilderness Trail Ride (407 824-2832). See "Sporting Activities," page 217.

ONE DAY BEFORE YOU LEAVE: Call Theme Park Restaurant Reservations (407 824-8800) and make 7:45 PM dinner reservations for DAY THREE at the Hollywood Brown Derby at Disney-MGM Studios. Call the Fireworks Factory (407 934-8989) and make 7 PM dinner reservations for DAY ONE.

★

DAY ONE: THE EVENING OF ARRIVAL

DAY / DATE

AFTER YOU CHECK INTO YOUR HOTEL: Stop at Guest Services, and if you do not have park admission tickets, consider purchasing a multiday pass that includes Typhoon Lagoon and Pleasure Island. Also at Guest Services, make 1 PM lunch reservations for DAY FOUR at the Rose & Crown Dining Room in the United Kingdom pavilion at the World Showcase, and make 7:30 PM dinner reservations for DAY FOUR at the Land Grille Room at Future World. (If you prefer another restaurant for dinner, consider the Coral Reef Restaurant.) Ask also for a *Times and Information* pamphlet showing the operating schedules at the Magic Kingdom, Epcot Center, and Disney-MGM Studios. Your reservations are now complete for the remainder of your vacation.

4:30 PM: Drive or take WDW transportation to DISNEY VILLAGE MARKETPLACE. Browse the shops and boutiques (check out The City for trendy attire), then step over to Cap'n Jack's Oyster Bar and find a seat at the bar for a convivial afternoon beverage and a great view of Buena Vista Lagoon.

6:30 PM: Stroll to the Fireworks Factory at Pleasure Island. Catch the last part of happy hour in the bar. (Thursday nights are Disney Cast Member nights.)

AFTER DINNER: Enter PLEASURE ISLAND through the back door of the Fireworks Factory and pick up an entertainment schedule. Tour the island, then head over to MANNEQUINS at 9 PM for the light show and dance performance that begins at about 9:30 PM. Afterward, sample the clubs, including NEON ARMADILLO for live country-western music and the ADVENTURERS CLUB for some friendly story swapping.

Join the crowd outside at the West End Stage at 10:45 PM (11:45 PM on weekends) for the **NEW YEAR'S EVE STREET PARTY**. It's guaranteed to launch your first evening in the Wild Kingdom.

BEFORE YOU RETIRE: If you played on Pleasure Island until the wee hours, you may want to leave a wake-up call and order a room-service breakfast for tomorrow. You'll leave for the Magic Kingdom at 9 AM.

★

DAY TWO

DAY / DATE

9 AM: Drive or take WDW transportation to the **MAGIC KINGDOM**. (If you are driving, park at the Contemporary resort and take the monorail from the Contemporary to the Magic Kingdom.) At Main Street, step into City Hall and make reservations for the 10:30 AM Guided Tour of the Magic Kingdom. Explore the Main Street shops and attractions until it's time for the guided tour.

10:30 AM: The **GUIDED TOUR OF THE MAGIC KINGDOM** lasts about $3^{1}/_{2}$ hours and takes you on the following attractions: **DREAMFLIGHT**; **IT'S A SMALL WORLD**; **THE HAUNTED MANSION**; **DIAMOND HORSESHOE JAMBOREE** (for lunch); **PIRATES OF THE CARIBBEAN**; and **JUNGLE CRUISE**. (Attractions visited on the tour may vary.) The tour is a great way to meet a variety of people from around the world.

OPTIONAL AFTERNOON COOL-DOWN: When the guided tour ends, you can continue touring the Magic Kingdom, return to your resort to relax, or go for the Optional Afternoon Cool-Down. Exit the park and take the monorail to the Contemporary resort. Check out the beach scene (there are coin lockers and changing rooms at the marina and towels near the pool), join a volleyball game, rent a Water Sprite to zip around Bay Lake and the Seven Seas Lagoon and quick-tour some of the other themed resorts, or drop into the Olympiad Health Club for a workout, tan, or massage. (You can also choose to cool off with a matinee at Pleasure Island's ten-screen multiplex theater.)

6:30 PM: Drive, taxi, or monorail to Disney's Grand Floridian Beach Resort. Tour the hotel lobby, enjoy the live entertainment, and stroll through the resort's Victorian gardens and courtyard.

7:45 PM DINNER: Narcoossee's is located on a pier behind the resort, at the edge of Seven Seas Lagoon. If you arrive early, take a seat in the bar where you can look out over the lagoon. (Light eaters and budget diners should try the Grand Floridian Cafe.)

AFTER DINNER: Step out onto the deck that surrounds Narcoossee's to catch the shimmering lights of the **ELECTRICAL WATER PAGEANT**, which floats by at about 9:15 PM, then hop the monorail from the Grand Floridian to the **MAGIC KINGDOM**. Pick up an entertainment schedule, then stroll down Main Street and find a good viewing spot for the **FANTASY IN THE SKY** fireworks show and Tinkerbell's flight over Cinderella's Castle (about 10 PM). Afterward, proceed to Frontierland and enjoy the following attractions: ❶ **SPLASH MOUNTAIN** (if you don't mind getting splashed) and ❷ **BIG THUNDER MOUNTAIN RAILROAD** (if you like thrill rides and the lines are not too long). Watch the **SPECTROMAGIC** parade in Frontierland, which passes by about 11 PM, then continue on to Fantasyland for ❸ **PETER PAN'S FLIGHT**. Cap your tour in Tomorrowland with ❹ **SPACE MOUNTAIN** (if you like thrill rides) and ❺ **MISSION TO MARS**. Or, check out the live entertainment at the **TOMORROWLAND THEATRE**.

★

DAY THREE

_____
DAY / DATE

ACTIVE MORNING: This morning, choose from a wild and wet expedition at Typhoon Lagoon or a morning engaged in waterskiing, fishing, horseback riding, or bicycling at Fort Wilderness.

If you select **TYPHOON LAGOON**, leave your hotel one hour before the park opens and get there by car or WDW bus. Rent towels at the entrance and set up camp in the shade on the beach across the creek from Typhoon Tilly's. Use the changing rooms and lockers at Typhoon Tilly's, and take in the following attractions: ❶ **CASTAWAY CREEK**, for a long, lazy inner-tube journey around the park; ❷ **SHARK REEF**, for a snorkeling experience among Caribbean undersea life; ❸ **GANG PLANK FALLS**, for a wild whitewater raft ride; ❹ **STORM SLIDES**, for serious thrill seekers; and ❺ **THE WAVES AT TYPHOON LAGOON**.

If you select an activity at **FORT WILDERNESS**, leave your hotel one hour before your scheduled activity and get there by car or taxi (do not use WDW public transportation to this destination).

• For **HORSEBACK RIDING**, proceed to the Fort Wilderness Guest Parking Lot and walk over to the Tri-Circle-D Livery, adjacent to the parking lot. Mount up and join the **FORT WILDERNESS TRAIL RIDE**.

• For **BICYCLING**, proceed to the Fort Wilderness Guest Parking Lot. Take a gray- or brown-flag bus from the Fort Wilderness Depot to the Meadow Recreation Area. Rent a bicycle at the Bike Barn, request a map, and take the **WILDERNESS RIDE** (see "Bicycle Paths," page 218).

• For **FISHING**, proceed to the Fort Wilderness Guest Parking Lot. Take an orange-flag bus from the Gateway Depot to the Settlement Recreation Area. At the Fort Wilderness Marina, join the **FORT WILDERNESS FISHING EXCURSION**. (Guests at the Contemporary resort can ferry to Fort Wilderness.)

• For **WATERSKIING**, proceed to the Fort Wilderness Guest Parking Lot. Take an orange-flag bus from the Gateway Depot to the Settlement Recreation Area. At the marina, board the **FORT WILDERNESS WATERSKIING EXCURSION** speedboat. (Guests at the Contemporary resort can ferry to Fort Wilderness.)

1 PM LUNCH: Return to your resort for lunch. Afterward, relax before the busy evening schedule ahead.

4 PM: Drive or take WDW transportation to **DISNEY-MGM STUDIOS**. As you enter, pick up an entertainment schedule at the Crossroads of the World kiosk. Stroll down Hollywood Boulevard and visit some the following attractions: ❶ **STAR TOURS** (if the line is too long, come back after dinner); ❷ **INDIANA JONES EPIC STUNT SPECTACULAR**; ❸ **JIM HENSON'S MUPPET*VISION 3D**; ❹ **MONSTER SOUND SHOW**; and ❺ **THE GREAT MOVIE RIDE**. If you have time before dinner, join the **BACKSTAGE STUDIO TOUR** (the tram portion) and/or the **INSIDE THE MAGIC** walking tour.

7:30 PM DINNER: The Hollywood Brown Derby is located at the end of Hollywood Boulevard. (Light eaters and budget diners should try Disney-MGM Studios Commissary, next to the Chinese Theater.)

AFTER DINNER: Continue your tour of the attractions, especially the **TWILIGHT ZONE TOWER OF TERROR** on Sunset Boulevard (if it's open) and **SUPERSTAR TELEVISION**. Before the **SORCERY IN THE SKY** fireworks show begins (about 9 or 10 PM), find a viewing spot at the end of Hollywood Boulevard, near the Hollywood Brown Derby.

Optional Night Owl Event: Drive or taxi to the Buena Vista Palace at Hotel Plaza for some late-night carousing with music and dance at the **Laughing Kookaburra**. Live bands and DJs entertain local residents, Disney Cast Members, and visitors and business travelers from around the world.

★

DAY FOUR

DAY / DATE

Before You Leave Your Hotel: You'll be touring all day today, with an afternoon break at Disney's Beach Club Resort, so pack a tote bag with whatever you'll need, including a hat or visor (and bathing suits and sunblock, if you plan to swim or sun at the Beach Club).

8:30 AM: Drive or taxi to Disney's Beach Club Resort. Walk through the hotel to the waterfront and stroll toward the International Gateway to the **World Showcase**. Pick up an entertainment schedule at the entrance and tour the pavilions in a counter-clockwise direction. Begin with **France**, where you can stop for a pastry and coffee at Boulangerie Pâtisserie, then on to **Morocco**, **Japan**, and the **U.S.A.** (for **The American Adventure** attraction). At **Italy**, catch the street theater, then continue to **Germany**, **China** (for the film **Wonders of China**), **Norway** (for the **Maelstrom** attraction), and finally **Mexico**, where you can cruise **El Rio del Tiempo**. Continue across the World Showcase Plaza to **Canada** and, if you have time before lunch, see **O Canada!** on your way to the **United Kingdom**.

1 PM Lunch: The Rose & Crown Dining Room is located at the United Kingdom pavilion on the edge of the World Showcase Lagoon. If you arrive early, enjoy a beverage in the Pub, which is usually filled with friendly people at this time of day. (Light eaters and budget diners should try Le Cellier in Canada.)

After Lunch: Exit at the International Gateway, just beyond the United Kingdom, and stroll back to the Beach Club to refresh and relax. If you want to lounge in a beach cabana on the white sands, there are changing rooms and lockers nearby. Or, enjoy the comfortable lobby bar or the extensive video arcade, tour the shops at the Beach Club and the adjacent Yacht Club, rent a boat and tour the lakes, or drop into the Crews Cup Lounge at the Yacht Club for a wide-screen-TV sports or entertainment interlude.

4 PM: Return to the International Gateway and walk past the United Kingdom toward **Future World**. Take in as many of the following attractions as you can before dinner (skip any with long lines; you can catch them later, if the park is open late): ❶ Journey Into Imagination pavilion — **Magic Eye Theater**; ❷ The Land pavilion — **Listen to The Land**; ❸ The Living Seas — **Caribbean Coral Reef Ride** (enter through the exit, if you just want to see the aquarium); ❹ **Spaceship Earth**; ❺ **Universe of Energy**; ❻ Wonders of Life pavilion — **Body Wars** (if you like thrill rides) and **Cranium Command**; and ❼ World of Motion pavilion — **It's Fun to be Free**.

7:30 PM Dinner: The Land Grille Room is located in The Land pavilion at Future World. (Light eaters and budget diners should try the Farmer's Market at The Land pavilion.)

After Dinner: If **IllumiNations** begins at 10 PM tonight, continue your tour where you left off. If IllumiNations begins at 9 PM, head back to the United Kingdom. There are good views along the promenade from the United Kingdom to France for this spectacular finale to your Wild Kingdom vacation. ◆

TICKETS & TIMING

ADMISSIONS

Tickets to the theme parks at Walt Disney World come in a variety of prices and touring styles. If you are staying at a WDW resort, you have the best admission option: the special-value Be Our Guest Pass, good for all parks for the length of your stay. If you are not staying on WDW property, then determine in advance what you would like to see and do during your visit and purchase accordingly. First-time visitors should keep in mind that it can take more than one day to see a single park, particularly during peak seasons. Ticket prices tend to change about twice each year, moving up incrementally. When purchasing tickets in advance, always ask about discounts that might be available during your visit (see also "Discount Travel Clubs," page 250).

ONE-DAY ONE-PARK TICKET: One day's admission to either the Magic Kingdom, Disney-MGM Studios, or Epcot Center — about $40 (about $30 for children).

FOUR-DAY SUPER PASS: Four days' admission to the Magic Kingdom, Disney-MGM Studios, and Epcot Center, including use of WDW transportation linking the parks — about $140 (about $110 for children). The Four-Day Super Pass has no expiration date.

FIVE-DAY SUPER DUPER PASS: Five days' admission to the Magic Kingdom, Disney-MGM Studios, and Epcot Center, including use of WDW transportation linking parks. After the ticket is first used, it is good for seven consecutive days at Typhoon Lagoon, Pleasure Island, River Country, and Discovery Island — about $190 (about $150 for children). The Five-Day Super Duper Pass has no expiration date.

BE OUR GUEST PASS: Available to guests staying at WDW resorts, this length-of-stay pass includes admission to the Magic Kingdom, Disney-MGM Studios, Epcot Center, Typhoon Lagoon, Pleasure Island, River Country, and Discovery Island. Guests may buy passes for any length of stay; for example, guests staying one night can buy a two-day Be Our Guest Pass for about $85 (about $70 for children); guests staying four nights can buy a five-day Be Our Guest Pass for about $170 (about $135 for children).

ONE-DAY ADMISSION TO ALL OTHER PARKS: Guests who do not have a Five-Day Super Duper Pass or a Be Our Guest Pass are charged admission at the following parks: Typhoon Lagoon — about $25 ($20 for children); River Country — about $16 ($13 for children); Discovery Island — about $10 ($6 for children); and Pleasure Island — about $16 for entry after 7 PM (includes all clubs and events).

ANNUAL PASSPORT: Guests who plan to visit for seven days or longer or who plan to return within the year should consider an Annual Passport, which includes unlimited admission for one year to the Magic Kingdom, Disney-MGM Studios, and Epcot Center, advance-restaurant-reservation privileges, free parking, and use of WDW transportation linking the parks — about $225.

PURCHASING TICKETS: Tickets can be purchased at Guest Services in all WDW resorts. Tickets may also be purchased by mail through Ticket Services, Walt Disney World Company, P. O. Box 10030, Lake Buena Vista, FL 32830. Call ahead (407 824-4321) for current prices, and allow six weeks for delivery. Tickets may also be purchased with a credit card by phone (407 824-4321). Allow twenty-one days for delivery. Walt Disney World accepts personal checks, money orders, traveler's checks, American Express, MasterCard, and Visa. ◆

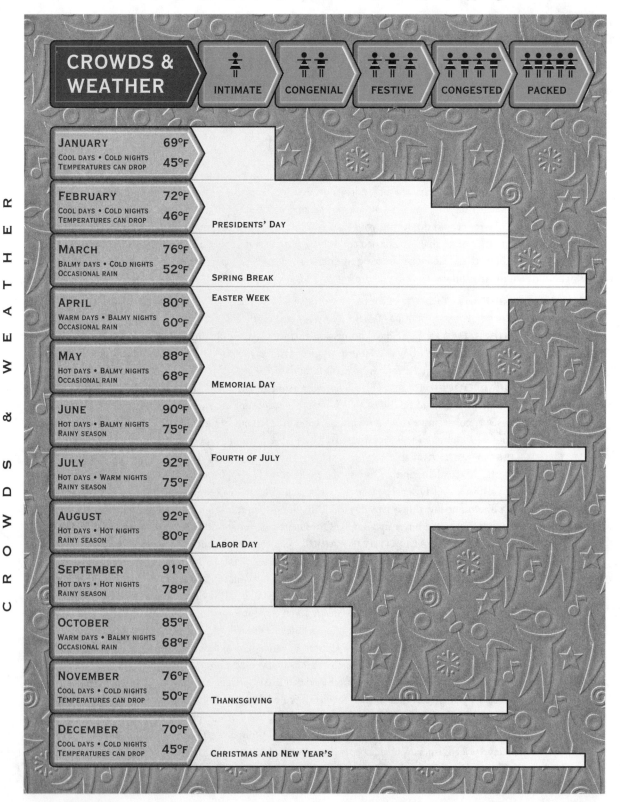

CROWDS & WEATHER

INTIMATE CONGENIAL FESTIVE CONGESTED PACKED

CROWDS & WEATHER

JANUARY 69°F
COOL DAYS • COLD NIGHTS 45°F
TEMPERATURES CAN DROP

FEBRUARY 72°F
COOL DAYS • COLD NIGHTS 46°F
TEMPERATURES CAN DROP
Presidents' Day

MARCH 76°F
BALMY DAYS • COLD NIGHTS 52°F
OCCASIONAL RAIN
Spring Break

APRIL 80°F
Easter Week
WARM DAYS • BALMY NIGHTS 60°F
OCCASIONAL RAIN

MAY 88°F
HOT DAYS • BALMY NIGHTS 68°F
OCCASIONAL RAIN
Memorial Day

JUNE 90°F
HOT DAYS • BALMY NIGHTS 75°F
RAINY SEASON

JULY 92°F
Fourth of July
HOT DAYS • WARM NIGHTS 75°F
RAINY SEASON

AUGUST 92°F
HOT DAYS • HOT NIGHTS 80°F
RAINY SEASON
Labor Day

SEPTEMBER 91°F
HOT DAYS • HOT NIGHTS 78°F
RAINY SEASON

OCTOBER 85°F
WARM DAYS • BALMY NIGHTS 68°F
OCCASIONAL RAIN

NOVEMBER 76°F
COOL DAYS • COLD NIGHTS 50°F
TEMPERATURES CAN DROP
Thanksgiving

DECEMBER 70°F
COOL DAYS • COLD NIGHTS 45°F
TEMPERATURES CAN DROP
Christmas and New Year's

CROWDS & WEATHER

As might be expected, crowd size is directly related to school vacations and national holidays. During peak-attendance times, the parks have extended hours with special parades and shows; however, unless you are traveling to WDW for a convention, seminar, or special event, arrange your vacation to avoid these busy times. In the summer, when school is out, it is not only crowded but uncomfortably hot and rainy here. During the winter months, unseasonable cold weather can move in, so winter visitors should pack accordingly (see "Packing," page 249). It may be a good idea to check with Disney Weather before you leave (407 824-4104).

WINTER: Christmas week kicks off the winter season, and all over Florida this is the busiest week of the year. The crowds at WDW can be awesome, the lines intimidating, and the shows and attractions inundated with children. During the three weeks preceding Christmas, however, WDW is sparsely attended, making this an ideal time to visit, since the holiday decor and festivities are underway. Attendance drops again after New Year's Eve and continues to be low until Presidents' Day, in mid-February. The temperature can drop to the mid-forties, even during the day, but there is little precipitation. Winter hours in the theme parks are shorter, but the smaller crowds make the attractions far more accessible.

SPRING: From early March until Easter and spring break, the crowds are light to moderate. After Easter and before the start of the summer season in early June, children are still in school and the weather is, for the most part, pleasant. There is little rain, and the temperatures range from the high sixties to the mid-eighties. During April, the days grow steadily warmer, although the nights remain balmy until June. This is an especially pleasant time for those interested in golf and other outdoor activities.

SUMMER: Summer is consistently busy at Walt Disney World. Vast crowds and long lines are the norm, and reservations for restaurants, shows, and hotels can be difficult to get. The weather can be brutal as well, climbing into the nineties with high humidity and almost daily tropical showers in the afternoon. These brief storms have a tendency to clear out the parks, and if you don't mind getting wet, it is a good time to tour. The first two weeks of June and last two weeks of August have lower attendance than the rest of the summer. Evenings can be balmy and delightful in June, but by August they are just plain hot.

FALL: The most pleasant times at WDW are from the beginning of October through the weekend preceding Thanksgiving, and the week after Thanksgiving until the week before Christmas. Although WDW is sparsely attended in September, the weather is still quite hot. Orlando's most pleasant weather is during the fall. There is less rain than at other times of the year, and the temperatures range from the fifties to the mid-eighties. The weather can get cold from after Thanksgiving until just before Christmas, but the holiday decor and entertainment and the nearly deserted theme parks make for an ideal vacation. Although Thanksgiving week is busy, on Thanksgiving day the crowd is almost always around the dinner tables. ◆

✠

SEASONAL SCHEDULES & EVENTS

The theme parks are open year round, although they close earlier from September through May. Epcot Center, however, is usually open until 9 PM or later. Resort rates drop about ten to fifteen percent during value seasons, which occur during winter, spring, and fall, except for the holiday periods. Throughout the year, WDW stages a number of special events and activities (see also "Holidays at Walt Disney World," page 259).

JANUARY: Special events include resort-wide New Year's Eve celebrations and the Walt Disney World Marathon. The Magic Kingdom and Disney-MGM Studios close early and do not offer fireworks or evening parades. Typhoon Lagoon is closed for refurbishing. Value-season resort rates begin after New Year's.

FEBRUARY: Special events include a Mardi Gras celebration at Pleasure Island. The Magic Kingdom and Disney-MGM Studios close early except on weekends and during Presidents' Day week, with limited fireworks and parades. Typhoon Lagoon is closed for refurbishing during the first two weeks of February; Discovery Island is closed for refurbishing during the second two weeks. Value-season resort rates continue until Presidents' Day week, when peak season begins.

MARCH: Large crowds arrive at WDW during spring break and Easter week. Special events include the Bryant Gumbel/WDW Pro-Am Golf Tournament. Disney-MGM Studios closes early and the Magic Kingdom closes early during the first two weeks. There are limited fireworks and parades, except during the week preceding Easter. Discovery Island is closed for refurbishing during the first two weeks of March. Peak-season resort rates continue until after Easter, when value season begins.

APRIL: Special events include the televised Easter Parade at the Magic Kingdom. Disney-MGM Studios closes early after Easter week, and there are limited fireworks and parades, except during the week before Easter through Easter week. Peak-season resort rates continue until after Easter, when value season begins.

MAY: The Magic Kingdom and Disney-MGM Studios close early and do not offer fireworks or evening parades, except during Memorial Day weekend. Value-season resort rates continue until Memorial Day week, when peak-season rates apply.

JUNE: Special events include the Classic Car Show at Disney Village Marketplace and the Walt Disney World Wine Festival. The theme parks are open late with a full schedule of parades and fireworks after the second week. Value-season resort rates continue until the second week of June, when peak season begins.

JULY: Special events include extended Fourth of July fireworks in all theme parks. The theme parks are open late with a full schedule of parades and fireworks. Peak-season resort rates apply throughout July.

AUGUST: The theme parks are open late with a full schedule of parades and fireworks until the week preceding Labor Day. Value-season resort rates begin the third week of August.

SEPTEMBER: Special events include the annual Night of Joy Christian music program at the Magic Kingdom. After Labor Day weekend, the Magic Kingdom and Disney-MGM Studios close early. Magic Kingdom fireworks and parades occur during Labor Day weekend only. Some attractions at the theme parks are closed for refurbishing during the fall. Value-season resort rates apply throughout September.

OCTOBER: Special events include the Boat Show at Disney Village Marketplace and the Walt Disney World/Oldsmobile Golf Classic. The Magic Kingdom and Disney-MGM Studios close early; Magic Kingdom fireworks and parades occur on Saturdays only. Some attractions at the theme parks are closed for refurbishing during the fall. Value-season resort rates apply throughout October.

NOVEMBER: Special events include the Festival of the Masters art show at Disney Village Marketplace. Resort-wide Christmas events begin after Thanksgiving. The Magic Kingdom and Disney-MGM Studios close early; Magic Kingdom fireworks and parades occur on Saturdays only. Some attractions at the theme parks are closed for refurbishing during the fall. Value-season resort rates apply throughout November.

DECEMBER: Christmas events and New Year's Eve celebrations are featured at the theme parks and at selected resorts. The Magic Kingdom and Disney-MGM Studios close early the first two weeks of December. A full schedule of fireworks and evening parades begins the week preceding Christmas, continuing through New Year's. Peak-season resort rates begin the week before Christmas. ◆

HOTELS

The Orlando metropolitan area has the largest concentration of hotel rooms in the United States, and one out of seven rooms is located at Walt Disney World. Although lower-priced accommodations are available elsewhere, the undeniable convenience and exclusive privileges offered to guests staying at a WDW resort far outweigh any additional expenses. Several of the newer Disney resorts are priced under $100 per night, and some of the campsites at Fort Wilderness are priced under $50 per night. In addition, WDW resort guests can purchase Be Our Guest Passes at a savings over regular park admission prices (see "Admissions," page 139).

THEME PARK ACCESS: WDW transportation — buses, trams, monorails, and water launches — travels between the resorts and theme parks and makes driving and parking unnecessary. WDW parking lots are free to resort guests who do drive. Guests can enter some theme parks up to an hour before the gates officially open, and no resort guest is ever turned away, even if the park has exceeded its visitor capacity.

INFORMATION ACCESS: Every hotel room provides the Disney Events Channel on television, an up-to-the-minute listing of shows, coming attractions, and special events. Guests receive brochures on dining, recreation, and transportation to help them with logistics. The Walt Disney World Switchboard connects guest rooms to every telephone on WDW property free of charge, and Guest Services at the resorts offers a wide range of services to streamline vacations, including reservations, banking, and ticket sales.

RESERVATION PRIVILEGES: Resort guests may book hard-to-get theme park restaurant reservations up to three days in advance and book dinner shows when they reserve their rooms. Resort guests may also book tee times at golf courses up to thirty days in advance and are given preference over non-resort guests.

RESORT IDENTIFICATION CARD: This card acts as a pass for WDW transportation and allows guests to charge purchases and meals in most of the full-service restaurants to their hotel rooms. (Charging privileges are not available to guests at the privately run Dolphin, Swan, and Hotel Plaza resorts.)

THE WALT DISNEY WORLD RESORT EXPERIENCE: The WDW resort environment is designed to be a total-immersion experience so that guests never have the feeling of leaving the "magic" at the end of the day. This is due in part to the carefully crafted atmosphere of each resort and also to the Disney Cast Members, who strive to offer guests the best possible vacation experience. In the reviews, the hotels are rated for atmosphere, attitude, freshness or quality of the rooms, and overall value as follows: ✗ = sub-standard, ✗✗ = adequate but unexceptional, ✗✗✗ = better than most, and ✗✗✗✗ = superior in every way.

PRICES: The Walt Disney World resorts offer a wide range of rates, depending on their amenities and location (see "Walt Disney World Overview," page 10, for resort locations). Prices at most resorts change during peak and value seasons (see "Seasonal Schedules & Events," page 141). The hotel reviews list each resort's amenities and indicate the average price of a standard room, before taxes, as follows:

$ – under $109
$$ – $110 to $149
$$$ – $150 to $199
$$$$ – $200 to $299
$$$$$ – over $300
$$$$$$ – over $500

RESERVATIONS: Reservations for all resorts at Walt Disney World can be made through Walt Disney World Reservations (407 934-7639). Reservations at the privately run WDW resorts can also be made directly; many have toll-free numbers. Vacation packages are available at all WDW resorts. ◆

BUENA VISTA PALACE

LOCATION: Buena Vista Palace is one of seven independently owned Hotel Plaza Resorts at Disney Village. The hotel is located on Walt Disney World property, across from Disney Village Marketplace. Guests enjoy most of the same transportation and reservations privileges as do guests at the Disney-owned hotels.

AMBIENCE: Large fountains mark the entrance to this imposing and majestic mirror-paneled high-rise hotel. The Buena Vista Palace is situated on twenty-seven acres of open land and pine forest and boasts its own private lagoon. An extensive convention center housed in the hotel attracts a professional crowd. The elegant multilevel lobby encircles a narrow twenty-seven-story atrium and is furnished traditionally with oil paintings, crystal chandeliers, and ornately framed mirrors. Guest rooms are spacious and all rooms have private balconies. The hotel prides itself on maintaining its upscale and uptown grandeur. In sales, the Buena Vista Palace ranks as one of the top five resorts in the United States.

RATES: Standard rooms **$$**. Crown-level concierge rooms **$$$$** (including Continental breakfast, late afternoon cocktails, evening cordials, and special room amenities). Palace Suites **$$$$** (including separate bedroom, wet bar, refrigerator, two baths, and in-room coffee maker). Rates vary with the season.

AMENITIES: Twenty-four-hour room service, mini bar, in-room safe, hair dryer, turndown service, voice mail, pay-per-view movies, and valet parking.

RESTAURANTS: *Watercress Cafe & Bake Shop* — Breakfast, lunch, and dinner with soup and salad bar. *Arthur's 27* — Elegant Continental dining in an award-winning rooftop restaurant. *Outback* — Steak and seafood dinners, Australian-style.

WDW PUBLIC TRANSPORTATION: Bus or walk to Disney Village Marketplace, Pleasure Island, and Buena Vista Golf Course. Bus to all other theme parks. Taxi service available.

RECREATION: Two pools, tennis, marina, health club, sauna, massage, and whirlpool.

FEATURES: The resort's very popular nightclub, the Laughing Kookaburra, features happy hour, live entertainment, and dancing. There is also a small nightclub on the top floor, the Palace Lounge, with live music and late-night dancing.

DRAWBACKS: Guests relying on WDW buses to reach attractions may find them inconvenient or overcrowded.

TIPS: The resort offers a number of vacation packages that include accommodations, some meals, WDW admission, and other amenities. To receive a brochure, call the hotel directly (800 327-2990).

The Buena Vista Palace offers discounts to members of several travel clubs, including Meritz Exclusively Yours and Orlando Magicard.

A rental car can save considerable commuting time from this location.

MAKING RESERVATIONS: Call the Buena Vista Palace toll-free number (800 327-2990) and inquire about special promotional rates, corporate rates, and senior discounts. Reservations may also be made through Walt Disney World Reservations (407 934-7639).

XXX ATMOSPHERE. **XXX** ATTITUDE. **XXX** FRESHNESS. **XXXX** VALUE.

BUENA VISTA PALACE
A PRIVATELY OWNED HOTEL
1900 BUENA VISTA DRIVE, LAKE BUENA VISTA, FLORIDA 32830
TELEPHONE (407) 827-2727 • FAX (407) 827-6034

THE DISNEY INN

LOCATION: The Disney Inn is one of six hotels in the Magic Kingdom Resorts Area. It is located adjacent to the Magnolia and Palm golf courses in a quiet, wooded area a short drive from the Magic Kingdom.

AMBIENCE: This hotel, with its old-fashioned, wood-shingled low-rise architecture, is oriented to golf fans and set apart from the rest of WDW by a long, winding driveway and impeccably manicured fairways. Snow White–themed topiaries flank the doors to the lobby, a comfortable, unpretentious ranch-style room with rock walls and windows overlooking the pool and golf course. Guest rooms, the fewest in number but the most spacious of any Disney resort, are quasi suites that have a pleasant country-inn atmosphere, with knotty pine furnishings and floral details. All rooms feature balconies or patios with views of the pools, the golf courses, or the resort's lush landscaping. The resort itself is very low-key and could be located anywhere — although the unmistakable whistle of the Walt Disney World Railroad steam trains at the Magic Kingdom can be heard from the grounds.

RATES: Standard rooms $$$. Rates vary with the season.

AMENITIES: Room service, voice mail, and valet parking.

RESTAURANTS: *The Garden Gallery* — Breakfast buffet, lunch, and dinner featuring American cuisine.

RECREATION: Two pools, tennis, nature walk, health club, two PGA golf courses, clubhouse, putting greens, driving ranges, and golf studio with private lessons.

WDW PUBLIC TRANSPORTATION: Bus to the Transportation and Ticket Center (TTC) to catch monorails to the Magic Kingdom and Epcot Center. From the Magic Kingdom, water launch to Discovery Island, Fort Wilderness, and River Country. Bus to all other theme parks. Taxi service available.

FEATURES: Conveniently located for guests primarily interested in golf. The eighteen-hole Magnolia and Palm golf courses are top-ranked PGA courses.

During the month of October, when the Walt Disney World/Oldsmobile Golf Classic is held, it is nearly impossible to book a room here, but it can be an exciting time for golf fans who manage to book well in advance.

The Disney Inn is one of the more serene and secluded hideaways in WDW. Garden-lovers will enjoy the resort's nature-walk tour of botanical specimens from around the world.

DRAWBACKS: WDW buses to attractions can be inconvenient and slow from this location.

The resort's restaurant offers a limited choice in dining for guests staying longer than a few days.

TIPS: A rental car is practically required for this out-of-the-way resort and can save considerable commuting time.

Rooms No. 101 to 113 on the ground floor (or 301 to 313 on the top floor) surround the quiet pool and have sweeping fairway views beyond.

MAKING RESERVATIONS: Call Walt Disney World Reservations (407 934-7639). Inquire about special promotional rates and vacation packages.

XX ATMOSPHERE. **XXX** ATTITUDE. **XXX** FRESHNESS. **XX** VALUE.

THE DISNEY INN
A DISNEY-OWNED HOTEL
1950 WEST MAGNOLIA PALM, LAKE BUENA VISTA, FLORIDA 32830
TELEPHONE (407) 824-2200 • FAX (407) 824-3229

DISNEY VACATION CLUB

LOCATION: Disney Vacation Club is one of four hotels in the Disney Village Resorts Area. The Vacation Club is located adjacent to the Lake Buena Vista Golf Course and is connected by waterway to Disney Village Marketplace and Pleasure Island.

AMBIENCE: The village atmosphere of Key West with a dash of Caribbean flair is the theme here, complete with a landmark lighthouse at the edge of the resort's private lagoon. Charming, tinned-roofed two- and three-story buildings, in pastel-colored clapboard with ornate white trim and picket fences, line the winding streets of the village. The accommodations feel like vacation homes and are furnished in shades of apricot, aqua, and celadon, colors used throughout the resort exteriors. All rooms have balconies that overlook waterways, golf greens, or woodlands. Clustered around the lagoon at the center of the resort is a small lobby, an inviting library, and all recreational facilities and services.

RATES: Studios $$$ (including refrigerator, microwave, and coffee maker). One-bedroom units $$$$. Two-bedroom units $$$$$. Three-bedroom units $$$$$$. All vacation homes except studios have wide-screen televisions, fully equipped kitchens, and laundry facilities. Rates vary with the season.

AMENITIES: Voice mail, in-room safe, VCR, and videocassette library.

RESTAURANTS: *Olivia's Cafe* — Breakfast, lunch, and dinner featuring Florida and Caribbean cuisine.

WDW PUBLIC TRANSPORTATION: Water launch or bus to Disney Village Marketplace and Pleasure Island. Bus to all theme parks, including the Magic Kingdom, Epcot Center, Disney-MGM Studios, and Typhoon Lagoon. To reach other destinations, bus to the Transportation and Ticket Center (TTC) or Disney Village Marketplace and connect to destination buses. Taxi service available.

RECREATION: Two pools, small beach, tennis, volleyball, shuffleboard, marina, bicycling, jogging path, health club, sauna, whirlpool, fitness training, and massage.

FEATURES: The resort is conveniently located for guests interested in golfing at WDW.

Guests may rent their own boats and commute by water to Disney Village Marketplace, Pleasure Island, and other Disney Village Resorts.

DRAWBACKS: WDW buses operate within the resort, but it is quite spread out. Guests relying on WDW buses to reach attractions may find them inconvenient or overcrowded.

TIPS: A rental car is a must for guests who want to see it all.

Room locations that are close to the recreation area and lobby are in buildings 12, 13, and 14. Buildings 11 and 15 are secluded, but still close to the common areas. Building 23 is near the quiet pool.

Disney Vacation Club is actually a time-share and a member of Resort Condominiums International. RCI members can exchange time at Disney Vacation Club. Units not used by time-share owners are available to guests as full-service hotel accommodations.

MAKING RESERVATIONS: Call Walt Disney World Reservations (407 934-7639). Inquire about special promotional rates and vacation packages.

XXX ATMOSPHERE. **XX** ATTITUDE. **XXXX** FRESHNESS. **XXX** VALUE.

DISNEY VACATION CLUB
A DISNEY-OWNED HOTEL
1510 NORTH COVE ROAD, LAKE BUENA VISTA, FLORIDA 32830
TELEPHONE (407) 827-7700 • FAX (407) 827-7710

DISNEY'S ALL-STAR RESORTS

LOCATION: Walt Disney World's newest resort area, All-Star Village, covers 240 acres of forest land at the southernmost point of Walt Disney World. It is located south of Disney-MGM Studios, adjacent to the site of the new Blizzard Beach water park and close to the area where WDW's fourth major theme park will be built over the next few years. All-Star Village will ultimately incorporate three distinct resort complexes, two of which are scheduled to open in 1994 and 1995: Disney's All-Star Sports Resort and Disney's All-Star Music Resort. From All-Star Village, it is a short drive to Disney-MGM Studios and Epcot Center.

AMBIENCE: This budget-priced resort complex, when it is complete, will be the largest at Walt Disney World, or any place in the world. Disney's All-Star Sports Resort has five separately themed hotel buildings, distinguished by massive three-dimensional entertainment architecture. The All-Star Sports hotels include Touchdown Hotel, Homerun Hotel, Surf Inn, Center Court, and Hoops Hotel. Disney's All-Star Music Resort also has five themed hotel buildings: Jazz Inn, Country Fair, Broadway, Calypso, and Rock Inn. The theme of each hotel building is carried over to the lobby and interior furnishings, as well as to the landscaping, pools, and other recreational amenities.

RATES: Standard rooms $.

AMENITIES: Mini bar and voice mail.

RESTAURANTS: *All-Star Sports and All-Star Music Food Courts* — Food court complexes with six to eight counter-service restaurants for breakfast, lunch, and dinner.

WDW PUBLIC TRANSPORTATION: Bus to all theme parks, including the Magic Kingdom, Epcot Center, Disney-MGM Studios, Pleasure Island, Disney Village Marketplace, and Typhoon Lagoon. To reach other destinations, bus to the Transportation and Ticket Center (TTC) and connect to destination buses. Taxi service available. A possible continuation of the monorail system to the area is on the master plan.

RECREATION: Pools, bicycling, jogging path, and themed sports areas including baseball, football, basketball, and tennis.

FEATURES: All recreational amenities are cleverly designed to reflect each hotel building's sport or music motif. The pool at Homerun Hotel, for example, is shaped like a baseball diamond, the one at Surf Inn like a wave, and the one at Calypso like a guitar.

DRAWBACKS: Because of the large number of rooms at the resort, WDW buses to attractions may be inconvenient or overcrowded.
  Guests primarily interested in the Magic Kingdom may find the commute from here tedious.
  Because the resort is very spread out, it can be a long trek from the guest rooms to the food courts.
  The resort has no full-service restaurants and attracts mainly families with young children.

TIPS: Request an upper-floor room in a building near the food court or main recreation complex.
  A rental car is essential to see all of WDW in a reasonable amount of time from this location.

MAKING RESERVATIONS: Disney's All-Star Sports Resort will open in mid-1994. Call Walt Disney World Reservations (407 934-7639). Inquire about special promotional rates and vacation packages.

DISNEY'S ALL-STAR RESORTS
A DISNEY-OWNED HOTEL
P. O. BOX 10,000, LAKE BUENA VISTA, FLORIDA 32830
TELEPHONE (407) 824-2222

DISNEY'S BEACH CLUB RESORT

LOCATION: Disney's Beach Club Resort is one of five hotels in the Epcot Resorts Area. It is located within walking distance of the International Gateway to the World Showcase at Epcot Center. It faces Stormalong Bay and shares a white sand beach and harbor waterfront with Disney's Yacht Club Resort.

AMBIENCE: This sky blue, multilevel resort was designed by architect Robert Stern and shares resort amenities with the more formal Yacht Club located next to it. The New England seacoast–style resort is beach oriented and has a sporty, casual decor, from the 1927 Chevrolet taxi parked in front to the pink marble floor tiles, striped wicker furnishings, and caged finches in the pastel-infused lobby. Guest rooms are cheerful and light, furnished with pink and white cabana-striped curtains and verdigris-finished wrought-iron bedsteads. Many rooms have verandas or small balconies.

RATES: Standard rooms $$$$.

AMENITIES: Twenty-four-hour room service, mini bar, hair dryer, in-room safe, newspaper delivery, turn-down service, voice mail, and valet parking.

RESTAURANTS: *Cape May Cafe* — Breakfast buffet and clambake dinner buffet featuring lobster.
Ariel's Restaurant — Dinner featuring fresh seafood in an aquarium-themed dining room.
Beaches and Cream — Breakfast and all-day hamburgers with soda fountain specialties.

WDW PUBLIC TRANSPORTATION: Walk to the World Showcase at Epcot Center. Water launch to Disney-MGM Studios. Bus to the Magic Kingdom, Pleasure Island, Disney Village Marketplace, and Typhoon Lagoon. To reach other destinations, bus to the Transportation and Ticket Center (TTC) and connect to destination buses. Taxi service available.

RECREATION: Pool, white sand beach, mini water park, marina, tennis, volleyball, jogging path, bocce ball (lawn bowling), croquet, health club, sauna, steam room, fitness classes, fitness training, whirlpool, and massage.

FEATURES: This full-amenity resort is conveniently located for guests primarily interested in Future World and the World Showcase at Epcot Center, and Disney-MGM Studios.

DRAWBACKS: WDW buses to the Magic Kingdom may be infrequent or overcrowded.
Although the more expensive lagoon-view rooms have lovely water views, they can be noisy since Stormalong Bay water park is filled with children late into the night.

TIPS: The rooms on the fourth floor were originally designated as concierge rooms, so they are more spacious and more generous in comforts. The rooms on the second and fourth floors have balconies.
Standard rooms that face the canal in front, but that are not above the parking portico, are a good value, while rooms located at the far end of the hotel facing the forest, although a bit of a trek from the lobby, offer pleasant views, quiet isolation, and fast access to the International Gateway at Epcot.

MAKING RESERVATIONS: Call Walt Disney World Reservations (407 934-7639). Inquire about special promotional rates and vacation packages.

XXX ATMOSPHERE. **XXXX** ATTITUDE. **XXXX** FRESHNESS. **XXX** VALUE.

DISNEY'S BEACH CLUB RESORT
A DISNEY-OWNED HOTEL
1800 EPCOT RESORT BOULEVARD, LAKE BUENA VISTA, FLORIDA 32830
TELEPHONE (407) 934-8000 • FAX (407) 934-3850

DISNEY'S CARIBBEAN BEACH RESORT

LOCATION: Disney's Caribbean Beach Resort is one of five hotels in the Epcot Resorts Area. The buildings of the resort encircle forty-acre Barefoot Bay, a series of three lakes created for the resort's exclusive use. From Disney's Caribbean Beach Resort it is a short drive to Epcot Center, Disney-MGM Studios, Typhoon Lagoon, Pleasure Island, and Disney Village Marketplace.

AMBIENCE: Built as Disney's first budget resort, the sprawling Caribbean Beach resort consists of clusters of pitched-roof two-story buildings painted in rather jarring colors and set in expertly designed tropical landscaping. The upper floors of the buildings are surrounded by walkways with white Caribbean-style railings. Instead of a formal lobby, the resort welcomes guests at its modest freestanding "Customs House," where overhead fans and wicker settees set a tropical note. The limited-amenity guest rooms, with subdued colors and wood furnishings, are functional and cozy. All resort activities are centered at Old Port Royale, on one side of Barefoot Bay.

RATES: Standard rooms $. Rates remain the same year round.

AMENITIES: Mini bar and voice mail.

RESTAURANTS: *Old Port Royale* — Food court with six counter-service restaurants.
Captain's Tavern — Dinner featuring prime rib and American cuisine.

WDW PUBLIC TRANSPORTATION: Disney's Caribbean Beach Resort has its own internal bus system. WDW shuttle bus to all theme parks, including the Magic Kingdom, Epcot Center, Disney-MGM Studios, Pleasure Island, Disney Village Marketplace, and Typhoon Lagoon. To reach other destinations, bus to the Transportation and Ticket Center (TTC) and connect to destination buses. Taxi service available.

RECREATION: Six pools, white sand beach, marina, bicycling, jogging path, nature walk, and whirlpool.

FEATURES: Parrot Cay, a small island in the middle of Barefoot Bay, has a fantasy Spanish-fort playground, a tropical nature walk, and an aviary stocked with colorful birds.

DRAWBACKS: The resort is especially popular with families with young children, making it an all-day noisy experience at the pools and beaches.

Because the resort sprawls over two hundred acres, it can be a long trek from guest rooms to the food court at Old Port Royale.

WDW buses to attractions are inconvenient, overcrowded, and slow from this location.

Guests primarily interested in the Magic Kingdom will find the commute long and tedious.

TIPS: To select a room close to Old Port Royale, request Trinidad North, next door, or Jamaica, just across the bridge. For isolation, request Trinidad South, which has its own private beach and pool.

The rooms on the second floor afford the most privacy.

A rental car can speed commuting time considerably from this location.

MAKING RESERVATIONS: Call Walt Disney World Reservations (407 934-7639). Inquire about special promotional rates and vacation packages.

XX ATMOSPHERE. **XX** ATTITUDE. **XXX** FRESHNESS. **XX** VALUE.

DISNEY'S CARIBBEAN BEACH RESORT
A DISNEY-OWNED HOTEL
900 CAYMAN WAY, LAKE BUENA VISTA, FLORIDA 32830
TELEPHONE (407) 934-3400 • FAX (407) 934-3288

DISNEY'S CONTEMPORARY RESORT

LOCATION: Disney's Contemporary Resort is one of six hotels in the Magic Kingdom Resorts Area. It is conveniently located on the monorail line that serves the Magic Kingdom and Epcot Center, and has a long white sand beach that fronts Bay Lake.

AMBIENCE: The elongated pyramidal structure of this resort has maintained its futuristic look, although its fourth-floor common area, the Concourse, has an incongruous American Southwest motif. Its minimalist-style lobby on the first floor is strictly functional, with sparse but brightly colored angular furniture. Most lobby amenities are actually located on the Concourse level, where the monorail glides through the glass-and-steel atrium. Tower rooms have been recently redecorated in sophisticated neutrals, geometric-patterned fabrics, and streamlined furniture. The garden wing rooms are spacious but not redecorated, and the buildings are set at some distance from the lobby. All rooms have a balcony or patio.

RATES: Garden rooms **$$$$**. Tower rooms **$$$$**. Tower-room concierge suites **$$$$$$** (including Continental breakfast, afternoon wine and cheese, evening cordials, and special room amenities). Rates vary with the season.

AMENITIES: Twenty-four-hour room service, in-room safe (tower rooms), newspaper delivery, voice mail, and valet parking.

RESTAURANTS: *Top of the World* — Dinner shows nightly and Sunday brunch buffet.
Contemporary Cafe — Breakfast buffet and alternating international-themed dinner buffets nightly.
Concourse Grille — Breakfast, lunch, and dinner with an American Southwest theme.

RECREATION: Two pools, white sand beach, marina, tennis, volleyball, shuffleboard, jogging path, health club, sauna, whirlpool, fitness training, and massage.

WDW PUBLIC TRANSPORTATION: Walk to the Magic Kingdom. Monorail to the Magic Kingdom, the Transportation and Ticket Center (TTC), and Epcot Center. Water launch to Discovery Island, Fort Wilderness, and River Country. Bus to all other theme parks. Taxi service available.

FEATURES: In this most tennis-oriented of the WDW resorts, the Racquet Club offers practice courts and personal instruction. The resort also offers private shuttles to all golf courses.

DRAWBACKS: WDW buses to Disney-MGM Studios, Pleasure Island, or Typhoon Lagoon can be inconvenient or overcrowded. Guests using monorails to reach Epcot Center must change trains at the TTC.

TIPS: Tower rooms are the most popular, convenient, and expensive. Higher-floor rooms facing the Magic Kingdom have a view of the fireworks shows.

Garden rooms, although less expensive, are some distance from the lobby. However, those on the first floor facing Bay Lake are popular, because they have glass doors that open onto small patios.

MAKING RESERVATIONS: Call Walt Disney World Reservations (407 934-7639). Inquire about special promotional rates and vacation packages.

XX ATMOSPHERE. **XX** ATTITUDE. **XXX** FRESHNESS. **XX** VALUE.

DISNEY'S CONTEMPORARY RESORT
A DISNEY-OWNED HOTEL
4600 NORTH WORLD DRIVE, LAKE BUENA VISTA, FLORIDA 32830
TELEPHONE (407) 824-1000 • FAX (407) 824-3539

DISNEY'S DIXIE LANDINGS RESORT

LOCATION: Disney's Dixie Landings Resort is one of four hotels in the Disney Village Resorts Area. It is connected by carriage path and waterway to nearby Port Orleans resort and by waterway to Disney Village Marketplace and Pleasure Island.

AMBIENCE: The rustic bayous and antebellum mansions of the Old South are recreated at Dixie Landings. The large, sprawling resort has two sections. On one side is Alligator Bayou with its two-story Cajun-style brick or stucco lodges sporting wide front porches and rough-hewn railings, all set a in dense moss-hung pine forest. On the other side is Magnolia Bend, with an array of elegant three-story plantation manors set apart by fountains, sweeping lawns, and weeping willows. The Sassagoula River loops through the resort and in the center is the reception area, designed as a riverboat depot, circa 1880. The rooms in this limited-amenity resort are simply decorated in soft neutral colors; furnishings in the Bayou rooms are more rustic than the Magnolia rooms. All rooms have a vanity-dressing area with two pedestal sinks.

RATES: Standard rooms $$. Rates remain the same year round.

AMENITIES: Voice mail, pizza delivery to rooms, and refrigerator on request.

RESTAURANTS: *Boatwright's Dining Hall* — Breakfast and dinner featuring Cajun specialties.
Colonel's Cotton Mill — Food court with five counter-service restaurants for breakfast, lunch, and dinner, housed in an old cotton mill.

WDW PUBLIC TRANSPORTATION: Water launch or bus to Disney Village Marketplace and Pleasure Island. Bus to all theme parks, including the Magic Kingdom, Epcot Center, Disney-MGM Studios, and Typhoon Lagoon. To reach other destinations, bus to the Transportation and Ticket Center (TTC) or Disney Village Marketplace and connect to destination buses. Taxi service available.

RECREATION: Five pools, theme pool, marina, bicycling, jogging path, whirlpool, and fishing hole.

FEATURES: Conveniently located for guests interested in golfing at WDW.
Guests may rent their own boats and commute by water to Disney Village Marketplace, Pleasure Island, and other Disney Village Resorts.

DRAWBACKS: WDW buses to attractions can be inconvenient or overcrowded.
This budget-priced hotel is popular with young families, although the buildings are very spread out and offer a great deal of privacy.

TIPS: This limited-amenity resort offers an excellent value for the price. Upgrade to a river-view room and you'll have a luxury setting for a fraction of the cost of WDW's premier resorts.
The most popular locations are those close to the common areas and lobby. If you prefer a plantation manor, request a room in the Oak Manor; if you prefer a rustic setting, request lodge house No. 14.
A rental car can save a great deal of commuting time from this location.

MAKING RESERVATIONS: Call Walt Disney World Reservations (407 934-7639). Inquire about special promotional rates and vacation packages.

XXX ATMOSPHERE. **XXX** ATTITUDE. **XXXX** FRESHNESS. **XXXX** VALUE.

DISNEY'S DIXIE LANDINGS RESORT
A DISNEY-OWNED HOTEL
1251 DIXIE DRIVE, LAKE BUENA VISTA, FLORIDA 32830
TELEPHONE (407) 934-6000 • FAX (407) 934-5777

DISNEY'S FORT WILDERNESS RESORT AND CAMPGROUND

LOCATION: Disney's Fort Wilderness Resort and Campground is one of six hotels in the Magic Kingdom Resorts Area. It stretches from Vista Boulevard to the shores of Bay Lake.

AMBIENCE: This is not a hotel but a seven-hundred-acre, forested full-amenity campground. Here, guests may rent campsites for tents, hookups for recreational vehicles, or one of the resort's permanent fully appointed trailers. Fort Wilderness offers a natural setting to return to after a hectic day at the theme parks and is itself a Disney World attraction (see "Fort Wilderness & River Country," page 68).

RATES: Wilderness homes (one-bedroom trailer homes) **$$$**. Campsites with full hookups **$**. Campsites with partial hookups **$**. Rates vary with the season.

AMENITIES: Wilderness homes include kitchen, cable TV, voice mail, housekeeping services, and outdoor grill. Full-hookup campsites include sanitary disposal, water, cable TV, electricity, and outdoor grill. Partial-hookup campsites include water, electricity, and outdoor grill. All campsite loops have air-conditioned rest rooms, showers, ice makers, laundry facilities, and telephones.

RESTAURANTS: *Trail's End Buffeteria* — Cafeteria-style breakfast, lunch, and dinner with entertainment. *Crockett's Tavern* — Dinner featuring steak and seafood in a Wild West setting.

RECREATION: Pool, lap pool, white sand beach, marina, tennis, bicycling, volleyball, basketball, tetherball, shuffleboard, jogging path, nature trail, horseback riding, waterskiing, and fishing.

WDW PUBLIC TRANSPORTATION: Fort Wilderness has its own internal bus system to all campsites, Fort Wilderness attractions, and River Country (where there is no parking). Electric carts or bikes can also be rented for use within the resort. Water launch to the Magic Kingdom, Discovery Island, and the Contemporary resort. Bus from the Fort Wilderness Guest Parking Lot to the theme parks, or to the Transportation and Ticket Center (TTC) to transfer to destination buses or monorails.

FEATURES: Fort Wilderness offers several entertainment events daily including the Hoop-Dee-Doo Musical Revue dinner show, hayrides, movies, and the nightly Electrical Water Pageant.

Two on-site convenience stores, Settlement Trading Post and Meadow Trading Post, carry a limited supply of groceries, deli items, and sundries.

DRAWBACKS: WDW buses to attractions can be inconvenient or overcrowded.

TIPS: A car is essential at this location, especially during the summer rainy season. Guests may drive to and from their campsites to all WDW attractions.

The most popular Wilderness Home locations are on loops 2500 and 2700 near the swimming pool. The most popular campsites are on loop 400, near the marina and River Country.

MAKING RESERVATIONS: Call Walt Disney World Reservations (407 934-7639). Inquire about special promotional rates and vacation packages.

XXX ATMOSPHERE. **X** ATTITUDE. **XX** FRESHNESS. **XX** VALUE.

DISNEY'S FORT WILDERNESS RESORT AND CAMPGROUND
A DISNEY-OWNED HOTEL
3500 N. FORT WILDERNESS, LAKE BUENA VISTA, FLORIDA 32830
TELEPHONE (407) 824-2900 • FAX (407) 824-3508

DISNEY'S GRAND FLORIDIAN BEACH RESORT

LOCATION: Disney's Grand Floridian Beach Resort is one of six hotels in the Magic Kingdom Resorts Area. It is conveniently located on the monorail line that serves the Magic Kingdom and Epcot Center, and it has a white sand beach that fronts Seven Seas Lagoon.

AMBIENCE: The most elegant and expensive of the WDW resorts, this rambling, romantic Victorian-style hotel is fashioned after the grand seaside resorts of the 1890s. With its white banisters and railings, paned glass windows, peaked red-shingled roofs, and formal flower and shrub gardens, this resort is a favorite with honeymooners. Its spacious and luxurious stained glass–domed lobby has ornate wrought-iron elevators, potted trees, and clusters of intimately placed settees, where guests can enjoy the live music that is ongoing in the common areas. The guest rooms are handsomely decorated and each has a patio or balcony.

RATES: Standard rooms **$$$$**. Concierge rooms **$$$$$** (including Continental breakfast, afternoon snacks, evening wine and appetizers, and special room amenities). Rates vary with the season.

AMENITIES: Twenty-four-hour room service, mini bar, in-room safe, hair dryers, robes, newspaper delivery, voice mail, and valet parking.

RESTAURANTS: *Victoria & Albert's* — Elegant, award-winning candlelight dinner, prix-fixe menu.
Flagler's — Italian dinners with singing servers; breakfast buffet on weekends.
Narcoossee's — Lunch and dinner featuring steaks and Florida seafood on the waterfront.
1900 Park Fare — Buffet-style breakfast and dinner; Disney characters drop by.
Grand Floridian Cafe — Breakfast, lunch, and dinner featuring Florida-style cuisine.

RECREATION: Pool, white sand beach, marina, tennis, volleyball, jogging path, health club, sauna, steam room, whirlpool, fitness classes, fitness training, and massage.

WDW PUBLIC TRANSPORTATION: Monorail or water launch to the Magic Kingdom. Monorail to the Transportation and Ticket Center (TTC) and Epcot Center. Monorail or water launch to the Magic Kingdom to transfer to water launch to Discovery Island, Fort Wilderness, and River Country. Bus to Pleasure Island. Bus or monorail to the TTC to transfer to destination buses for all other theme parks. Taxi service available.

FEATURES: The resort offers shuttles to all golf courses and has the only clay tennis courts at WDW.
A very good high tea is served at 3 PM in the Garden View Lounge.

DRAWBACKS: WDW buses to Disney-MGM Studios, Pleasure Island, or Typhoon Lagoon can be inconvenient or overcrowded. Guests using monorails to reach Epcot Center must change trains at the TTC.

TIPS: While all the rooms are graciously appointed, the rooms on the upper floors are more private.
The lagoon-view rooms are the most popular, but the rooms overlooking the central courtyard help maintain the enchantment of the Victorian-themed architecture, especially at night.

MAKING RESERVATIONS: Call Walt Disney World Reservations (407 934-7639). Inquire about special promotional rates and vacation packages.

XXXX ATMOSPHERE. **XXXX** ATTITUDE. **XXXX** FRESHNESS. **XXX** VALUE.

DISNEY'S GRAND FLORIDIAN BEACH RESORT
A DISNEY-OWNED HOTEL
4401 FLORIDIAN WAY, LAKE BUENA VISTA, FLORIDA 32830
TELEPHONE (407) 824-3000 • FAX (407) 824-3186

DISNEY'S POLYNESIAN RESORT

LOCATION: Disney's Polynesian Resort is one of six hotels in the Magic Kingdom Resorts Area. It is conveniently located on the monorail line that serves the Magic Kingdom and Epcot Center, and it has a white sand beach that fronts Seven Seas Lagoon.

AMBIENCE: This aptly named resort, situated in an extensive tropical garden, features South Pacific lodge architecture. The hotel is a cluster of two- and three-story dark-beamed buildings scattered throughout the expertly landscaped grounds. The lobby entrance and atrium have a lush garden with a carp pond, parrots, bamboo, and blooming orchids. Guest rooms have ceiling fans and canopied beds and are decorated with batik and tapa-cloth prints in shades of green and brown. Most upper-floor rooms have balconies.

RATES: Standard rooms **$$$**. Royal Polynesian concierge-service rooms **$$$$** (including Continental breakfast, afternoon snacks, evening wine and appetizers, and special room amenities). Rates vary with the season.

AMENITIES: Room service, voice mail, and valet parking.

RESTAURANTS: *Papeete Bay Verandah* — A la carte and buffet Polynesian-style dinner and Sunday brunch. *Coral Isle Cafe* — Breakfast, lunch, and dinner featuring Polynesian and Asian selections. *Tangaroa Terrace* — A la carte and buffet Polynesia-themed breakfast.

RECREATION: Two pools, white sand beach, marina, volleyball, and jogging path.

WDW PUBLIC TRANSPORTATION: Monorail or water launch to the Magic Kingdom. Walk to the Transportation and Ticket Center (TTC) and monorail to Epcot Center or transfer to destination buses for all other theme parks. Monorail or water launch to the Magic Kingdom and transfer to the water launch to Discovery Island, Fort Wilderness, and River Country. Taxi service available.

FEATURES: The Polynesian Luau dinner show is held nightly at the resort's Luau Cove.

Carefully landscaped gardens with tropical plant specimens and torch lighting at night create an enchanting island atmosphere.

Windows in the resort's Tambu Lounge overlook the Seven Seas Lagoon and have good views of the nighttime Electric Water Pageant and the fireworks show over the Magic Kingdom.

DRAWBACKS: WDW buses to Disney-MGM Studios, Pleasure Island, or Typhoon Lagoon can be inconvenient or overcrowded. Guests using monorails to reach Epcot Center must change trains at the TTC.

This is a very popular hotel for families and can be heavily populated with children.

TIPS: The Polynesian resort creates a convincing ambience for a tropical-style vacation. The most popular rooms are those with views of the lagoon or the pools. To make the most of it, request one of the rooms farthest out, on the newest side of the hotel, facing the lagoon. Upper-floor rooms offer the most privacy.

MAKING RESERVATIONS: Call Walt Disney World Reservations (407 934-7639). Inquire about special promotional rates and vacation packages.

XXX ATMOSPHERE. **XX** ATTITUDE. **XX** FRESHNESS. **XXX** VALUE.

DISNEY'S POLYNESIAN RESORT
A DISNEY-OWNED HOTEL
1600 SOUTH SEAS DRIVE, LAKE BUENA VISTA, FLORIDA 32830
TELEPHONE (407) 824-2000 • FAX (407) 824-3174

DISNEY'S PORT ORLEANS RESORT

LOCATION: Disney's Port Orleans Resort is one of four hotels in the Disney Village Resorts Area. It is connected by carriage path and waterway to nearby Dixie Landings resort and by waterway to Disney Village Marketplace and Pleasure Island.

AMBIENCE: Port Orleans is designed to capture the atmosphere of the New Orleans's French Quarter preparing for Mardi Gras. Beyond the large steel-and-glass atrium lobby is a courtyard where a Dixieland band entertains guests. The resort is arranged in a complex grid of cobblestone streets with names like Rue D'Baga and Reveler's Row. The three-story row house–style buildings, some in red brick and others painted shades of ocher, peach, aqua, and French blue, mimic the diversity of New Orleans' architectural styles. Ornate wrought-iron railings, varying rooflines, louvered shutters, French doors, and small front-yard gardens all amplify the atmosphere. At night old-fashioned street lamps form atmospheric pools of light among the magnolia and willow trees. The rooms are simply decorated in soft neutral colors with ceiling fans. A small vanity area features two old-fashioned pedestal sinks.

RATES: Standard rooms **$$**. Rates remain the same year round.

AMENITIES: Voice mail, pizza delivery to rooms, and refrigerator upon request.

RESTAURANTS: *Bonfamille's Café* — Breakfast and dinner featuring Creole and American cuisine.
Sassagoula Floatworks and Food Factory — Mardi Gras–themed food court with four counter-service restaurants for breakfast, lunch, and dinner.

WDW PUBLIC TRANSPORTATION: Water launch or bus to Disney Village Marketplace and Pleasure Island. Bus to all theme parks, including the Magic Kingdom, Epcot Center, Disney-MGM Studios, and Typhoon Lagoon. To reach other destinations, bus to the Transportation and Ticket Center (TTC) or Disney Village Marketplace and connect to destination buses. Taxi service available.

RECREATION: Theme pool, marina, bicycling, croquet, jogging path, and whirlpool.

FEATURES: Guests may rent their own boats and commute by water to Disney Village Marketplace, Pleasure Island, and other Disney Village Resorts.
The resort is conveniently located for guests interested in golfing at WDW.

DRAWBACKS: This budget-priced hotel is oriented to young families, although the resort layout does have areas of privacy and quiet. The fantasy-themed pool scene is designed strictly for the young at heart.
WDW buses to attractions can be inconvenient or overcrowded.

TIPS: This limited-amenity resort offers an excellent value for the price. Upgrade to a top-floor river-view room and you'll have a luxury view for a fraction of the cost of WDW's premier resorts.
A rental car will save considerable commuting time from this location.

MAKING RESERVATIONS: Call Walt Disney World Reservations (407 934-7639). Inquire about special promotional rates and vacation packages.

XXX ATMOSPHERE. **XXX** ATTITUDE. **XXXX** FRESHNESS. **XXXX** VALUE.

DISNEY'S PORT ORLEANS RESORT
A DISNEY-OWNED HOTEL
2201 ORLEANS DRIVE, LAKE BUENA VISTA, FLORIDA 32830
TELEPHONE (407) 934-5000 • FAX (407) 934-5353

DISNEY'S VILLAGE RESORT

LOCATION: Disney's Village Resort is one of four hotels in the Disney Village Resorts Area. The resort is spread out across 250 acres of woodlands, waterways, and golf greens, and fronts Buena Vista Lagoon along with Disney Village Marketplace and Pleasure Island.

AMBIENCE: Disney's Village Resort is designed like a large country club and surrounds the fairways of the Lake Buena Vista Golf Course. The resort area is so spread out that guests are provided with an atlas to help them find their way. The dark brown villas are widely scattered along tree-lined lanes and in thickly forested glades. Some are quite isolated, overlooking the bayoulike waterways, while others are perched at the edge of the fairways. Floor plans vary and many units have skylights and lofts; the decor is standard, with an occasional rustic touch. A small lodge at the resort entrance serves as a lobby; the social center is Lake Buena Vista Clubhouse, where the restaurant and recreational facilities can be found.

RATES: Club suites $$$ (including refrigerator, microwave, and coffee maker). One- and two-bedroom villas $$$$. Two-bedroom treehouse villas $$$$$. Two- and three-bedroom grand vista homes $$$$$$. All villas have fully equipped kitchens. Rates vary with the season.

AMENITIES: Room service and voice mail.

RESTAURANTS: *Lake Buena Vista Restaurant* — Breakfast buffet, lunch, and dinner, and Sunday brunch overlooking the Buena Vista Lagoon.

WDW PUBLIC TRANSPORTATION: Walk, bus, water launch, or rent an electric cart to travel to Disney Village Marketplace and Pleasure Island. Bus to all theme parks, including the Magic Kingdom, Epcot Center, Disney-MGM Studios, and Typhoon Lagoon. To reach other destinations, connect with destination buses at Disney Village Marketplace. Taxi service available.

RECREATION: Six pools, nearby marina, bicycling, tennis, jogging path, health club, whirlpools, PGA golf course, putting green, driving range, and golf clinic with private lessons.

FEATURES: Disney's Village Resort is especially oriented to golfers, with its own eighteen-hole championship golf course, clubhouse, and pro shop.

The Gourmet Pantry at nearby Disney Village Marketplace has a delicatessen, a bakery, and a fair selection of groceries. Groceries may be ordered by phone and delivered to rooms free of charge.

Electric carts may be rented both for use within the resort and at Disney Village Marketplace.

DRAWBACKS: WDW buses to theme parks are very inconvenient to use from this resort.

TIPS: The interesting circular treehouse villas are ideal for larger groups, romantic getaways, or longer stays. Request a water view. The area that is within walking distance of Disney Village Marketplace is called the Vacation Villas area.

Although WDW buses operate within the resort, a rental car is essential at this location.

MAKING RESERVATIONS: Call Walt Disney World Reservations (407 934-7639). Inquire about special promotional rates and vacation packages.

XX ATMOSPHERE. **XX** ATTITUDE. **XX** FRESHNESS. **XX** VALUE.

DISNEY'S VILLAGE RESORT
A DISNEY-OWNED HOTEL
1901 BUENA VISTA DRIVE, LAKE BUENA VISTA, FLORIDA 32830
TELEPHONE (407) 827-1100 • FAX (407) 934-2741

DISNEY'S WILDERNESS LODGE

LOCATION: Disney's Wilderness Lodge is one of six hotels in the Magic Kingdom Resorts Area. It is located in the forest on the southwest shore of Bay Lake between Disney's Contemporary Resort and Fort Wilderness & River Country.

AMBIENCE: Designed by noted architect Peter Dominick, Jr., Disney's Wilderness Lodge was inspired by the U.S. National Park lodges built in the early 1900s. The six-story quarry-stone building is surrounded by forests and relies on heavy wooden beams and natural light to create a convincing lodge-retreat atmosphere. The spacious atrium lobby features unusual hanging lighting sculptures, a massive rock fireplace, and two gigantic totem poles from the coastal Northwest. A hot spring bubbles from the lobby to the outdoor areas, where it is transformed into a waterfall that cascades into the resort's rock-carved swimming pools and spas. The furnishings and decor have a rustic theme and feature Native American motifs of the Pacific Northwest.

RATES: Standard rooms **$$$**. Rates vary with the season.

AMENITIES: Room service, mini bar, hair dryer, in-room safe, voice mail, and valet parking.

RESTAURANTS: *Artist Point Dining Room* — Dinner featuring American cuisine and game such as buffalo and elk, in a setting highlighted by classic landscape paintings of the Pacific Northwest.

Whispering Canyon Cafe — Hearty family-style breakfast, lunch, and dinner in a setting accented by silhouette cutouts of cowboys at work.

Roaring Fork — All-day self-service dining and snacks in a rock-carved fishing lodge setting.

Territory Lounge — Cocktails and snacks in an ambience that honors the explorers and trappers who inspired the westward migration.

WDW PUBLIC TRANSPORTATION: Bus to the Transportation and Ticket Center (TTC) and transfer to monorails to Epcot Center and the Magic Kingdom. Water launch to the Magic Kingdom and Discovery Island. Walk or bus to Fort Wilderness and River Country. Bus to all other theme parks. Taxi service available.

RECREATION: Pool, hot and cold mineral pools, white sand beach, marina, bicycling, and jogging path.

FEATURES: The resort is adjacent to Fort Wilderness & River Country, providing numerous recreational options including nature trails, eight miles of bicycling paths, fishing and waterskiing excursions, tennis, volleyball, basketball, tetherball, shuffleboard, and horseback riding.

TIPS: Although more expensive than the standard rooms, the Bay Lake view rooms offer an unparalleled view of Walt Disney World's largest lake and Discovery Island.

Although the hotel is close to the monorail, a rental car in this location can be very convenient.

MAKING RESERVATIONS: Disney's Wilderness Lodge is scheduled to open in the early summer of 1994. Call Walt Disney World Reservations (407 934-7639). Inquire about special promotional rates and vacation packages.

DISNEY'S WILDERNESS LODGE
A DISNEY-OWNED HOTEL
P. O. BOX 10,000, LAKE BUENA VISTA, FLORIDA 32830
TELEPHONE (407) 824-2222

DISNEY'S YACHT CLUB RESORT

LOCATION: Disney's Yacht Club Resort is one of five hotels in the Epcot Resorts Area. It is located within walking distance of the International Gateway to the World Showcase at Epcot Center. It faces Storm-along Bay and shares a white sand beach and harbor waterfront with Disney's Beach Club Resort.

AMBIENCE: Designed by architect Robert Stern, the gray and white clapboard-sided Yacht Club has rope-slung boardwalks and a picturesque lighthouse along its waterfront. It has a decidedly nautical motif and shares resort amenities with the more casually decorated Beach Club, next door. The lobby has dark wood floors, polished brass details, and tufted leather couches — the feeling is sophisticated yet comfortable. Guest rooms, with their white furniture, old-fashioned armoires, ceiling fans, and large balconies have a pleasant, home-away-from-home feeling.

RATES: Standard rooms **$$$$**. Concierge rooms **$$$$$** (including Continental breakfast, afternoon snacks, evening wine and appetizers, and special room amenities). Rates vary with the season.

AMENITIES: Twenty-four-hour room service, mini bar, in-room safe, hair dryer, newspaper delivery, turn-down service, voice mail, and valet parking. In-room checkers and chess games available on request.

RESTAURANTS: *Yacht Club Galley* — Breakfast buffet or a la carte; lunch and dinner with emphasis on New England specialties.
Yachtsman Steakhouse — Dinner featuring prime-cut steaks and a small selection of seafood and poultry dishes.

WDW PUBLIC TRANSPORTATION: Walk or tram to the World Showcase at Epcot Center. Water launch to Disney-MGM Studios. Bus to the Magic Kingdom, Pleasure Island, Disney Village Marketplace, and Typhoon Lagoon. To reach other destinations, bus to the Transportation and Ticket Center (TTC) and connect to destination buses. Taxi service available.

RECREATION: Pool, white sand beach, mini water park, marina, tennis, volleyball, jogging path, bocce ball, croquet, health club, sauna, steam room, whirlpool, fitness classes, fitness training, and massage.

FEATURES: This full-amenity resort is conveniently located for guests primarily interested in Future World and the World Showcase at Epcot Center, and Disney-MGM Studios.
The Yacht Club's location between the Beach Club and the Dolphin hotel makes the amenities at either resort easily accessible.

DRAWBACKS: WDW buses to the Magic Kingdom may be infrequent or overcrowded.
Although the more-expensive lagoon-view rooms have water views, they can be noisy since Stormalong Bay water park is filled with children late into the night.

TIPS: Rooms surrounding the "quiet pool" are popular for their seclusion. Upper-floor standard rooms to either side of the entrance are a good value.

MAKING RESERVATIONS: Call Walt Disney World Reservations (407 934-7639). Inquire about special promotional rates and vacation packages.

XXXX ATMOSPHERE. **XXXX** ATTITUDE. **XXXX** FRESHNESS. **XXX** VALUE.

DISNEY'S YACHT CLUB RESORT
A DISNEY-OWNED HOTEL
1700 EPCOT RESORTS BOULEVARD, LAKE BUENA VISTA, FLORIDA 32830
TELEPHONE (407) 934-7000 • FAX (407) 934-3450

GROSVENOR RESORT

LOCATION: The Grosvenor Resort is one of seven independently owned Hotel Plaza Resorts at Disney Village. The hotel is located on Walt Disney World property, and guests enjoy most of the same transportation and reservations privileges as do guests at the Disney-owned hotels.

AMBIENCE: The resort's boxy exterior architecture belies the graceful interior of this high-rise hotel with its two low-rise garden wings. The decor is colonial British, and the dark green carpets, soft peach walls, and rattan furnishings give the spacious lobby a clubby, comfortable feel. Large square pillars hold up the lobby's arched ceiling, which is hung with understated chandeliers. The Grosvenor features its own Sherlock Holmes Museum and is frequented by European travelers.

RATES: Standard rooms **$$**. Rates vary with the season.

AMENITIES: Room service, refrigerator (unstocked), in-room safe, VCR, videocassette library, video camera rentals, and valet parking.

RESTAURANTS: *Baskervilles Restaurant* — British-themed dining room serving a la carte lunch and buffet dinners featuring all-you-can-eat prime rib.
Crumpets Cafe — Lobby deli market for light snacks; open twenty-four hours daily.

WDW PUBLIC TRANSPORTATION: Bus or walk to Disney Village Marketplace, Pleasure Island, and Lake Buena Vista Golf Course. Bus to all other attractions. Taxi service available.

RECREATION: Two pools, tennis, volleyball, basketball, handball, shuffleboard, whirlpool, and massage.

FEATURES: In-room VCRs allow guests to relax in the afternoons with movies from the hotel's video library or their own videos taken during the day.

On Saturday nights, the Grosvenor presents MurderWatch Mystery Dinner Theater, a very popular dinner show in which guests solve a murder mystery staged by professional actors.

Hotel guests may use nearby Disney World recreation facilities, including the Disney Village Marketplace Marina, and the jogging paths, health club, and golfing facilities at Disney's Village Resort.

DRAWBACKS: Guests relying on WDW buses to reach attractions may find them inconvenient.

TIPS: The garden-wing rooms have private balconies; tower rooms do not, but the higher floors offer sweeping views. The garden-wing rooms with a pool view (odd-numbered rooms) are the most popular.

The Grosvenor offers discounts to members of several travel clubs, including the American Automobile Association and the American Association of Retired Persons.

The Grosvenor offers a vacation package that includes accommodations, daily breakfast, WDW admission, and other amenities. For a brochure, call the resort's toll-free number (800 624-4109).

A rental car can save considerable commuting time from this location.

MAKING RESERVATIONS: First call Best Western central reservations (800 528-1234), then call the hotel directly and compare rates (800 624-4109). Inquire about promotional rates, corporate rates, and senior discounts. Reservations may also be made through Walt Disney World Reservations (407 934-7639).

XX ATMOSPHERE. **XXX** ATTITUDE. **XX** FRESHNESS. **XXXX** VALUE.

GROSVENOR RESORT
A BEST WESTERN HOTEL
1850 HOTEL PLAZA BOULEVARD, LAKE BUENA VISTA, FLORIDA 32830
TELEPHONE (407) 828-4444 • FAX (407) 828-8120

GUEST QUARTERS SUITE RESORT

LOCATION: The Guest Quarters Suite Resort is one of seven independently owned Hotel Plaza Resorts at Disney Village. The hotel is located on Walt Disney World property, and guests enjoy most of the same transportation and reservations privileges as do guests at the Disney-owned hotels.

AMBIENCE: The mirror-glassed hotel is a contemporary, quasi-pyramidal, seven-story beige-stuccoed building with blue awnings all along the ground floor. Its small lobby, decorated with Disney posters and light marble tiles, features an indoor atrium with a huge, verdigris-finished bird cage stocked with small birds. The guest suites are generously proportioned and simply furnished in shades of peach and green, and feature separate bedrooms and a mini-kitchen area.

RATES: One-bedroom suites **$$**. Two-bedroom suites **$$$$**. Rates remain the same year round.

AMENITIES: Room service, refrigerator (unstocked), in-room coffee maker, hair dryer, and three televisions (two color, one black and white) in each suite. Microwave on request.

RESTAURANTS: *Parrot Patch* — Large family-style restaurant for breakfast, lunch, and dinner.

WDW PUBLIC TRANSPORTATION: Bus or walk to Disney Village Marketplace, Pleasure Island, and Lake Buena Vista Golf Course. Bus to all other attractions. Taxi service available.

RECREATION: Pool, tennis, fitness room, and whirlpool.

FEATURES: Guest Quarters offers a good value for a suite at WDW. Each suite has a spacious living room that includes a dining area and limited kitchen facilities. Grocery stores are located nearby.

Guest Quarters has a very pleasant pool area with fountains and a congenial poolside bar environment. The pool's free-form shape is large enough for swimming laps.

Resort guests may take advantage of nearby Disney World recreational facilities, including the Disney Village Marketplace Marina and the jogging paths and golfing facilities at Disney's Village Resort.

DRAWBACKS: Guests relying on WDW buses to reach attractions may find them inconvenient or overcrowded.

TIPS: Rooms with a pool view are especially pleasant. Ground-floor rooms have sliding glass doors that open onto small open patios. Disney-view rooms are the most frequently requested.

Guest Quarters offers discounts to members of several travel clubs, including the American Automobile Association, the American Association of Retired Persons, and Orlando Magicard.

The hotel offers vacation packages that include accommodations, WDW admission, and other amenities. To receive a brochure, call the hotel directly (407 934-1000).

A rental car can save considerable commuting time from this location.

MAKING RESERVATIONS: First call Guest Quarters central reservations (800 424-2900), then call the hotel directly and compare rates (407 934-1000). Inquire about special promotional rates, corporate rates, and senior discounts. Reservations may also be made through Walt Disney World Reservations (407 934-7639).

XX ATMOSPHERE. **X** ATTITUDE. **XXX** FRESHNESS. **XXX** VALUE.

GUEST QUARTERS SUITE RESORT
GUEST QUARTERS SUITE HOTELS, INC.
2305 HOTEL PLAZA BOULEVARD, LAKE BUENA VISTA, FLORIDA 32830
TELEPHONE (407) 934-1000 • FAX (407) 934-1011

THE HILTON RESORT

LOCATION: The Hilton Resort is one of seven independently owned Hotel Plaza Resorts at Disney Village. The hotel is located on Walt Disney World property, across from Disney Village Marketplace. Guests enjoy most of the same transportation and reservations privileges as do guests at the Disney-owned hotels.

AMBIENCE: This hotel, one of the largest in the Hotel Plaza area, is a sprawling, medium high-rise with wings angling off to each side of the central structure. It is situated on acres of open land, with a duck pond and fountains in front. The angular lobby, has muted tropical decor, with brass-railed staircases, pink conch-shell wall sconces, and a long, rose-colored marble reception desk. The guest rooms are pleasantly decorated with aqua, peach, and green accents and peach and rose floral bedspreads. The hotel caters to business travelers and seminar attendees.

RATES: Standard rooms $$$. Tower concierge rooms $$$$ (including Continental breakfast; all-day snacks, no-host cocktails and appetizers; evening tea, coffee, and petits fours; and special room amenities). Rates vary with the season.

AMENITIES: Room service, mini bar, voice mail, pay-per-view movies, and valet parking.

RESTAURANTS: *American Vineyards* — Dinner featuring regional American cuisine and wines.
 Country Fair Restaurant — Breakfast, lunch, and dinner buffet-style or full service, indoors or on the terrace.
 Benihana's — Steak or seafood dinners grilled by Japanese teppan chefs at communal tables.

WDW PUBLIC TRANSPORTATION: Bus or walk to Disney Village Marketplace, Pleasure Island, and Lake Buena Vista Golf Course. Bus to all other attractions. Taxi service available.

RECREATION: Two pools, tennis, health club, sauna, and whirlpools.

FEATURES: Hilton Honors members can earn points and upgrade rooms.
 Hotel guests may take advantage of nearby Disney World recreational facilities, including the Disney Village Marketplace Marina and the jogging paths and golfing facilities at Disney's Village Resort.

DRAWBACKS: Guests relying on WDW buses to reach attractions may find them inconvenient.

TIPS: Almost all rooms have nice views, but the most popular rooms are those with views of the pool or of Walt Disney World and the evening fireworks show at Pleasure Island.
 The Hilton offers vacation packages that include accommodations, daily breakfast, WDW admission, and other amenities. To receive a brochure, call the resort's toll-free number (800 782-4414).
 The Hilton offers discounts to members of the American Automobile Association.
 A rental car can save considerable commuting time from this location.

MAKING RESERVATIONS: First call Hilton central reservations (800 445-8667), then call the hotel's toll-free number (800 782-4414) to compare rates. Inquire about promotional rates, corporate rates, and senior discounts. Reservations may also be made through Walt Disney World Reservations (407 934-7639).

✗✗ ATMOSPHERE. **✗** ATTITUDE. **✗✗✗** FRESHNESS. **✗✗** VALUE.

THE HILTON RESORT
A HILTON HOTEL
1751 HOTEL PLAZA BOULEVARD, LAKE BUENA VISTA, FLORIDA 32830
TELEPHONE (407) 827-4000 • FAX (407) 827-6369

HOTEL ROYAL PLAZA

LOCATION: Hotel Royal Plaza is one of seven independently owned Hotel Plaza Resorts at Disney Village. The hotel is located on Walt Disney World property, and guests enjoy most of the same transportation and reservations privileges as do guests at the Disney-owned hotels.

AMBIENCE: Metallic gold windows and balconies accent this white masonry high-rise hotel with its garden wing. The lobby is sparse and straightforward, with rattan furniture and sea-foam green carpets. Despite a recent partial remodeling, the hotel still has a down-at-the-heels feeling to it, although it is slated for a major modernization incorporating a Bermuda–style design inside and out. Guest rooms are modestly sized and simply furnished, with flame-stitched blue and ocher bedspreads and neutral walls. Each tower room has its own small half moon–shaped balcony, offering sweeping views of Walt Disney World.

RATES: Standard rooms $$. Celebrity Signature Suites $$$$$$ (including a fully stocked kitchen, stereo, sauna, and Jacuzzi). Rates vary with the season.

AMENITIES: Room service, mini bar, in-room safe, VCR, videocassette library, and video camera rentals.

RESTAURANTS: *The Plaza Diner* — Breakfast, lunch, and dinner; open twenty-four hours daily.

WDW PUBLIC TRANSPORTATION: Bus or walk to Disney Village Marketplace, Pleasure Island, and Lake Buena Vista Golf Course. Bus to all other attractions. Taxi service available.

RECREATION: Pool, tennis, shuffleboard, sauna, tanning salon, and whirlpool.

FEATURES: Giraffe, the hotel's late-night dance club, has a live DJ and a happy hour with complimentary snacks.

Hotel Royal Plaza boasts three Celebrity Signature Suites, specially designed for Burt Reynolds, Barbara Mandrell, and Michael Jackson. Each includes custom decor and personal memorabilia.

Hotel guests may take advantage of nearby Disney World recreational facilities, including the Disney Village Marketplace Marina and the jogging paths and golfing facilities at Disney's Village Resort.

DRAWBACKS: Guests relying on WDW buses to reach attractions may find them inconvenient.

TIPS: The most popular rooms are those on the higher floors, with views of Walt Disney World and the evening fireworks show at Pleasure Island. Also popular are the ground-floor poolside lanai rooms.

Hotel Royal Plaza offers discounts to members of many travel clubs, including the American Automobile Association, Encore, Quest, the American Association of Retired Persons, Entertainment Publications, and Orlando Magicard.

The Royal Plaza offers several vacation packages that include accommodations, breakfast daily, WDW admission, and other amenities. To receive a brochure, call the hotel directly (407 828-2828).

A rental car can save considerable commuting time from this location.

MAKING RESERVATIONS: Call Hotel Royal Plaza's toll-free number (800 248-7890) and inquire about special promotional rates, corporate rates, and senior discounts. Reservations may also be made through Walt Disney World Reservations (407 934-7639).

✗ ATMOSPHERE. ✗ ATTITUDE. ✗ FRESHNESS. ✗ VALUE.

HOTEL ROYAL PLAZA
A PRIVATELY OWNED HOTEL
1905 HOTEL PLAZA BOULEVARD, LAKE BUENA VISTA, FLORIDA 32830
TELEPHONE (407) 828-2828 • FAX (407) 827-3977

HOWARD JOHNSON RESORT HOTEL

LOCATION: Howard Johnson Resort Hotel is one of seven independently owned Hotel Plaza Resorts at Disney Village. The hotel is located on Walt Disney World property, and guests enjoy most of the same transportation and reservations privileges as do guests at the Disney-owned hotels.

AMBIENCE: This high-rise hotel has a modern white-stuccoed exterior, with traditional terra-cotta mission tiles on the roof. Inside, the narrow fourteen-story atrium lobby has an indoor reflecting pool and glass elevators. It is furnished to evoke a cool Caribbean mood, and beneath the atrium stands a free-form, open-sided, tent-roofed lobby lounge. Despite the atrium, the lobby has a motel feel about it. The turquoise, coral, and sand colored guest rooms have unexceptional hotel-style furnishings with tropical accents. All rooms have balconies, many with views of Disney World.

RATES: Standard rooms $. Rates vary with the season.

AMENITIES: Room service, mini bar, in-room safe, coffee maker, VCR, and videocassette library.

RESTAURANTS: *Howard Johnson Restaurant* — Breakfast, lunch, and dinner, featuring Howard Johnson's specialties.

WDW PUBLIC TRANSPORTATION: Bus or walk to Disney Village Marketplace, Pleasure Island, and Lake Buena Vista Golf Course. Bus to all other attractions. Taxi service available.

RECREATION: Two pools, fitness room, and whirlpool.

FEATURES: Hotel guests may take advantage of nearby Disney World recreational facilities, including the Disney Village Marketplace Marina and jogging, tennis, and golfing at Disney's Village Resort.

In-room VCRs allow guests to relax in the afternoon with movies available from the hotel's videocassette library, or their own videos taken during the day.

DRAWBACKS: Guests relying on WDW buses to reach attractions may find them inconvenient.

TIPS: Higher floors offer sweeping views. Request a room with a view of Pleasure Island, with its nightly New Year's Eve fireworks display.

Howard Johnson hotels offer discounts to members of many travel clubs, including the American Automobile Association, Entertainment Publications, Encore, Quest, the American Association of Retired Persons, Great American Traveler, See America, Travel World Leisure Club, and Orlando Magicard.

Howard Johnson Resort Hotel offers vacation packages that include accommodations, WDW admission, some meals, and other amenities. To receive a brochure, call the hotel toll-free number directly (800 223-9930).

A rental car can save considerable commuting time from this location.

MAKING RESERVATIONS: First call Howard Johnson central reservations (800 654-2000), then call the hotel toll-free number directly and compare rates (800 223-9930). Inquire about special promotional rates, corporate rates, and senior discounts. Reservations may also be made through Walt Disney World Reservations (407 934-7639).

✗ ATMOSPHERE. ✗✗ ATTITUDE. ✗ FRESHNESS. ✗✗ VALUE.

HOWARD JOHNSON RESORT HOTEL
A HOWARD JOHNSON HOTEL
1805 HOTEL PLAZA BOULEVARD, LAKE BUENA VISTA, FLORIDA 32830
TELEPHONE (407) 828-8888 • FAX (407) 827-4623

TRAVELODGE HOTEL

LOCATION: Travelodge Hotel is one of seven independently owned Hotel Plaza Resorts at Disney Village. The hotel is located on Walt Disney World property, and guests enjoy most of the same transportation and reservations privileges as do guests at the Disney-owned hotels.

AMBIENCE: The interior theme of this single-tower high-rise hotel is vaguely Caribbean, with rattan furniture, green faux-marble pillars, and a huge bird cage holding two desultory-looking lovebirds. In the center of the round lobby, a circular staircase leads up to the meeting rooms on the mezzanine level. The guest rooms are serene and pleasantly decorated, and all rooms have balconies, many with impressive views, especially on the the higher floors. The grounds are artfully landscaped with tropical foliage.

RATES: Standard rooms **$$**. Rates vary with the season.

AMENITIES: Room service, mini bar, in-room safe, hair dryers, coffee maker, newspaper delivery, and pay-per-view movies.

RESTAURANTS: *Traders Restaurant* — Breakfast and dinner, a la carte or buffet, indoors or on the terrace. *Parakeet Cafe* — Lobby deli serving light meals all day.

WDW PUBLIC TRANSPORTATION: Bus or walk to Disney Village Marketplace, Pleasure Island, and Lake Buena Vista Golf Course. Bus to all other attractions. Taxi service available.

RECREATION: Pool.

FEATURES: Toppers night club on the eighteenth floor offers dance music until 2 AM and has sweeping views of Walt Disney World and the evening fireworks shows. The club is popular with Disney employees.
Members of Travelodge Business Break Club and Classic Travel Club (for seniors) receive room and rental car discounts and additional amenities.
Hotel guests may take advantage of nearby Walt Disney World recreation facilities, including the Disney Village Marketplace Marina, and jogging, tennis, and golfing at Disney's Village Resort.

DRAWBACKS: Guests relying on WDW buses to reach attractions may find them inconvenient.
Guests looking for the recreational features of a full-scale resort will be disappointed here.

TIPS: For the best room location, request a high floor with a Walt Disney World view.
Travelodge offers a selection of vacation packages that include accommodations, WDW admission, some meals, and other amenities. To receive a brochure, call the hotel directly (800 348-3765).
Travelodge offers discounts to members of several travel clubs, including the American Automobile Association, Entertainment Publications, and the American Association of Retired Persons.
A rental car can save considerable commuting time from this location.

MAKING RESERVATIONS: First call Travelodge Hotels central reservations (800 255-3050), then call the hotel toll-free number directly and compare rates (800 348-3765). Inquire about special promotional rates, corporate rates, and senior discounts. Reservations may also be made through Walt Disney World Reservations (407 934-7639).

✗ ATMOSPHERE. ✗✗ ATTITUDE. ✗✗ FRESHNESS. ✗✗✗ VALUE.

TRAVELODGE HOTEL
TRUSTHOUSE FORTE HOTELS, INC.
2000 HOTEL PLAZA BOULEVARD, LAKE BUENA VISTA, FLORIDA 32830
TELEPHONE (407) 828-2424 • FAX (407) 828-8933

WALT DISNEY WORLD DOLPHIN

LOCATION: The Dolphin is one of five Epcot Resorts. It is located a short distance from the International Gateway to the World Showcase at Epcot Center. It faces Crescent Lake and shares a waterfront plaza and white sand beach with the Swan hotel.

AMBIENCE: Designed by architect Michael Graves, this strikingly colored postmodern high-rise hotel features a fanciful multistory fountain cascading into a giant clam shell. The lobby is a larger-than-life striped circus tent with a dolphin-motif fountain and islands of wicker seating. Guest rooms are entertainingly detailed with cabana-striped bedspreads and painted tropical headboards.

RATES: Standard rooms $$$$. Dolphin Towers concierge rooms $$$$$ (including Continental breakfast, evening cocktails and appetizers, and special room amenities). Rates vary with the season.

AMENITIES: Twenty-four-hour room service, mini bar, in-room safe, turndown service, newspaper delivery, voice mail, pay-per-view movies, and valet parking.

RESTAURANTS: *Ristorante Carnevale* — Dinner and Sunday brunch featuring Italian specialties.
Sum Chow's — Elegant dinner with innovative Chinese nouvelle cuisine.
Harry's Safari Bar & Grille — Dinner featuring grilled steaks and seafood in a Congo-adventure setting.
Coral Cafe — All-day dining and breakfast and dinner buffets.
Tubbi Checkers Buffeteria — Twenty-four-hour family-oriented cafeteria and market.

WDW PUBLIC TRANSPORTATION: Tram to the World Showcase at Epcot Center. Water launch to Disney-MGM Studios. Bus to the Magic Kingdom, Pleasure Island, Disney Village Marketplace, and Typhoon Lagoon. To reach other destinations, bus to the Transportation and Ticket Center (TTC) and connect to destination buses. Taxi service available.

RECREATION: Pool, grotto pool, small beach, marina, tennis, volleyball, jogging path, health club, sauna, steam room, whirlpool, fitness classes, fitness training, and massage.

FEATURES: Members of the ITT Sheraton Club earn points and may upgrade rooms.
Conveniently located for guests primarily interested in Epcot Center and Disney-MGM Studios.
The Body by Jake Health Studio on premises is one of the best at Walt Disney World.

DRAWBACKS: WDW buses to the Magic Kingdom can be infrequent or overcrowded.

TIPS: The Dolphin offers several vacation packages that include accommodations, WDW admission, some meals, car rental, and other amenities. To receive a brochure, call the hotel directly (800 227-1500).
The most popular room locations are those with a view of IllumiNations and the pool-view rooms.

MAKING RESERVATIONS: First call Sheraton central reservations (800 325-3535), then call the hotel toll-free number directly and compare rates (800 227-1500). Inquire about special promotional rates, corporate rates, and senior discounts. Reservations may also be made through Walt Disney World Reservations (407 934-7639).

XXX ATMOSPHERE. **XX** ATTITUDE. **XXXX** FRESHNESS. **XX** VALUE.

WALT DISNEY WORLD DOLPHIN
A SHERATON HOTEL
1500 EPCOT RESORT BOULEVARD, LAKE BUENA VISTA, FLORIDA 32830
TELEPHONE (407) 934-4000 • FAX (407) 934-4099

WALT DISNEY WORLD SWAN

LOCATION: The Swan is one of five Epcot Resorts. It is located a short distance from the International Gateway to the World Showcase at Epcot Center. It faces Crescent Lake and shares a waterfront plaza and white sand beach with the Dolphin hotel.

AMBIENCE: This contemporary high-rise hotel, designed by noted architect Michael Graves, is a standout example of entertainment architecture. The Swan's water-fantasy theme is expressed in soft shades of turquoise and coral, which extend to the guest rooms decorated with a pineapple motif. The large lobby is divided into smaller alcoves, giving an impression of privacy and sophistication. The Swan houses an extensive convention center and caters to business travelers and seminar attendees, rather than families.

RATES: Standard rooms **$$$$**. Royal Beach Club concierge rooms **$$$$$** (including Continental breakfast, complimentary open bar, evening appetizers, and special room amenities). Rates vary with the season.

AMENITIES: Twenty-four-hour room service, mini bar, in-room safe, turndown service, bathrobes, newspaper delivery, voice mail, pay-per-view movies, and valet parking.

RESTAURANTS: *Palio* — Dinner with light entertainment in an Italian bistro.
Garden Grove Cafe — Breakfast and dinner buffets and all-day dining, emphasizing Florida seafood.
Splash Grill & Deli — Breakfast buffet and all-day light meals.

WDW PUBLIC TRANSPORTATION: Tram to the World Showcase at Epcot Center. Water launch to Disney-MGM Studios. Bus to the Magic Kingdom, Pleasure Island, Disney Village Marketplace, and Typhoon Lagoon. To reach other destinations, bus to the Transportation and Ticket Center (TTC) and connect to destination buses. Taxi service available.

RECREATION: Lap pool, small beach, marina, tennis, jogging path, health club, sauna, whirlpool, and massage.

FEATURES: The resort is conveniently located for guests who are primarily interested in Epcot Center and Disney-MGM Studios.
Westin Premier members earn points and may upgrade rooms.

DRAWBACKS: WDW buses to the Magic Kingdom can be infrequent or overcrowded.

TIPS: The Swan offers a selection of resort packages that include accommodations, WDW admission, some meals, and other amenities. Some packages include car rental. To receive a brochure, call the hotel and ask for the resort-package desk (407 934-3000).
For a good room value, request a standard resort room with a balcony, facing the pool.

MAKING RESERVATIONS: First call Westin central reservations (800 228-3000), then call the hotel directly and compare rates (407 934-3000). Inquire about special promotional rates, corporate rates, and senior discounts. Reservations may also be made through Walt Disney World Reservations (407 934-7639).

XXX ATMOSPHERE. **XX** ATTITUDE. **XXXX** FRESHNESS. **XX** VALUE.

WALT DISNEY WORLD SWAN
A WESTIN HOTEL
1200 EPCOT RESORT BOULEVARD, LAKE BUENA VISTA, FLORIDA 32830
TELEPHONE (407) 934-3000 • FAX (407) 934-4499

RESTAURANTS

Walt Disney World is one of the few places where guests can arrive at an elegant restaurant in tee-shirts, shorts, and tennis shoes and be treated like dignitaries; most theme park restaurants do not expect guests to return to their hotel rooms to change before dinner. The only exception to this casual dress code is at the better resort restaurants and the Empress Room at Pleasure Island, where guests tend to dress up.

THEME PARK DINING

There are hundreds of restaurants, fast-food counters, and food vendors throughout the theme parks for on-the-go visitors. The full-service theme park restaurants, however, are designed to be an extension of the Walt Disney World experience. The unique dining atmospheres are created with great attention to detail, and the service is competent and courteous. The food may not be up to epicurean standards overall, but most visitors will enjoy pleasant dining experiences here. Alcohol is served in all theme park restaurants except those in the Magic Kingdom, and a few of the restaurants have extensive wine lists. Smoking is prohibited in theme park restaurants, except where noted in the restaurant reviews. Most of the menus offer low-fat selections, and many indicate "Healthy Choices" next to listings. Vegetarians will find a selection of salads and vegetable, pasta, and seafood entrees on most menus. Kosher, vegan, or other special meals at the theme park restaurants can be requested when reservations are made, or twenty-four hours in advance through Special Activities (560-6233).

PRICES: The prices at Walt Disney World restaurants tend to be high. Entrees average $9 to $15 for lunch and $16 to $23 for dinner. Each restaurant review includes a section indicating the average price range for entrees as follows:

$ – under $8
$$ – $9 to $15
$$$ – $16 to $23
$$$$ – $24 to $33
$$$$$ – over $34

RESERVATIONS FOR WALT DISNEY WORLD RESORT GUESTS: Most full-service restaurants at the theme parks accept reservations and are usually booked early, especially during peak seasons. Guests staying at a Walt Disney World resort can make restaurant reservations three days in advance at the major theme parks by calling Theme Park Restaurant Reservations (407 824-8800). Guests may also make advance reservations through Guest Services at their resort. The restaurants at Pleasure Island and Disney Village Marketplace accept reservations up to thirty days in advance through Village Restaurant Reservations (407 828-3900). If the restaurant is already booked, Guest Services at your resort may be able to place you on a waiting list or suggest acceptable alternatives.

RESERVATIONS FOR DAY VISITORS: The theme park restaurants accept only same-day bookings from day visitors who are not staying at a WDW resort. Some strategy is required to book seating in the major theme parks' restaurants and, in every case, it is necessary to arrive at the park before it officially opens.

WALT DISNEY WORLD DINING

✦ **EPCOT CENTER RESTAURANTS:** *Same-Day Reservations* — When the park opens, head quickly to Earth Station and use the WorldKey Information Service system to make your reservation. If you are entering through the International Gateway, use the WorldKey Information Service kiosks near the World Showcase Plaza or at the Germany pavilion.

✦ **DISNEY-MGM STUDIOS RESTAURANTS:** *Same-Day Reservations* — When the park opens, go directly to the Restaurant Reservation Desk, located at the end of Hollywood Boulevard.

✦ **MAGIC KINGDOM RESTAURANTS:** *Same-Day Reservations* — When the park opens, proceed directly to the restaurant of your choice. At the Magic Kingdom, dining reservations are taken at the door.

✦ **PLEASURE ISLAND AND DISNEY VILLAGE MARKETPLACE RESTAURANTS:** Any visitor to WDW can make dining reservations up to thirty days in advance through Village Restaurant Reservations (407 828-3900). Reservations at the Fireworks Factory may be made by calling 407 934-8989.

✦ **IF THE RESTAURANT IS ALREADY BOOKED:** Make backup reservations, then proceed to the restaurant of your choice and ask the host or hostess if seatings are available (some restaurants hold tables for walk-ins), or ask if you may put your name on a waiting list in the event of no-shows or a cancellation.

GUIDE TO LOCATION AND CUISINE AT
WALT DISNEY WORLD'S FULL-SERVICE RESTAURANTS

The guide below lists the full-service restaurants both by location and by the type of cuisine served. Restaurants highlighted with a star have sophisticated atmospheres or intimate settings, or they are especially conducive to relaxing between the whirlwind of attractions.

WORLD SHOWCASE AT EPCOT

AU PETIT CAFÉ
BIERGARTEN
BISTRO DE PARIS ★
CHEFS DE FRANCE ★
LE CELLIER
L'ORIGINALE ALFREDO DI ROMA RISTORANTE ★
NINE DRAGONS RESTAURANT ★
RESTAURANT AKERSHUS
RESTAURANT MARRAKESH ★
ROSE & CROWN DINING ROOM ★
SAN ANGEL INN RESTAURANTE ★
TEMPURA KIKU
TEPPANYAKI DINING

FUTURE WORLD AT EPCOT

CORAL REEF RESTAURANT ★
THE LAND GRILLE ROOM ★

DISNEY-MGM STUDIOS

50'S PRIME TIME CAFE
THE HOLLYWOOD BROWN DERBY ★
HOLLYWOOD & VINE CAFETERIA
MAMA MELROSE'S RISTORANTE ITALIANO ★
SCI-FI DRIVE-IN DINER

MAGIC KINGDOM

THE CRYSTAL PALACE
KING STEFAN'S BANQUET HALL ★
LIBERTY TREE TAVERN
THE PLAZA RESTAURANT
TONY'S TOWN SQUARE RESTAURANT ★

DISNEY VILLAGE MARKETPLACE

EMPRESS ROOM ★
CAP'N JACK'S OYSTER BAR ★
CHEF MICKEY'S VILLAGE RESTAURANT
FISHERMAN'S DECK ★
STEERMAN'S QUARTERS ★

PLEASURE ISLAND

EMPRESS ROOM ★
THE FIREWORKS FACTORY
FISHERMAN'S DECK ★
PORTOBELLO YACHT CLUB ★
STEERMAN'S QUARTERS ★

FORT WILDERNESS

CROCKETT'S TAVERN
TRAIL'S END BUFFETERIA

WALT DISNEY WORLD DINING

WDW RESORT RESTAURANTS

American Vineyards ★
Ariel's ★
Arthur's 27 ★
Baskervilles
Boatwright's Dining Hall
Bonfamille's Cafe
Cape May Cafe
Flagler's ★
Harry's Safari Bar & Grille ★
Lake Buena Vista Restaurant ★
Narcoossee's ★
Outback ★
Palio ★
Papeete Bay Verandah
Ristorante Carnevale ★
Sum Chow's ★
Victoria & Albert's ★
Yachtsman Steakhouse ★

AMERICAN

Baskervilles
Chef Mickey's Village Restaurant
Crockett's Tavern
The Crystal Palace
50's Prime Time Cafe
The Fireworks Factory
The Hollywood Brown Derby ★
Hollywood & Vine Cafeteria
King Stefan's Banquet Hall ★
Lake Buena Vista Restaurant ★
The Land Grille Room ★
Liberty Tree Tavern
The Plaza Restaurant
Sci-Fi Drive-In Diner
Trail's End Buffeteria

CONTINENTAL

American Vineyards ★
Arthur's 27 ★
Empress Room ★
Victoria & Albert's ★

SEAFOOD

Ariel's ★
Cape May Cafe
Cap'n Jack's Oyster Bar ★
Coral Reef Restaurant ★
Fisherman's Deck ★
Harry's Safari Bar & Grille ★
Narcoossee's ★
Outback ★

STEAK & PRIME RIB

Baskervilles
Crockett's Tavern
Harry's Safari Bar & Grille ★
Narcoossee's ★
Outback ★
Steerman's Quarters ★
Yachtsman Steakhouse ★

CAJUN, CREOLE, & BARBECUE

Boatwright's Dining Hall
Bonfamille's Cafe
The Fireworks Factory

ITALIAN

Flagler's ★
L'Originale Alfredo di Roma Ristorante ★
Mama Melrose's Ristorante Italiano ★
Palio ★
Portobello Yacht Club ★
Ristorante Carnevale ★
Tony's Town Square Restaurant ★

FRENCH

Au Petit Café
Bistro de Paris ★
Chefs de France ★

JAPANESE

Tempura Kiku
Teppanyaki Dining

INTERNATIONAL

Biergarten (German)
Le Cellier (Canadian)
Nine Dragons Restaurant (Chinese) ★
Papeete Bay Verandah (Polynesian)
Restaurant Akershus (Norwegian)
Restaurant Marrakesh (Moroccan) ★
Rose & Crown Dining Room (British) ★
San Angel Inn Restaurante (Mexican) ★
Sum Chows (Asian) ★

CAFETERIAS & BUFFETS

Baskervilles
Cape May Cafe
Le Cellier
The Crystal Palace
Hollywood & Vine Cafeteria
Restaurant Akershus
Trail's End Buffeteria

AU PETIT CAFÉ

FOOD: Au Petit Café serves light French-style a la carte dishes including crepes, quiches, sandwiches served on croissants and French baguettes, and soups and salads.

LOCATION: Au Petit Café is an outdoor restaurant located at the Chefs de France building in front of the France pavilion in the World Showcase at Epcot Center. Look for the brick-red awning, under which diners are seated facing the promenade and the World Showcase Lagoon.

DINING HOURS: Open all day from 11:30 AM until park closing.

AMBIENCE: Guests enjoy outdoor dining Parisian-style while sitting at small tables in this sidewalk cafe. White marble tables surrounded by delicate black iron chairs are situated under an open-sided awning supported by green pillars. Servers wear black bolero-style jackets and are wonderfully attentive. This cafe is an excellent spot to watch passersby and to view the FriendShip water launches plying the waters of the World Showcase Lagoon.

SAMPLE ENTREES: *Le Tartare de Saumon Légèrement Fumé aux Concombres Croquants Sauce Douce aux Herbes* (fresh and smoked salmon chopped and garnished with cucumbers, served with herb sauce and brioche); *La Salade de Blanc de Volaille aux Légumes Frais Sauce Curry* (sliced breast of chicken on bed of greens, with Gruyère cheese, fresh vegetables, and a light curry sauce, served chilled); *La Crêpe de Jambon Savoyarde* (a crepe filled with mushrooms and ham with a Gruyère cheese sauce).

HEALTHY-CHOICE ENTREES: *La Salade Niçoise* (mixed green salad arranged with white tuna, tomato, cucumber, potatoes, celery, and black olives, served with vinaigrette dressing); *L'Assiette Végétarienne* (vegetable plate).

LUNCH: The menu is the same for lunch and dinner.

BEVERAGES: French beer and wines are served, as are spirits. Soft drinks, mineral water, and *café express*, a hearty espressolike coffee, are offered. *Café Grand Marnier,* the restaurant's specialty drink, is made with café express, Grand Marnier liqueur, and whipped cream.

AVERAGE PRICE RANGE: Entrees $$.

FEATURES: The cafe dishes offered here are created by the celebrated chefs responsible for designing the menu at the Chefs de France restaurant. The desserts are fine examples of the art of Gaston Lenôtre, who is considered to be France's premier pastry and dessert chef.

The most popular dishes among frequent diners are the *Coq au Vin* and *Le Sandwich de Saumon.*

On a beautiful day, outdoor dining along the World Showcase promenade can be an extraordinarily pleasant experience, especially during low-attendance times.

DRAWBACKS: Because of its outdoor location, Au Petit Café is not the best dining atmosphere on very hot or cold days, despite the view.

Since no reservations are taken, there can be a lengthy wait, especially during peak dining hours.

RESERVATIONS: No reservations are accepted; diners are seated on a first-come, first-served basis. Because the restaurant is outdoors, smoking is permitted.

REVIEWERS' RATINGS

XXXX – As good as it gets. **XXX** – Better than most. **XX** – Adequate. **X** – Of limited appeal.

XXX FOOD *(Well-executed dishes and an excellent value for light eaters.)*
XXX SERVICE *(Friendly, helpful, and fast.)*
XXX AMBIENCE *(Very pleasant outdoor dining, depending on the weather and the wait.)*

BIERGARTEN

FOOD: The Biergarten serves traditional German cuisine, including roasted meats, sauerbraten (a marinated beef dish), German sausages (weisswurst, bratwurst, and knockwurst), and seafood, along with dumplings, red cabbage, and potato salad.

LOCATION: The entrance to the restaurant is tucked in the back of the Germany pavilion in the World Showcase at Epcot Center. Guests can reach it by strolling through the platz, past St. George's fountain.

DINING HOURS: 11:30 AM for lunch, 4 PM for dinner.

AMBIENCE: The Biergarten is a spacious dining room fashioned after the famous beer halls of Munich. Ornate street lamps, balconies overflowing with geraniums, and water cascading from an old mill lend an outdoor air to the restaurant, creating an instant German vacation for guests. Bavarian-costumed servers carry giant steins of beer and great platters of food. On the stage at the front of the hall, performances of German music, folk dancing, singing, and yodeling are featured at dinner. The festive atmosphere of the Biergarten captures the essence of Oktoberfest, one of Germany's traditional celebrations.

SAMPLE DINNER ENTREES: *Sauerbraten mit Knödeln und Rotkohl* (marinated beef, dumplings, and red cabbage); *Heiße Kombinationsplatte mit Knödeln und Wein Kraut* (bratwurst, smoked pork loin, and sauerbraten, with dumplings in sauerbraten sauce, wine kraut); *Rouladen mit Spätzle und Rotkohl* (beef rolls stuffed with pickle, bacon, and onions, served with noodles and red cabbage). All entrees are served with choice of goulash soup or tossed green salad.

HEALTHY-CHOICE ENTREES: *Vegetarier Teller* (assorted seasonal vegetables served hot); *Halbes Huhn, am Spieß gebraten mit Petersilienkartoffel und Rotkohl* (one-half roasted chicken, with boiled potatoes and red cabbage); *Frische Fischplatte* (fresh fish prepared in a traditional German style).

LUNCH: Lunch and dinner menus are very similar, although lunch does not include soup or salad and prices are quite a bit lower. There is no entertainment at lunch.

BEVERAGES: A selection of fine wines from Germany is offered, along with Beck's beer on tap, served in thirty-three-ounce steins. Spirits, including German liqueurs such as Jägermeister and Kirschwasser, are available, as are soft drinks, coffee, and tea.

AVERAGE PRICE RANGE: Lunch entrees **$$**, dinner entrees **$$$**.

FEATURES: Diners in the late afternoon and evening can enjoy a lively stage show of German music and dance at 4:30, 5:45, 7, 8:15, and 9:15 PM (when the park is open late).

DRAWBACKS: The long tables are arranged communally, so guests seeking an intimate conversation will find little privacy when the restaurant is busy. The large dining hall, when it is full, can also be very noisy. The Biergarten offers a very limited selection for vegetarians.

RESERVATIONS: Walt Disney World resort guests may make reservations three days in advance by calling Theme Park Restaurant Reservations (407 824-8800) or by contacting Guest Services at their resort. Same-day reservations can be made at Earth Station, at any WorldKey Information Service kiosk, or at the restaurant itself.

REVIEWERS' RATINGS

XXXX – As good as it gets. **XXX** – Better than most. **XX** – Adequate. **X** – Of limited appeal.

X FOOD *(The heavy German dishes are generally disappointing.)*
XXX SERVICE *(Bustling, friendly, and fast, given the large crowded tables.)*
XXX AMBIENCE *(A beautifully designed atmosphere, but the dining experience can be loud.)*

BISTRO DE PARIS

FOOD: Bistro de Paris features French haute cuisine, including appetizers such as pâté de fois gras and smoked salmon, and entrees consisting of seafood, meats, and vegetables served with a variety of unique light sauces. Despite its name, which suggests casual food, Bistro de Paris is the most upscale of the restaurants in the France pavilion and more gourmet than Chefs de France downstairs.

LOCATION: The restaurant is located on the second floor of the Chefs de France building in the World Showcase at Epcot Center. Guests can find the restaurant by walking down the cobblestone street of the pavilion. The entrance is at the rear of the Chefs de France building.

DINING HOURS: 5:30 PM for dinner. The restaurant opens for lunch seasonally at noon, during peak-attendance times at the park.

AMBIENCE: Guests ascend a dramatic spiraling stairway to the restaurant. Hanging brass and milk glass chandeliers fill the dining room with soft, romantic light. Mirrors and artwork in ornate gold frames adorn the walls, giving the place a Parisian turn-of-the-century atmosphere. The bistro motif is reflected in the seating arrangements, with long banquettes and red upholstered chairs.

SAMPLE DINNER ENTREES: *La Bouillabaisse Marseillaise avec sa Rouille et ses Croûtons* (seafood casserole from the South of France, served with garlic sauce and croutons); *Le Suprême de Canard aux Griottes, Sauce Bigarade* (sautéed breast of duck garnished with French Griotte cherries and a red wine sauce); *Le Carré d'Agneau pour Deux à la Sariette en Persillade sur son Tian de Légumes Provençal* (rack of lamb for two, roasted and flavored with herb butter and served with vegetables).

HEALTHY-CHOICE ENTREES: *L'Espadon Grillé, Sauce Choron* (grilled swordfish with a tomato-bearnaise sauce and fresh vegetables). A vegetable plate is available on request.

LUNCH: Lunch is served seasonally, during peak attendance times. Lunch entrees are lighter, and prices are considerably lower than at dinner.

BEVERAGES: French wine and beer, as well as spirits, are served. Soft drinks, mineral water, tea, coffee, and café express are also available. The restaurant's popular after-dinner drink, *Café Grand Marnier,* is made with café express, Grand Marnier, and whipped cream.

AVERAGE PRICE RANGE: Lunch entrees **$$$**, dinner entrees **$$$$**.

FEATURES: Three of France's premier *cuisiniers,* Paul Bocuse, Roger Vergé, and Gaston Lenôtre, have created the dishes for Bistro de Paris.

With its intimate lighting and decor, the award-winning Bistro de Paris is especially romantic.

DRAWBACKS: Bistro de Paris is one of the most popular of the World Showcase restaurants and, because it is very small, same-day reservations are difficult to secure.

RESERVATIONS: Walt Disney World resort guests can make reservations three days in advance by calling Theme Park Restaurant Reservations (407 824-8800) or by contacting Guest Services at their resort. Same-day reservations can be made at Earth Station, at any WorldKey Information Service kiosk, or at the restaurant itself.

REVIEWERS' RATINGS

XXXX – As good as it gets.   **XXX** – Better than most.   **XX** – Adequate.   **X** – Of limited appeal.

XXXX FOOD *(Very good food beautifully presented — a fairly good value overall.)*
XXXX SERVICE *(Friendly and professional, more relaxed than Chefs de France, downstairs.)*
XXXX AMBIENCE *(Elegant, pretty, and very French.)*

CAP'N JACK'S OYSTER BAR

FOOD: Cap'n Jack's serves an assortment of fresh seafood including shrimp, oysters, crab meat, clams, and scallops. The seafood is served fresh on the half-shell, in salads, or cooked into crab cakes, seafood soups, and pasta dishes.

LOCATION: The restaurant is located at the end of a pier in the center of Disney Village Marketplace. It sits on Buena Vista Lagoon, and guests can reach it by walking along the waterfront.

DINING HOURS: Open all day from 11:30 AM.

AMBIENCE: The galley-style entrance at Cap'n Jack's has a glass-fronted display of the day's fresh seafood. The restaurant has two dining areas, one to the left of the galley and another surrounding the large, hexagonal copper-topped bar in the restaurant's center. Both dining rooms are small, but offer delightful views of Buena Vista Lagoon and the *Empress Lilly* riverboat. A boathouse atmosphere has been achieved with plank wood flooring, thickly varnished wooden tables, and leather-slung chairs.

SAMPLE ENTREES: *Jack's Shrimp Ziti* (baby shrimp and ziti tossed with garlic butter and topped with Parmesan cheese, served with garlic bread); *Zesty Crab Cakes* (crab meat patties seasoned with onions and herbs, served with coleslaw and garlic bread); *Some Like it Cold* (oysters and clams on the half-shell, peel-and-eat shrimp, and marinated scallops); *Some Like it Hot* (a cup of chowder, crab cakes, and smoked fish with garlic bread).

HEALTHY-CHOICE ENTREES: *Cap'ns Sampler* (a salad plate of smoked fish, marinated scallops, and shrimp on assorted greens, served with house dressing and cocktail sauce).

LUNCH: The menu is the same for lunch and dinner.

BEVERAGES: Cold beer is served in Mason jars with handles. Wine and spirits are also offered, as are coffee, tea, and soft drinks. The restaurant features a *Strawberry Margarita,* made with strawberries and served in a large frosted glass.

AVERAGE PRICE RANGE: Entrees $$.

FEATURES: Cap'n Jack's is a casual lively restaurant, with a friendly atmosphere. The circular bar is a great place to meet fellow vacationers while waiting for a table. Guests can also enjoy drinks and seafood delicacies at the bar.

The favorite entrees among regulars are the *Zesty Crab Cakes* and *Jack's Shrimp Ziti.*

If you are visiting at the right time of year, be sure to order stone crab from the Florida coast, which is wonderful and very hard to find.

The desserts at Cap'n Jack's, especially the *Key Lime Pie* and *Something Chocolate* (chocolate on chocolate cake), are superior.

DRAWBACKS: It is unclear from the signs in front of the restaurant how guests are seated. Guests must wait in line at the podium. If you just want to sit at the bar for a snack or beverage, bypass the line.

There can be a long wait for a table during peak dining times.

RESERVATIONS: No reservations are accepted; diners are seated on a first-come, first-served basis.

REVIEWERS' RATINGS
XXXX – As good as it gets. **XXX** – Better than most. **XX** – Adequate. **X** – Of limited appeal.

XXXX FOOD *(Very good seafood at reasonable prices.)*

XX SERVICE *(Service is efficient, although servers can be surly at times.)*

XXX AMBIENCE *(Beautiful views and casual atmosphere, but it can get busy and loud.)*

CHEF MICKEY'S VILLAGE RESTAURANT

FOOD: Chef Mickey's Village Restaurant serves up satisfying country-style cuisine. Breakfast entrees include eggs Benedict, corned beef hash, and French toast. Lunch and dinner menus feature beef, chicken, seafood, and pasta as well as sandwiches and hamburgers.

LOCATION: The restaurant is located at the far end of Disney Village Marketplace, adjacent to Disney's Village Resort. There is a cul-de-sac driveway at the side where guests can be dropped off.

DINING HOURS: Open all day from 9 AM. Lunch is served at 11:30 PM, dinner at 5:30 PM.

AMBIENCE: Chef Mickey's Village Restaurant is a two-tiered, light-filled modern dining room containing many flourishing plants and two immense ficus trees. The walls are covered with pictures of Mickey's friends, and Chef Mickey himself puts in an appearance at dinnertime. The peaked ceilings and skylights allow sunshine to pour in, and the tall, slender windows provide a great view of Buena Vista Lagoon and the *Empress Lilly* riverboat. Servers wear white chef's jackets with Mickey Mouse bandanas.

SAMPLE DINNER ENTREES: *Smoked Baby Back Ribs* (barbecued ribs served with coleslaw, corn on the cob, and corn bread); *Steak Oscar* (broiled fillets topped with crab meat, asparagus tips, and bearnaise sauce, served with rice pilaf); *Chicken & Scampi Combo* (boneless chicken and Gulf shrimp, sautéed in garlic butter and served over rice pilaf). *Seafood Pasta Primavera* (pasta in a cream sauce, tossed with sea scallops and fresh vegetables).

HEALTHY CHOICE ENTREES: *Chicken Mediterranean* (boneless chunks of chicken stewed with tomatoes, onions, green peppers, and olives, served over rice pilaf); *Salmon Lasagna* (served with a spinach and pine nut sauce and fresh vegetables); *Captain's Catch* (selection of fresh seafood daily).

BREAKFAST AND LUNCH: Breakfasts feature egg dishes, waffles, and *Suns-Up* (a blend of fruit, fruit juice, and yogurt served as a breakfast drink). Lunch and dinner menus are similar, although the popular *Fajita Sizzler* (choice of beef or chicken with grilled peppers and onions, served with Cheddar cheese, guacamole, diced tomatoes, sour cream, and flour tortillas) is available only at lunch. Lunch prices are somewhat lower.

BEVERAGES: Wine, beer, and spirits are served, as are coffee, tea, and soft drinks. Specialty drinks, named after Disney movies, include *Outrageous Fortune,* a combination of gin, peach schnapps, grenadine, and ginger ale.

AVERAGE PRICE RANGE: Breakfast entrees $; lunch entrees $$; dinner entrees $$$.

FEATURES: Guests waiting to dine can enjoy a before-dinner beverage and wide-screen TVs at the Village Lounge, adjoining Chef Mickey's Village Restaurant.

DRAWBACKS: Chef Mickey's presence every evening makes this restaurant a very popular place for families. Dinners can get quite noisy. Expect lots of kids.

RESERVATIONS: Visitors can make reservations up to thirty days in advance by calling Village Restaurant Reservations (407 828-3900). Same-day reservations can be made at Disney Village Marketplace Guest Services or at the restaurant itself.

REVIEWERS' RATINGS
XXXX – As good as it gets. **XXX** – Better than most. **XX** – Adequate. **X** – Of limited appeal.

XX FOOD *(Ordinary, simple kid-pleasing food.)*
XX SERVICE *(Patient with kids; sometimes slow, sometimes frenzied.)*
X AMBIENCE *(Homey but crowded. Don't come here if you're avoiding Mickey.)*

CHEFS DE FRANCE

FOOD: Chefs de France features traditional French cuisine consisting of seafood, meat, poultry, and vegetables accompanied with distinctive sauces created by three of France's premier chefs. One or two of the beautifully prepared appetizers and a salad, ordered together, can serve as a meal.

LOCATION: The mansard-roofed building housing Chefs de France stands on the corner at the entrance to the France pavilion in the World Showcase at Epcot Center. Diners pass under a brick-red awning across from the fountain to enter this restaurant.

DINING HOURS: 12 PM for lunch, 4:30 PM for dinner.

AMBIENCE: In this restaurant, accented with white linen tablecloths and fresh flowers on each table, guests can choose to dine in the formal dining room with its etched-glass partitions, wood-beamed ceilings, traditional patterned carpeting, and gilt-framed mirrors, or on the black and white tiled veranda, which is hung with pots of flowers and has tall arched windows overlooking the pavilion streets.

SAMPLE DINNER ENTREES: *Le vol au vent de rouget frais, les coquilles St. Jacques* (fillet of red snapper and fresh spinach baked in pastry, with sautéed scallops and crab dumplings with lobster cream sauce); *Le demi canard, sauce au chaud parfum et son gâteau de pomme de terre douce* (a half duck braised in red wine, served with cranberry and sweet potato mousse); *Le filet de boeuf mathurini* (tenderloin of beef sautéed with raisins in a brandy sauce); *Le saumon a l'oseille* (broiled fresh salmon with sorrel cream sauce, served with fresh vegetables).

HEALTHY-CHOICE ENTREES: *Le traditionnel coq au vin du beaujolais* (chicken braised in red wine with pearl onions and mushrooms, served with angel hair pasta); *L'assiette végétarienne* (vegetable plate).

LUNCH: Entree selections differ slightly at lunch and prices are lower.

BEVERAGES: French wine and beer are served, as are spirits, soft drinks, and mineral water. Thick and strong café express, very similar to espresso, is also offered. The comprehensive wine list includes vintages specially selected by the chefs who designed the cuisine.

AVERAGE PRICE RANGE: Lunch entrees **$$**, dinner entrees **$$$**.

FEATURES: Three of France's premier *cuisiniers*, Paul Bocuse, Roger Vergé, and Gaston Lenôtre, have created the dishes for Chefs de France.

A magnificent array of not-to-be-missed, reasonably priced desserts is offered.

The escargot with parsley and butter is a favorite appetizer among frequent diners here.

DRAWBACKS: Because this is one of the most popular restaurants at Epcot, it is difficult to get same-day reservations.

Tables are placed very close together, so be prepared to overhear conversations.

RESERVATIONS: Walt Disney World resort guests can make reservations three days in advance by calling Theme Park Restaurant Reservations (407 824-8800) or by contacting Guest Services at their resort. Same-day reservations can be made at Earth Station, at any WorldKey Information Service kiosk, or at the restaurant itself.

REVIEWERS' RATINGS

XXXX – As good as it gets. **XXX** – Better than most. **XX** – Adequate. **X** – Of limited appeal.

XXX FOOD *(Fine cuisine, although most sauces are cream-based. A very good food value.)*

XXX SERVICE *(Bustling and oblique, but efficient and ultimately professional.)*

XXX AMBIENCE *(Light, bright, and busy rather than romantic.)*

CORAL REEF RESTAURANT

FOOD: The Coral Reef Restaurant serves an extensive array of seafood that is smoked, sautéed, or grilled. New American–style cuisine featuring chicken, beef, and pasta is also available.

LOCATION: The Coral Reef Restaurant is located in the Living Seas pavilion, in Future World at Epcot Center. The restaurant has its own entrance at the side of the pavilion, where painted blue waves lead guests inside.

DINING HOURS: 11:30 AM for lunch, 4:30 PM for dinner.

AMBIENCE: The multitiered restaurant is adjacent to one of the largest saltwater aquariums in the world, holding more than 5.7 million gallons of sea water and nearly eight thousand underwater inhabitants. The coral reef sea life is visible to all diners through eight-foot-high acrylic windows, and diners are given a brochure as they enter to help them identify the fish. The undersea dining atmosphere is augmented by the dark blue walls, place mats, and carpeting, the dim lighting, and the fascinating view.

SAMPLE DINNER ENTREES: *Pan-smoked Grouper* (grouper marinated in lemon, cooked over hickory, and served with braised cabbage and a tomato-basil sauce); *Salmon Fillet* (salmon grilled with mesquite seasonings and topped with corn relish, or poached and topped with a light basil sauce); *Seafood Fettuccine* (shrimp and scallops served Alfredo-style with butter and Parmesan cheese). All entrees served with soup or salad.

HEALTHY-CHOICE ENTREES: *Mixed Seafood Grill* (portions of grilled tuna, salmon, and shrimp); *Caribbean Tuna* (grilled tuna seasoned with Jamaican jerk spices, served with a Caribbean coulee); *Woodsman Chicken* (boneless chicken breast, broiled and served with whole-grain rice).

LUNCH: The lunch and dinner menus are very similar, and prices are only slightly lower at lunch. Soup or salad are not included with lunch.

BEVERAGES: A selection of beers from seven countries is offered, along with domestic and imported wines and spirits. Soft drinks, tea, coffee, and espresso are served. Specialty drinks are offered in alcoholic and nonalcoholic forms, including the *Sea Star*, a blend of Chablis wine, strawberries, lime juice, banana, and club soda.

AVERAGE PRICE RANGE: Lunch entrees **$$$$**, dinner entrees **$$$$**.

FEATURES: Diners sit eye-to-eye with an array of Caribbean reef fish, including sharks and barracuda. Keep an eye out for the grouper, weighing in at more than five hundred pounds.

  The most popular dishes among frequent diners here are the *Maine Lobster* and the *Caribbean Tuna*.

DRAWBACKS: The high prices of the food do not reflect the quality, which is generally unexceptional.

  Coral Reef fills its dinner reservations quickly, making it difficult to get same-day reservations.

RESERVATIONS: Walt Disney World resort guests may make reservations three days in advance by calling Theme Park Restaurant Reservations (407 824-8800) or by contacting Guest Services at their resort. Same-day reservations can be made at Earth Station, at any WorldKey Information Service kiosk, or at the restaurant itself.

REVIEWERS' RATINGS

XXXX – As good as it gets. **XXX** – Better than most. **XX** – Adequate. **X** – Of limited appeal.

XX FOOD *(A large selection of seafood, with standard preparations and above-average prices.)*

XX SERVICE *(Efficient but impersonal and occasionally uninformed.)*

XXXX AMBIENCE *(Subdued lighting and great fish-watching — a memorable experience.)*

CROCKETT'S TAVERN

FOOD: Crockett's Tavern serves frontier-style American cuisine and Mexican specialties. The menu features a large selection of hickory-smoked and charbroiled meats, including beef and beef ribs, chicken, fresh fish, and seafood.

LOCATION: Crockett's Tavern is located in Pioneer Hall in the Settlement Recreation Area at Fort Wilderness. Guests can reach Pioneer Hall by ferrying to the Fort Wilderness Marina or by taking a bus from the Fort Wilderness Guest Parking Lot.

DINING HOURS: Dinner only from 5 PM.

AMBIENCE: A dozen rocking chairs, sure to be filled by evening, sit on the sturdy plank wood front porch of Crockett's Tavern. After being greeted by the huge stuffed bear at the entrance, guests will notice that this log cabin restaurant overflows with the trappings of Davy Crockett. An Indian birch bark canoe is suspended from the ceiling, and Davy's rifle and coonskin hat and an array of wilderness artifacts can be found throughout the restaurant. The dining room is furnished with rattan chairs, wide overhead fans, bright red tablecloths, and hurricane lanterns.

SAMPLE DINNER ENTREES: *Georgie Russel's Bourbon Tenderloin* (beef tenderloin fillet marinated in whiskey, charbroiled, and served with oven-roasted garlic); *Busted Luck's Buffalo Burger* (ground buffalo served on a fresh-baked roll with baked beans); *Homeplace Rib and Chicken Dinner* (barbecued beef ribs, fried chicken breast, baked beans, and corn on the cob); *New Orleans Seafood Sampler* (shrimp, clams, scallops, and fresh fish, either fried or oven-broiled, served with coleslaw and hush puppies); *Mexican Fiesta Platter for Two* (charbroiled Gulf shrimp, beef and chicken burritos, Mexican rice, and pinto beans).

HEALTHY-CHOICE ENTREES: *Davy's Dockside Catch* (fresh catch of the day served with coleslaw and hush puppies); *Barnyard Chicken* (chicken marinated and charbroiled or fried).

BEVERAGES: Soft drinks, coffee, and tea are served, as are wine, beer, and spirits. The restaurant's specialty drinks include the *Gunslinger,* a blend of tropical fruit juices and rum, and *Davy's Lemonade,* made with Jack Daniels, Triple Sec, sour mix, half a lemon, and a touch of lime.

PRICE RANGE: Dinner entrees $$.

FEATURES: Nightly entertainment, usually in the form of folk singing, is performed in the adjacent Trail's End Buffeteria, which opens onto the restaurant.

Guests can unwind wilderness-style before or after dinner by soaking up the atmosphere at the long saloon bar in Crockett's Tavern.

DRAWBACKS: The restaurant enjoys a reputation for rowdy dinners filled with kids. If you're looking for a quiet evening, try another restaurant.

Due to the isolation of Pioneer Hall within Fort Wilderness, Crockett's Tavern is difficult to reach from other locations in Walt Disney World.

RESERVATIONS: No reservations. Guests are seated on a first-come, first-served basis.

REVIEWERS' RATINGS

XXXX – As good as it gets.   **XXX** – Better than most.   **XX** – Adequate.   **X** – Of limited appeal.

XX   FOOD   *(Down-home American charbroiled meats with mediocre accompaniments.)*

XX   SERVICE   *(Polite but harried. Food arrives quickly.)*

XX   AMBIENCE   *(Rustic cabin setting; probably not worth the trip if you're not already there.)*

THE CRYSTAL PALACE

FOOD: The Crystal Palace is a self-service restaurant that offers hot entrees incorporating beef, chicken, pasta, and fresh fish. Also available are a number of salads and sandwiches.

LOCATION: The Crystal Palace, a Magic Kingdom landmark, is located at the end of Main Street on the left, facing Cinderella's Castle. It can be approached from the bridge that leads into Adventureland.

DINING HOURS: Breakfast from park opening; 11 AM for lunch, 5 PM for dinner when park is open late.

AMBIENCE: This spacious, light-filled restaurant resembles the Victorian-era glass conservatory in San Francisco's Golden Gate Park, and gives guests the feeling that they're dining inside a giant greenhouse. In the gazebo atrium, an octagonal banquette surrounds a growing mass of greenery. A glass dome in the ceiling adds to the greenhouse experience. The food counter is located in the center of the restaurant, where guests order and pay for their meals before being seated in dining areas to either side. The tables along the window walls offer diners a view of the beautifully landscaped gardens and Cinderella's Castle beyond. The Victorian decor is enhanced with stained glass, mint green lattice-work ceilings, ornate mirrors, and wrought-iron tables and chairs.

SAMPLE DINNER ENTREES: *Prime Rib* (a slice of prime rib served with fresh vegetables, rice or mashed potatoes, and a fresh-baked roll); *Beef Burgundy* (beef sautéed with mushrooms and wine, served in a pastry shell with fresh vegetables and a fresh-baked roll); *Italian Pasta Plate* (pasta with tomato sauce and meatballs, served with garlic bread); *Country Breaded Fish* (fresh fish lightly breaded and fried, served with fresh vegetables, rice or mashed potatoes, and a fresh baked roll).

HEALTHY-CHOICE ENTREES: *Spit-roasted Chicken* (a half chicken roasted and basted with rosemary and thyme, served with garden vegetables, rice or mashed potatoes, and a fresh-baked roll). A selection of salads and fresh fruit is also available.

BREAKFAST AND LUNCH: Breakfast entrees include eggs and hashed brown potatoes, hotcakes, French toast, Danish pastry, and cereal. Lunch entrees are similar to dinner offerings, although the lunch menu features a selection of hot and cold sandwiches, including grilled turkey, barbecued pork, and a Mexican club sandwich. A variety of large salads is also offered at lunch. Lunch prices are only slightly lower than dinner.

BEVERAGES: Coffee, tea, and soft drinks are served.

AVERAGE PRICE RANGE: Breakfast entrees $; lunch entrees $$; dinner entrees $$.

FEATURES: This restaurant has a wide selection of good desserts and is an excellent place for a midday break when the lunch crowd has thinned.

Health-conscious diners may order breakfast dishes made with EggBeaters, and at dinner a selection of salads is offered.

DRAWBACKS: Because the Crystal Palace attracts a lot of families, there can be a long wait for tables during peak dining hours.

RESERVATIONS: No reservations taken. Guests are seated on a first-come, first-served basis.

REVIEWERS' RATINGS

XXXX – As good as it gets. **XXX** – Better than most. **XX** – Adequate. **X** – Of limited appeal.

XX FOOD *(A good selection of standard dishes are offered here at reasonable prices.)*

XX SERVICE *(Self-service.)*

XX AMBIENCE *(A pleasant and light-filled, turn-of-the-century garden atmosphere.)*

EMPRESS ROOM

FOOD: The Empress Room features one of Walt Disney World's most elegant presentations of French and Continental cuisine. Beef, seafood, pheasant, duck, venison, and pasta are prepared with culinary artistry and expertise.

LOCATION: The restaurant is on the second deck of the *Empress Lilly* riverboat, which is docked at Pleasure Island. Guests will find it near the main entrance to Pleasure Island. It is also adjacent to Disney Village Marketplace.

DINING HOURS: Dinner only from 6 PM.

AMBIENCE: This small, quiet dining room is by far the most elegant and romantic in Walt Disney World. Tables are isolated by etched-glass partitions, and a large crystal chandelier suffuses the room with a soft peach glow. Secluded tables line the walls of the room, which has no view. Larger parties are seated in the center of the dining room.

SAMPLE DINNER ENTREES: The menu in this restaurant changes from day to day. Typical entrees can include *Carré d'Agneau Parfum au Thym* (roasted rack of lamb prepared with fresh thyme); *Medaillons de Veau Forestière* (roast loin of veal served with wild mushroom sausage and a vermouth sauce); *Crevettes et Saints-Jacques aux Pâtes Blanches et Noires, Sauce au Safran* (shrimp and sea scallops served over black and white linguine with saffron sauce).

HEALTHY-CHOICE ENTREES: *Poulet Nature Poele a l'Estragon et aux Echalottes* (free-range chicken breast braised with tarragon and shallots, served with three-grain pilaf); *Filet St. Pierre, Sauce Cressonière* (fillet of John Dory with Maine lobster and watercress sauce). An exquisite vegetable plate can be prepared upon request.

BEVERAGES: Wine, beer, spirits, and soft drinks are served, as are coffee and tea. The restaurant features an excellent selection of French wines and champagnes.

AVERAGE PRICE RANGE: Dinner entrees $$$$$. A 20 percent gratuity is added to the bill.

FEATURES: The handsome Empress Lounge, adjacent to the dining room, is also the waiting area and is available to Empress Room guests only. The lounge windows overlook the *Empress Lilly's* slowly turning paddle wheel.

The Empress Room holds a Mobil Four-Star Award and is a recipient of the restaurant industry's Ivy Award.

The desserts at the Empress Room are delightful, and guests will enjoy the presentation of after-dinner coffee, which is a culinary event in itself.

DRAWBACKS: This restaurant is small and tables are in demand, so reservations may be difficult to secure during peak season, unless they are made well in advance.

RESERVATIONS: Advance reservations are required. Visitors can make reservations up to thirty days in advance by calling Village Restaurant Reservations (407 828-3900). Same-day reservations can be made only if there is a cancellation. Jackets are required for gentlemen.

REVIEWERS' RATINGS

XXXX – As good as it gets. **XXX** – Better than most. **XX** – Adequate. **X** – Of limited appeal.

XXXX FOOD *(Creative, fresh presentations with emphasis on presentation and style.)*

XXX SERVICE *(Accomplished tableside preparation and presentation, at times obtrusive.)*

XXXX AMBIENCE *(Diners are pampered in traditional elegance.)*

50's Prime Time Cafe

FOOD: The 50's Prime Time Cafe serves cuisine popular in that era, such as pot roast, meat loaf, chicken, and lamb, prepared from family-style recipes and topped with lots of gravy. Steaks, seafood, hamburgers, and sandwiches are also available.

LOCATION: The restaurant is located on Vine Street, across from Echo Lake at Disney-MGM Studios. Guests will find it by looking for the sign above it in the shape of a giant TV.

DINING HOURS: 11 AM for lunch, 4 PM for dinner.

AMBIENCE: Family-style dining in a unique mini-kitchenette is the feature at the 50's Prime Time Cafe. There are ruffled curtains, festive wallpaper, a black and white checkerboard tile floor, and plenty of plastic, vinyl, and chrome. Jello molds, rolling pins, calendars, clocks, and other old-fashioned fifties kitchen paraphernalia decorate the walls, along with pictures of stars from early TV shows. Servers known as "Brother" or "Sis" act as bratty siblings and snitch to "Mom" about diners' manners or whether or not they clean their plates. Meals are served on dinner trays and colorful Fiestaware dishes. During meals, diners can watch "I Love Lucy" or "The Honeymooners" on the old-fashioned black and white TVs scattered throughout the restaurant.

SAMPLE DINNER ENTREES: *Magnificent Meatloaf* (veal meat loaf prepared with mushrooms and peppers, served with mashed potatoes and mushroom gravy); *Granny's Pot Roast* (old-fashioned pot roast served with mashed potatoes); *Auntie's Roasted Lamb* (lamb shank served with mashed potatoes and gravy).

HEALTHY-CHOICE ENTREES: *Mom's Shrimp or Chicken Spectacular* (shrimp, fresh chicken breast, or a combination of the two, charbroiled and served with avocado salsa); *Dad's Fishin' Trip* (seasonal fresh fish, served with garden vegetables); *Aunt Selma's Lobster Salad* (fresh vegetable salad and lobster meat).

LUNCH: Lunch and dinner menus are similar, although prices are slightly lower at lunch.

BEVERAGES: Coffee, tea, and soft drinks are served, and refills are complimentary. The restaurant's soda fountain features such specialties as root beer floats, ice cream sodas, and milk shakes, including a peanut-butter-and-jelly-flavored shake. Beer, spirits, and wine are also available, and the wine list has a fairly good selection of Napa Valley and Sonoma County vintages.

AVERAGE PRICE RANGE: Lunch entrees **$$,** dinner entrees **$$$.**

FEATURES: The Prime Time Lounge, which can be entered through the restaurant, has a huge wrap-around bar with a stack of TVs. It's a unique and entertaining setting for before-dinner cocktails.

DRAWBACKS: The 50's Prime Time Cafe is very popular during peak seasons, and same-day reservations can be difficult to secure.

RESERVATIONS: Walt Disney World resort guests can make reservations three days in advance by calling Theme Park Restaurant Reservations (407 824-8800) or by contacting Guest Services at their resort. Same-day reservations can be made at the Restaurant Reservation Desk on Hollywood Boulevard or at the restaurant itself.

REVIEWERS' RATINGS

XXXX – As good as it gets. **XXX** – Better than most. **XX** – Adequate. **X** – Of limited appeal.

XXX FOOD *(Good and hearty home cooking.)*

XXX SERVICE *(Servers love role-playing with guests. Not a place for low-profile dining.)*

XXX AMBIENCE *(A total fifties experience; good fun if you're in the mood.)*

THE FIREWORKS FACTORY

FOOD: The Fireworks Factory is known for its "secret recipe" barbecue sauce used to flavor meats as they slowly cook over the applewood grill. The menu features smoked and grilled meats, seafood specialties, and pasta dishes and salads.

LOCATION: The restaurant is located on Pleasure Island, across from the *Empress Lilly* riverboat. It is also adjacent to Disney Village Marketplace.

DINING HOURS: Open all day. Lunch from 11:30 AM, dinner from 4 PM.

AMBIENCE: Signs of destruction are rampant at the Fireworks Factory, which looks like an ammunitions warehouse blown sky-high. All that's left standing is a marred steel substructure with partially blown-apart brick walls and corrugated tin siding. Stacked cases of beer partition off tables in alcoves, and scaffolding stairs lead to a second level, which offers diners a view of Buena Vista Lagoon. This popular eatery attracts a lively crowd.

SAMPLE DINNER ENTREES: *The Pyro's Pork Chops* (grilled pork chops served with braised cabbage, mashed potatoes, and bacon butter); *Select Aged Ribeye Steak* (ribeye served with herb butter and mushroom caps); *Bluegrass Chicken* (boneless breast of chicken sautéed with bacon, onions, and mushrooms, with natural-reduction sour cream sauce, served with rice and fresh vegetables); *Buster's Last Crusade* (a half pound of Dungeness crab with a small portion of baby back ribs or barbecued chicken, served with choice of potato or corn on the cob).

HEALTHY-CHOICE ENTREES: *Rocket Shrimp Salad* (Alaskan shrimp over romaine lettuce with tomatoes, cucumbers, and egg wedges); *Sunsoaked Citrus Chicken* (breast of chicken, marinated and grilled, topped with citrus butter, and served with rice and fresh vegetables); *The Rainbow Trout* (fresh Idaho trout pan fried with fresh spinach and tomato butter, served with rice and fresh vegetables); *Fresh Fruit Paradise* (seasonal fruits served with cottage cheese or sherbet).

LUNCH: Lunch and dinner menus are similar, although prices are slightly lower at lunch.

BEVERAGES: Wine, beer, spirits, and soft drinks are served, as are coffee and tea. A wide variety of domestic and imported beer is available along with a standard selection of wine, including a few good California wines. The Fireworks Factory offers a selection of speciality drinks, including the *21 Rum Salute,* consisting of Bacardi 151 rum, Myers's dark rum, and a blend of secret ingredients, and the *Coconut Beach Explosion,* a pyrotechnic combination of coconut, Malibu rum, and peach schnapps.

AVERAGE PRICE RANGE: Lunch entrees **$$**, dinner entrees **$$$**.

FEATURES: The Fireworks Factory happy hour offers drinks at reduced prices between 3 and 7 PM. The is one of the few late-night eating places at WDW, open until 3 AM.

DRAWBACKS: Expect a noisy meal in this restaurant. Avoid the crush on Thursday nights (Cast-Member night for WDW employees), unless that's what you're looking for.

RESERVATIONS: Reservations can be made by calling the restaurant directly (407 934-8989) or at the restaurant itself. The restaurant has a smoking section.

REVIEWERS' RATINGS
XXXX – As good as it gets. **XXX** – Better than most. **XX** – Adequate. **X** – Of limited appeal.

XX FOOD *(Unexceptional barbecue specialties; generous portions.)*
XXX SERVICE *(Cheerful and very efficient, given the crush.)*
XX AMBIENCE *(Noisy from happy hour into the night. Appeals to a party crowd.)*

FISHERMAN'S DECK

FOOD: The Fisherman's Deck features fresh seafood that is served grilled, sautéed, stir-fried with pasta, tucked into crepes, or tossed with romaine. Steak and chicken dishes are also available.

LOCATION: The restaurant is on the second deck of the *Empress Lilly* riverboat, which is docked at Pleasure Island. It is also adjacent to Disney Village Marketplace.

DINING HOURS: 11:30 AM for lunch, 5:30 PM for dinner.

AMBIENCE: At Fisherman's Deck, guests enjoy an incomparable view of Buena Vista Lagoon from the windows across the *Empress Lilly's* bow. The semicircular dining room has light-colored walls, patterned earth-toned carpeting, and copper light fixtures. The restaurant is filled with sunlight during the day and offers a relaxing, quiet environment for lunch and dinner.

SAMPLE DINNER ENTREES: *Fresh Speckled Trout* (trout sautéed with cashews, cilantro, and Key lime, served with seasonal vegetables); *Steamed Whole Maine Lobster* (lobster served with seasonal vegetables and drawn butter); *Fresh Catfish* (marinated catfish dusted in corn flour, pan-fried and served with seasonal vegetables); *Fisherman's Selection* (baked jumbo shrimp, conch fritters, and fresh fish, served with seasonal vegetables).

HEALTHY-CHOICE ENTREES: *Whole Baby Chicken* (chicken marinated in peppercorns, tarragon, and garlic, served with roasted potato and grilled vegetables); *Seafood Primavera* (shrimp and scallops stir-fried with pasta and seasonal vegetables); *Fresh Seafood of the Day* (one of a variety of imaginatively prepared fresh fish offered daily).

LUNCH: Lunch and dinner menus are similar, although only the lunch menu includes the not-to-be-missed *Chicken Pot Pie* (chicken, fresh vegetables and mushrooms, baked in a pastry crust) and *Crepes Carmen* (rolled pancakes filled with shrimp and scallops, topped with hollandaise, and served with stir-fried vegetables). Prices are considerably lower at lunch.

BEVERAGES: Beer and spirits are served and an extensive wine list is featured here. Coffee, tea, soft drinks, and espresso are also available, as is an extensive collection of after-dinner cordials.

AVERAGE PRICE RANGE: Lunch entrees **$$**, dinner entrees **$$$**.

FEATURES: The Baton Rouge Lounge, which features live musical comedy nightly, is only a few steps away, and makes an entertaining before- or after-dinner stop.

   On hot days, this is a great spot for Disney Village Marketplace shoppers to relax and cool off. Drop in about 2 PM, after the lunch crowd has thinned out. Light eaters are welcome to order just salads, appetizers, or desserts.

DRAWBACKS: The restaurant books early during peak season, and it can be difficult to secure same-day reservations.

RESERVATIONS: Visitors can make reservations up to thirty days in advance by calling Village Restaurant Reservations (407 828-3900). Same-day reservations can be made at Disney Village Marketplace Guest Services or at the restaurant itself.

REVIEWERS' RATINGS

XXXX – As good as it gets. **XXX** – Better than most. **XX** – Adequate. **X** – Of limited appeal.

    XXX FOOD *(A wide variety of seafood dishes, many light and healthful.)*

    XXX SERVICE *(Polite servers in riverboat attire.)*

    XXX AMBIENCE *(A wonderful view, relaxing after a hectic day.)*

HOLLYWOOD & VINE CAFETERIA

FOOD: Hollywood & Vine Cafeteria serves American-style beef, chicken, veal, seafood, and pasta dishes along with sandwiches and a variety of large salads.

LOCATION: The restaurant is located on Vine Street across from Echo Lake at Disney-MGM Studios, next door to the 50's Prime Time Cafe.

DINING HOURS: Open all day. Breakfast begins at park opening; lunch from 11 AM until 4 PM. Dinner is served only during the summer and on holidays, when the park stays open late.

AMBIENCE: Hollywood & Vine "Cafeteria of the Stars" is a replica of a Tinseltown diner from the 1950s. In one room, a sprawling forty-foot mural features famous landmarks from Hollywood and the San Fernando Valley. Another very vivid mural features a detailed nighttime view of Hollywood Boulevard. Black and white photographs with scenes from early Hollywood hang on the walls. The dining room, furnished with pink geometric-patterned carpeting and black Venetian blinds, is divided into two sections with a long chrome cafeteria counter center stage. Guests select their food at the cafeteria, pay at the cashier, and dine in the restaurant's pale pink Naugahyde booths or at Formica-topped tables surrounded by chrome dinette chairs. Outdoor patio dining is also available with pleasant umbrella-shaded tables.

SAMPLE ENTREES: *Back Lot Ribs* (baby back ribs with barbecue sauce, served with vegetables and rice); *Academy Special* (cheese-stuffed pasta shells with tomato herb sauce, served with vegetables); *Sunset Steak* (tenderloin tips simmered in a mushroom sauce, served with rice); *Carved Sirloin* (beef sirloin served with green beans, rice, and horseradish sauce).

HEALTHY-CHOICE ENTREES: *Serenade of Life* (cold salad of shrimp, grilled chicken breast, mixed greens, and fresh fruit); *Malibu Marina* (assorted seafood and vegetables in a tomato sauce, served with rice); *Cahuenga Chicken* (roasted half chicken, served with vegetables and rice).

BREAKFAST AND LUNCH: The breakfast menu includes egg dishes, pancakes, French toast, and the restaurant's special *Rodeo Drive Blintzes* (cheese-filled crepes served with a choice of strawberry, blueberry, or pineapple topping). Lunch and dinner entrees are identical, although additional entrees are added in the evening. Prices are the same for lunch and dinner.

BEVERAGES: Wine and beer are available at the cafeteria, as are coffee, tea, and soft drinks.

AVERAGE PRICE RANGE: Breakfast **$**, lunch and dinner entrees **$$**.

FEATURES: Hollywood & Vine Cafeteria is a good choice for a quick meal or for light eaters. The line usually moves fast, even during busy times.

The Tune In Lounge, which can be entered from within the restaurant, is an entertaining and relaxing stop for a before- or after-dinner drink.

DRAWBACKS: Hollywood & Vine Cafeteria is very large and attracts families with young children, so it can get very crowded and noisy during busy mealtimes.

RESERVATIONS: Cafeteria service. No reservations.

REVIEWERS' RATINGS

XXXX – As good as it gets. **XXX** – Better than most. **XX** – Adequate. **X** – Of limited appeal.

XX FOOD *(Not bad for cafeteria-style food.)*

XX SERVICE *(Self-service.)*

XX AMBIENCE *(Interesting decor, but it can be a madhouse during peak dining hours.)*

THE HOLLYWOOD BROWN DERBY

FOOD: The Hollywood Brown Derby serves charbroiled beef, grilled lamb and pork, sautéed veal, roasted chicken, seafood, pasta, and the restaurant's famous Cobb salad.

LOCATION: The Hollywood Brown Derby is housed in a Los Angeles–style Mediterranean building at the end of Hollywood Boulevard next to the Disney-MGM working studios. The entrance is under a long, brown awning.

DINING HOURS: 11:30 AM for lunch, 4 PM for dinner.

AMBIENCE: Red carpet paves the way through the two-tiered Hollywood Brown Derby, which is divided into several distinct dining areas. The tiled indoor veranda at the front of the restaurant is favored by visiting celebrities. Outdoor dining is also available, with guests seated on the patio under maroon umbrellas. In the main dining room, booths line the walls of the upper and lower tiers, and white linen-covered tables occupy the central floor. The room is accented with mahogany wainscoting and hanging chandeliers. The windows at the front of the restaurant have airy lace curtains; other sections have velvet drapes or dark wood shutters. The restaurant's signature collection of caricatures adorns the walls, and Streetmosphere actors playing characters such as Hedda Hopper seeking good gossip mingle with diners at times.

SAMPLE DINNER ENTREES: *Pasta and Seafood* (pasta with sea scallops and shrimp in a feta cheese sauce, served with garlic bread sticks); *Stuffed Chicken Breast* (sautéed chicken breast stuffed with shrimp mousse, served with champagne sauce and fresh vegetables); *Mixed Grill* (grilled lamb, tenderloin of beef, pork, veal liver and pork sausage, served with fresh vegetables).

HEALTHY-CHOICE ENTREES: *Vegetable Medley* (sautéed fresh vegetables, served with angel hair pasta, seasoned with herbs and raspberry vinegar); *Roast Chicken* (roasted half chicken served with fresh vegetables); *Baked Grouper* (baked grouper fillet topped with meunière butter and served with pasta).

LUNCH: The lunch and dinner menus are very similar, and prices are only slightly lower at lunch.

BEVERAGES: A large selection of California wines are featured at the Hollywood Brown Derby, along with beer and spirits. Coffee, tea, and soft drinks are available, as are espresso and cappuccino. The Hollywood Brown Derby features after-dinner drinks including vintage port and its specialty drink *Cafe Henry III,* a blend of Kahlúa, brandy, Galliano, Grand Marnier, and coffee.

AVERAGE PRICE RANGE: Lunch entrees $$, dinner entrees $$$.

FEATURES: The Hollywood Brown Derby does not have a lounge, but the Catwalk Bar, upstairs, is a great place for before-dinner cocktails. There is an elevator adjacent to the waiting area.

DRAWBACKS: The restaurant is usually very busy, especially during peak seasons, making it difficult to secure same-day reservations.

RESERVATIONS: Walt Disney World resort guests can make reservations three days in advance by calling Theme Park Restaurant Reservations (407 824-8800) or by contacting Guest Services at their resort. Same-day reservations can be made at the Restaurant Reservation Desk on Hollywood Boulevard or at the restaurant itself.

REVIEWERS' RATINGS

XXXX – As good as it gets.   **XXX** – Better than most.   **XX** – Adequate.   **X** – Of limited appeal.

XXX FOOD *(Sometimes quite good, sometimes unexceptional. Try the Cobb salad.)*

XXX SERVICE *(Very fast, very efficient, always professional.)*

XXXX AMBIENCE *(Very Hollywood, very comfortable and adult. Ask for a booth.)*

KING STEFAN'S BANQUET HALL

FOOD: King Stefan's Banquet Hall serves hearty portions of beef, chicken, and fish, prepared in a standard quasi-British-American fashion. A variety of large salads is also on the menu.

LOCATION: The restaurant is perched high atop Cinderella's Castle in Fantasyland at the Magic Kingdom. Guests will find the entrance at the rear of the castle, facing Fantasyland.

DINING HOURS: 11:30 AM for lunch, 4 PM for dinner.

AMBIENCE: Approaching King Stefan's from Main Street, guests walk through the castle archway, which is lined with a mosaic in tiny tiles that tells Cinderella's story. The entrance lobby of King Stefan's Banquet Hall recalls the medieval splendor of centuries long past. Stone archways are lit by wall torches, and shields, swords, and suits of armor glint above the fireplace. A burgundy-carpeted turret stairway leads guests up to the large two-tiered dining room, where cathedral ceilings, beautifully carved wooden beams and arches, chairs upholstered in tapestry, and fleur-de-lys carpeting create a royal atmosphere. Tall, narrow arched windows inset with stained glass afford guests an overview of Fantasyland. Servers are decked out in brocade medieval attire.

SAMPLE DINNER ENTREES: *Grand Duke* (steak grilled with green peppercorn sauce, served with roasted potatoes and sautéed vegetables); *Queen's Cut* (roast prime rib served with a baked potato and sautéed fresh vegetables); *Friar's Fowl* (chicken breast stuffed with ham, spinach, and mozzarella cheese, breaded and sautéed, served over fettuccine with fresh mushrooms, tomatoes, and cilantro). Dinner entrees include a choice of soup or salad.

HEALTHY-CHOICE ENTREES: *The Royal Mariner* (fresh fish of the day, served with parsley potatoes and sautéed fresh vegetables); *Cinderella Salad* (assorted salad greens and vegetables, topped with tomatoes, cheese, and sautéed chicken, served with a dill vinaigrette).

LUNCH: Lunch and dinner menus are similar; however, the lunch menu also features large lunch salads and sandwiches, including *The Coachman* (sliced turkey, turkey ham, turkey bacon, and Swiss cheese served with marinated fresh vegetables). Lunch entrees include soup but not salad, and prices are considerably lower at lunch.

BEVERAGES: Coffee, tea, and soft drinks are served. All chilled beverages except bottled water and orange juice may be ordered in a King Stefan's souvenir glass.

AVERAGE PRICE RANGE: Lunch entrees $$, dinner entrees $$$$.

FEATURES: Cinderella herself visits King Stefan's Banquet Hall periodically throughout the day.
King Stefan's Banquet Hall has the only second-story view in the Magic Kingdom.

DRAWBACKS: Families are attracted to this restaurant, and reservations are required for both lunch and dinner, so it may be difficult to get tables during peak season.

RESERVATIONS: Walt Disney World resort guests can make reservations three days in advance by calling Theme Park Restaurant Reservations (407 824-8800) or by contacting Guest Services at their resort. Same-day reservations can be made at the restaurant itself.

REVIEWERS' RATINGS

XXXX – As good as it gets. **XXX** – Better than most. **XX** – Adequate. **X** – Of limited appeal.

XX FOOD (*Very expensive unexceptional food. You're paying for the view.*)

XX SERVICE (*Polite and attentive, but often slow at busy times.*)

XXXX AMBIENCE (*A unique atmosphere that provides a memorable experience.*)

THE LAND GRILLE ROOM

FOOD: The Land Grille Room serves regional American cuisine, including dishes from the South, the Southwest, and New England. The menu offers seafood, meats, and poultry, prepared by broiling, barbecuing, and stir-frying. Some of the fish and vegetables are actually grown in The Land pavilion.

LOCATION: The restaurant is located inside The Land pavilion in Future World at Epcot Center. To reach it, guests walk to the back of the pavilion, along the balcony overlooking the Farmer's Market, below.

DINING HOURS: 9 AM for breakfast; 11:30 AM for lunch; 4:30 PM for dinner.

AMBIENCE: This two-tiered revolving restaurant gives diners a chance to view the environmental exhibits in the Listen to The Land attraction. The restaurant revolves past scenes of a rain forest, a desert, and a prairie complete with buffalo, and diners can even catch a glimpse inside a farmhouse window. Roomy upholstered booths make the excursion comfortable and, at the same time, intimate.

SAMPLE DINNER ENTREES: *Steak and Lobster* (broiled Maine lobster and beef tenderloin served with fresh vegetables); *Barbecue Pork Spare Ribs* (ribs served with corn on the cob); *Stir-Fry Chicken* (chicken strips with pea pods, broccoli, mushrooms, peppers, and pasta); *Roast Prime Rib of Beef* (prime rib served with fresh vegetables). Entrees include soup or salad.

HEALTHY-CHOICE ENTREES: *Broiled Fresh Salmon* (salmon served with raspberry vinaigrette sauce and pasta); *Stir-Fried Shrimp* (shrimp with pea pods, broccoli, mushrooms, peppers, and pasta); *Key West Chicken* (chicken marinated in lime juice, served with fresh vegetables).

BREAKFAST AND LUNCH: The breakfast menu includes egg dishes and waffles. Lunch and dinner menus are somewhat similar, although lunch does not include a salad with entrees and prices are slightly lower. The lunch menu also offers sandwiches and hamburgers prepared in the styles of various regions.

BEVERAGES: A variety of regional American beers is available, and the wine list includes selections from American vineyards. The restaurant's full bar features *The Land Grille's Bloody Mary,* a popular house specialty that is garnished with celery from The Land's own greenhouses. Coffee, tea, espresso, and soft drinks are also served.

AVERAGE PRICE RANGE: Breakfast entrees $$; lunch entrees $$$; dinner entrees $$$$.

FEATURES: The revolving restaurant provides an entertaining atmosphere at meals. For the best view, request a table on the lower tier.

This is the only full-service restaurant in Epcot that serves breakfast (reservations accepted).

DRAWBACKS: During peak attendance times, it is very difficult to get same-day reservations for lunch, although dinner reservations are easier to secure. Guests holding reservations may bypass the occasional long lines waiting to enter The Land pavilion by notifying an attendant.

RESERVATIONS: Walt Disney World resort guests may make reservations three days in advance by calling Theme Park Restaurant Reservations (407 824-8800) or by contacting Guest Services at their resort. Same-day reservations can be made at Earth Station, at any WorldKey Information Service kiosk, or at the restaurant itself.

REVIEWERS' RATINGS

XXXX – As good as it gets.   **XXX** – Better than most.   **XX** – Adequate.   **X** – Of limited appeal.

   XXX   FOOD   *(Inventive American cuisine. The food seems expensive for the quality.)*
   XXX   SERVICE   *(The servers here are pleasant and professional.)*
  XXXX   AMBIENCE   *(Interesting, ever-changing scenery with comfortable, roomy booths.)*

LE CELLIER

FOOD: Le Cellier serves an assortment of regional specialties from various provinces of Canada. Cheddar cheese soup, meat pies, stews, and fresh poached salmon are some of the staple offerings of this cafeteria-style restaurant.

LOCATION: The entrance to Le Cellier is at the side of the Canada pavilion in the World Showcase at Epcot Center. Guests can reach it by walking down the ramp along the river flowing through the flowering Victoria gardens.

DINING HOURS: Open all day. Lunch from 11 AM, dinner from 4:30 PM.

AMBIENCE: The cool, comfortable feeling of dining inside a giant wine cellar is conveyed to guests in Le Cellier restaurant. Wrought-iron lanterns adorn the thick stone walls, and dramatic archways divide the dining room into smaller, more intimate areas. Dark wood panels line the walls, topped here and there by ironwork fashioned into a Canadian maple leaf pattern. Guests line up and serve themselves at the cafeteria, pay the cashier, and seat themselves at pleasant wooden tables with elegant, tapestry-upholstered high-back chairs.

SAMPLE DINNER ENTREES: *Prime Rib* (served with garden vegetables and potatoes or rice); *Chicken & Meatball Stew* (served over a bed of rice); *Cold Cutters* (prime rib, ham, Canadian Cheddar cheese, and marinated mushrooms); *Seafood Stew* (shrimp, scrod, salmon, mussels, and scallops, served over rice in a velouté sauce with garden vegetables); *Fried Chicken* (served with garden vegetables and potatoes or rice).

HEALTHY-CHOICE ENTREES: *Poached Salmon* (served with garden spinach and rice or potatoes).

LUNCH: The foods available only at lunch include *Pork Pie* (served with garden vegetables) and a selection of deli sandwiches. Most entrees are available at both lunch and dinner. Lunch and dinner prices vary only slightly.

BEVERAGES: La Batt's and Molson's beer are served along with a variety of Canadian wines. Coffee, tea, mineral water, and soft drinks are also offered.

AVERAGE PRICE RANGE: Lunch entrees **$$**, dinner entrees **$$**.

FEATURES: The most popular dish among frequent guests at Le Cellier is the *Chicken and Meatball Stew.*

Le Cellier may have one of the best approaches in the World Showcase, requiring guests to meander through gorgeous flowering gardens, often accompanied by the music of a bagpipe band.

On hot afternoons, this dimly lit serve-yourself restaurant is a great place to relax and cool off. Go after 2 PM, when the lunch crowd has thinned out. Try the *Maple Syrup Pie* or *Sherry Trifle.*

The cafeteria format allows light eaters to create smaller meals.

DRAWBACKS: Because no reservations are taken, lines can be long and slow during peak dining hours. Dinner is usually a better bet than lunch.

Vegetarians may find the entree selection limited at Le Cellier.

RESERVATIONS: Cafeteria-style service; no reservations are taken.

REVIEWERS' RATINGS
XXXX – As good as it gets. **XXX** – Better than most. **XX** – Adequate. **X** – Of limited appeal.

XX FOOD *(Hearty and flavorful, but with an unmistakable steam-table aroma.)*

XX SERVICE *(Self-service; servers bring water and clear tables.)*

XX AMBIENCE *(The pleasant dining room feels more like a restaurant than a cafeteria.)*

LIBERTY TREE TAVERN

FOOD: Liberty Tree Tavern features a New England–style menu consisting of meats, poultry, and seafood sautéed or prepared with sauces. A traditional roast turkey dinner accompanied with all the trimmings is available every day.

LOCATION: The restaurant is located at Liberty Square in the Magic Kingdom. Guests will find it in a white-pillared colonial-style building across from the Liberty Square Riverboat landing.

DINING HOURS: 11:30 AM for lunch, 4:30 PM for dinner.

AMBIENCE: The Liberty Square Tavern immerses guests in the atmosphere of an early-American dining hall, with pegged wood flooring, sparkling paned windows, and spindle-back chairs. The multitiered restaurant is divided into several dining areas, and light green wainscoting lines the walls throughout. One wall is fashioned from rough-cut mortared stone, and features a massive fireplace with an oak beam mantel. Iron candelabra hang from the beamed ceilings, and pewter and copper artifacts decorate the walls here and there. Servers wear early-American colonial garb.

SAMPLE DINNER ENTREES: *Freedom Fighter Chicken* (sautéed strips of chicken breast simmered in a seasoned sauce, served with sautéed vegetables); *Fresh Whole Maine Lobster* (steamed whole lobster served with drawn butter or margarine and a twice-baked potato); *New England Pot Roast* (beef braised in a wine sauce, served with sautéed vegetables and mashed potatoes); *Land and Sea* (roast prime rib served with half a steamed Maine lobster and garden vegetables.) Dinner entrees are served with a choice of soup or salad.

HEALTHY-CHOICE ENTREES: *Cape Cod Pasta* (fresh sea scallops sautéed with vegetables and tossed with spinach linguine); *Catch of the Day* (sautéed fresh fillet of fish served with fresh vegetables).

LUNCH: During off-peak seasons, the menu is the same for lunch and dinner and includes sandwiches and salads; during peak seasons, a separate lunch menu is offered, and prices are considerably lower at lunch.

BEVERAGES: Coffee, tea, soft drinks, and juice are served. *Sherbet Punch,* the restaurant's special non-alcoholic thirst quencher, may be ordered in a Liberty Tree Tavern souvenir glass.

AVERAGE PRICE RANGE: Lunch entrees **$$**, dinner entrees **$$$$**.

FEATURES: *New England Clam Chowder* is offered with some of the entrees and is a favorite among frequent diners here.

On hot days, this dimly lit restaurant is a great place to relax and cool off. At about 2 PM, the lunch crowds have gone and seating is often available. Light eaters can order appetizers.

DRAWBACKS: The familiar American dishes here make this restaurant a Magic Kingdom favorite; reservations are difficult to get during peak seasons.

During lunch hours, the restaurant is filled with families and noise levels can be quite high.

RESERVATIONS: Walt Disney World resort guests can make reservations three days in advance by calling Theme Park Restaurant Reservations (407 824-8800) or by contacting Guest Services at their resort. Same-day reservations can be made at the restaurant itself.

REVIEWERS' RATINGS

XXXX – As good as it gets. **XXX** – Better than most. **XX** – Adequate. **X** – Of limited appeal.

XX FOOD *(Generous portions of uninspired preparations. Try the turkey dinner.)*

XX SERVICE *(Polite, but can be rushed and abrupt at busy times.)*

XX AMBIENCE *(Pleasant dimly lit decor, but packed with kids at mealtimes.)*

L'ORIGINALE ALFREDO DI ROMA RISTORANTE

FOOD: L'Originale Alfredo di Roma serves Italian cuisine and freshly made pasta accompanied with a selection of sauces. The featured pasta is *Le Originali Fettuccine all'Alfredo,* a creation of the namesake restaurant in Rome. Also on the menu are chicken, veal, and seafood prepared in regional styles.

LOCATION: The restaurant is located across from the Fontana di Nettuno fountain, at the back of the Italy pavilion in the World Showcase at Epcot Center. Guests pass under the white-pillared portico lit by hanging lanterns to enter the palatial pink-stuccoed building.

DINING HOURS: 12 PM for lunch, 4 PM for dinner.

AMBIENCE: Photographs of international celebrities cover the walls of the restaurant's spacious entry area, where waiting guests are seated beneath an elaborate crystal chandelier. The elegant dining area, with mauve velvet chairs and pink tablecloths, has windows facing the piazza. The walls are covered with masterful trompe l'oeil murals depicting scenes from Italian country estates. Multitalented servers in crisp white coats periodically break into Italian ballads and operatic arias to create a festive dining experience.

SAMPLE DINNER ENTREES: *Le Originali Fettuccine all'Alfredo* (wide-noodle pasta tossed with butter and Parmesan cheese); *Pollo alla Parmigiana* (boneless chicken breast breaded and pan-fried, topped with tomato sauce and mozzarella cheese, served with ziti); *Cotoletta di Vitello Alfredo* (veal chop sautéed in black truffles and wine, served with fresh asparagus and mushrooms); *Saltimbocca alla Romana* (veal and Italian-style ham, thinly sliced, seasoned with sage, and pan-fried).

HEALTHY-CHOICE ENTREES: *Pollo alla Cacciatora* (chicken breast simmered with tomatoes, mushrooms, and onions, served with ziti); *Scaloppine of Veal al Marsala* (sliced veal in a mushroom and Marsala wine sauce).

LUNCH: Lunch and dinner menus are similar, although there are many more veal dishes at dinner. Prices are only slightly lower at lunch.

BEVERAGES: Wine, beer, spirits, soft drinks, coffee, and tea are served. The wine list includes selections from various regions of Italy. A special after-dinner drink, *Caffè Alfredo,* is made of espresso with Sambuca, brandy, and Amaretto, topped with whipped cream.

AVERAGE PRICE RANGE: Lunch entrees **$$$**, dinner entrees **$$$$**.

FEATURES: The restaurant's pasta is made fresh daily on the premises. Guests can watch the pasta-making process through the kitchen windows.

DRAWBACKS: This is the most popular restaurant in the World Showcase, so it is extremely difficult to book same-day reservations for dinner.

RESERVATIONS: Walt Disney World resort guests may make reservations three days in advance by calling Theme Park Restaurant Reservations (407 824-8800) or by contacting Guest Services at their resort. Same-day reservations can be made at Earth Station, at any WorldKey Information Service kiosk, or at the restaurant itself.

REVIEWERS' RATINGS

XXXX – As good as it gets. **XXX** – Better than most. **XX** – Adequate. **X** – Of limited appeal.

XXX FOOD *(Good overall. The meat and fish dishes outshine the pasta.)*

XXX SERVICE *(Generally efficient, spirited, and helpful.)*

XXX AMBIENCE *(Beautiful decor, but the room can feel crowded during peak dining times.)*

MAMA MELROSE'S RISTORANTE ITALIANO

FOOD: Mama Melrose's Ristorante Italiano serves Italian cuisine with California-style touches. The thin cracker-crust pizzas are baked in a hickory wood–burning oven. Beef, veal, fresh fish, and chicken are prepared with a variety of Italian sauces. All-you-can-eat pasta is featured, topped with a choice of sauces.

LOCATION: The restaurant is tucked away in the the New York City Set around the corner from Muppet*Vision 3D at Disney-MGM Studios. Guests can reach it by walking past the Studio Showcase.

DINING HOURS: 11:30 AM for lunch, 4 PM for dinner.

AMBIENCE: The waiting area at Mama Melrose's is permeated with delicious smells from the woodburning ovens. As they are led down the long hallway to their tables, guests can catch a view of the chefs preparing meals. The walls and rafters are festooned with grapevines, hanging bottles, tiny lights, and other paraphernalia. The dim lighting evokes the feeling of twilight. Hardwood floors, red-checked tablecloths, and loud good humor create an offbeat trattoria atmosphere.

SAMPLE DINNER ENTREES: *Vitello alla Piccata* (veal piccata served with pasta); *Pasta con Conchiglie e Gamberi alla Panna* (pasta tossed with shrimp and scallops, in a cream sauce); *Bistecca alla Pizzaiola* (grilled tenderloin of beef with pizzaiola sauce and provolone cheese, served with pasta); *Quattro Fromaggi* (individual-sized pizza topped with fresh tomato, Brie, romano, mozzarella, and Gorgonzola cheeses).

HEALTHY-CHOICE ENTREES: *Pesce del Giorno* (fresh fish of the day); *Lasagne Vegetariane* (vegetable lasagna); *Pollo alla Marsala* (chicken Marsala, served with pasta); *Pasta e Pollo con Verdura del Giardino* (pasta served with assorted fresh vegetables and chicken in tomato sauce).

LUNCH: Lunch and dinner menus are similar, although prices are slightly lower at lunch.

BEVERAGES: Fine Californian, Italian, and French wines are featured at Mama Melrose's. Coffee, tea, soft drinks, and espresso are offered, as are beer and spirits. *Bella Cappuccino,* a house favorite, consists of cappuccino with Frangelico and Bailey's Irish Cream, topped with a touch of cinnamon.

AVERAGE PRICE RANGE: Lunch entrees **$$**, dinner entrees **$$$**.

FEATURES: The hickory wood–burning brick ovens and a hardwood charbroiler enable chefs to produce top-quality pizzas and grilled meats.

The dessert most popular with frequent diners here is *Tiramisù,* a delicious Italian favorite.

Mama Melrose's is a great place to drop in for a midday beverage, once the mealtime crowds have gone. Guests are seated at a dinner table and given fresh-baked bread and olive oil to snack on.

DRAWBACKS: Although decorated in a cozy way, with candles and red-checked tablecloths, the restaurant is very large and can get crowded and noisy during peak dining hours.

RESERVATIONS: Walt Disney World resort guests can make reservations three days in advance by calling Theme Park Restaurant Reservations (407 824-8800) or by contacting Guest Services at their resort. Same-day reservations can be made at the Restaurant Reservation Desk on Hollywood Boulevard or at the restaurant itself.

REVIEWERS' RATINGS

XXXX – As good as it gets. **XXX** – Better than most. **XX** – Adequate. **X** – Of limited appeal.

XX FOOD *(Italian dishes may not deliver to real Italian-food buffs. Stick to the pizza.)*

XXX SERVICE *(Snappy and efficient, servers must do the equivalent of twenty laps a night.)*

XX AMBIENCE *(The large dining room can get very noisy during peak hours.)*

NINE DRAGONS RESTAURANT

FOOD: The Nine Dragons Restaurant serves Chinese cuisine from several regions of China: Light and mild Mandarin, hot and spicy Szechuan and Hunan, subtly flavored Cantonese, and internationally inspired Kiangche from Shanghai. Meats, poultry, seafood, and vegetables are prepared with a variety of seasonings and sauces. The menu was created by the chefs at the Beijing Hotel.

LOCATION: The restaurant is just past the Gate of the Golden Sun, a replica of Beijing's summer palace at the China pavilion in the World Showcase at Epcot Center. It is entered through an elaborately carved, arched doorway.

DINING HOURS: Open all day. Lunch from 11 AM, dinner from 4 PM.

AMBIENCE: An elaborately carved rosewood partition dominates the entry to the large open dining room of the Nine Dragons Restaurant. Plush, dark cranberry-colored carpeting, black-lacquered chairs, intricately painted ceilings, and white linen tablecloths give the restaurant a very formal atmosphere. Ornate paper lanterns supplement the light that pours in from octagonally shaped windows. The tables in the front of the restaurant offer a good view of the World Showcase promenade.

SAMPLE DINNER ENTREES: *Beef in Spicy Sha Cha Sauce* (beef strips stir-fried with bamboo shoots and snow peas); *Kang Bao Chicken* (stir-fried chicken, peanuts, and dried hot peppers); *Baby Back Pork Ribs* (honey-roasted ribs, served with pork and shrimp fried rice); *Jasmine Duck* (steamed duck marinated in jasmine tea and fried); *Shrimp or Scallops Royale* (stir-fried shrimp or scallops, in spicy black bean sauce with green peppers). All entrees are served with rice and tea.

HEALTHY-CHOICE ENTREES: *Stir-Fried Grouper and Garden Vegetables* (fresh grouper stir-fried with vegetables); *Lemon Chicken* (chicken breast braised in a lemon sauce); *Imperial String Beans* (string beans cooked in a lightly oiled wok).

LUNCH: Lunch and dinner menus are similar, although prices of some dishes are quite a bit lower at lunch.

BEVERAGES: Wine, Tsing Tao beer, and spirits are served. Fresh melon juice is available, as are soft drinks, mineral water, coffee, and tea. The restaurant features several specialty drinks including the *Shanghai Surprise,* made with ginseng brandy, rum, grapefruit, lemon, and orange juice; and the *Xian Quencher,* a mixture of fresh melon juice and rum or vodka.

AVERAGE PRICE RANGE: Lunch entrees $$$, dinner entrees $$$$.

FEATURES: It is fairly easy to secure last-minute reservations for Nine Dragons at Epcot Center.
Popular dishes among frequent diners are the *Beef in Spicy Sha Cha Sauce* and *Kang Bao Chicken.*

DRAWBACKS: Dishes are served as full meals, rather than family-style as in most Chinese restaurants. Many visitors consider the restaurant overpriced given the average quality of the food.

RESERVATIONS: Walt Disney World resort guests can make reservations three days in advance by calling Theme Park Restaurant Reservations (407 824-8800) or by contacting Guest Services at their resort. Same-day reservations can be made at Earth Station, at any WorldKey Information Service kiosk, or at the restaurant itself.

REVIEWERS' RATINGS

XXXX – As good as it gets. **XXX** – Better than most. **XX** – Adequate. **X** – Of limited appeal.

XX FOOD *(Consistently average-quality cuisine at high prices.)*

X SERVICE *(Efficient but indifferent, and sometimes intrusive.)*

XX AMBIENCE *(A formal setting in an elegant room, but unexceptional overall.)*

THE PLAZA RESTAURANT

FOOD: The Plaza Restaurant offers a typical American lunchroom menu of grilled and cold sandwiches and hamburgers. Its main bill of fare, however, is a whimsical selection of soda fountain treats, including the largest ice cream sundae in the Magic Kingdom.

LOCATION: The restaurant is located at the end of Main Street to the right, facing Cinderella's Castle. It can also be reached from the bridge leading into Tomorrowland.

DINING HOURS: Open all day from 11 AM.

AMBIENCE: The Plaza Restaurant is housed in an ornate Victorian building with a showcase atrium veranda off to the side. The interior has splendid Art Nouveau touches, with carved white wall panels, an array of gold-etched mirrors, and intricate brass and glass chandeliers. Marble-topped tables are scattered throughout the cheerful dining room, which has an abundance of windows framed in gauzy white valances. The view from the round veranda takes in Cinderella's Castle and the lovely rose and topiary gardens leading to Tomorrowland. As a tribute to the turn-of-the-century atmosphere, waitresses wear long black Victorian dresses with crisp white aprons.

SAMPLE ENTREES: *Reuben Sandwich* (grilled sandwich with corned beef, Swiss cheese, sauerkraut, and Thousand Island dressing); *Pastrami Sandwich* (sliced pastrami on rye bread); *Hot Roast Beef Sandwich* (slices of roast beef with melted Muenster cheese, bacon, shredded lettuce, and Thousand Island dressing, served on rye bread); *Cold Roast Beef Sandwich* (sliced roast beef, lettuce, tomato, onion, and horserad-ish sauce on pumpernickel bread). Sandwiches are served with German potato salad.

HEALTHY-CHOICE ENTREES: *Fresh Vegetable Sandwich* (sliced cucumber, squash, alfalfa sprouts, tomato, and Swiss cheese on whole-wheat bread with dill spread); *Turkey Burger* (grilled ground turkey with mozzarella cheese); *Fruit Plate* (fresh seasonal fruits served with bread and strawberry cream cheese).

LUNCH: The same menu is used throughout the day.

BEVERAGES: Coffee, tea, soft drinks, and juice are served, and espresso, cappuccino, and cafe mocha are also featured. The Plaza's popular specialty, *Creamy Hand Dipped Milk Shakes,* come in vanilla, choco-late, and strawberry. Ice cream floats and sodas are available as well.

AVERAGE PRICE RANGE: Entrees $$.

FEATURES: Ice cream–lovers will feel right at home in the Plaza Restaurant. In addition to the listed spe-cialties, guests can take advantage of the *Bicycle Built for Two,* a create-your-own-fantasy ice cream treat.

This is a great place to come in and cool off on hot afternoons, after the lunch crowd has thinned out. Ask for a table on the veranda.

For health-conscious diners, fountain specialties can be prepared with nonfat ice cream.

DRAWBACKS: No advance reservations are taken, so there can be long lines waiting to get in during peak dining times. Waits can be up to an hour.

RESERVATIONS: No reservations taken. Diners are seated on a first-come, first-served basis.

REVIEWERS' RATINGS
XXXX – As good as it gets. **XXX** – Better than most. **XX** – Adequate. **X** – Of limited appeal.

XX FOOD (*Expensive lunchroom sandwiches and kid-pleasing specialties.*)

XX SERVICE (*Efficient but impersonal, seemingly memorized, politeness.*)

XX AMBIENCE (*Pretty, but at busy times it's noisy with hungry kids.*)

PORTOBELLO YACHT CLUB

FOOD: The Portobello Yacht Club has an interesting menu featuring Northern Italian cuisine, including thin-crust pizzas, original pasta creations, and seafood flown in fresh daily. Also available are charcoal-grilled steaks, chicken, and pork chops flavored with fresh herbs and roasted in the restaurant's wood-burning oven.

LOCATION: The restaurant is located on Pleasure Island across from the *Empress Lilly* riverboat. It is also adjacent to Disney Village Marketplace and can be reached by walking along the waterfront.

DINING HOURS: Open all day. Lunch from 11:30 AM, dinner from 4 PM.

AMBIENCE: Despite its Italian name, the Portobello Yacht Club seems to capture the atmosphere of a New England yacht club. High-beamed ceilings shelter an array of model ships, nautical paraphernalia, and an entire wall of yachting photos. The tables are covered in white and mint-green tablecloths, with a decorative Italian plate gracing each setting. The long, comfortable mahogany bar is accented with brass and surrounded with black leather stools. This restaurant also has terrace dining, offering guests a view of Buena Vista Lagoon.

SAMPLE ENTREES: *Costoletta di Maiale* (center-cut pork chop marinated with herbs, roasted in the wood-burning oven, and served with roasted potatoes and seasonal vegetables); *Spaghettini alla Portobello* (Alaskan crab legs, scallops, clams, shrimp and mussels with tomatoes, garlic, olive oil, wine, and herbs, tossed with thin spaghetti); *Vitello Milanese* (sautéed breaded veal served with fresh arugula, spinach, red onion, and tomato with balsamic vinaigrette); *Vitello con Granchio* (veal flank steak on angel hair pasta with crab meat, tossed with tomato-basil cream).

HEALTHY-CHOICE ENTREES: *Pollo alla Griglia* (half chicken marinated in olive oil, garlic, and rosemary, charcoal grilled and served with oven-roasted potatoes and seasonal vegetables); *Bucatini all'Amatriciana* (tube pasta with plum tomatoes, Italian bacon, garlic, and fresh basil); *Saltimbocca di Pollo* (boneless chicken breast with prosciutto, sage, lemon, and garlic, served with pasta and vegetables).

LUNCH: The lunch menu has a limited selection of entrees, and prices are quite a bit lower.

BEVERAGES: Wine, beer, and spirits are served. The impressive wine selection features a number of fine California and Italian wines. Coffee, tea, and espresso are offered, as is a tempting choice of house cappuccinos. *Caesar's Secret,* a specialty of the house, is concocted with Amaretto and Frangelico.

AVERAGE PRICE RANGE: Lunch entrees $$, dinner entrees $$$.

FEATURES: The restaurant features one of Walt Disney World's most extensive selections of grappas, single-malt scotches, Cognacs, and brandies.
  This is one of the few late-night full-service restaurants at Walt Disney World, open until 1:30 AM. Portobello features a number of interesting desserts; the espresso ice cream is especially popular.

DRAWBACKS: Tables for two are very hard to get when the restaurant is crowded, and there are long waits.

RESERVATIONS: No reservations are accepted; diners are seated on a first-come, first-served basis. The restaurant has a smoking section.

REVIEWERS' RATINGS
XXXX – As good as it gets. **XXX** – Better than most. **XX** – Adequate. **X** – Of limited appeal.

XXX FOOD *(An ambitious array of Northern Italian dishes, creatively prepared.)*
XXX SERVICE *(Very friendly, helpful, and fast.)*
XXX AMBIENCE *(Pleasant but crowded at peak dining hours. Good for a quiet lunch.)*

RESTAURANT AKERSHUS

FOOD: Restaurant Akershus features an all-you-can-eat Norwegian buffet known as a *koldtbord*. The cold selections include an array of Norwegian salads and smoked fish, and the hot dishes incorporate meat, poultry, seafood, and vegetables. Diners are encouraged to return to the buffet for separate courses beginning with appetizers, continuing with the cold buffet, and ending with hot entrees and cheeses.

LOCATION: The restaurant is tucked inside the Norway pavilion in the World Showcase at Epcot Center. The entrance is located across the traditional town square from Kringla Bakeri og Kafé.

DINING HOURS: 11:30 AM for lunch, 4:30 PM for dinner.

AMBIENCE: The Restaurant Akershus is fashioned after the medieval castle fortress that spans most of Oslo's harbor. Its four dining areas feature medieval touches such as tall clerestory-style leaded-glass windows with lace curtains, walls of large white-washed bricks, wooden cathedral ceilings with iron chandeliers, and dramatic stone archways. Tables are set with red napkins and crisp white tablecloths.

SAMPLE DINNER ENTREES: Cold selections: *kyllingsalat* (chicken salad), *kjottsalat* (meat salad), *potetsalat* (potato salad), *egg ogs kinkesalat* (egg and ham salad), *karrisild* (curried herring), *glassmestersild* (glass master herring), *sildesalat* (herring salad), *tomatsilde* (tomato herring), *røkelaks og eggerøre* (smoked salmon and scrambled eggs), *fisketerrin* (fish mousse), *roastbiff* (roast beef), *ostefat* (cheese platter), *fylt svinekam* (stuffed pork loin). Vegetarian salads include mixed green salad, pasta salad, cucumber salad, cabbage salad, vegetable salad, and tomato salad.

    Hot selections: *kjøttkaker* (meatballs), *få'r I Kål* (lamb and cabbage), *røke svinekam* (smoked pork), *skinkegrateng* (pork and noodles). Side dishes include mashed rutabaga, red cabbage, and potatoes.

HEALTHY-CHOICE ENTREES: *Røkt kalkun* (smoked turkey), *steinbit I dillsaus* (wolffish with dill sauce), and poached salmon.

LUNCH: The food selection available at lunch and dinner varies slightly, although the price is quite a bit lower at lunch.

BEVERAGES: Soft drinks, mineral water, coffee, and tea are available, as is Ringnes beer on tap. The wine list features a good selection from California vineyards, along with a more limited selection from France, Italy, and Portugal. Spirits are served, featuring Norway's Linie aquavit.

AVERAGE PRICE RANGE: Lunch buffet **$$,** dinner buffet **$$$.**

FEATURES: Because this is not a widely known cuisine, guests will find it easy to get same-day seating.
    The food is served as an all-you-can-eat buffet, which diners can return to as often as they wish.

DRAWBACKS: The selection of heavy desserts, ordered a la carte from the servers, is disappointing.
    Vegetarian diners may find the hot selections quite limited.

RESERVATIONS: Walt Disney World resort guests may make reservations three days in advance by calling Theme Park Restaurant Reservations (407 824-8800) or by contacting Guest Services at their resort. Same-day reservations can be made at Earth Station, at any WorldKey Information Service kiosk, or at the restaurant itself.

REVIEWERS' RATINGS
XXXX – As good as it gets. **XXX** – Better than most. **XX** – Adequate. **X** – Of limited appeal.

    XX FOOD *(Good quality, but some foods may be unappealing to some diners. Skip the desserts.)*
    XX SERVICE *(Informal and, at times, uneven. Drinks and desserts are served a la carte.)*
    XX AMBIENCE *(Spacious medieval-style interior with lots of room between tables.)*

RESTAURANT MARRAKESH

FOOD: Restaurant Marrakesh serves North African cuisine featuring meats and fish cooked with aromatic spices, as well as couscous, a light and flavorful steamed-grain dish that is regarded as the national dish of Morocco.

LOCATION: The restaurant is tucked away in the back of the Morocco pavilion in the World Showcase at Epcot Center. Guests can reach it by wandering through Morocco's shopping bazaar.

DINING HOURS: 11 AM for lunch, 5 PM for dinner.

AMBIENCE: The opulent multilevel Restaurant Marrakesh has slim carved pillars reaching up to the high ceiling, which is painted in colorful geometrics and hung with chandeliers. Red velvet banquettes against the tiled walls provide seating in the upper-level dining areas, while the tables in the main room, below, surround a small stage and tiled dance floor where belly dancers and musicians perform. The waiters wear *djellabas,* the traditional long robes of Morocco.

SAMPLE DINNER ENTREES: *Tagine of Chicken* (braised half chicken flavored with cumin, paprika, garlic, green olives, and preserved lemon, served with sliced potatoes); *Shish Kebab* (grilled brochettes of lamb flavored with Moroccan spices, served with rice with almonds and raisins); *Meshoui* (lamb roasted with almonds and raisins); *Couscous* (semolina steamed and served with garden vegetables and a choice of chicken or lamb).

HEALTHY-CHOICE ENTREES: *Tagine of Grouper* (fillet of grouper baked with green peppers and tomatoes, served with rice with almonds and raisins); *Vegetable Couscous* (semolina steamed and served with garden vegetables).

LUNCH: Lunch and dinner menus are very similar, and prices are only slightly lower at lunch.

BEVERAGES: Wine, beer, spirits, soft drinks, and mineral water are served. Besides coffee and espresso, *atai benna'na',* or fresh brewed mint tea, is offered. The restaurant features a special cocktail called *Marrakesh Express,* containing gin, citrus juices, and orange-blossom water. The wine list offers an interesting selection of French and Moroccan wines.

AVERAGE PRICE RANGE: Lunch entrees **$$$**, dinner entrees **$$$**.

FEATURES: Moroccan musicians and belly dancers entertain at both lunch and dinner. Entertainment begins twenty minutes after the hour, so schedule your meal accordingly.

Because many guests are unfamiliar with the cuisine, it is easier to secure reservations at the Restaurant Marrakesh or dine without a reservation.

DRAWBACKS: Service is much too fast and the meats are sometimes dry, suggesting that much of the food is precooked. Delay your order if you wish to settle in first.

RESERVATIONS: Walt Disney World resort guests may make reservations three days in advance by calling Theme Park Restaurant Reservations (407 824-8800) or by contacting Guest Services at their resort. Same-day reservations can be made at Earth Station, at any WorldKey Information Service kiosk, or at the restaurant itself.

REVIEWERS' RATINGS
XXXX – As good as it gets. **XXX** – Better than most. **XX** – Adequate. **X** – Of limited appeal.

XXX FOOD *(Delicious flavors, but brochettes and other meats can be dry.)*
XX SERVICE *(Polite and helpful, but a bit too fast.)*
XXX AMBIENCE *(Memorable surroundings and interesting entertainment.)*

ROSE & CROWN DINING ROOM

FOOD: The Rose & Crown Dining Room serves traditional British fare including steak and kidney pie, bangers and mash, prime rib, and London-style fish and chips wrapped in waxed newspaper.

LOCATION: The Rose & Crown Pub & Dining Room is the only full-service restaurant that sits on the edge of the World Showcase Lagoon. It is located directly across the promenade from the United Kingdom pavilion in the World Showcase at Epcot Center.

DINING HOURS: 11:30 AM for lunch, 4:30 PM for dinner.

AMBIENCE: The Rose & Crown Dining Room has a generous touch of neighborhood pub–style architecture, with wood plank flooring, mahogany wainscoting, and hardwood tables and chairs. Hanging milk glass chandeliers, white pressed-tin ceilings, and stained-glass room dividers provide atmospheric highlights. The Rose & Crown Pub, in the front of the restaurant, has a stand-up wraparound mahogany bar with etched-glass paneling. The restaurant and its adjoining terrace overlook the World Showcase lagoon.

SAMPLE DINNER ENTREES: *Cottage Pie* (spiced ground beef and carrots topped with mashed potato and Cheddar cheese); *London Style Fish & Chips* (cod fried in ale batter, served with fried potatoes and malt vinegar); *Argyle Prime Rib* (served with Yorkshire pudding and garden vegetables); *Northern Irish Styled Chicken* (breast of chicken, sautéed and served with mushroom sauce, mashed potatoes, and garden vegetables.) Traditional British pies are served with soup or salad.

HEALTHY-CHOICE ENTREES: *Grimsby* (broiled fillet of fresh fish served with garden vegetables); *Traditional British Vegetarian Pie* (served with soup or salad).

LUNCH: The lunch menu differs from dinner and includes the *Hampton Lighter Appetite* (chilled vegetables served with Stilton cheese and walnut dressing). At lunch, British pies do not include soup or salad, and prices are lower.

BEVERAGES: Bass ale, Guinness stout, and lager are served chilled or at room temperature. Wine and spirits are offered, as are coffee, tea, and soft drinks. Specialty drinks include the *Shandy,* consisting of Bass ale and ginger beer, and *Irish Coffee,* made with Irish whiskey, coffee, and whipped cream.

AVERAGE PRICE RANGE: Lunch entrees $$, dinner entrees $$$.

FEATURES: The adjacent Rose & Crown Pub is a great spot to enjoy cocktails before dinner and soak up the convivial atmosphere.

Dining tables on the outdoor terrace provide an excellent view of the World Showcase Lagoon.

Popular entrees among those in the know are the *Cottage Pie* and the *London Style Fish & Chips.*

DRAWBACKS: The restaurant fills its reservations quickly during peak seasons, and it can be difficult to secure same-day reservations.

RESERVATIONS: Walt Disney World resort guests can make reservations three days in advance by calling Theme Park Restaurant Reservations (407 824-8800) or by contacting Guest Services at their resort. Same-day reservations can be made at Earth Station, at any WorldKey Information Service kiosk, or at the restaurant itself.

REVIEWERS' RATINGS

XXXX – As good as it gets. **XXX** – Better than most. **XX** – Adequate. **X** – Of limited appeal.

XXX FOOD *(Unexpectedly good food and value. Try the fish and chips.)*
XXX SERVICE *(Servers, in nineteenth-century pub costume, are charming and efficient.)*
XXX AMBIENCE *(A lively crowd and comfortable, cozy decor.)*

SAN ANGEL INN RESTAURANTE

FOOD: The San Angel Inn Restaurante specializes in regional Mexican dishes. Seafood, beef, and chicken are prepared in savory sauces enhanced with chilies and a wealth of Mexican spices. The original San Angel Inn is one of Mexico City's historic showplaces.

LOCATION: San Angel Inn Restaurante is located, overlooking the indoor river, in the rear of the Mexico pavilion in the World Showcase at Epcot Center.

DINING HOURS: 11 AM for lunch, 4:30 PM for dinner.

AMBIENCE: Entering the Mexico pavilion, guests walk through a Mexican colonial village at twilight to reach the restaurant at the edge of the river. Red-sashed servers attend guests seated in colonial-style chairs at tables covered with pale pink cloths. The restaurant is very dark and lit with lanterns (bring a penlight to read the menus). A distant view of a smoking volcano and an exotic Mayan pyramid lend an aura of mystery to this romantic dining room.

SAMPLE DINNER ENTREES: *Filete Ranchero* (grilled beef tenderloin served over corn tortillas, topped with ranchera sauce, poblano chili strips, Mexican cheese, and onions and served with refried beans); *Huachinango a la Veracruzana* (fillet of red snapper poached in wine with onions, tomatoes, and Mexican peppers); *Enchiladas de Pollo* (corn tortillas filled with chicken, topped with tomato-chili sauce, cheese, sour cream, onions, and green tomatillo sauce or mole sauce). Entrees are served with a choice of soup or salad and Mexican rice.

HEALTHY-CHOICE ENTREES: *Pescado Dorado* (fillet of mahi-mahi marinated in chili sauce, grilled and served with Mexican rice and vegetables); *Mole Poblano* (chicken simmered with Mexican spices and a hint of chocolate, served with refried beans).

LUNCH: Lunch and dinner menus are very similar, although lunch does not include soup or salad, and prices are much lower.

BEVERAGES: Classic Mexican beers such as Dos Equis, Bohemia, and Tecate are served, as are wine and spirits. After-dinner drinks include *Mexican Coffee* (Kahlúa, tequila, and cream) and *Café de Olla* (coffee with cinnamon and brown sugar). Juice, soft drinks, mineral water, coffee, and tea are also available.

AVERAGE PRICE RANGE: Lunch entrees **$$**, dinner entrees **$$$**.

FEATURES: The San Angel Inn Restaurante has a small adjacent lounge where diners can unwind, wait for a table, and enjoy a Margarita with chips and salsa.

Many visitors find the San Angel Inn Restaurante to be the most romantic in the World Showcase.

DRAWBACKS: Guests who love their salsa hot will be disappointed — even the jalapeños seem denatured.

San Angel Inn Restaurante's reservations fill quickly, so it is difficult to make same-day reservations.

RESERVATIONS: Walt Disney World resort guests may make reservations three days in advance by calling Theme Park Restaurant Reservations (407 824-8800) or by contacting Guest Services at their resort. Same-day reservations can be made at Earth Station, at any WorldKey Information Service kiosk, or at the restaurant itself.

REVIEWERS' RATINGS
XXXX – As good as it gets. **XXX** – Better than most. **XX** – Adequate. **X** – Of limited appeal.

XX FOOD *(Not as good as it was at one time, but still flavorful and satisfying.)*

XXX SERVICE *(Polite, fast, and eager to please.)*

XXX AMBIENCE *(Enchanting and romantic; a memorable dining atmosphere.)*

SCI FI DRIVE-IN DINER

FOOD: The Sci-Fi Drive-In Diner features hot entrees including prime rib, ribeye steaks, oven-roasted turkey, smoked barbecue chicken, broiled fresh fish, pasta, and a selection of hot and cold sandwiches and large salads.

LOCATION: The restaurant is located adjacent to the Chinese Theater, next door to the Disney-MGM Studios Commissary. Guests can find it by looking for the restaurant's movie theater marquee sign.

DINING HOURS: 11 AM for lunch, 4 PM for dinner.

AMBIENCE: The waiting area of Sci-Fi Drive-In Diner resembles the back of a typical movie set, with exposed wall studs and bolts. Guests enter the large dining room through what looks like a movie ticket booth and are seated at tables built into fifties-style convertibles. It's always evening at the Sci Fi Drive-In Diner, and make-believe stars glisten in the sky against a moonlit Hollywood Hills mural. Clips from campy science fiction films and cartoons play continuously on the giant movie screen; sound is provided through drive-in speakers mounted at each car. All cars and most seats face forward. The drive-in snack bar–style kitchen is located in the back of the fenced-in theater, where servers dressed as carhops pick up the food and deliver it to the cars.

SAMPLE DINNER ENTREES: *The Towering Terror* (prime rib of beef au jus, served with green beans and a choice of potato); *Return to The Red Planet* (linguine with crab and shrimp in a tomato-herb sauce, served with garlic sticks); *Saucer Sightings* (ribeye steak served with green beans and a choice of potato); *Journey to the Center of the Pasta* (vegetable lasagna with tomato sauce, served with garlic bread sticks).

HEALTHY-CHOICE ENTREES: *Cosmic Creation* (roasted barbecue chicken, served with corn on the cob and a choice of potato); *Monster Mash* (roasted turkey served with dressing, mashed potatoes, green beans, and cranberry relish); *Terror of the Tides* (broiled fresh fish fillet with orange tamarind sauce, served with green beans and a choice of potato).

LUNCH: The lunch menu has fewer hot entrees and features lower-priced sandwiches and salads.

BEVERAGES: Coffee, tea, juice, soft drinks, and milk shakes are served, as are beer and wine. The wine list includes a surprisingly good selection of California vintages.

AVERAGE PRICE RANGE: Lunch entrees **$$**, dinner entrees **$$$**.

FEATURES: Dining here can be a memorable experience for those who enjoy unique environments.

DRAWBACKS: Keep in mind that entertainment is the feature here, not the food, which is standard at best. Watching science fiction and horror films while eating is literally out of this world, but forget social conversation; most guests face forward except for a few cars with facing seats. The atmosphere is somewhat eerie and quiet because of the attention paid to the flicks onscreen.

RESERVATIONS: Walt Disney World resort guests can make reservations three days in advance by calling Theme Park Restaurant Reservations (407 824-8800) or by contacting Guest Services at their resort. Same-day reservations can be made at the Restaurant Reservation Desk on Hollywood Boulevard or at the restaurant itself.

REVIEWERS' RATINGS

XXXX – As good as it gets. **XXX** – Better than most. **XX** – Adequate. **X** – Of limited appeal.

    XX FOOD *(Average food, although the desserts can be quite good.)*

    XX SERVICE *(Carhop servers do their best to serve efficiently while staying down in front.)*

    XXX AMBIENCE *(An eat-in-your-car experience. Entertaining if you're in the mood.)*

STEERMAN'S QUARTERS

FOOD: Steerman's Quarters features high-quality certified Angus beef, including prime rib, filet mignon, and Porterhouse steak, as well as lamb, veal chops, chicken, and seafood.

LOCATION: The restaurant is on the main deck of the *Empress Lilly* riverboat, which is docked near the main entrance to Pleasure Island. It is also adjacent to Disney Village Marketplace, and can be reached by walking along the waterfront.

DINING HOURS: Dinner only from 5:30 PM.

AMBIENCE: The riverboat dining room of America's past is re-created at Steerman's Quarters. The large one-room dining area has teal blue beams and pillars, and tapestry-covered banquettes line the walls. The white linen–covered tables are surrounded by comfortable black leather chairs. A wall of windows across the stern of the boat offers guests a view of the *Empress Lilly's* huge red paddle wheel, which turns continuously. The pleasant waiting area is furnished with plush, blue velvet–upholstered Victorian setees and dark wood plank flooring.

SAMPLE DINNER ENTREES: *Mixed Grille* (filet mignon, broiled lamb chop, and roasted chicken, served with red-skinned potatoes); *Kansas City Strip* (broiled strip steak, served with baked potato); *Filet Mignon* (tenderloin of beef, served with baked potato); *Lamb Chops* (French-cut chops, served with baked potato); *Veal Empress* (broiled veal chop, served with baked potato); *Roast Prime Ribs of Beef au jus* (served with baked potato and creamed horseradish).

HEALTHY-CHOICE ENTREES: *Whole Roasted Chicken* (served with seasonal vegetables); *Lilly's Fresh Seafood* (catch of the day, served with seasonal vegetables).

BEVERAGES: Wine, beer, and spirits are served, as are coffee, tea, and soft drinks. The restaurant's wine list features a few fine French wines and an impressive selection of Californian wines, including several celebrated Opus One Mondavi-Rothschild vintages. The list also features a selection of American and French champagnes.

AVERAGE PRICE RANGE: Dinner entrees $$$$.

FEATURES: The desserts are quite good in this restaurant; especially popular are the *Crème Brulée* and the *Key Lime Pie.*

The Baton Rouge Lounge, which features live musical comedy nightly, is only a few steps away, and makes an entertaining before- or after-dinner stop.

DRAWBACKS: Steerman's Quarters is a meat-lover's paradise, and vegetarians will find very few items on the menu to select from here.

Dinner reservations fill quickly during peak seasons, and it can be very difficult to secure same-day reservations.

RESERVATIONS: Visitors can make reservations up to thirty days in advance by calling Village Restaurant Reservations (407 828-3900). Same-day reservations can be made at Disney Village Marketplace Guest Services or at the restaurant itself.

REVIEWERS' RATINGS
XXXX – As good as it gets. **XXX** – Better than most. **XX** – Adequate. **X** – Of limited appeal.

XXX FOOD *(Good preparations and portions for meat-and-potato lovers.)*
XXX SERVICE *(Well informed, helpful, and efficient without being hurried.)*
XXX AMBIENCE *(A comfortable room with a warm and pleasant decor.)*

TEMPURA KIKU

FOOD: Tempura Kiku features seafood, chicken, beef, and vegetables dipped in a light batter, deep-fried, and served with a dipping sauce. While tempura is considered by many to be a traditional Japanese dish, it actually originated with the Portuguese, who opened Western trade with Japan. Sushi and sashimi are also available.

LOCATION: Tempura Kiku is located in the Japan pavilion in the World Showcase at Epcot Center. The restaurant is on the second floor, above the Mitsukoshi Department Store.

DINING HOURS: 11:30 AM for lunch, 5 PM for dinner. Closed between 3 and 5 PM.

AMBIENCE: This small dining room is just off the waiting room for the larger restaurant next door, Teppanyaki Dining. Warm gold-toned walls, traditional wood detailing, and short blue-gray doorway curtains contrast pleasantly with high-tech cookware in the center of this sushi bar–style restaurant. Guests are seated at the counter surrounding the cooking area, where they can enjoy the personal attention of their own white-hatted chef. Questions regarding ingredients and cooking styles are welcomed, and chefs will gladly suggest meals for newcomers to Japanese cuisine.

SAMPLE DINNER ENTREES: *Tori* (deep-fried chicken strips and fresh vegetables); *Sakana* (deep-fried shrimp, scallop, lobster, fish, and fresh vegetables); *Ume* (deep-fried shrimp, chicken strips, and fresh vegetables); *Take* (shrimp, skewered beef, and chicken strips with fresh vegetables); *Ebi* (shrimp with fresh vegetables). Soup, salad, and rice are included with the meal.

HEALTHY-CHOICE ENTREES: Although most Japanese foods are low in fat, several of the accompaniments make an excellent choice for light eaters. *Sashimi* (assorted raw fish); *Nigiri-zushi* (assorted raw fish on seasoned rice; tuna rolled in rice and seaweed); *Gosho-maki* (crab meat, avocado, cucumber, and smelt roe rolled in seasoned rice with sesame seeds and seaweed).

LUNCH: Lunch and dinner menus are very similar, although lunch does not include a salad and prices are much lower.

BEVERAGES: Wine, plum wine, sake, Kirin beer, and soft drinks are served, along with coffee and traditional Japanese green tea. The wine list offers a small but interesting selection of California wines. Specialty drinks offered from the full bar in the adjacent Matsu No Ma Lounge include the *Matsu*, made from gin, melon liqueur, pineapple, and lemon juices.

AVERAGE PRICE RANGE: Lunch entrees **$$**, dinner entrees **$$$**.

FEATURES: Since no reservations are taken, Tempura Kiku is a good choice for visitors who do not have dining reservations, especially during off-peak hours. Guests waiting for seats can enjoy the view of the World Showcase Lagoon from the Matsu No Ma Lounge.

The counter service is fast and efficient, making Tempura Kiku an excellent choice for lunch.

DRAWBACKS: Groups of more than three will find it difficult to conduct conversations because of the counter seating.

RESERVATIONS: No reservations are taken in this restaurant. The counter seats twenty-five.

REVIEWERS' RATINGS
XXXX – As good as it gets. **XXX** – Better than most. **XX** – Adequate. **X** – Of limited appeal.

XX FOOD *(Very typical, modern tempura-style cooking.)*
XXXX SERVICE *(Fast, pleasant, and professional.)*
XXX AMBIENCE *(Friendly Japanese-style counter dining with interesting goings-on.)*

TEPPANYAKI DINING

FOOD: Teppanyaki Dining offers meat, seafood, poultry, and vegetable dishes deftly prepared at the table by a white-hatted stir-fry chef. All the entrees are fresh and sizzling, with a crisp, quick-cooked flavor.

LOCATION: Teppanyaki Dining is located in the Japan pavilion in the World Showcase at Epcot Center. Guests enter this second-floor restaurant from the wide staircase at the side of the Mitsukoshi Department Store.

DINING HOURS: 11:30 AM for lunch, 4:30 PM for dinner.

AMBIENCE: Guests are seated in one of the five tatami-floored rooms, which are separated by movable hand-painted shoji screens. Each dining room has four black-lacquered tables under gleaming copper venting hoods. The tables accommodate eight guests around the teppan grill, where the stir-fry chef prepares the meals. Once the orders are placed, the entertainment begins. The chef dons a large white hat, pulls knives from a holster, and artfully slices, dices, seasons, and stir-fries each order. Those familiar with the Benihana of Tokyo restaurant chain will notice a striking but more low-key similarity. In the background are the sounds of traditional *koto* music of Japan.

SAMPLE DINNER ENTREES: *Ebi* (grilled shrimp); *Beef Tenderloin* (grilled steak); *Fujiyama* (grilled sirloin and shrimp); *Nihon-kai* (grilled shrimp, scallops, and lobster). All entrees are served with salad, grilled fresh vegetables with udon noodles, and steamed rice.

HEALTHY-CHOICE ENTREES: *Tori* (grilled chicken); *Kaibashira* (grilled scallops). Chefs will prepare vegetarian meals on request.

LUNCH: Lunch and dinner menus are very similar, although lunch does not include a salad, and prices are much lower, almost by half.

BEVERAGES: A fair selection of American wines is offered, as is plum wine from Japan. Kirin beer and hot sake are also available, as are cocktails from the full bar. A popular specialty drink, *Tachibana*, is concocted from light rum, orange Curaçao, mandarin orange, and orange juice. Soft drinks, green tea, and coffee are also available.

AVERAGE PRICE RANGE: Lunch entrees $$, dinner entrees $$$.

FEATURES: With their speedy chopping and clever techniques, the stir-fry chefs provide memorable mealtime entertainment.

The nearby Matsu No Ma Lounge, overlooking the World Showcase Lagoon, makes waiting for tables painless.

It is frequently possible to get seating for individuals and parties of two without reservations.

DRAWBACKS: The communal seating may disappoint those looking for an intimate meal.

RESERVATIONS: Walt Disney World resort guests may make reservations three days in advance by calling Theme Park Restaurant Reservations (407 824-8800) or by contacting Guest Services at their resort. Same-day reservations can be made at Earth Station, at any WorldKey Information Service kiosk, or at the restaurant itself.

REVIEWERS' RATINGS

XXXX – As good as it gets. **XXX** – Better than most. **XX** – Adequate. **X** – Of limited appeal.

XX   FOOD *(Americanized cuisine; may be disappointing for those who expect the real thing.)*

XXXX   SERVICE *(Entertaining service, fast and efficient.)*

XXX   AMBIENCE *(Plenty of camaraderie, if you're in the mood for communal dining.)*

TONY'S TOWN SQUARE RESTAURANT

FOOD: Tony's Town Square Restaurant offers Italian-style hot entrees and lighter dishes such as pizza, calzone, pasta, frittatas, and Italian sandwiches.

LOCATION: Tony's Town Square Restaurant is located at the beginning of Main Street in the Magic Kingdom, across the Town Square from City Hall and next to Disneyana Collectibles.

DINING HOURS: Open all day. Breakfast from park opening; lunch from 12 PM, dinner from 4:30 PM.

AMBIENCE: The welcoming centerpiece at Tony's Town Square Restaurant is a large statue of the Lady and the Tramp. Other reminders of that delightful Walt Disney film are placed throughout the comfortable waiting area and dining rooms, which have been recently remodeled. Guests may choose seating in the main dining room with its stained-glass windows, mahogany-beamed ceilings, and banquette seating. They may also choose to dine in the restaurant's skylit atrium, decorated with ceiling fans and striped green terrazzo floors. The atrium offers a view of bustling Town Square.

SAMPLE DINNER ENTREES: *Sirloin Steak with Lobster and Pasta* (sirloin steak seasoned with garlic and served with lobster sautéed and tossed with linguine and cream sauce); *Chicken Florentine* (grilled chicken breast with spinach sauce and a blend of cheeses); *Tony's Scampi-Style Shrimp* (shrimp sautéed with garlic and fresh vegetables, tossed with linguine and a cream sauce); *Seafood Linguine* (sautéed lobster, scallops, and mussels tossed with tomato sauce and fresh pesto); *Joe's Linguine* (sautéed prosciutto, plum tomatoes, artichoke hearts, garlic, and linguine tossed with a blend of cheeses and cream).

HEALTHY-CHOICE ENTREES: *Turkey Piccata with Pasta* (sliced turkey breast sautéed with lemon juice, white wine, and mushrooms); *Seafood Grill* (grilled fresh fish served with pasta, spinach-basil sauce, and red bell pepper–cream sauce).

BREAKFAST AND LUNCH: *Tony's Italian Toast* and *Lady and the Tramp Waffles* are the breakfast specialties at Tony's, along with a selection of egg dishes. The lunch menu has fewer hot entrees than the dinner menu, and features frittatas, salads, and hot sandwiches. Prices are considerably lower at lunch.

BEVERAGES: Coffee, espresso, cappuccino, tea, and soft drinks are served.

AVERAGE PRICE RANGE: Breakfast entrees **$$**; lunch entrees **$$**; dinner entrees **$$$**.

FEATURES: The lunch menu has a large selection for light eaters, including a variety of healthful salads.

Among the Magic Kingdom restaurants, Tony's is a good choice for those who enjoy Italian food. Although the cuisine is quite Americanized, it's a better value than most of what's available here.

Tony's Town Square Restaurant has compiled a menu for guests with special dietary needs.

On hot afternoons, Tony's is a great place to relax and cool off. After 2:30 PM, there are many empty tables and guests can order beverages or appetizers only, if they wish. Tony's *Fried Calamari with Marinara Sauce* is popular among frequent diners here.

DRAWBACKS: The restaurant is situated in a very busy part of the Magic Kingdom and attracts many families; it is not the best choice for a quiet lunch or dinner.

RESERVATIONS: Same-day reservations only, taken at the restaurant door.

REVIEWERS' RATINGS

XXXX – As good as it gets. **XXX** – Better than most. **XX** – Adequate. **X** – Of limited appeal.

XX FOOD *(Fair Italian food with a wide selection of entrees. A good bet for breakfast.)*

XXX SERVICE *(Polite, snappy, and informed.)*

XX AMBIENCE *(Pleasant, but often filled with children during mealtimes.)*

TRAIL'S END BUFFETERIA

FOOD: The Trail's End Buffeteria serves hearty country-style dishes for breakfast, lunch, and dinner. The offerings include freshly made soup, sandwiches, pizza, casseroles, and an all-you-can-eat taco-salad bar.

LOCATION: Trail's End Buffeteria is located at Pioneer Hall in the Settlement Recreation Area at Fort Wilderness. Guests can reach Pioneer Hall by ferrying to the Fort Wilderness Marina or by taking a bus from the Fort Wilderness Guest Parking Lot.

DINING HOURS: Open all day. Breakfast from 7 AM; lunch from 1:30 PM; dinner from 4:30 PM.

AMBIENCE: The Trail's End Buffeteria offers cafeteria-style dining in an Old West, log cabin atmosphere. Painted animal hides, antlers, and horseshoes decorate the walls of this casual restaurant. The small dining room has Formica-topped early-American tables and a rustic log-beamed ceiling. At the cafeteria in the back, guests select from a variety of hot and cold foods, pay at the cashier, and seat themselves.

SAMPLE DINNER ENTREES: *Carved Steamship Round of Beef; Chicken and Dumplings; Sweet and Sour Pork Spareribs; Fried Chicken; Shrimp Creole; Pasta with Meatballs.* All entrees are served with vegetables, and a complimentary salad bar.

HEALTHY-CHOICE ENTREES: *Fresh Catch of the Day; Assorted Fresh Garden Vegetables; Salad Bar.*

BREAKFAST AND LUNCH: A Continental breakfast is served, as are egg dishes, grits, biscuits, and a seven-inch breakfast pizza. Lunch features a la carte entrees, and an all-you-can-eat taco-salad bar.

BEVERAGES: Beer and wine are available, as are coffee, tea, and soft drinks. Dinner guests can also purchase cocktails at Crockett's Tavern, next door, and bring them into the restaurant.

AVERAGE PRICE RANGE: Breakfast $; lunch $; dinner buffet $$.

FEATURES: Trail's End offers guests two theme dinners weekly: Friday night is Southern Night, featuring smoked whitefish, steak, and other Southern specialties. Saturday night is Italian night, featuring pasta, seafood, and pizza. Late-night pizza service starts at 9 PM every night of the week.

Trail's End offers entertainment nightly, when a folksinger performs on a small stage in the restaurant. Show times are at 6:30, 8, and 10 PM.

The restaurant opens at 7 AM, giving early birds who are camping at Fort Wilderness a head start to theme parks, or providing early arrivals for Fort Wilderness activities with a convenient breakfast spot.

Trail's End will prepare foods to go, which makes it an ideal choice for visitors who would like to picnic at the beach or along the nature trails of Fort Wilderness.

DRAWBACKS: Trail's End Buffeteria attracts lots of families and can get very noisy and crowded.

Since the cafeteria area in this restaurant is very small, the line can move slowly during peak dining hours, except at lunch, when most Fort Wilderness guests are at the theme parks.

Due to the isolation of Pioneer Hall within Fort Wilderness, Trail's End Buffeteria is difficult to locate when coming from elsewhere in Walt Disney World. Since the food here is unexceptional, it is only a worthwhile meal destination for visitors who are participating in Fort Wilderness activities.

RESERVATIONS: Cafeteria-style service. No reservations.

REVIEWERS' RATINGS
✗✗✗✗ – As good as it gets. **✗✗✗** – Better than most. **✗✗** – Adequate. **✗** – Of limited appeal.

✗ **FOOD** *(Ordinary and plenty of it. A good price value, everything considered.)*

✗ **SERVICE** *(Self-service. Not the brightest bunch at WDW, but nice all the same.)*

✗ **AMBIENCE** *(Rustic and plain. Don't go out of your way.)*

RESORT DINING

The resort restaurants offer some of the best dining experiences to be had at Walt Disney World. Very often, the resort coffee shops are also surprisingly good, especially in the premier resorts, and the prices are reasonable. Any WDW visitor can make advance reservations at the resort restaurants. On holidays such as Thanksgiving and Easter, reservations should be made thirty days ahead. Resort restaurant reservations can be made by calling the Walt Disney World Switchboard (407 824-2222) and asking to be transferred to the resort where the restaurant is located. Kosher, vegan, and other special meals can be requested when reservations are made, or can be requested twenty-four hours or more in advance at each restaurant. Resort restaurants are open every day. Listed below are some of the favorite resort eating spots among frequent visitors. Wine, beer, and spirits are served in all resort restaurants; unless otherwise noted, however, smoking is not permitted in the Disney-owned restaurants.

AMERICAN VINEYARDS: *The Hilton Resort* — American Vineyards serves up regional American cuisine in an elegant setting, with entrees including prime rib, steak, seafood, venison, and rabbit. Meats and seafood can be broiled, grilled, blackened, sautéed, or roasted, and are served with a choice of the restaurant's special sauces, including green peppercorn or brandy sauce. The extensive wine list reflects the restaurant's theme, and there is entertainment nightly.

> **DINING HOURS:** American Vineyards is open for dinner from 6 until 10:30 PM.
> **AVERAGE PRICE RANGE:** Entrees $$$$.
> **RESERVATIONS:** Reservations are recommended. The restaurant has a smoking section.

ARIEL'S: *Disney's Beach Club Resort* — Named after the feisty princess in *The Little Mermaid,* Ariel's is a first-rate choice for seafood. Entrees also include pasta, beef, and chicken, and there is a separate menu section for the specialty of the house, lobster. The wine list features vintage California wines and the dining room is decorated with an undersea theme.

> **DINING HOURS:** Ariel's is open for dinner from 6 until 10 PM.
> **AVERAGE PRICE RANGE:** Entrees $$$$.
> **RESERVATIONS:** Reservations are recommended.

ARTHUR'S 27: *Buena Vista Palace* — Arthur's 27 serves elegant international cuisine in a traditional decor with a panoramic view. Specialty entrees include Dover sole, venison, and duck. A seven-course prix-fixe banquet is also available. The wine list is extensive and well developed, and special dietary requests are accommodated with alacrity and style. The service at Arthur's 27 is impeccable, and the restaurant has won numerous awards, including a four-diamond rating from the American Automobile Association.

> **DINING HOURS:** Arthur's 27 is open for dinner from 6 until 10:30 PM.
> **AVERAGE PRICE RANGE:** Entrees $$$$.
> **RESERVATIONS:** Reservations are highly recommended. Jackets are required for men; evening attire for women. Smoking is permitted in the restaurant.

BASKERVILLES: *Grosvenor Resort* — Complete with a replica of Sherlock Holmes' Baker Street study, Baskervilles challenges diners to keep an observant eye out for Sherlock Holmes memorabilia throughout

the dining room as they enjoy daily all-you-can-eat buffets at breakfast and dinner. Prime rib is the stand-out dinner-buffet feature; a la carte entrees include pasta, veal, beef, chicken, seafood, and stir-fry specialties. Lunch is a la carte only and features salads, sandwiches, and light meals.

> **DINING HOURS:** Baskervilles is open for breakfast from 7 until 11 AM, lunch from 11:30 AM until 1 PM, and dinner from 5 until 10 PM. Sunday brunch is served from 7 AM until 12:30 PM. The MurderWatch Mystery Dinner Theater is held here on Saturday nights (see "Dinner Shows," page 209).

> **AVERAGE PRICE RANGE:** Breakfast entrees **$$**; lunch entrees **$$**; dinner entrees **$$**.

> **RESERVATIONS:** Dinner reservations are recommended. Smoking is permitted in the restaurant.

BOATWRIGHT'S DINING HALL: *Disney's Dixie Landings Resort* — The hospitality and cooking of the Old South dominate the entrees at Boatwright's Dining Hall, including tin-pan breakfasts, seafood jambalaya, steaks, prime rib, and Cajun specialties. Also featured are family-style dinners of chicken, ribs, or catfish, and fresh-baked breads and pastries.

> **DINING HOURS:** Boatwright's Dining Hall is open for breakfast from 7 until 11:30 AM and dinner from 5 until 10 PM.

> **AVERAGE PRICE RANGE:** Breakfast entrees **$**, dinner entrees **$$**.

> **RESERVATIONS:** Dinner reservations are recommended.

BONFAMILLE'S CAFE: *Disney's Port Orleans Resort* — First conceived in the Disney movie *The Aristocats,* Bonfamille's Cafe is a casual restaurant that evokes the Old French Quarter of New Orleans in its decor. Dinner entrees include steaks, seafood, and Creole specialties such as seafood jambalaya and spicy shrimp, crawfish, and oyster dishes. Breakfasts are lively and tend to be crowded.

> **DINING HOURS:** Bonfamille's Cafe is open for breakfast from 7 until 11:30 AM and dinner from 5 until 10 PM.

> **AVERAGE PRICE RANGE:** Breakfast entrees **$**, dinner entrees **$$**.

> **RESERVATIONS:** Dinner reservations are recommended.

CAPE MAY CAFE: *Disney's Beach Club Resort* — Beach scenes and striped umbrellas create a casual seashore atmosphere and friendly mood at the Cape May Cafe. The buffet-style meals feature a daily New England–style clambake including fish, mussels, oysters, and shrimp, along with a variety of chowders. Whole steamed lobster can be ordered as a separate entree.

> **DINING HOURS:** Cape May Cafe is open for dinner from 5:30 until 9:30 PM.

> **AVERAGE PRICE RANGE:** Buffet **$$$**.

> **RESERVATIONS:** Reservations are recommended.

FLAGLER'S: *Disney's Grand Floridian Beach Resort* — Singing waiters with guitars and tambourines enliven the elegant, upscale atmosphere at Flagler's. Entrees are prepared Italian-style and include pasta, seafood, chicken, beef, and veal dishes. The wine list offers selections that complement the menu. Weekend breakfast buffets are lively and very popular with families.

> **DINING HOURS:** Flagler's is open for dinner from 5:30 until 10 PM. A breakfast buffet is offered on Saturdays and Sundays from 8 AM until 1 PM.

> **AVERAGE PRICE RANGE:** Dinner entrees **$$$$**, breakfast buffet **$$**.

> **RESERVATIONS:** Reservations are recommended.

HARRY'S SAFARI BAR & GRILLE: *Walt Disney World Dolphin* — Tropical murals, tiger-stripe carpets, and prices in British pounds as well as U.S. dollars impart an international jungle explorer flavor to a civilized dining experience at Harry's Safari Bar & Grille. Entrees feature beef, chicken, and seafood specialties grilled to order. A "yard of beer" is also available for the intrepid bon vivant.

  DINING HOURS: Harry's Safari Bar & Grille is open for dinner from 6 until 11 PM.

  AVERAGE PRICE RANGE: Entrees $$$$.

  RESERVATIONS: Reservations are recommended. The restaurant has a smoking section.

LAKE BUENA VISTA RESTAURANT: *Disney's Village Resort* — Comfortably ensconced in the Lake Buena Vista Clubhouse, the Lake Buena Vista Restaurant is known among Walt Disney World "insiders" as a great place to relax in a private setting with a beautiful view of the Disney Village Water-ways. A very popular breakfast buffet is served, as is a Sunday brunch. Lunch and dinner entrees include chicken, steaks, salads, and seafood such as Maine lobster.

  DINING HOURS: The Lake Buena Vista Restaurant is open for breakfast from 7 until 11 AM, lunch from 11:30 AM until 3 PM, and dinner from 5:30 until 10 PM. Snacks are served from 3 until 10 PM. Sunday brunch is served from 9 AM until 2 PM.

  AVERAGE PRICE RANGE: Breakfast buffet $$; lunch entrees $$; dinner entrees $$$; Sunday brunch $$.

  RESERVATIONS: Dinner reservations are recommended.

NARCOOSSEE'S: *Disney's Grand Floridian Beach Resort* — An octagonal shape, open central kitchen, outdoor deck, and sensational waterside view of the Seven Seas Lagoon and the Magic Kingdom create an upbeat mood for diners at Narcoossee's. The restaurant features blackened alligator steak along with entrees that include seafood, chicken, veal, lamb, and beef dishes.

  DINING HOURS: Narcoossee's is open for lunch from 11:30 AM until 3 PM and dinner from 5 until 10 PM. Snacks and appetizers are served from 3 until 5 PM.

  AVERAGE PRICE RANGE: Lunch entrees $$, dinner entrees $$$$.

  RESERVATIONS: Reservations are recommended.

OUTBACK: *Buena Vista Palace* — An indoor waterfall cascades down three stories at Outback, where servers wearing Australian bush outfits dish up surf-and-turf specialties grilled over pits in the middle of the restaurant. Huge steaks, chicken, and seafood, including lobster, are offered as generously sized entrees. Also featured are ninety-nine varieties of beer from all over the world.

  DINING HOURS: Outback is open for dinner from 6 until 11 PM.

  AVERAGE PRICE RANGE: Entrees $$$$.

  RESERVATIONS: Reservations are recommended. The restaurant has a smoking section.

PALIO: *Walt Disney World Swan* — Palio serves a variety of fine Italian cuisine in an elegant and festive atmosphere. Entrees include specialty pizzas baked in wood-burning ovens and a variety of veal, pasta, and seafood dishes. Italian pastries and other desserts are also offered. An open kitchen lets diners watch their chefs at work, and strolling musicians provide tableside entertainment.

  DINING HOURS: Palio is open for dinner from 6 until 11 PM.

  AVERAGE PRICE RANGE: Entrees $$$.

  RESERVATIONS: Reservations are recommended. The restaurant has a smoking section.

PAPEETE BAY VERANDAH: *Disney's Polynesian Resort* — The restaurant features a unique blend of Polynesian and Asian cuisines in a casual atmosphere with a magnificent view of Seven Seas Lagoon and the Magic Kingdom. Beef, pork, and seafood such as salmon and lobster are offered as baked, steamed, stir-fried, or grilled entrees. A Polynesian combo plays soft island music for dinner guests.

> **DINING HOURS:** Papeete Bay Verandah is open for dinner from 5:30 until 10 PM. Sunday brunch is served from 11 AM until 2 PM.
>
> **AVERAGE PRICE RANGE:** Dinner entrees **$$$**, Sunday brunch **$$$**.
>
> **RESERVATIONS:** Reservations are recommended.

RISTORANTE CARNEVALE: *Walt Disney World Dolphin* — Venice during Carnival is the festive atmosphere of Ristorante Carnevale, which showcases dishes from Italy's Tuscany region. Entrees include large portions of pasta, seafood, sausage, veal, or quail, served up with a burst of song. Strolling jugglers and musicians also provide tableside entertainment.

> **DINING HOURS:** Ristorante Carnevale is open for dinner from 6 until 11 PM.
>
> **AVERAGE PRICE RANGE:** Entrees **$$$$**.
>
> **RESERVATIONS:** Reservations are recommended. The restaurant has a smoking section.

SUM CHOW'S: *Walt Disney World Dolphin* — Sum Chow's serves a sophisticated selection of regional Asian dishes in an elegant environment with white paper lanterns, black lacquer chairs, and deep red tablecloths. Specialty entrees incorporate seafood, beef, pork, lamb, chicken, and duck prepared in a variety of ways and served with great attention to style. A five-course prix-fixe dinner is also available.

> **DINING HOURS:** Sum Chow's is open for dinner from 6 until 10 PM.
>
> **AVERAGE PRICE RANGE:** Dinner entrees **$$$$**, prix-fixe dinner **$$$$$**.
>
> **RESERVATIONS:** Reservations are recommended. The restaurant has a smoking section.

VICTORIA & ALBERT'S: *Disney's Grand Floridian Beach Resort* — Award-winning Victoria & Albert's preserves the grand dining tradition in a formal, elegant setting with Royal Doulton china, individual servers at each table, and pleasant harp music wafting through the air. A seven-course prix-fixe meal is served that changes nightly and reflects the foods of the season. Entrees incorporate seafood, poultry, beef, veal, lamb, and game. Soups, salads, appetizers, and desserts round out the prix-fixe menu. An excellent selection of wines, aperitifs, and cordials is also available.

> **DINING HOURS:** Victoria & Albert's has two dinner seatings, 6 PM and 9 PM.
>
> **AVERAGE PRICE RANGE:** Prix-fixe dinner **$$$$$** (excluding wine and gratuities).
>
> **RESERVATIONS:** Advance reservations are required. Jackets and ties are required for men; evening attire for women.

YACHTSMAN STEAKHOUSE: *Disney's Yacht Club Resort* — Wood plank flooring, strolling musicians, and private booths and dining areas provide an intimate, clubby atmosphere for meat-lovers at the Yachtsman Steakhouse. Entrees include prime cuts of beef, lamb, and pork specially selected and prepared in a glassed-in kitchen. A limited selection of chicken and seafood dishes is also available. The restaurant offers an impressive list of wines and domestic and international beers.

> **DINING HOURS:** Yachtsman Steakhouse is open for dinner from 6 until 10 PM.
>
> **AVERAGE PRICE RANGE:** Entrees **$$$$**.
>
> **RESERVATIONS:** Reservations are recommended. ◆

DINNER SHOWS

Dinner shows are one of the most popular entertainment offerings at Walt Disney World, so if you want to attend one, be sure to reserve a seating well in advance of your visit. The dinner shows reviewed in the pages that follow also include the Diamond Horseshoe Jamboree, which is staged throughout the day at the Magic Kingdom. Over the years, WDW has added more evening entertainment to the lineup of events for adult visitors, and the premier late-night scene is still Pleasure Island (see "Pleasure Island," page 61). Popular with insiders, but less well known among visitors, are the unique dance clubs at Hotel Plaza. Frequented by locals and Disney Cast Members, the clubs listed below are ideal for an inexpensive, casual night out.

LAUGHING KOOKABURRA: *Buena Vista Palace* — This energetic dance club, the largest at Hotel Plaza, is located in the lower level of the hotel. Starting at 4 PM, DJs play a mix of soft rock, seventies disco, and Top 40 tunes. At 10 PM, the featured band comes onstage and the dancing heats up. The crowds are usually thirty-something convention attendees and guests staying at Hotel Plaza.

> **HOURS:** Nightly from 4 PM until 2:30 AM.
>
> **FEATURES:** Happy hour from 4 until 8 PM, including a complimentary buffet. On Ladies' Night Tuesdays, women receive free drinks; Cast Member discounts are on Mondays. Free valet parking.

TOP OF THE PALACE LOUNGE: *Buena Vista Palace* — Located on the hotel's twenty-seventh floor, this elegant lounge provides a perfect setting for guests seeking an intimate spot for cocktails or after-dinner drinks. Guests can dance to live jazz or watch the evening fireworks over the Magic Kingdom, Epcot Center, and Disney-MGM Studios. Live entertainment begins at 9 PM; a singer accompanied by piano appears on weeknights, and a jazz trio is featured on Fridays and Saturdays. The lounge attracts a sophisticated crowd, which spills over from the elegant Arthur's 27. Attire ranges from casual to dressy.

> **HOURS:** Nightly from 5 PM until 1 AM.
>
> **FEATURES:** Nightly Champagne Sunsets feature a complimentary champagne toast every evening, followed by an excellent view of WDW's fireworks shows. Appetizers and desserts from Arthur's 27 are served. Free valet parking at the Laughing Kookaburra entrance, downstairs.

TOPPERS: *Travelodge Hotel* — This popular club, on the hotel's top floor, is a favorite of the locals and Cast Members who flock there after work to watch WDW's fireworks shows, enjoy Margaritas by the pitcher, and dance to modern rock hits played by Toppers' skillful DJs. The club's energy varies throughout the night: Between 8 and 10 PM, it's packed with fireworks spectators; after 10 PM, a lively dance crowd forms; and after midnight, the dance action really begins, making this a great late-night spot.

> **HOURS:** Nightly from 4 PM until 3 AM.
>
> **FEATURES:** Happy hour from 4 until 7 PM, including a complimentary buffet. Snack foods are available from 8 PM until midnight, and the club has an excellent view of all theme park fireworks. On selected nights, Toppers offers two-for-one drink specials; Cast Member discounts are on Tuesdays.

GIRAFFE: *Hotel Royal Plaza* — Giraffe offers solid, basic dance-club entertainment, and guests can drink, dance, throw darts, and shoot pool surrounded by funky early-seventies decor. DJs play new wave and modern rock tunes for a crowd composed largely of the hotel's guests.

> **HOURS:** Nightly from 4 PM until 3 AM.
>
> **FEATURES:** Happy hour from 4 until 9:30 PM. Wednesday is a two-for-one drink night. ◆

BROADWAY AT THE TOP

LOCATION: The Broadway at the Top dinner show is staged nightly at the Top of the World Supper Club on the fifteenth floor of Disney's Contemporary Resort. NOTE: The Top of the World is scheduled to be remodeled in 1994, and the dinner show may not be shown during that time.

ENTERTAINMENT: This cabaret-style show begins after dinner, with three women and two men in sequined evening gowns and white dinner jackets singing and dancing to classic and modern Broadway hits. They are accompanied by a jazzy quintet playing modern renditions of Big Band–style dance music. The intricately choreographed medley of show tunes features some of Walt Disney World's best talent, who perform numbers from *The Music Man, West Side Story, 42nd Street,* and *A Chorus Line.* The show is periodically updated with hit tunes from the latest Broadway performances. Unlike most dinner shows, guests who enjoy dancing are welcome on the dance floor between acts.

DINING ROOM: This moderately sized three-tiered dining room conveys an intimate supper club feeling. Elegant, plush red booths and well-spaced tables comfortably accommodate dinner guests. The better seats are directly in front of the stage, alongside the dance floor, or in booths on the second tier.

SAMPLE MENU: The four-course dinner includes *Appetizer* (Jumbo Shrimp Cocktail, Rainbow Fruit Melody, Consommé du Jour, Crab and Corn Bisque, or Show Stopping Ravioli); *Salad* (butter lettuce, alfalfa sprouts, enoki mushrooms, tomato, and seafood dressing); *Entree* (Prime Rib of Beef au Jus, Chicken Broadway, Shrimp Primavera, Fresh Seasonal Catch, or Contemporary Duo); and *Dessert* (Rich Chocolate Cheesecake, Baked Apple en Croûte, White Chocolate Mousse Cake, or Florida Orange Snow).

Kosher, vegetarian, or low-fat meals may be ordered twenty-four hours in advance through Guest Services at the Contemporary resort (824-1000).

BEVERAGES: Soft drinks, coffee, and iced tea are included with the meal. Guests may also purchase beverages from the extensive wine list, and there is a full-service bar in the adjoining lounge.

PRICE: Ticket price is about $45 (about $20 for children). Tax, gratuities, and alcoholic beverages are not included in the ticket price, and servers expect a 15 to 20 percent tip.

SHOW TIMES: The early show seating is at 6 PM; the late show seating is at 9:15 PM.

MAKING RESERVATIONS: Reservations should be made as far in advance as possible. Guests staying at WDW resorts can reserve the show at the time they book their rooms. Visitors staying in one of the Hotel Plaza resorts can make reservations forty-five days ahead. Day visitors can make reservations thirty days in advance through Walt Disney World Reservations (407 934-7639).

The dinner show is paid for after the meal, and tickets are not purchased in advance. For same-day reservations, call 824-3611.

TIPS: Try to arrive early, as tables are given away on a first-come, first-served basis. Guests who are celebrating a birthday or anniversary should mention it when they make reservations.

NOTE: There is no smoking permitted at Broadway at the Top. Guests will feel most comfortable in evening wear. Jackets (but not ties) are required for gentlemen.

REVIEWERS' RATINGS

XXX – Really makes the evening worthwhile.   **XX** – Pleasant if not memorable.   **X** – Of limited merit.

XX	ENTERTAINMENT	*(Polished routines that are, at times, too intense for this small club.)*
XX	FOOD	*(Fancy food with creative presentations.)*
XXX	SERVICE	*(An elegant, professional, and helpful staff in formal attire.)*
XXX	AMBIENCE	*(Intimate and private. Good for a romantic evening or upscale celebration.)*

DIAMOND HORSESHOE JAMBOREE

LOCATION: The Diamond Horseshoe Jamboree is held at the Diamond Horseshoe Saloon, located at the Magic Kingdom in Frontierland.

ENTERTAINMENT: The show opens with a selection of Gay Nineties music performed by a live band. The musicians perform throughout the show, adding fills and reactions to the on- and off-stage activities. Miss Lilly then sweeps into the saloon with her girls, who perform a series of rollicking tunes, athletic can-can dances, and comic vignettes on both the stage and the saloon's main floor. Intermittently, Miss Lilly entertains with songs, a surprisingly provocative striptease behind a screen as she changes out of her traveling clothes into a red satin dress, and flirtatious exchanges with members of the audience, some of whom are invited onto the stage to play an array of cowbells, clackers, and other musical items. An easy flow of well-timed humor and innocent and not-quite-so-innocent naughtiness entertains both adults and children.

DINING ROOM: The Diamond Horseshoe Saloon, with its white-framed arched windows and a large front porch, is a replica of an eighteenth-century frontier dance hall. The main floor has an elegant stage at one end, and a long wooden bar with a polished brass rail runs along the wall. The horseshoe-shaped balcony is set off with white wooden railings. Guests are seated on both levels at rustic wooden tables.

SAMPLE MENU: *Snacks* (popcorn and potato chips), *Smoked Turkey Sandwich* or *Smoked Ham and Swiss Sandwich* (served with pickles and potato chips), *Peanut Butter and Jelly Sandwich* (served with potato chips and brownie), and a house special, *The Horseshoe* (pastrami, salami, and cheese on rye, served with pickles and potato chips). Desserts include ice cream and brownies.

BEVERAGES: Soft drinks, milk, punch, and iced tea are available for purchase. Coffee and other hot beverages are not available, as there have been accidental spills from the balcony.

PRICE: There is no charge to see the show. Food prices are as follows: sandwiches about $6, snacks and desserts about $3, and beverages about $2. Gratuities are not included in the food or beverage prices, and servers expect a 15 to 20 percent tip.

SHOW TIMES: Shows are scheduled daily at 10:45 AM, 12:15 PM, 1:45 PM, 3:30 PM, and 4:45 PM.

MAKING RESERVATIONS: You must make reservations in person on the day you wish to see the show. The shows fill quickly, so reservations should be made as early in the day as possible — preferably as soon as the Magic Kingdom opens (between 8 and 9 AM). To reserve a table, go to the podium in front of Disneyana Collectibles on Main Street, across the Town Square from City Hall. At that time, you will be given a ticket and table number — if you have a special seating request, make it then.

TIPS: If you are unable to get a confirmed reservation, go to the saloon forty-five minutes before the scheduled show time. Guests without reservations are seated at empty tables on a first-come, first-served basis.
Diamond Horseshoe Jamboree is sometimes included on the Guided Tour of the Magic Kingdom. The tables on the balcony offer the best view of the show — ask for table 204 or 209 or one nearby. Guests at the 3:30 PM show can watch the Surprise Celebration parade while waiting to be seated.

NOTE: Smoking is not permitted at the Diamond Horseshoe Jamboree.

REVIEWERS' RATINGS

XXX – Really makes the event worthwhile.   **XX** – Pleasant if not memorable.   **X** – Of limited merit.

XXX   ENTERTAINMENT   *(A vivacious performance by skilled singers and dancers.)*
X   FOOD   *(The quality and limited selection are unexceptional. The feature is the show.)*
XXX   SERVICE   *(Polite, good-humored, and professional.)*
XXX   AMBIENCE   *(A boisterous, Gay Nineties saloon atmosphere, meticulously designed.)*

HOOP-DEE-DOO MUSICAL REVUE

LOCATION: The Hoop-Dee-Doo Musical Revue is held nightly at Pioneer Hall, in the heart of 740-acre Fort Wilderness. Visitors can catch shuttle buses to Pioneer Hall from the Fort Wilderness Guest Parking Lot, or ferry across Bay Lake from the Contemporary Marina or the Magic Kingdom Dock.

ENTERTAINMENT: The dinner show, performed by the enthusiastic Pioneer Hall Players, starts with a banjo and piano serenade followed by a song-and-dance vaudeville performance that relies heavily on broad humor, sight gags, pratfalls, puns, and audience participation. The colorfully costumed performers mingle with the audience, asking them where they're from, then sing little ditties based on the replies. Guests with birthdays or anniversaries are singled out for special attention, as are newlyweds. For the finale, washboards are handed out to the audience, who are encouraged to play them with their spoons.

DINING ROOM: The large pine-log lodge has two levels: a ground floor with a stage at one end, and a balcony supported by large rock pillars. The room is lit with hanging wagon-wheel fixtures and decorated in a wilderness motif with stuffed animal heads, snowshoes, and antlers.

SAMPLE MENU: The family-style all-you-can-eat dinner includes *Appetizer* (chips and salsa, and a small loaf of white bread); *Salad* (lettuce, slices of cucumber, carrot, and cabbage) with *Vinaigrette Dressing; Barbecued Beef Ribs and Chicken* (served in a metal pail); *Corn on the Cob;* and *Strawberry Shortcake.*

Kosher, vegetarian, or low-sodium meals may be ordered twenty-four hours in advance through the Hoop-Dee-Doo Musical Revue Office (824-2748).

BEVERAGES: Soft drinks, coffee, and iced tea are included with the meal. Beer and a very mild sangría are also offered.

PRICE: Ticket price is about $35 ($26 for juniors, $18 for children). Gratuities are not included in the ticket price, and servers expect a 15 to 20 percent tip.

SHOW TIMES: Shows are scheduled at 5 PM, 7:15 PM, and 9:30 PM. Families frequent the early show.

MAKING RESERVATIONS: Reservations for the popular Hoop-Dee-Doo Musical Revue should be made as far in advance as possible. WDW resort guests can reserve the show at the time they book their rooms. Visitors staying in one of the Hotel Plaza resorts can make reservations forty-five days ahead. Day visitors can make reservations thirty days in advance through Walt Disney World Reservations (407 934-7639).

Reserved dinner-show tickets can be purchased at Guest Services in any WDW resort, or at the Guest Services Window at Pioneer Hall. You are assigned a table number at that time. The better tables are on the balcony or in the center of the ground floor. For same-day reservations, call 824-2748.

TIPS: Pioneer Hall is not easy to find at night, and it takes longer than you think to get there. See "Fort Wilderness & River Country," page 68, for a map of Fort Wilderness and transportation details.

Seating begins about twenty minutes before show time. If you arrive early, relax in the comfortable rocking chairs on the porch, or enjoy a pre-dinner beverage at Crockett's Tavern next door.

NOTE: There is no smoking permitted at the Hoop-Dee-Doo Musical Revue. Dress is very casual. During the summer, it may be a good idea to wear mosquito repellent.

REVIEWERS' RATINGS

✗✗✗ – Really makes the evening worthwhile.   **✗✗** – Pleasant if not memorable.   **✗** – Of limited merit.

✗   ENTERTAINMENT   *(Very weak material executed by talented performers.)*
✗   FOOD   *(Ample amounts, but the meats are greasy and the corn on the cob soggy.)*
✗✗✗   SERVICE   *(Polite, fast, friendly, and professional.)*
✗✗   AMBIENCE   *(A boisterous, family-steakhouse atmosphere. Kids have a great time here.)*

JOLLY HOLIDAYS

LOCATION: The Jolly Holidays dinner show and Christmas celebration is staged in the Fantasia Ballroom at Disney's Contemporary Resort, which is located on the monorail line in the Magic Kingdom Resorts Area.

ENTERTAINMENT: Guests are entertained periodically during dinner by carolers, but it is after dinner that the action really begins. The lights go down and all four stages in the ballroom are used, which keeps guests swiveling in their seats. Toyland on Christmas Eve is the theme of the show, and throughout the room, toys come to life, including a parade of toy soldiers, Raggedy Ann and Andy, Goofy dressed as Santa, Minnie and Mickey Mouse, and a cast of more than one hundred elaborately costumed singers and dancers. The show runs heavy on the sentimental, but what could be more appropriate for Christmas? The entertainment is modified and new elements are added each year.

DINING ROOM: The Fantasia Ballroom is on the ground floor of the Contemporary's new convention center. The four walls of this vast ballroom are turned into elaborate stages, and the room is filled with round tables that seat twelve and are festively decorated with green tablecloths, red napkins, and a center-piece of brightly wrapped gifts. Most tables are near at least one stage, and the aisles between tables are also used by the performers, so everyone has a unique view. The ballroom's prismatic mirrored ceiling is used to created special lighting effects with spotlights, lasers, and strobes.

SAMPLE MENU: The all-you-can-eat turkey dinner, with all the trimmings, is served family-style at each table. The menu includes *Platters of Sliced Roast Turkey, Gravy, Mashed Potatoes, Sweet Potatoes, Green Beans, Cranberry Sauce,* and *Hot Apple Cobbler with Fresh Whipped Cream.* Food and beverages are frequently replenished by servers.

BEVERAGES: Unlimited soft drinks, coffee, tea, and red and white wine are included with the meal.

PRICE: Ticket price is about $50 ($45 for juniors, $30 for children). Gratuities and taxes are included in the ticket price.

SHOW TIMES: Jolly Holidays plays nightly from just after Thanksgiving until just before Christmas. Shows are scheduled at either 5 or 7:30 PM. Families with young children frequent the early shows.

MAKING RESERVATIONS: Reservations for Jolly Holidays can be made beginning around October through Walt Disney World Reservations (407 934-7639). The show is paid for at the time it is booked, with a credit card or by mail order. There is a forty-eight-hour cancellation policy. Walt Disney World also offers a Jolly Holiday Vacation Package that includes accommodations, admission to the Jolly Holidays dinner show, themed holiday receptions at specially decorated resorts throughout the property, and admission to all Walt Disney World theme parks. Same-day reservations can be made through Guest Services at any WDW resort.

TIPS: Seating begins about twenty minutes before show time. If you arrive early, several no-host bars dispense Christmas spirits in the large lobby outside the ballroom.

Guests are seated communally at tables for twelve on a first-come, first-served basis.

NOTE: There is no smoking permitted at Jolly Holidays. Dress tends to be festive.

REVIEWERS' RATINGS

XXX – Really makes the evening worthwhile. **XX** – Pleasant if not memorable. **X** – Of limited merit.

XXX ENTERTAINMENT *(Great sound, lighting, and performances. A pleaser for all ages.)*

XXX FOOD *(If you like turkey dinners, this is the best food at any Disney dinner show.)*

XXX SERVICE *(The servers are unobtrusive and skilled professional convention workers.)*

XX AMBIENCE *(It's remarkable that a ballroom can be made to feel so cozy and homey.)*

MurderWatch Mystery Dinner Theater

LOCATION: MurderWatch Mystery Dinner Theater is staged on Saturday nights at the Grosvenor Resort, located on Hotel Plaza at Disney Village. The show is held in Baskervilles restaurant.

ENTERTAINMENT: Guests are asked to help solve a murder with a zany and animated group of players, some of whom are clandestinely planted in the audience before the show. Most of the action takes place after guests have served themselves at the buffet. Some subtle altercations occur while guests are dining, to attract attention to the large cast and to create suspicion. After witnessing a murder, compiling clues, guessing at motives, and listening to a number of hilarious, heartrending confessions, guests are asked to choose the most likely suspect. The winners receive their awards on stage.

DINING ROOM: Guests are seated at tables for two, four, or six in a spacious but intimately proportioned Edwardian-style dining room. The walls of the restaurant are decorated with framed plates from Sherlock Holmes editions, drawn for London's *Strand Magazine* in the 1890s.

MENU: The all-you-can-eat buffet includes *Roast Prime Rib of Beef, Yorkshire Pudding, Asian Stir-fried Vegetables, Baked Chicken with Mushrooms and Peppers, Baked Fish with Spinach and Tomatoes, Stuffed Shells,* and a complete *Salad Bar.* Side dishes include *Rice Pilaf with Raisins and Almonds* and *Corn Fritters.* Guests select from an array of desserts at the *Dessert Buffet.*

BEVERAGES: Coffee and tea are available at the buffet. Soft drinks, wine, and beer are brought to the table by servers. Guests can order cocktails from Moriarty's Pub, next door.

PRICE: Ticket price is about $25 (about $12.50 for children). The admission price includes gratuities. Guests pay as they enter the restaurant.

SHOW TIMES: There is one show nightly at 6:30 PM; during peak seasons, show times are at 6 and 9 PM.

MAKING RESERVATIONS: Reservations for the MurderWatch Mystery Dinner Theater should be made well in advance of your visit. There is no preference for guests at the Grosvenor Resort, and reservations are taken on a first-come, first-served basis. During peak seasons and holidays, reservations should be made at least two to four weeks in advance. Reservations made during low-attendance times require a two-day advance notice. Reservations can be made by calling the Grosvenor Resort (800 624-4109).

TIPS: The dining room has several large square pillars in the center, which can obscure the action taking place throughout the show. Ask for a table on the perimeter of the room when booking reservations.

Don't miss the Grosvenor's Sherlock Holmes Museum, an exact replica of the famous detective's 221B Baker Street digs, tucked in the back of the restaurant. It includes such props as the famous Stradivarius, Holmes' purple dressing gown and Meerschaum pipe, and the remains of a meal interrupted by a client in distress. Give yourself a little extra time before or after the show to view it.

There are very few children at these shows; the atmosphere is more like a supper club. The few children who do attend are usually nine or older and are rounded up as clue hunters by the hosts.

NOTE: The Grosvenor caters to a European clientele, and smoking is allowed throughout the dining room. Avid nonsmokers might want to pass on this show. Guests should dress for a sit-down dinner.

REVIEWERS' RATINGS

XXX – Really makes the evening worthwhile.   **XX** – Pleasant if not memorable.   **X** – Of limited merit.

XX   ENTERTAINMENT   *(A quick and professional cast. The jokes can be insensitive at times.)*

XX   FOOD   *(Above-average buffet-style food, good prime rib, and a very good value.)*

XX   SERVICE   *(Self-service. Servers bring beverages and clear plates.)*

XX   AMBIENCE   *(Fun if you're in the mood. The audience gets involved in solving the crime.)*

POLYNESIAN LUAU

LOCATION: The Polynesian Luau dinner show is staged nightly in Luau Cove, an open-air dinner theater near the beach at Seven Seas Lagoon, behind Disney's Polynesian Resort.

ENTERTAINMENT: The show begins after dinner, with a South Seas island fashion show and the music of a five-piece Hawaiian band. After a brief intermission, the talented dancers appear on stage: women wearing skirts of ti leaves interpreting a graceful hula, men performing a tribal dance from the kingdom of Tonga, the staccato drums and fast-moving dances of Tahiti, and a dramatic Samoan fire-dance finale with burning torches and a great deal of good humor.

DINING ROOM: A partial roof covers the large fan-shaped dining room, protecting guests from the occasional rains but leaving the stage open to the sky. Guests are seated at long, candlelit quasi-communal tables that radiate out from the stage.

SAMPLE MENU: The family-style all-you-can-eat dinner includes *Salad* (lettuce, tomatoes, radicchio, carrots, orange segments, and banana chips) with *Cucumber Dressing; Stir-Fried Vegetables with Scallops and Shrimp; Barbecued Pork Ribs; Roasted Chicken; Herbed Rice; Dessert of Fresh Fruit* (pineapple, strawberries, melons, and kiwi) with *Chocolate Dipping Sauce.* The menu may vary.

Kosher, vegetarian, or low-fat meals may be ordered twenty-four hours in advance through the Polynesian Luau Office (824-1335).

BEVERAGES: Soft drinks, coffee, and iced tea are included with the meal. You may also select a *Mai Tai* (tropical fruit juices, orange liqueur, and rum) or *Melon Colada* (pineapple juice, coconut milk, melon liqueur, and rum). They may sound potent but they're very mild. Beer and wine are also offered.

PRICE: Ticket price is about $35 (about $25 for juniors and $20 for children). Gratuities are not included in the ticket price, and servers expect a 15 to 20 percent tip.

SHOW TIMES: The early show seating is at 6:45 PM; the late show seating is at 9:30 PM.

MAKING RESERVATIONS: Reservations for the Polynesian Luau should be made well in advance. Guests staying at WDW resorts can reserve the show at the time they book their rooms. Visitors staying in one of the Hotel Plaza Resorts can make reservations forty-five days ahead. Day visitors can make reservations thirty days in advance through Walt Disney World Reservations (407 934-7639).

Reserved dinner-show tickets can be purchased at Guest Services at the Polynesian or any other WDW resort. You are assigned a table number at that time.

TIPS: The performance is most dramatic when it is dark, so try to book the late show during the summer. If your timing is right, you can see the Magic Kingdom fireworks show during dinner.

Visitors who would like a sneak preview of the Polynesian Luau should venture out to Luau Cove at 8 or 10:45 PM. The stage may be viewed from the courtyard at the entrance, which is part of the hotel common area.

NOTE: There is no smoking permitted at the Polynesian Luau. Dress casually for an outdoor setting. Shows are rarely cancelled, even in the rain, but if the weather is very cold, call 824-1335 to confirm.

REVIEWERS' RATINGS

XXX – Really makes the evening worthwhile.   **XX** – Pleasant if not memorable.   **X** – Of limited appeal.

XX	ENTERTAINMENT	*(A pleasant, well-crafted show with professional dance and music.)*
XX	FOOD	*(Not exactly a gourmet feast, but enjoyable and filling.)*
X	SERVICE	*(Family-style service by polite but rushed and impersonal staff.)*
XXX	AMBIENCE	*(The tropical atmosphere is especially nice after dark.)*

SPORTING ACTIVITIES

Travelers who like to combine sporting activities with their vacations will find plenty of options at Walt Disney World, which prides itself on the quality and diversity of its recreational facilities. Walt Disney World has devoted years of planning and development to meet the needs of its sporting guests, positioning itself as a premier sports vacation destination (see also "Sporting Life Vacation," page 107). If you are interested in specific sports or recreation activities, you may want to stay at a resort that features them (see "Hotels," page 143, for recreation facilities at individual resorts). Day visitors also have access to most outdoor activities.

BICYCLING: There are more than fifteen miles of bicycle paths at WDW, many in wilderness and other unique settings. The best resorts for bicycling are the Vacation Club, Village Resort, and Fort Wilderness.

BOATING: Thirteen marinas offer rentals of sailboats, pedal boats, motorboats, and canoes, and provide access to over 750 acres of WDW lakes and waterways. Some of the best resorts for boating are the Contemporary, Grand Floridian, Polynesian, and Fort Wilderness.

FISHING: The Fort Wilderness and Buena Vista Lagoon Fishing Excursions are led by professionals, who take guests to the best spots to angle for largemouth bass, bluegill, and brown bullhead catfish. Guests may also fish the Fort Wilderness Waterways.

GOLF: Five outstanding PGA golf courses make Walt Disney World the largest golf resort in the world and the site of more than a thousand golf tournaments each year. The best resorts for golf vacations include the Vacation Club, Village Resort, and Disney Inn.

HEALTH CLUBS: Many of the WDW resorts are outfitted with the latest in exercise equipment and services, including personal trainers. The resorts with the best health clubs are the Vacation Club, Yacht Club, Beach Club, Dolphin, Contemporary, and Grand Floridian.

HORSEBACK RIDING: At the Tri-Circle-D Livery, visitors can mount one of the well-trained quarterhorses, paints, or Appaloosas for a pleasant trail ride through the back country of Fort Wilderness.

JOGGING: The many jogging paths and designated runs at WDW include both scenic meandering trails and strenuous courses with exercise stations — all well maintained. The resorts with the best jogging paths are the Village Resort and Fort Wilderness.

NATURE WALKS: The self-led nature walks at WDW take visitors through forests, wetlands, specimen gardens, and jungle environments, and provide encounters with an abundance of exotic plants and wildlife.

SWIMMING: Sun- and water-lovers can work out or cool down in numerous lap pools and lounge pools, on white sand beaches, and in water parks throughout Walt Disney World. Among the resorts with the best pool and beach scenes are the Grand Floridian, Contemporary, Beach Club, and Polynesian.

TENNIS: WDW's two tennis clubs, forty courts, and professional instructors are available to both serious and casual players. The best tennis resorts are Contemporary, Swan, Dolphin, and Grand Floridian.

VOLLEYBALL: Several recreation areas and resorts offer sand courts and volleyballs for both friendly and competitive games. The resorts with the best volleyball courts are the Beach Club and Vacation Club.

WATERSKIING: Professional instructors at Fort Wilderness take groups out into Bay Lake for waterskiing excursions throughout the day, providing both equipment and skiing instruction. ◆

BICYCLE PATHS

Bicycling is one of the more pleasant exercise diversions at Walt Disney World and offers an array of scenic views and landscapes. Six Walt Disney World resorts have bicycling areas ranging from beach promenades and wilderness areas to manicured fairways and flower-lined streets. Rental fees range from about $3 to $5 per hour and $6 to $10 per day, depending on the resort and type of bike. Florida weather permits bicycling at any time of the year. During the summer months, visitors will find early-morning rides the most pleasant, since afternoons tend to be hot, humid, and often rainy. During the rest of the year, however, bicyclists can enjoy rides at any time of day. Bicycle rentals end at sundown.

◆

WILDERNESS RIDE
Disney's Fort Wilderness Resort and Campground

Eight miles of roads and trails throughout Fort Wilderness are available to visitors riding either single or tandem bicycles. The lightly traveled paved roads have occasional cars and buses, but the off-road trail system is a biker's dream. It meanders along waterways, past beaches, through shady forests, and across bridges and boardwalks.

WHERE TO RENT: Bicycles, including tandem bikes, can be rented at the Bike Barn, located at the Meadow Recreation Area in Fort Wilderness.

WHO MAY RENT: Bicycles are available to both WDW resort guests and day visitors.

BIKING AREAS: Bikers may use all roads, paths, and trails throughout Fort Wilderness. The overall path length is about eight miles.

MAPS: Maps showing the roads and trails of Fort Wilderness are available at the Bike Barn, where bicycles are rented. (See also "Fort Wilderness & River Country," page 68.)

NOTE: Paths are shared with pedestrians and electric carts. Roads are also traveled by cars and WDW buses, so bikers should use caution.

◆

COUNTRY CLUB AND OLD KEY WEST RIDE
Disney's Village Resort and Disney Vacation Club

Combining the features of two adjoining resorts, this pleasant ride for the leisurely biker travels through the sprawling Village Resort, past spacious green fairways, across bridges and waterways, and along shady forest lanes. The path continues into the Vacation Club, following the winding streets lined with sun-bleached, Key West–style vacation cottages.

WHERE TO RENT: Bicycles may be rented at either resort and ridden through both. Disney's Village Resort rents bicycles at the bell stand in the Reception Center. The Disney Vacation Club rents both regular and tandem bicycles at Hank's Rent N' Return.

WHO MAY RENT: Only guests staying at a WDW resort may rent bicycles at these two resorts.

BIKING AREAS: At Disney's Village Resort, bikes may use the resort roadways and all paths designated for joggers, but may not leave the paved areas or travel on the golf paths. At Disney Vacation Club, bicycles may use any of the streets. The overall path length is about three miles.

MAPS: Maps showing the roadways and golf cart paths at the Village Resort are available at the bell stand in the Reception Center, where bicycles are rented. Maps of the Vacation Club roadways are available at Hank's Rent N' Return, where bicycles are rented.

NOTE: Paths are shared with pedestrians and electric carts. Roads are also traveled by cars and WDW buses, so bikers should use caution.

TROPICAL ISLAND CRUISE
Disney's Caribbean Beach Resort

The paved promenade encircling forty-acre Barefoot Bay lake lets bikers meander casually along white sand beaches and sample a range of exotic tropical landscaping and colorful Caribbean-style lodges. Bicycles may cross the wooden bridges leading to Parrot Cay island and travel past the aviaries and themed architecture of an old Caribbean fort.

WHERE TO RENT: Bicycles may be rented at the Barefoot Bay Boat Yard, located in the center of the Caribbean Beach Resort at Old Port Royale.

WHO MAY RENT: Bicycles are available to both WDW resort guests and day visitors.

BIKING AREAS: Bicycles may use the promenade that encircles Barefoot Bay and the sidewalks of the individual island villages. Bicycles are not permitted on the perimeter roads of the resort. The overall path length is about $1\frac{1}{2}$ miles.

MAPS: Maps of the promenade at Disney's Caribbean Beach Resort are available at the Barefoot Boat Yard, where bicycles are rented.

NOTE: Joggers and pedestrians share the promenade with bikers. The best time for a bicycle ride is mid-morning, after resort guests have departed for the theme parks.

EASY RIDER
Disney's Port Orleans and Dixie Landings Resorts

The paved areas and rustic paths of these two resorts take bikers riding single or tandem bicycles on a town-and-country tour through the Old South. The path follows the Carriage Path encircling Port Orleans, a replica of the French Quarter in New Orleans. It continues along the riverfront to Dixie Landings, meandering past plantation mansions and deep-country bayou lodges sheltered by tall trees draped with Spanish moss.

WHERE TO RENT: Single and tandem bikes are available at both resorts. At Port Orleans, bicycles can be rented at Port Orleans Landing, near the marina. At Dixie Landings, bicycles can be rented at Dixie Levee, near the marina.

WHO MAY RENT: Bicycles are available to both WDW resort guests and day visitors.

BIKING AREAS: Bikers may ride on any of the sidewalks and inner roadways of both resorts, as well as all along the Carriage Path. Bicycles are not permitted on the perimeter roads of the resorts. The overall path length is about $2\frac{1}{2}$ miles.

MAPS: Resort maps are available at Guest Services in both resorts.

NOTE: Pedestrians, joggers, and luggage-conveyance carts share this path, although it is generally deserted during the day. ◆

BOATING & MARINAS

Walt Disney World is home to the largest privately owned fleet of watercraft in the world — and much of it is available to visitors who would like to explore the extensive waterways and interconnected lakes that span the forty-three square miles of Walt Disney World. A variety of rental boats is available at all of the Walt Disney World lakes: Bay Lake, Seven Seas Lagoon, Buena Vista Lagoon, Lake Buena Vista, Crescent Lake, Stormalong Bay, and Barefoot Bay. Boats may also be rented to explore Walt Disney World's canal and inland waterway systems. Disney's Fort Wilderness Resort and Campground and the marinas in the Disney Village Resorts Area provide access to these waterways.

LAKES, WATERWAYS, AND MARINAS

The Walt Disney World marinas are open every day from about 10 AM until sundown. Visitors who rent boats at one marina can dock at other marinas in the area to tour various theme resorts or explore recreation facilities. Each lake and waterway has unique characteristics and touring opportunities. The watercraft are available on a first-come, first-served basis.

SEVEN SEAS LAGOON AND BAY LAKE: Together, these lakes make up the largest body of water at Walt Disney World, covering 650 acres. The lakes are connected by a unique water bridge and are also used by ferries, waterskiers, and fishing excursions. Forests and wetlands surround the lakes, which are accented by miles of white sand beaches. The wetlands are home to a large population of native waterfowl, including great white egrets, herons, and pelicans. Discovery Island zoological park lies in the middle of Bay Lake, and although boaters cannot dock at Discovery Island, they can dock their craft at the following marinas during their excursion (boats must be returned to the marina where rented):

- Marina Pavilion at Disney's Contemporary Resort
- The Marina at Disney's Fort Wilderness Resort and Campground
- Catamaran Corner at Disney's Polynesian Resort
- Captain's Shipyard at Disney's Grand Floridian Beach Resort.

BUENA VISTA LAGOON AND THE DISNEY VILLAGE WATERWAYS: Buena Vista Lagoon, thirty-five acres of man-made lake, is the showcase lake of the Disney Village Resorts Area. Along its shores are the Disney Village Marketplace shopping center and Pleasure Island. A Mississippi riverboat replica, the *Empress Lilly,* is docked at Buena Vista Lagoon, and the lagoon's waters are used by ferries and fishing excursions. The narrow Disney Village Waterways lead off from the lagoon and meander through pine forests and bayous where the trees are overhung by vines. The waterways pass under footbridges and flow by fairways populated with golfers trying to make par, while snowy white long-necked egrets pose among the water reeds, hoping the boat wake will wash something edible their way. The waterways lead to the Trumbo Canal and the Sassagoula River, and boaters can dock their craft at the following marinas during their excursion:

- The Marina at Disney Village Marketplace
- Hank's Rent N' Return at Disney Vacation Club
- The Landing at Disney's Port Orleans Resort
- Dixie Levee at Disney's Dixie Landings Resort.

CRESCENT LAKE AND STORMALONG BAY: These two small interconnected lakes are surrounded by some of the most intriguing architecture at Walt Disney World, including the fanciful Dolphin and Swan resorts, and the faithfully replicated New England seaside architecture of the Yacht Club and Beach Club resorts. On the other side of the lakes, in the World Showcase, the tops of the replicas of the Eiffel Tower and the Campanile of St. Mark's Square in Venice can be seen. Along the shores are white sand beaches, arched bridges, and boardwalks filled with strolling pedestrians and colorful trams on their way to the International Gateway. The lakes are also used by ferries. Boaters can rent their craft at the following marinas:

- The Hot Spot at Walt Disney World's Dolphin and Swan
- Bayside Marina at Disney's Yacht Club and Beach Club Resorts.

BAREFOOT BAY: This forty-acre lake is actually three interconnected lakes, one of which has Parrot Cay island in its center, spanned on both sides by wooden footbridges. A white sand beach follows the shoreline and, just beyond it, a promenade of pedestrians and bicyclists encircles the lake. On all sides of the lake, clusters of brightly colored Caribbean cottages are nestled in the extensive tropical landscaping. Boaters can rent their craft at the following marina:

- Barefoot Bay Boat Yard at Disney's Caribbean Beach Resort.

FORT WILDERNESS WATERWAYS: Friendly ducks and not-so-friendly swans share these narrow waterways with native waterfowl and canoers. At times, the waterways give way to open grassy banks where hopeful fishers patiently hold their poles. More often, the canals become bayoulike, closed in by pine forests hung with gray-green Spanish moss. Here and there, canoers will find picnic-perfect shady inlets filled with water reeds and an occasional blue heron standing guard. Canoers may rent their craft at the following marina:

- The Bike Barn at Disney's Fort Wilderness Resort and Campground.

LAKE BUENA VISTA: No one seems to know the name of this lake, which local residents claim was originally called Black Lake before the land was developed by Disney. It is both a natural lake and an extension of the man-made Buena Vista Lagoon, nearby. Lake Buena Vista is on the grounds of the Buena Vista Palace hotel in the Disney Village Resorts Area. The shores are surrounded by dark green water reeds with a dense stand of pine forest beyond. The glassy surface of the lake's dark waters is ideal for the Sunkats that use it exclusively, and, of course, ideal for the swans and ducks that populate it prettily. Boaters can rent their craft at the following marina:

- Recreation Island Marina at Buena Vista Palace.

WATERCRAFT

Visitors can select from a wide variety of watercraft at the Walt Disney World marinas including speedboats, sailboats, canopy boats, pontoon boats, pedal boats, canoes, rowboats, and a selection of floatable flotsam such as Toobies (motorized inner tubes) and sailboards. Boats can be rented by the hour or half hour and are available to both Walt Disney World resort guests and day visitors with a valid driver's license (a few exceptions are noted below). The fees for rentals and the types of boats available vary from marina to marina. Generally, the least expensive rentals are at the lower-priced resorts. Boats are rented on a first-come, first-served basis and cannot be reserved.

WATER SPRITES: These tiny, two-passenger mini speedboats sit low in the water and zip along at about ten miles per hour. Water Sprites are used exclusively on the lakes and are not allowed in the canals or narrow waterways.

CAPACITY: Water Sprites hold two passengers (weighing up to three-hundred pounds total).

RENTAL FEE: Depending on the marina, Water Sprite rentals start at about $24 per hour.

WHO MAY RENT: Water Sprites are available to both WDW resort guests and day visitors.

MARINAS: Water Sprites are available at the following marinas and resorts: Contemporary, Polynesian, Grand Floridian, Yacht Club, Beach Club, Fort Wilderness Marina, and Disney Village Marketplace Marina.

SAILBOATS: Sailboats and catamarans are available in a variety of sizes and styles, including Sunfish, Com-Pacs, Capris, and Hobie Cats. Visitors who wish to rent catamarans must be experienced sailors.

CAPACITY: The Sunfish holds two passengers; the Com-Pac holds four passengers; the Capri holds up to six passengers; the Hobie Cat 14 holds two passengers; the Hobie Cat 16 holds three.

RENTAL FEE: Depending on the marina, sailboat rentals start at about $12 per hour.

WHO MAY RENT: Sailboats are available to both WDW resort guests and day visitors. The sailboats at the Dolphin and Swan are available to WDW resort guests only.

MARINAS: Sailboats are available at the following marinas and resorts: Contemporary, Polynesian, Grand Floridian, Yacht Club, Beach Club, Caribbean Beach, Swan, Dolphin, and Fort Wilderness Marina.

PONTOON BOATS: These motor-powered watercraft, also known as float boats, are canopied and sit high in the water atop gleaming stainless-steel pontoons. They are available in twenty- and twenty-four-foot lengths and may cruise either the lakes or the waterways. They are ideal for larger groups.

CAPACITY: Twenty-foot pontoon boats hold eight to ten passengers; twenty-four-foot pontoon boats hold up to twenty passengers.

RENTAL FEE: Depending on the marina, pontoon boat rentals start at about $30 per hour for twenty-foot boats and about $50 per hour for twenty-four-foot boats. Reservations are required for the large pontoon boats, which include a driver.

WHO MAY RENT: Pontoon boats are available to both WDW resort guests and day visitors.

MARINAS: Pontoon boats are available at the following marinas and resorts: Contemporary, Polynesian, Grand Floridian, Yacht Club, Beach Club, Vacation Club, Port Orleans, Dixie Landings, Caribbean Beach, Disney Village Marketplace Marina, and Fort Wilderness Marina.

CANOPY BOATS: Motorized canopy boats may be used on both the lakes and waterways. Their striped canvas canopies provide shade and they are ideal sightseeing craft for small groups. At some marinas, larger canopy boats are available.

CAPACITY: Small canopy boats hold four passengers; large canopy boats hold six passengers.

RENTAL FEE: Depending on the marina, rental fees for canopy boats range from about $20 to $26 per hour. Large canopy boats rent for about $35 per hour.

WHO MAY RENT: Canopy boats are available to both WDW resort guests and day visitors.

MARINAS: Canopy boats are available at the following marinas and resorts: Contemporary, Polynesian, Grand Floridian, Yacht Club, Beach Club, Vacation Club, Port Orleans, Dixie Landings, Caribbean Beach, Disney Village Marketplace Marina, and Fort Wilderness Marina.

PEDAL BOATS: These small, colorful, human-powered watercraft, also called paddle boats, will cruise along as fast as you can pedal. They're very light and are ideal for lazy explorations of the shoreline and for sneaking up on waterfowl for a closer look. Only the front seats have pedals, so passengers in the back get a free ride.

    CAPACITY: Pedal boats hold up to four passengers.

    RENTAL FEE: Depending on the marina, pedal boat rentals start at about $10 per hour.

    WHO MAY RENT: Pedal boats are available to both WDW resort guests and day visitors. Pedal boats at the Dolphin and Swan are available to WDW resort guests only.

    MARINAS: Pedal boats are available at the following marinas and resorts: Polynesian, Yacht Club, Beach Club, Port Orleans, Dixie Landings, Vacation Club, Caribbean Beach, Swan, Dolphin, and the Bike Barn at Fort Wilderness.

ROWBOATS: A few resorts maintain a small fleet of rowboats for visitors who want to see if that rowing machine at the gym actually pays off. These nifty boats are great for getting in close to the shore or exploring small inlets that other boats cannot reach.

    CAPACITY: Rowboats hold up to two passengers.

    RENTAL FEE: Depending on the marina, rowboats rentals start at about $5 per hour.

    WHO MAY RENT: Rowboats are available to both WDW resort guests and day visitors.

    MARINAS: Rowboats are available at the following resorts: Yacht Club, Beach Club, Vacation Club, Port Orleans, and Dixie Landings.

CANOES: Canoes are the official watercraft of the Fort Wilderness Waterways. These canals are a favorite spot for fishing, and canoers can buy bait and rent fishing poles, as well. The canoes at the Caribbean Beach resort are for use on forty-acre Barefoot Bay lake.

    CAPACITY: Canoes hold up to three passengers.

    RENTAL FEE: Depending on the marina, canoe rentals start at about $5 per hour.

    WHO MAY RENT: Canoes are available to both WDW resort guests and day visitors.

    MARINAS: Canoes are available at the following marinas and resorts: Caribbean Beach and the Bike Barn at Fort Wilderness. (See also "Fishing Excursions," page 224.)

OUTRIGGER CANOES: These are the canoes that were fashioned by the Polynesians for steady travel through the pounding surf. Outrigger canoes are restricted to Seven Seas Lagoon, and they require a minimum of six persons to row.

    CAPACITY: Outrigger canoes hold up to eight passengers.

    RENTAL FEE: Rental fees for outrigger canoes start at about $2 per person per hour.

    WHO MAY RENT: Outrigger canoes are available to both WDW resort guests and day visitors.

    MARINAS: Outrigger canoes are available at the Polynesian resort.

SUNKATS: These motorized lounge chairs for two are ideal for drifting along and soaking up the sun on a lazy afternoon. They float high above the water on rubber pontoons.

    CAPACITY: Sunkats hold up to two passengers.

    RENTAL FEE: Depending on the marina, Sunkat rentals start at about $22 per hour.

    WHO MAY RENT: Sunkats are available only to WDW resort guests.

    MARINAS: Sunkats are available at the following resorts: Buena Vista Palace, Swan, and Dolphin. ◆

FISHING EXCURSIONS

In recent years, the fishing excursions at Walt Disney World have become increasingly popular. In fact, during the summer months, excursions are reserved many months in advance. The fishing guides who lead the excursions are professional fishers, and they know well the best fishing spots in the lakes they tour. There are two main fishing areas at Walt Disney World: Bay Lake and Buena Vista Lagoon. A large number of native fish were found in Bay Lake at the time that Disney began development, including largemouth bass, bluegill, Seminole killfish, lake chubsuckers, and spotted gar. As new lakes, lagoons, and waterways were created in order to drain parts of the swampland, the waters were further stocked with brown bullhead catfish and at least eight species of sunfish. The lakes and waterways are no longer stocked, since the fish now propagate well and provide a naturally balanced ecology that feeds the large waterfowl population and other local denizens.

Visitors who would like to join one of the fishing excursions should make reservations well in advance of their trip. They can use their own equipment, if they wish, although tackle is provided and bait is readily available. No fishing license is required at Walt Disney World. Catch-and-release is the official policy here, although the fish in Bay Lake and the Fort Wilderness Waterways may be kept by visitors who have their own kitchens.

◆

FORT WILDERNESS FISHING EXCURSION

Bay Lake, the largest natural lake at Walt Disney World, is the fishing ground of the Fort Wilderness Fishing Excursion. Forests and wetlands surround the lake; the wetlands are home to a large population of native waterfowl, including great white egrets, herons, and pelicans. Bay Lake is large and well aerated, and the fish here are relatively free of pesticides and bacteria. Some of the largemouth bass that have been caught here weigh as much as thirteen pounds. Pontoon boats are used for the excursions, and there is a maximum of five participants on each trip. The excursions leave three times daily from the Fort Wilderness Marina.

EXCURSION FEES: About $120 for two hours, which includes boat, guide, bait, tackle, and refreshments. Participants may bring their own equipment.

TIMES: 8 AM, 12 PM, and 3 PM. Times vary throughout the year.

RESERVATIONS: Space can be reserved up to two weeks in advance (407 824-2757). Reservations are recommended, and during the busy summer months they are essential.

NOTE: Excursion boats will also pick up guests at the following resorts: Polynesian, Grand Floridian, and Contemporary.

◆

BUENA VISTA LAGOON FISHING EXCURSION

The waters of both Buena Vista Lagoon and the Disney Village Waterways are the fishing grounds for this excursion. Buena Vista Lagoon is man-made, as are the waterways that feed it. Because this system is smaller and less aerated than the water system at Bay Lake, the fish caught here may not be kept to eat. However, the excursion does provide a mounting service for visitors who catch fish weighing in over eight pounds. Pontoon boats are used for the excursion and there is a maximum of five participants on each trip. The excursions leave twice daily from the Disney Village Marketplace Marina. The afternoon tour is popular with repeat visitors, because it goes out after the rental boats have been returned and the fish are stirred up and hungry.

EXCURSION FEES: About $110 for two hours, which includes boat, guide, bait, and tackle. Visitors who get caught up in the experience can keep right on fishing for $30 for each additional hour. Participants can bring their own equipment.

TIMES: 7 AM and 6 PM. Times vary throughout the year.

RESERVATIONS: Reservations are required at least twenty-four hours in advance, but can be made up to three months ahead (407 828-2204). This popular excursion fills quickly in the summer, so visitors should book reservations far in advance of a summer visit.

NOTE: Excursion boats will also pick up guests at the following resorts: Vacation Club, Port Orleans, and Dixie Landings.

FISHING THE FORT WILDERNESS WATERWAYS

Fishing is permitted in the miles of picturesque waterways that traverse Fort Wilderness. Fish may be caught from the grassy banks of the canals, or visitors can rent canoes to paddle out to likely looking fishing holes in the heavily forested areas. Fish caught in these waterways can be kept only by guests with kitchens.

EQUIPMENT: Fishers can use their own equipment, if they wish. Canoes and cane poles can be rented at the Bike Barn in the Meadow Recreation Area at Fort Wilderness. Bait is sold at the Meadow Trading Post, nearby.

RENTAL FEES: Canoes rent for about $4 per hour or $10 per day. Poles rent for about $2 per per hour or $8 per day.

TIMES: The Bike Barn is open from 8 AM until sundown.

RESERVATIONS: No reservations are taken for canoes.

NOTE: Canoes hold up to three persons. Fishing is best in the early morning or late afternoon.

THE FISHING HOLE AT DIXIE LANDINGS

Disney's Dixie Landings Resort has its very own stocked fishing hole on the Sassagoula River, which is part of the Disney Village Waterways. Visitors fish from an old-fashioned roped-off dock. A catch-and-release policy is encouraged. Guests can keep their fish if they clean them there and provide a cooler, although this is not advised, since these waterways may contain a residue of the pesticides used to control mosquitoes. The fishing hole is stocked with bass, bluegill, and catfish. So far, the biggest catfish pulled from the hole weighed in at seven pounds.

EQUIPMENT: Cane poles can be rented at the Fishing Hole. Bait is provided and worm-hooking instructions are offered.

RENTAL FEES: Poles rent for about $3 per hour, including bait.

TIMES: The Fishing Hole is open from 7 AM until sundown.

RESERVATIONS: No reservations are taken.

NOTE: A large book of photographs on display at the rental desk shows some of the fish taken out of the Fishing Hole. For about $2 visitors can get a souvenir Polaroid of themselves and their catch. ◆

GOLF COURSES

Walt Disney World sometimes calls itself *The Magic Linkdom,* and with good reason: It boasts five outstanding PGA golf courses, as well as a par-36 practice course. With ninety-nine holes of golf and twenty thousand guest rooms, Walt Disney World is the largest golf resort in the world. The golf courses here host more than a thousand golf tournaments each year, including the world's biggest: the PGA Tour's Walt Disney World/Oldsmobile Golf Classic.

The golf courses are available to all visitors at Walt Disney World. Advance reservations are necessary for all courses, especially during peak seasons and holidays. Vacationers who would like to golf frequently during their stay should inquire about WDW's all-inclusive Golf Package Vacations (407 827-7200).

MAGNOLIA GOLF COURSE

Designed by Joe Lee, the Magnolia Golf Course is long and tight and requires a great deal of accuracy. It is planted with more than fifteen hundred magnolia trees and features the unique "mousetrap" on the sixth hole, a sand trap shaped like Mickey. In fact, the course has a preponderance of sand and water, with large greens on a rolling terrain. The layout covers 6,642 yards from the middle tees. The final round of the PGA Tour's Walt Disney World/Oldsmobile Golf Classic is played on this course, and the Disney pros rate the Magnolia the third toughest of the five courses at WDW.

GREENS FEES: About $75; twilight (after 3 PM) $35. Includes cart and taxes.

EQUIPMENT RENTAL: Clubs, shoes, and range balls are available at the Disney Inn Pro Shop.

FACILITIES: The golf course has two driving ranges, a putting green, locker rooms, a beverage cart on the course, and a complimentary health club at the Disney Inn. The Pro Shop carries golf apparel, equipment, and accessories. The Garden Gallery restaurant, nearby, is open for breakfast, lunch, and dinner, and the adjoining lounge is open all day. The Disney Inn Golf Studio offers personalized swing analysis using videotape, and both private and group lessons with PGA and LPGA instructors. Call 407 824-2270 for Golf Studio reservations.

RESERVATIONS: To reserve tee times, call the Walt Disney World Master Starter (407 824-2270) between 8 AM and 5 PM, EST. Guests staying at WDW resorts may reserve tee times up to thirty days in advance. Day visitors may reserve seven days ahead. Same-day reservations may be made by calling the Pro Shop directly (824-2288).

HOW TO GET THERE: The Magnolia Golf Course is located at the Disney Inn, in the Magic Kingdom Resorts Area. There is free parking at the Pro Shop. Complimentary shuttles are available to guests staying at the Magic Kingdom resorts. Guests at other WDW resorts should check with Guest Services for transportation options.

NEAREST RESORTS: Disney Inn, Grand Floridian, Polynesian, and Contemporary.

PALM GOLF COURSE

Like the Magnolia, the Palm is tree-lined and the greens are mature. It is a picturesque course on which it is not unusual to see deer and other wildlife in the early mornings, including a certain alligator known to stroll along the outlying fairways. This Joe Lee–designed course is a challenging one, with narrow greens, plenty of water hazards, and some difficult doglegs. The layout covers 6,461 yards from the middle tees. The eighteenth hole has been rated the fourth toughest on the PGA Tour, and the Disney pros rate the Palm the second toughest of the five courses at WDW.

GREENS FEES: About $75; twilight (after 3 PM) $35. Includes cart and taxes.

EQUIPMENT RENTAL: Clubs, shoes, and range balls are available at the Disney Inn Pro Shop.

FACILITIES: The golf course has two driving ranges, a putting green, locker rooms, a beverage cart on the course, and a complimentary health club at the Disney Inn. The Pro Shop carries golf apparel, equipment, and accessories. The Garden Gallery restaurant, nearby, is open for breakfast, lunch, and dinner, and the adjoining lounge is open all day. The Disney Inn Golf Studio offers personalized swing analysis using videotape, and both private and group lessons with PGA and LPGA instructors. Call 407 824-2270 for Golf Studio reservations.

RESERVATIONS: To reserve tee times, call the Walt Disney World Master Starter (407 824-2270) between 8 AM and 5 PM, EST. Guests staying at WDW resorts may reserve tee times up to thirty days in advance. Day visitors may reserve seven days ahead. Same-day reservations may be made by calling the Pro Shop directly (824-2288).

HOW TO GET THERE: The Palm Golf Course is located at the Disney Inn, in the Magic Kingdom Resorts Area. There is free parking at the Pro Shop. Complimentary shuttles are available to guests staying at the Magic Kingdom resorts. Guests at other WDW resorts should check with Guest Services for transportation options.

NEAREST RESORTS: Disney Inn, Grand Floridian, Polynesian, and Contemporary.

◆

LAKE BUENA VISTA GOLF COURSE

The play on the Lake Buena Vista Golf Course is short and tight, but the views and fairways are wide and open. The greens are fully mature on this course, although they can be bumpy at times because many beginners play here. The beautiful country club–like course, designed by Joe Lee, is lined with pine forests, oaks, and magnolias. The layout covers 6,655 yards from the middle tees, and the Disney pros rate Lake Buena Vista the fifth toughest of the five courses at WDW.

GREENS FEES: About $75; twilight (after 3 PM) $35. Includes cart and taxes.

EQUIPMENT RENTAL: Clubs, shoes, and range balls are available at the Lake Buena Vista Pro Shop.

FACILITIES: The golf course has a driving range, a putting green, locker rooms, a beverage cart on the course, and a complimentary health club at the Lake Buena Vista Clubhouse. The Pro Shop carries golf apparel, equipment, and accessories. The Lake Buena Vista Restaurant in the Clubhouse is open for breakfast, lunch, and dinner; the adjoining lounge is open all day. The Lake Buena Vista Golf Studio offers personalized swing analysis using videotape, and both private and group lessons with PGA and LPGA instructors. Call 407 824-2270 for Golf Studio reservations.

RESERVATIONS: To reserve tee times, call the Walt Disney World Master Starter (407 824-2270) between 8 AM and 5 PM, EST. Guests staying at WDW resorts may reserve tee times up to thirty days in advance. Day visitors may reserve seven days ahead. Same-day reservations may be made by calling the Pro Shop directly (828-3741).

HOW TO GET THERE: The Lake Buena Vista Golf Course is located at Disney's Village Resort in the Village Resorts Area. There is free parking at the Lake Buena Vista Clubhouse. It is within walking

GOLF COURSES

distance of most of the Hotel Plaza resorts. Guests at other WDW resorts should check with Guest Services for transportation options.

NEAREST RESORTS: Village Resort, Buena Vista Palace, Hilton, Vacation Club, Port Orleans, Dixie Landings, Grosvenor, Hotel Royal Plaza, Travelodge, Howard Johnson, and Guest Quarters.

OSPREY RIDGE GOLF COURSE

This extra-long course was designed by Tom Fazio, with plenty of berms and mounds as well as some excellent par-3s. The lakes and creeks were excavated to create the elevated ridge that is the central feature of this course. Recently, eight nesting platforms were set in place by helicopter to attract ospreys to the area. The course features large greens that are not fully mature, yet the course is fast becoming a favorite with experienced golfers. The layout covers 6,705 yards from the middle tees, and the Disney pros rate Osprey Ridge the toughest of the five courses at WDW.

GREENS FEES: About $85; twilight (after 3 PM) $45. Includes cart and taxes.

EQUIPMENT RENTAL: Clubs, shoes, and range balls are available at Bonnet Creek Golf Club Pro Shop.

FACILITIES: The golf course has a driving range, a putting green, locker rooms, and a beverage cart on the course. The Pro Shop carries golf apparel, equipment, and accessories. The Sand Trap restaurant in the Bonnet Creek Golf Club is open for lunch, and the adjoining lounge is open all day. The Bonnet Creek Golf Studio offers personalized swing analysis using videotape, and both private and group lessons with PGA and LPGA instructors. Call 407 824-2675 for Golf Studio reservations.

RESERVATIONS: To reserve tee times, call the Walt Disney World Master Starter (407 824-2270) between 8 AM and 5 PM, EST. Guests staying at WDW resorts may reserve tee times up to thirty days in advance. Day visitors may reserve seven days ahead. Same-day reservations may be made by calling the Pro Shop directly (824-2675).

HOW TO GET THERE: The Osprey Ridge Golf Course is located at the Bonnet Creek Golf Club, which lies between Fort Wilderness and the Village Resorts Area. There is free parking in the large lot. The Bonnet Creek Golf Club offers complimentary taxies from all WDW resorts (699-9999).

NEAREST RESORTS: Fort Wilderness, Dixie Landings, Port Orleans, Vacation Club, and Village Resort.

EAGLE PINES GOLF COURSE

This challenging course, designed by Pete Dye, requires strategic play. Golfers must think their way from tee to green through the undulating, low-profile terrain. Water comes into play at sixteen holes, and instead of rough, the fairways are lined with pine needles and sand, giving the course a distinctive look and allowing for fast play. The layout covers 6,224 yards from the middle tees, and the Disney pros rate Eagle Pines the fourth toughest of the five courses at WDW.

GREENS FEES: About $85; twilight (after 3 PM) $45. Includes cart and taxes.

EQUIPMENT RENTAL: Clubs, shoes, and range balls are available at Bonnet Creek Golf Club Pro Shop.

FACILITIES: The golf course has a driving range, a putting green, locker rooms, and a beverage cart on the course. The Pro Shop carries golf apparel, equipment, and accessories. The Sand Trap restaurant in the Bonnet Creek Golf Club is open for lunch, and the adjoining lounge is open all day. The Bonnet Creek Golf Studio offers personalized swing analysis using videotape, and both private and group lessons with PGA and LPGA instructors. Call 407 824-2675 for Golf Studio reservations.

RESERVATIONS: To reserve tee times, call the Walt Disney World Master Starter (407 824-2270) between 8 AM and 5 PM, EST. Guests staying at WDW resorts may reserve tee times up to thirty days in advance. Day visitors may reserve seven days ahead. Same-day reservations may be made by calling the Pro Shop directly (824-2675).

HOW TO GET THERE: The Eagle Pines Golf Course is located at the Bonnet Creek Golf Club, which lies between Fort Wilderness and the Village Resorts Area. There is free parking in the large lot. The Bonnet Creek Golf Club offers complimentary taxis from all WDW resorts (699-9999).

NEAREST RESORTS: Fort Wilderness, Dixie Landings, Port Orleans, Vacation Club, and Village Resort.

◆

OAK TRAIL GOLF COURSE

Oak Trail Golf Course, also called the Executive or Family Course, has some of the most challenging holes at Walt Disney World. The course features two par-5s, two par-3s, and five par-4s, and the local pros play here to work on their game. The layout of this 9-hole, par-36 course covers 2,913 yards from the middle tees.

GREENS FEES: About $25 for nine holes; $35 for repeat play. Includes cart and taxes. Walking only.

EQUIPMENT RENTAL: Clubs and shoes are available at the Disney Inn Pro Shop.

FACILITIES: The Pro Shop carries golf apparel, equipment, and accessories. The Garden Gallery restaurant, nearby, is open for breakfast, lunch, and dinner, and the adjoining lounge is open all day.

RESERVATIONS: To reserve tee times, call the Walt Disney World Master Starter (407 824-2270) between 8 AM and 5 PM, EST. Guests staying at WDW resorts may reserve tee times up to thirty days in advance. Day visitors may reserve seven days ahead. Same-day reservations may be made by calling the Pro Shop directly (824-2288).

HOW TO GET THERE: Oak Trail Course is located at the Disney Inn, in the Magic Kingdom Resorts Area. There is free parking at the Pro Shop. Complimentary shuttles are available to guests staying at the Magic Kingdom resorts. Other resort guests should check at Guest Services for transportation.

NEAREST RESORTS: Disney Inn, Grand Floridian, Polynesian, and Contemporary.

◆

TOURNAMENTS

The Walt Disney World golf courses are the sites for a number of nationally prominent tournaments, including the Bryant Gumbel/Walt Disney World Pro-Am Tournament. By far the most famous, and the world's biggest, is the PGA Tour's Walt Disney World/Oldsmobile Golf Classic. Each October since 1971, about 130,000 participants and 200,000 onlookers populate the Magnolia, Palm, and Lake Buena Vista courses during this nationally televised event. Running concurrently is the Classic Club Pro-Am, which gives golf enthusiasts a chance to play alongside pros in the Walt Disney World/Oldsmobile Golf Classic. Membership in the Golf Classic Club costs about $5,000, and includes greens fees (excluding cart fees) for one year, accommodations, park admissions during Pro-Am week, and a chance to play with a PGA Tour pro. For more information call the Classic Club Office at 407 824-2270. ◆

HEALTH CLUBS

A number of the resorts at Walt Disney World have full-service health clubs that offer a range of equipment and services. Visitors for whom a health club is an important resort amenity might want to review the club facilities before booking a room, since many of the clubs can be used only by registered guests. These include health clubs at the following resorts: Grand Floridian, Yacht Club, Beach Club, Vacation Club, Swan, Buena Vista Palace, and Hilton. The Dolphin and Contemporary resorts have health clubs that can be used by any WDW resort guest. Day visitors may use the exercise facilities at Disney's Village Resort and the Disney Inn. The most handsomely appointed health clubs are the Grand Floridian's St. John's Health Club, the Dolphin's Body by Jake Health Studio, and the Yacht and Beach Club's Ship Shape Health Club. These resorts are good choices for visitors who would like to incorporate a spa getaway into their vacation plans.

BUENA VISTA PALACE: *Buena Vista Palace Health Club* — The health club is located near the tennis courts and swimming pools, on Buena Vista Palace's Recreation Island behind the hotel. The handsome spacious club is housed in a pitched-roof octagonal building with mirrors on three walls and windows on the others, filling the room with light. The equipment is well spaced, so several persons can work out at once. There is a television, but no staff.

    EQUIPMENT AND FACILITIES: Paramount, Liferower, Lifestep, Lifecycle, free weights, sauna (coed), and whirlpool (outside).

    SERVICES: Massage by appointment (407 827-2727: hotel).

    FEES: Complimentary.

    HOURS: 6 AM until 10 PM.

    WHO MAY ATTEND: The health club is available only to registered guests.

THE DISNEY INN: *Magic Mirror Health Club* — This exercise facility is located at the far end of the hotel's Mickey Mouse–shaped swimming pool. The large rectangular room has mirrored walls and windows overlooking the pool. Although the equipment is modern, the decor is very 1950s. The exercise room has a television, but no staff.

    EQUIPMENT AND FACILITIES: Nautilus, Powerstep, Aerobicycle, treadmill, and free weights.

    SERVICES: Personal training by appointment (407 934-3454).

    FEES: Complimentary.

    HOURS: Daily 7:30 AM until 7 PM.

    WHO MAY ATTEND: The health club is available to both WDW resort guests and day visitors.

DISNEY'S YACHT CLUB AND BEACH CLUB RESORTS: *Ship Shape Health Club* — The main room of this elegant, fully staffed health club has French doors and large windows looking out over Stormalong Bay. The whirlpool is in its own room, with a domed portico overhead and baskets of flowers and plants surrounding the bathing area. All the rooms are furnished in blue and white, and the sauna and steam rooms are off to the side. Televisions are interspersed throughout the main exercise room, which is furnished with state-of-the-art equipment.

    EQUIPMENT AND FACILITIES: Lifecircuit, Nautilus, Lifestep, Lifecycle, Liferower, Gravitron, NordicTrack, StairMaster, treadmill, free weights, steam room (coed), sauna, and whirlpool.

SERVICES: Massage and personal training by appointment (407 934-3256).

FEES: About $5 per visit; $10 for an entire stay; $15 per family stay.

HOURS: 6:30 AM until 9:30 PM.

WHO MAY ATTEND: The health club is available only to registered guests.

DISNEY'S CONTEMPORARY RESORT: *Olympiad Health Club* — The Olympiad Health Club is located on the third floor of the Contemporary resort, near the hotel's executive offices. The moderately sized carpeted room has mirrored walls, low ceilings, and no television. The club is staffed and has a good selection of modern equipment and adjacent tanning and massage rooms.

EQUIPMENT AND FACILITIES: Nautilus, StairMaster, Lifecycle, Aerobicycle, NordicTrack, rowing machine, treadmill, free weights, sauna (coed), whirlpool (outside), and tanning booth.

SERVICES: Personal training and massage by appointment (407 824-3410).

FEES: About $5 per visit; $10 for an entire stay; $15 per family stay. Tanning booth $4 for ten minutes.

HOURS: 6:30 AM until 8 PM.

WHO MAY ATTEND: The health club is available to guests staying at any WDW resort.

DISNEY'S GRAND FLORIDIAN BEACH: *St. John's Health Club* — This fully staffed health club is located in a freestanding white Victorian cottage overlooking the pool. Although modest in size, the room has mirrored walls and paned-glass windows, which create a spacious, airy atmosphere. There are two televisions and pink-upholstered Nautilus equipment to match the pink-and-black multicolored floor. A large basket of fresh fruit is provided daily for exercising guests.

EQUIPMENT AND FACILITIES: Nautilus, StairMaster, Liferower, Lifestep, Aerobicycle, treadmill, free weights, sauna, and whirlpool (outside).

SERVICES: Personal training, fitness classes, nutrition and exercise counseling, and massage by appointment (407 824-2433).

FEES: About $5 per visit; $10 for an entire stay; $15 per family stay.

HOURS: 6 AM until 10 PM.

WHO MAY ATTEND: The health club is available only to registered guests.

DISNEY VACATION CLUB: *R.E.S.T. Fitness Center* — The Vacation Club health club is unstaffed and is located in the resort's recreation complex, facing the pool area and lagoon. A mirrored wall and French doors create an impression of spaciousness in this otherwise modest-sized, equipment-filled room. There is one television and a separate massage room off to the side. The sauna-steam room is outside the club, in the cute red lighthouse at the edge of the lagoon.

EQUIPMENT AND FACILITIES: Nautilus, Liferower, Lifestep, Lifecycle, free weights, combination sauna and steam room (coed), and whirlpool (outside).

SERVICES: Massage and personal training by appointment (407 827-7700: hotel).

FEES: Complimentary.

HOURS: 7 AM until 12 AM.

WHO MAY ATTEND: The health club is available only to registered guests.

DISNEY'S VILLAGE RESORT: *Lake Buena Vista Health Club* — This somewhat cramped, windowless exercise room is located at the Lake Buena Vista Clubhouse. Although the equipment is positioned closely, there is enough of a selection for a good workout. The room is carpeted and there is a television. There is no staff on site, and the door opens by combination, available from the Pro Shop nearby.

EQUIPMENT AND FACILITIES: Nautilus, StairMaster, Aerobicycle, free weights, and whirlpool (outside).

SERVICES: Personal training by appointment (407 934-3454).

FEES: Complimentary to registered guests. All others pay about $5 per visit or $10 for an entire stay.

HOURS: 7 AM until 10 PM.

WHO MAY ATTEND: The health club is available to both WDW resort guests and day visitors.

THE HILTON RESORT: *Hilton Health Club* — This modestly sized green-carpeted exercise room is located behind the hotel near the pools and tennis courts. Mirrors and tiles cover the walls and, on one side, large windows overlook the pool area. The health club has one television, but no staff.

EQUIPMENT AND FACILITIES: Nautilus, Lifestep, exercise bikes, treadmill, free weights, sauna (coed), and whirlpool (outside).

SERVICES: Massage by appointment (407 827-4000: hotel).

FEES: Complimentary.

HOURS: 6 AM until 10 PM.

WHO MAY ATTEND: The health club is available only to registered guests.

WALT DISNEY WORLD DOLPHIN: *Body by Jake Health Studio* — This handsome, fully staffed fitness center is operated by television workout professional Jake Steinfeld, who is occasionally on the premises and available for personal training. The carpeted weight room has windows overlooking Crescent Lake. The coed whirlpool is in a spacious tiled room furnished with blue rattan seating, and the club features its own workout studio with classes held throughout the day. There are no televisions in the weight room, although there is a wide screen TV-video setup in the exercise studio.

EQUIPMENT AND FACILITIES: Polaris, Lifestep, Lifecycle, Liferower, treadmill, free weights, sauna, and whirlpool (coed).

SERVICES: Fitness classes, personal training, massage, and body wraps by appointment (407 934-4264).

FEES: About $8 per visit; $16 for an entire stay; $26 per family stay.

HOURS: 6 AM until 8 PM.

WHO MAY ATTEND: The health club is available to guests staying at any WDW resort.

WALT DISNEY WORLD SWAN RESORT: *Swan Health Club* — This modest but fully staffed health club is entered from outside the hotel through large glass doors overlooking the lap pool. Potted plants and peach and blue trim create a sense of openness in the rectangular exercise room, which contains a selection of Sprint Circuit machines and one television. A massage room is attached and saunas are located in the adjoining locker rooms.

EQUIPMENT AND FACILITIES: Sprint Circuit machines, treadmill, free weights, sauna, and whirlpool (outside).

SERVICES: Massage by appointment (407 934-1360).

FEES: Complimentary.

HOURS: 7 AM until 11 PM.

WHO MAY ATTEND: The health club is available only to registered guests. ◆

HORSEBACK RIDING

At the Tri-Circle-D Ranch Livery and Trail Blaze Corral — a rustic stable and corral with the unmistakable smell of horseflesh — Walt Disney World maintains a herd of quarterhorses, paints, and Appaloosas that visitors can ride through the back country of Fort Wilderness. Groups of riders are led by guides on a packed-sand trail that meanders through a shady slash-pine and palmetto forest and past small sunny glades. The horses, which are sometimes used in the parades and special events in the Magic Kingdom, follow the trails in two single-file lines (there is no trotting or galloping). Riders must stay with the group and may not go off on their own. The horses are quite easy to handle, although the less-well-behaved ones will occasionally detour to take a nip off the palmetto bushes along the trail. Seasoned riders may find the wilderness scenery more interesting than the riding, but inexperienced riders will feel comfortable with the well-trained, gentle horses. The entire excursion takes about forty-five minutes and is available to both WDW resort guests and day visitors.

LOCATION: The Fort Wilderness Trail Ride begins at the Tri-Circle-D Livery, adjacent to the Fort Wilderness Guest Parking Lot. Visitors who are driving can park in the Fort Wilderness Guest Parking Lot, which is free to guests staying at WDW resorts. (Day visitors are charged a nominal fee.) WDW buses service Fort Wilderness from the theme parks and the Transportation and Ticket and Center (TTC), where visitors from other WDW resorts can transfer to Fort Wilderness buses.

FEE: About $15.

TIMES: Rides leave daily at 9 AM, 10:30 AM, 12 PM, and 2 PM. Times may vary with the season.

RESERVATIONS: Reservations for the Fort Wilderness Trail Ride can be made up to five days in advance by calling 407 824-2832 between 8 AM and 5 PM, EST. Riders must be at least nine years old and some weight restrictions may apply. Same-day reservations can be made at Guest Services in any Walt Disney World resort or theme park. Instant reservations can also be made from the house phone at the Gateway Depot in the Fort Wilderness Guest Parking Lot. Trail ride fees can be paid at the ticket booth directly in front of the Gateway Depot. Check-in time for rides is thirty minutes prior to ride time at the Fort Wilderness Trail Blaze Corral. Trail rides may be cancelled due to inclement weather.

HORSEBACK TRAIL RIDE TIPS

✦ Fall and spring are the most pleasant times of the year for trail rides. If you're visiting during hot weather, reserve the 9 AM ride, the coolest time of the day.

✦ Riders should wear long pants and shoes (not thongs, or high heels). Do not bring cameras, hats, or pocketbooks on the ride. There are coin-operated lockers near the bus stop in the parking lot, where you can store your belongings while you ride.

✦ If you are using Walt Disney World buses to reach Fort Wilderness, allow for travel time to reach the Trail Blaze Corral. Give yourself forty minutes if you are staying at the following resorts: Contemporary, Polynesian, Grand Floridian, or the Disney Inn. Allow one hour for transportation if you are staying at any other hotel on Disney property. The most efficient way to reach the Fort Wilderness Guest Parking Lot without a car is by taxi, via Vista Boulevard, the shortcut route. ✦

JOGGING PATHS

Most of the resorts at Walt Disney World have jogging courses or designated paths located on their grounds or nearby. Some of the courses are serious and spectacular, such as the exercise courses at Disney's Village Resort and in Fort Wilderness, while others meander through specially themed environments such as the promenade at the Caribbean Beach resort and the carriage path at Port Orleans. Maps of designated jogging paths are available at Guest Services in each resort. Any visitor to Walt Disney World can use the jogging paths. Resort guests who jog daily may want to vary their runs to take advantage of the splendidly executed themed architecture, landscaping, and natural wonders that Walt Disney World has to offer.

◆

CRESCENT LAKE AND BOARDWALK RUN
Walt Disney World Swan and Dolphin

The trail begins at the Beach Hut near the Grotto Pool between the Swan and Dolphin. The path loops through the promenade that connects the two hotels and then circles Crescent Lake, crossing the wood-slatted boardwalk to Epcot and returning along the Stormalong Bay beach in front of the Yacht Club and Beach Club resorts. It circles the parking area of the Swan, runs past the tennis courts, and continues along the perimeter of the Dolphin, Yacht Club, and Beach Club parking areas before returning.

LENGTH: The trail is designed in three lengths, depending on the turnaround: 3.1 miles (5K), 1.86 miles (3K), and 1.24 miles (2K).

MAPS: Jogging maps are available at the Swan and Dolphin resorts Guest Services, at the Body by Jake Health Studio in the Dolphin, and at the Swan Health Club in the Swan.

NOTE: Trams transporting visitors to Epcot Center use portions of this path.

◆

COUNTRY CLUB FITNESS COURSE AT LAKE BUENA VISTA
Disney's Village Resort, Disney Vacation Club, and Hotel Plaza at Disney Village

The trail begins at the Lake Buena Vista Clubhouse and winds its way through the Village Resort, a country club–like scattering of vacation villas surrounding the fairways of the Buena Vista Golf Course. The path follows the resort lanes to the Vacation Club, where it loops back and plunges into the forest along Tree-house Lane. Emerging from the forest, it crosses a grassy-banked waterway and follows a path lined with exercise stations. A footbridge takes the path back across the water to the starting point.

LENGTH: The course is designed in two lengths, depending on the turnaround: 3.4 miles and 2.4 miles. A section of the trail — 1.8 miles — has thirty-two exercise stations with instructions.

MAPS: Jogging maps are available at the Village Resort Guest Services, at the Pro Shop at the Lake Buena Vista Clubhouse, at the Vacation Club Guest Services, and at Guest Services at the Hotel Plaza resorts.

NOTE: Electric golf carts and bicycles may also use parts of the path. This is one of the most popular and professionally maintained jogging paths at Walt Disney World.

◆

SPORTING ACTIVITIES

BAREFOOT BAY BEACH AND ISLAND RUN
Disney's Caribbean Beach Resort

The path begins at any point along the promenade encircling forty-acre Barefoot Bay lake. The promenade meanders along the beach in front of the Caribbean-style lodges and tropical landscaping of the resort. For a sightseeing break from the promenade, joggers may run the path encircling Parrot Cay, a Caribbean-themed garden island in the center of the lake, complete with parrots and other colorful birds. Wooden footbridges connect Parrot Cay to the promenade from either side of the lake.

LENGTH: The promenade around the lake is approximately 1.4 miles long, and slightly longer if you loop through Parrot Cay island.

MAPS: Resort maps showing the jogging path are available at the Caribbean Beach resort Guest Services.

NOTE: Bicycles also use the promenade. The best time to run this trail is early in the morning, before hotel guests fill the promenade on their way to breakfast.

TOWN AND COUNTRY RUN THROUGH THE OLD SOUTH
Disney's Port Orleans and Dixie Landings Resorts

The trail starts at any point in either resort. It follows the Carriage Path that encircles Port Orleans resort and winds through the streets designed after New Orleans's French Quarter, with row house brick buildings and pleasant park squares. The run follows the banks of the Sassagoula River, and enters the Old South at Dixie Landings resort. The trail follows the river past large plantation mansions with sweeping lawns, then winds through a shady, wooded area where rustic bayou lodges are tucked among the cypresses and pines. The path crosses the river to Ol' Man Island, runs along the opposite shore past the Dixie Landings marina, and returns to the Port Orleans Carriage Path.

LENGTH: The trail length varies according to the winding paths chosen through the Dixie Landings resort, but averages about 1.5 miles.

MAPS: Jogging maps are available at the Port Orleans and Dixie Landings resorts Guest Services.

NOTE: Bicycles and luggage-conveyance carts also use this path, although it is generally deserted, especially during early-morning hours.

ADVANCED TIMBER CHALLENGE COURSE
Disney's Fort Wilderness Resort and Campground

The trailhead to the Challenge Course can be found across the road from the Tri-Circle-D Ranch near the Fort Wilderness Marina. The asphalt-surfaced course enters the cool shade of a dense pine forest, which conveys a sense of quiet isolation. Ferns and palmettos line the course, giving way every so often to the exercise stations placed alongside the path. Birds, marsh rabbits, and small lizards populate the area and watch the goings-on from the sidelines.

LENGTH: The fitness course is currently about 1 mile round trip, with exercise stations about every quarter mile along the way. It was 2.3 miles long before Disney's Wilderness Lodge was constructed and may reopen to that length.

MAPS: Fort Wilderness maps showing the exercise trail are available at Guest Services in the Fort Wilderness Reception Outpost, located in Fort Wilderness Guest Parking Lot, and at the Pioneer Hall Ticket and Information Window, near the Fort Wilderness Marina.

NOTE: Bicycles and electric carts may also use this path.

LAGOON RUN THROUGH TURN-OF-THE-CENTURY FLORIDA
Disney's Grand Floridian Beach Resort

The path starts at the Grand Floridian's wood-planked dock and shoreline restaurant, Narcoossee's, at Seven Seas Lagoon, and heads inland to wind past the resort's elegant lawns and flower gardens in the wide court-yard. Passing by the free-form Courtyard Pool, the path travels between the Summer House and the majestic Victorian lobby building, continuing along the white sand beach at the edge of the lagoon and past the tennis courts before looping back to the Grand Floridian dock.

LENGTH: The path is about 1.3 miles long.

MAPS: Jogging maps are available at the Grand Floridian resort Guest Services.

NOTE: Luggage-conveyance carts also use this path.

POLYNESIAN RUN
Disney's Polynesian Resort and The Disney Inn

The trail starts in the exotic tropical landscaping at the Polynesian resort's Luau Cove, and runs past the long South Pacific–style lodges. It emerges at the fairways of the Magnolia Golf Course, then travels alongside them before looping back at the Disney Inn. Passing under the monorail tracks, the path again enters the Polynesian's jungle environment, goes by the huge cross-beamed Great Ceremonial House, and exits on the beach at Seven Seas Lagoon. The trail runs along the beach, past the marina, and returns to Luau Cove.

LENGTH: The path is about 1.5 miles long.

MAPS: Jogging maps are available at the Polynesian resort Guest Services.

NOTE: Luggage-conveyance carts also share this path.

THE SURF AND TURF RUN
Disney's Yacht Club and Beach Club Resorts

The trail begins on the waterfront walkway at the shore of Stormalong Bay and curves along the beach past a long stretch of red and white cabanas. It continues across the wood-slatted boardwalk leading to Epcot's World Showcase and runs past Crescent Lake. The trail circles the parking area of the Swan hotel, runs past the tennis courts, and continues along the perimeter of the Dolphin, Yacht Club, and Beach Club parking areas, ending at the front entrances of the Yacht Club and Beach Club resorts.

LENGTH: The trail has two lengths, 2 miles and 1 mile, depending on the turnaround.

MAPS: Jogging maps are available at the Yacht Club and Beach Club resorts Guest Services.

NOTE: Trams transporting visitors to Epcot Center use portions of this path. ◆

Nature Walks

Visitors who would like a change of pace from the intense stimulation of the theme parks can enjoy leisurely strolls along some of Walt Disney World's nature walks. The trails explore a variety of environments including wooded wilderness areas, carefully landscaped specimen gardens, marshy wetlands, and lush tropical groves, populated with birds, rabbits, squirrels, deer, lizards, and numerous other creatures. Although some of the animals are tame, most are not, and visitors should enjoy them from a distance and resist the urge to pet or feed them.

Florida weather permits nature walks at any time of the year. In the summer months, early-morning walks are the most pleasant, since afternoons tend to be hot, humid, and often rainy (taking along an umbrella in the summer is a good idea, since it provides shelter from both sun and rain). During the rest of the year, visitors can enjoy walks at any time during daylight hours.

Most nature trails have refreshment stands nearby where picnic supplies may be purchased. Most also have shaded picnic areas with tables and trash receptacles.

The nature walks at Walt Disney World can be used by all visitors. Most are incorporated into the Disney resorts, but two, Discovery Island and River Country, are located in parks that charge admission.

Visitors who would like to get out into nature but do not wish to walk may rent electric carts for touring the extensive landscaping at Disney's Village Resort or the heavily forested back country at Disney's Fort Wilderness Resort and Campground.

◆

WILDERNESS SWAMP TRAIL
Disney's Fort Wilderness Resort and Campground

The Wilderness Swamp Trail is one of the most serene and varied of the nature trails at Walt Disney World, and one of the least traveled. The 2.2-mile-long trail starts in an old-growth forest of tall, moss-draped trees. Ferns, vines, and low shrubs grow untamed along the trail, which emerges on the shore of an estuary. Here, a secluded sitting area provides the perfect spot for a picnic. The trail plunges back into the dense forest before leading onto a boardwalk that crosses the wetlands of a wilderness swamp. Water reeds and cattails grow among the partially submerged cypress forest, where wild waterfowl live. The trail once again enters the tree-canopied forest. Wildflowers, berries, woodpeckers, fluttering butterflies, chirping birds, humming insects, and tiny yellow-striped lizards add splashes of color, sound, and movement. The trail crosses the grassy banks of Chickasaw Creek and returns through the forest.

MAPS: A map of Fort Wilderness showing the trailhead is available at Guest Services in the Fort Wilderness Reception Outpost (located in the Fort Wilderness Guest Parking Lot) and at the Pioneer Hall Ticket and Information Window (near the Fort Wilderness Marina). (See also "Fort Wilderness & River Country," page 68.)

NOTE: Snacks, beverages, and picnic supplies are available at the Settlement Trading Post, located between Pioneer Hall and the beginning of the Wilderness Swamp Trail. The Trail's End Buffeteria at Pioneer Hall also will prepare meals to go for those who wish to picnic. The Wilderness Swamp Trail is a wonderful walk at any time of the day, but the early mornings and dusky evenings are the most dramatic, with deep shadows and much animal activity.

THE GARDEN WALK
The Disney Inn

Trees, shrubs, and flowering plants from all over the world mix with native Florida species to create a delightful nature walk through about half a mile of carefully landscaped gardens and shady overgrown marshlands. Small plaques on low wooden posts identify many of the trees and plants and provide tidbits of information about them. Starting by the laurel oak next to Snow White's Reflecting Pool, with the scents of white gardenias and large-blossomed Southern magnolias wafting through the air, the walk leads to a forest glade with palms and ferns and tiny rivulets running through it. Here, a sweet bay tree from Massachusetts and a red maple from Nova Scotia contrast dramatically with the bald cypresses native to the Florida swamps. The walk passes a stand of yellow African irises, a long-needled slash pine native to the area, and a liriope, or evergreen giant, and continues over a stone bridge and past a small windmill by which a weeping willow from China gracefully drapes its branches. The walk crosses a wide lawn toward a crape myrtle from China that blossoms with lavender, pink, red, and white flowers in the spring. A pleasant gazebo nearby provides a view of the hotel's continuously blooming flower beds. The walk passes a pond, where waterfowl stretch their wings, before returning to the Disney Inn's entrance, with its signature topiary of the Seven Dwarfs.

MAPS: A map of the Garden Walk is available at the Disney Inn Guest Services.

NOTE: Nature-lovers will especially like exploring the marsh behind the red maple tree. This area is off the beaten path (and off the map), but it offers a glimpse of how the land must have looked before it was drained and developed.

PARROT CAY ISLAND AND AVIARY WALK
Disney's Caribbean Beach Resort

The walk through Parrot Cay, a Caribbean-themed garden island in the center of forty-acre Barefoot Bay lake, is a short, leisurely stroll that covers about a quarter mile and is sure to delight bird-lovers. The walk starts at either of the wooden footbridges that connect the island to the promenade encircling the lake, and twists and turns through a lush tropical garden of palm and banana trees and bamboo. As it meanders along the shore, the walk passes clusters of waterlilies and reeds that ring the island and travels by a picnic area and Caribbean fortress wall, complete with cannons pointing out over the lake. The walk continues past a rustic octagonal gazebo fashioned of lodgepoles, and over to Parrot Cay's highlight, an aviary populated with a variety of exotic birds. Here, cherry-headed conures and gold-cap conures from South America preen and display their colorful feathers, while a blue-front Amazon from Central America talks to visitors astute enough to greet him. Try opening the conversation with a simple "Hello!"

MAPS: There is no map available that focuses on Parrot Cay; however, a map of the resort is available at the Caribbean Beach resort Guest Services.

NOTE: Snacks, beverages, and other picnic supplies are available at the food court in Old Port Royale, located just across the footbridge to Parrot Cay. The Parrot Cay Island and Aviary Walk is pleasant at any time of the day, but the island's playground attracts large groups of children in the afternoons, so early mornings and evenings are best for quiet strolls. Parrot Cay is wheelchair accessible.

ZOOLOGICAL GARDENS WALK
Discovery Island

Discovery Island was designed to be the quintessential nature walk at Walt Disney World. Ferries carry visitors to the island from the Magic Kingdom Dock, the Contemporary Marina, and the Fort Wilderness Marina. The island's tree-canopied path starts at the dock and meanders through a jungle lush with palm trees, flowering plants, curling vines, and exotic shrubs from around the world. Tweets, chirps, screams, honks, and caws can be heard all over the island as the path travels by bright-plumaged macaws and cockatoos and enters a pleasant glade with cascading waterfalls. Emerging from a whispering bamboo grove, the path passes rare ring-tailed lemurs from Madagascar and yellow-furred golden lion tamarins from the American tropics. Tiny muntjac deer from Southeast Asia nibble on leaves, delicate cranes and hornbills stalk and catch fish, and large-beaked toucans squawk at passersby. The path enters a vast walk-through aviary that houses an incredible variety of birds and exits at an inlet that is the home to brown pelicans, birds once endangered by the pesticide DDT. A boardwalk to the right offers a beachside stroll with native birds that drop in for a visit. On the beach, a wrecked pirate ship points to a picnic spot hidden in the forest. The path to the left runs alongside a flamingo-filled lagoon and a section of beach favored by giant Galapagos tortoises. As the path returns to the dock, visitors can catch an up-close view of the island's resident alligators.

MAPS: A map of the trail is available at the Discovery Island dock where the ferries land. (See also "Discovery Island," page 76.)

NOTE: Admission is charged at Discovery Island, but it may be included already in some multiday passes. Sandwiches, salads, hot dogs, and other picnic supplies are available at the Thirsty Perch. Animal-lovers should try to see one of the bird or reptile shows scheduled throughout the day. Discovery Island is wheelchair accessible.

CYPRESS POINT NATURE TRAIL
River Country

This trail is actually a roped wooden walkway that leads visitors on a quarter-mile walk along the shoreline of Bay Lake and out into the the wetlands. Moss-hung bald cypresses grow up out of the water and shade the path. These trees are native to the wetlands and were here long before the land was developed. In the shallow water, among the roots of the trees, are colonies of freshwater mollusks, extremely important to the food chain in this ecosystem. Small fish dart through the water, and egrets and heron stand among the water reeds fishing. One aviary along the way holds a white-necked raven and another is the home of a red-tailed hawk. The birds at Cypress Point have been injured in the wild and rehabilitated and cannot survive unaided.

MAPS: There are no official maps of the trail or of River Country. See "Fort Wilderness & River County," page 68, for a detailed map of the area.

NOTE: Admission is charged at River Country, but may be included already in some multiday passes and special resort packages. Sandwiches, salads, hot dogs, and other picnic supplies are available at Pop's Place or the Waterin' Hole. There is a shaded picnic area at the end of the trail on the white sand beach. ◆

SWIMMING POOLS & BEACHES

All Walt Disney World resorts have swimming pools, usually more than one. The WDW resort pools are generally restricted to guests registered at a particular resort. Day visitors who want to engage in serious water play should visit the extensive water parks at River Country (see "Fort Wilderness & River Country," page 68), Typhoon Lagoon (see "Typhoon Lagoon," page 84), or Disney's newest water park, Blizzard Beach. Admission is charged at the water parks. There is also an extensive beach scene at the Walt Disney World resorts, and anyone bringing along a towel can venture out and stake a place in the sand. All beaches have snack bars, rest rooms, and coin-lockers nearby, although only Bay Lake and Seven Seas Lagoon are suitable for swimming year round.

◆

LAP POOLS

Serious swimmers who would like to exercise during their vacation should consider staying at a resort that offers a lap pool. Lap pools at Walt Disney World resorts are usually one of several pools, and are set apart from the family swimming pools. Nonetheless, it is best to swim in the morning, when the pools are virtually deserted. Lap pools or Olympic-sized pools can be found at:

- Disney's Contemporary Resort (a seventy-five-foot pool)
- Walt Disney World Swan (shared by guests at the Walt Disney World Dolphin).

Walt Disney World resorts with pools large enough for lap swimming include:

- Lake Buena Vista Clubhouse at Disney's Village Resort (the loveliest at Walt Disney World)
- Fort Wilderness Resort and Campground (in the Meadow Recreation Area)
- Buena Vista Palace (on Recreation Island)
- Disney's Yacht Club Resort (the "quiet pool")
- Disney's Beach Club Resort (the "quiet pool").

◆

WHITE SAND BEACHES

Most of the Walt Disney World resorts offer stretches of pure white sand beach for the enjoyment of guests. Many of the beaches are equipped with comfortable lounge chairs to relax in, or rows of jaunty striped cabanas for shelter from the sun. Besides the resort beaches listed below, there is also a charming deserted beach on Discovery Island, although swimming is not permitted there. During the hot summer months, when bacteria counts rise, all beaches at Florida lakes are closed. Beaches can be found at the following resorts and parks:

- Fort Wilderness Marina and Beach (a large beach on Bay Lake)
- Disney's Contemporary Resort (a large beach on Bay Lake)
- Disney's Polynesian Resort (a large beach on Seven Seas Lagoon)
- Disney's Grand Floridian Beach Club Resort (a large beach on Seven Seas Lagoon)
- Disney's Beach Club Resort (a large beach on Stormalong Bay — no swimming)
- Walt Disney World Swan and Dolphin (a small beach on Crescent Lake — no swimming)
- Disney's Caribbean Beach Resort (a large beach on Barefoot Bay)
- Disney Vacation Club (a small beach on the Trumbo Canal — no swimming). ◆

SWIMMING POOLS & BEACHES

TENNIS COURTS

Visitors who enjoy tennis can choose from a variety of tennis environments at Walt Disney World. Most of the resorts have well-designed tennis courts in a number of interesting settings — tucked into the forest, or overlooking beaches, lakes, golf courses, and pools. For casual play, the tennis courts at the resorts are well kept and pleasant; however, serious tennis players may want to take advantage of the professional facilities at Walt Disney World's full-service tennis clubs.

TENNIS CLUBS

The full-service tennis clubs at Walt Disney World are staffed by tennis pros, who offer private tennis lessons and challenging tennis clinics. Tennis equipment and ball machines can be rented at the pro shops, and the clubs will arrange tournaments for groups. Appropriate tennis attire is required.

THE RACQUET CLUB AT DISNEY'S CONTEMPORARY RESORT: The tennis courts at the Racquet Club are located next to the resort's north garden wing, on the shores of Bay Lake. The Contemporary is one of the most tennis-oriented resorts at Walt Disney World, and several of the courts are set up for competition play, complete with bleacher areas.

    COURTS: Six, lighted.

    HOURS: 7 AM until 10 PM.

    FEES: About $10 per hour ($25 for an entire stay), complimentary before 9 AM and after 8 PM.

    RESERVATIONS: Recommended. Courts can be reserved twenty-four hours in advance (824-3578).

    NOTE: Courts are available to both Walt Disney World resort guests and day visitors. Rental equipment is available at the Racquet Club, which also has two practice courts. The Racquet Club features a "Tennis Anyone" program that matches players with tennis partners. The pro shop, open from 9 AM until 8 PM, carries a wide selection of tennis apparel and equipment and offers a restringing service.

THE TENNIS CLUB AT WALT DISNEY WORLD DOLPHIN: The Dolphin shares a deluxe, full-service tennis club with the adjacent Swan resort. The Tennis Club is located on its own parcel of land across Epcot Resorts Boulevard from the two resorts, which are connected to the tennis courts by a walkway. There is parking behind the tennis courts, although the lot is unmarked. The Tennis Club has a comfortable waiting area under a striped cabana.

    COURTS: Eight, lighted.

    HOURS: 8 AM until 11 PM.

    FEES: About $12 per hour, complimentary after 7 PM.

    RESERVATIONS: Recommended. Courts can be reserved twenty-four hours in advance (934-4396).

    NOTE: Courts are available to both Walt Disney World resort guests and day visitors. The Tennis Club offers a match-up service for players looking for partners. Instruction for both individuals and groups is available, and themed round-robin tournaments are scheduled weekly. The pro shop, open from 8 AM until 7 PM, carries tennis apparel and equipment and offers a restringing service.

TENNIS COURTS

The tennis courts at most of the resorts are available to players on a first-come, first-served basis, although some do accept reservations, and some may be used only by registered guests. Day visitors as well as guests at any Walt Disney World resort usually can play the courts at the following resorts: Disney's Village Resort, the Disney Inn, Fort Wilderness, Guest Quarters Suite Resort, Hotel Royal Plaza, and Grosvenor Resort, although policies may change. Except for the tennis courts at Disney's Grand Floridian Beach Resort, resort tennis courts are complimentary. Appropriate tennis attire is required at all courts, and most resorts offer equipment rentals or loaners.

BUENA VISTA PALACE: Located on the resort's large Recreation Island, these tennis courts overlook Lake Buena Vista. A wide lawn leads from the pool area to the courts.

    COURTS: Three, lighted.

    HOURS: 6 AM until 10 PM.

    FEES: Complimentary.

    RESERVATIONS: None; courts are available on a first-come, first-served basis. There is no time limit for players.

    NOTE: Courts are available to registered guests only. Complimentary tennis equipment is available at the concierge desk in the Palace Suites, adjacent to the pool. Tennis lessons and tournaments can be arranged by the concierge.

THE DISNEY INN: The tennis courts are located at the edge of the Palm Golf Course near the south wing of the resort. A small landscaped area, shaded by a smattering of palm trees, provides guests with a pleasant place to wait for a game. The courts are banked by forest on two sides, with a view of the fairways in the distance.

    COURTS: Two, lighted.

    HOURS: Dawn until 10 PM.

    FEES: Complimentary.

    RESERVATIONS: None.

    NOTE: Courts are available to both Walt Disney World resort guests and day visitors. Rental equipment is available at the the Disney Inn Pro Shop.

DISNEY VACATION CLUB: The tennis courts at the Vacation Club are located on the edge of the Trumbo Canal, in the resort's recreation complex. The courts are surrounded by a palmetto and pine tree grove and lie within viewing distance of the pool. Although the courts themselves have no viewing area, there are benches nearby for those waiting to play.

    COURTS: Two, lighted.

    HOURS: 7 AM until 11 PM.

    FEES: Complimentary.

    RESERVATIONS: None; courts are available on a first-come, first-served basis.

    NOTE: Courts are available to registered guests only. Rental equipment is available at Hank's Rent N' Return.

◆ T E N N I S   C O U R T S ◆

DISNEY'S GRAND FLORIDIAN BEACH RESORT: The tennis courts at Disney's Grand Floridian Beach Resort have the distinction of being the only clay-surfaced courts in Walt Disney World. Located on the south side of the resort, the courts are secluded in a charming tree-banked setting. The monorail track is located between the courts and the Seven Seas Lagoon, and players can see and hear the trains gliding by as they play.

    COURTS: Two, lighted.

    HOURS: 7 AM until 9 PM.

    FEES: About $13 per hour.

    RESERVATIONS: Required, twenty-four hours in advance (824-2433).

    NOTE: Courts are available to Walt Disney World resort guests only. Rental equipment is available at the St. John's Health Club. Tennis lessons can be arranged by appointment.

DISNEY'S VILLAGE RESORT: The tennis courts at Disney's Village Resort are at the Lake Buena Vista Clubhouse, overlooking the Buena Vista Lagoon. Tennis enthusiasts can take in a panoramic view of the water as they play or wait for a court. Although the Village Resort is oriented to golfers, the Lake Buena Vista Pro Shop also carries tennis equipment and apparel.

    COURTS: Three, lighted.

    HOURS: 6 AM until 11 PM.

    FEES: Complimentary.

    RESERVATIONS: None; courts are available on a first-come, first-served basis.

    NOTE: Courts are available to both Walt Disney World resort guests and day visitors. Rental equipment is available at the Lake Buena Vista Pro Shop.

DISNEY'S YACHT CLUB AND BEACH CLUB RESORTS: These two resorts share a set of tennis courts, located on the far side of the Beach Club. The courts are surrounded on three sides by a forest of pine trees and low-growing mulberry and jasmine bushes. In the nearby waiting area, players can view ongoing games in the shade of a large canvas awning.

    COURTS: Two, lighted.

    HOURS: 9 AM until 10 PM.

    FEES: Complimentary.

    RESERVATIONS: None; courts are available on a first-come, first-served basis.

    NOTE: Courts are available to registered guests only. Rental equipment is available at the Ship Shape Health Club.

FORT WILDERNESS: At Fort Wilderness, players can enjoy a quiet country setting for their tennis game. To reach the courts, guests must take a Fort Wilderness shuttle (gray- or brown-flag bus) to the Meadow Recreation Area. The tennis courts are located adjacent to the Meadow swimming pool. Pine forests bank the courts on three sides, and there is a small waiting area near the pool.

    COURTS: Two, lighted.

    HOURS: 8 AM until 10 PM.

    FEES: Complimentary.

    RESERVATIONS: None; courts are available on a first-come, first-served basis. There is a one-hour playing-time limit if others are waiting to play.

TENNIS COURTS

NOTE: Courts are available to both Walt Disney World resort guests and day visitors. Rental equipment is available at the Bike Barn, nearby.

GROSVENOR RESORT: The tennis courts at the Grosvenor Resort are located behind the pool area, and adjacent to the resort's handball and volleyball courts. The area beyond the courts has patches of pine forest leading down to the shores of Lake Buena Vista. There is a small waiting area with shaded tables, nearby.

> **COURTS:** Two, lighted.
>
> **HOURS:** 9 AM until 10 PM.
>
> **FEES:** Complimentary.
>
> **RESERVATIONS:** None; courts are available on a first-come, first-served basis.
>
> **NOTE:** Courts are available to both Walt Disney World resort guests and day visitors. Complimentary loaner equipment is available at the Recreation Office near the pool.

GUEST QUARTERS SUITE RESORT: The resort's tennis courts are located behind the hotel, near the pool. A lawn stretches out in front of the courts, which are surrounded by tall palms and pines. Although the belt of trees acts as a buffer, players can hear the sounds of the freeway behind the courts. A wood-shingled gazebo provides players with a shaded waiting and viewing area.

> **COURTS:** Two, lighted.
>
> **HOURS:** 7 AM until 11 PM.
>
> **FEES:** Complimentary.
>
> **RESERVATIONS:** None; courts are available on a first-come, first-served basis.
>
> **NOTE:** Courts are available to both Walt Disney World resort guests and day visitors. Complimentary racquets are available at the hotel bell desk.

THE HILTON RESORT: The tennis courts at the Hilton Resort are located at the far end of this sprawling resort complex, a short distance from the pools. The courts are surrounded by a hibiscus hedge and tall slash-pine forest. There is no waiting area.

> **COURTS:** Two, lighted.
>
> **HOURS:** 8 AM until 10 PM.
>
> **FEES:** Complimentary.
>
> **RESERVATIONS:** Required. Courts can be reserved twenty-four hours in advance. (827-4000: hotel).
>
> **NOTE:** Courts are available to registered guests only. Racquets are available for rent at the Pool Hut. Tennis lessons can be arranged for registered guests.

HOTEL ROYAL PLAZA: The courts at this hotel are located at the far end of the property, across from the parking lot. They are backed up against the freeway, with little landscaping to offer a buffer from the noise. There is a small waiting area on the lawn in front of the courts.

> **COURTS:** Four, lighted.
>
> **HOURS:** 7 AM until 11 PM.
>
> **FEES:** Complimentary.
>
> **RESERVATIONS:** None; courts are available on a first-come, first-served basis.
>
> **NOTE:** Courts are available to both Walt Disney World resort guests and day visitors. No equipment is available for rent. The hotel can arrange tennis lessons for registered guests. ◆

VOLLEYBALL COURTS

The current popularity of volleyball throughout the United States is reflected in the number of courts available at Walt Disney World: There are more than a dozen courts scattered throughout the property. Volleyball is a "pickup" sport, so visitors who start playing on a deserted court or beach may find they pick up more players as they go along, or that if there is a game in progress, they can wait on the sidelines to be picked. The volleyball courts at Fort Wilderness are open to all visitors to Walt Disney World. The courts at Typhoon Lagoon and River Country, where admission is charged, can be used by any guest. A few of the courts at the WDW resorts supposedly are reserved for registered guests, but they are under-used and no one seems to check. All volleyball courts are available on a first-come, first-served basis.

◆

FORT WILDERNESS: There are a number of sand volleyball courts throughout Fort Wilderness. The court at the Meadow Recreation Area and the volleyball setup at the Fort Wilderness beach are the easiest to find. At the Meadow Recreation Area, the volleyball court is grouped with a shuffleboard court, tennis courts, and swimming pool. The beach court is located near the Fort Wilderness Marina.

> **EQUIPMENT:** Balls are usually kept in a box next to the net at the Meadow Recreation Area. Ask at the Bike Barn if no ball is available. Players at the Fort Wilderness beach court can get a ball free of charge at the Fort Wilderness Marina.

> **NOTE:** Volleyball courts are available to both WDW resort guests and day visitors.

◆

TYPHOON LAGOON: There is a permanently installed sand volleyball court at Typhoon Lagoon in the Getaway Glen Picnic Area. The court, which has a comfortable grassy berm for spectators, is a serious volleyball player's dream. It is secluded in a tropical grove, so a wild serve will not end up in someone's picnic lunch. The Leaning Palms, nearby, provides beverages and snacks for players.

> **EQUIPMENT:** Balls are available free of charge at Raft Rentals; a small deposit is required.

> **NOTE:** Admission is charged at Typhoon Lagoon. (See also "Typhoon Lagoon," page 84.)

◆

RIVER COUNTRY: The volleyball court in River Country is set up on the beach near Pop's Willow Picnic Area. Pop's Place snack bar can provide refreshments and picnic tables are nearby. The court over-looks Bay Lake.

> **EQUIPMENT:** Balls are available free of charge at Towel Rentals; a small deposit is required.

> **NOTE:** Admission is charged at River Country. (See also "Fort Wilderness & River Country," page 68.)

◆

DISNEY'S BEACH CLUB RESORT: The sand volleyball court at the Beach Club is located in a secluded grassy courtyard of the building. The open side of the courtyard faces the beach at Stormalong Bay. The volleyball court is shared by guests at the neighboring Yacht Club resort.

> **EQUIPMENT:** Balls are available free of charge at the Ship Shape Health Club.

> **NOTE:** The volleyball court is available only to registered guests.

◆ **VOLLEYBALL COURTS** ◆

DISNEY'S CONTEMPORARY RESORT: The Contemporary resort's sand volleyball court is located on the beach adjacent to the marina, on the shores of Bay Lake. The resort's swimming pool is nearby.
EQUIPMENT: Balls are available free of charge at the Contemporary Marina.
NOTE: The volleyball court is available to both WDW resort guests and day visitors.

DISNEY'S GRAND FLORIDIAN BEACH RESORT: The Grand Floridian's sand volleyball court is located on the beach along Seven Seas Lagoon. The setting is particularly lovely in the late afternoon.
EQUIPMENT: Balls are available free of charge at the St. John's Health Club.
NOTE: The volleyball court is available only to guests staying at a WDW resort.

DISNEY'S POLYNESIAN RESORT: The Polynesian, with its distinctly tropical setting, has one volleyball court. It is located on the white sand beach along Seven Seas Lagoon.
EQUIPMENT: Balls are available free of charge at Catamaran Corner marina.
NOTE: The volleyball court is available only to guests staying at a WDW resort.

DISNEY'S CARIBBEAN BEACH RESORT: The sand volleyball court at the Caribbean Beach resort is located on the beach in front of Old Port Royale, the main recreation area, on the shore of Barefoot Bay.
EQUIPMENT: Balls are available free of charge at Barefoot Bay Boatyard.
NOTE: The volleyball court is available only to guests staying at a WDW resort.

WALT DISNEY WORLD DOLPHIN AND SWAN: Guests at the Swan and Dolphin share a white sand beach on Crescent Lake, where an area is set aside for volleyball. The court is set up on request at the Hot Spot, where recreation equipment is rented.
EQUIPMENT: Balls are available free of charge at the Hot Spot.
NOTE: The volleyball court is available only to registered guests.

DISNEY VACATION CLUB: The Vacation Club has one sand volleyball court located in the resort's recreation complex. This picturesque court is set off from the nearby viewing stands with thick nautical rope. The court is grouped with the resort's tennis and shuffleboard courts.
EQUIPMENT: Balls are available free of charge at Hank's Rent N' Return.
NOTE: The volleyball court is available only to registered guests.

GROSVENOR RESORT: The Grosvenor Resort has one sand volleyball court located just behind the pool area, surrounded by lawn and pine forest. Handball, basketball, and tennis courts are nearby.
EQUIPMENT: Balls are available free of charge at the Pool Hut.
NOTE: The volleyball court is available only to registered guests. ◆

WATERSKIING EXCURSIONS

Waterskiers fly across the surface of Bay Lake all year long. Everyone from novices to experts can make use of Walt Disney World's fleet of speedboats and professional waterskiing instructors. The instructors are certified by the American Waterski Association, and they offer instruction and helpful tips to both beginning and advanced skiers — from helping novices to get up on skis the first time to expert instructions on how to perform complex turns and daredevil stunts. Besides standard waterskis, the excursion boats carry Scurfers (mini surfboards), Hydraslides (knee boards), and slalom skis. The ski boats cruise along at about fifty miles per hour and excursions last one hour. Groups of up to five people can waterski together and, since the fee is per hour rather than per person, it can be economical to team up with other waterskiers.

SKIING LOCATION: The waterski boats depart from the Fort Wilderness Marina, where participants usually join the excursion. Instructors will also pick up waterskiers at the Contemporary resort, or cross the water bridge to Seven Seas Lagoon to pick up skiers at the Grand Floridian and Polynesian resorts. The boats return to Bay Lake to commence waterskiing.

FEE: About $70 per hour, which includes ski boat, driver-instructor, and all waterskiing equipment. Participants may bring their own waterskis, if they wish. There is a limit of five persons per boat, but groups are not mixed, except by request.

RESERVATIONS: Reservations must be made at least one day in advance, but may be made up to two weeks in advance. During peak seasons, on warm weekends, and during holidays, reservations should be made as far in advance as possible (407 824-2621).

EXCURSION SCHEDULE: There are at least two waterskiing boats in operation at all times. Excursions depart daily at 8:45 AM, 9:45 AM, 10 AM, 11 AM, 1:15 PM, 1:30 PM, 2:30 PM, 2:45 PM, and 3:45 PM. Times may vary with the season.

WATERSKIING TIPS

✦ The best time of day to waterski is in the morning, when the water is calm and there is little interference from rental boats. Bay Lake can sometimes get foggy in the early morning, however, and it may be necessary to wait until visibility is adequate. Afternoon excursions can sometimes run into winds and choppy water.

✦ The Florida sun can be brutal, especially reflected off water. Don't forget sunblock, sunglasses, and visors.

✦ Waterskiing excursions, unlike fishing excursions, do not provide beverages or snacks, so plan on bringing your own. At the Settlement Trading Post, near the Fort Wilderness Marina, you can purchase beverages, including beer and wine, as well as snacks and sandwiches.

✦ Most of the instructors who lead the excursions belong to professional waterskiing associations, and many were waterski athletes or performers before becoming Cast Members at Walt Disney World. Experienced skiers may be able to pick up advanced techniques from the instructors, or at the very least hear a tall tale or two. ◆

TOURING TIPS

PACKING

Casual clothes are the norm throughout Walt Disney World. The only exceptions are in some of the more elegant restaurants and, if you want to make an impression, the nightclubs on Pleasure Island. Most resorts provide shampoo and conditioner; the premier resorts also supply hand lotion, toothpaste, toothbrushes, shaving lotion, sunblock, and hair dryers. In the fall and winter months, Orlando can get surprisingly cold, so before packing, you may want to check with Disney Weather (407 824-4104). The items listed below are absolute musts for touring Walt Disney World in comfort.

CLOTHING: Pack comfortable, well-broken-in walking shoes — you will be spending much of your time on your feet. Forget sandals except for poolside use, as these can cause blisters, and problems when boarding and disembarking rides. During the warm months, water sports are big at Walt Disney World, so if you plan to swim, don't forget your bathing suit. Women should bring a one-piece bathing suit for the wild water slides at Typhoon Lagoon. In the winter, bring a sweatshirt or sweater for layering, and pack a jacket that is lined for warmth. Don't forget gloves to keep off the chill when standing in line and touring out of doors.

SUN & WEATHER PROTECTION: Pack a lightweight hat that shades your eyes; visors are also a good choice and are easy to pack and carry around. Sunglasses are a must, the larger the better. Bring a pair that provides full protection from UV rays. Choose a sunblock rated SPF 15 or higher; the Florida sun will burn you even in the winter. (Sunburn is the most frequently treated problem at first-aid stations in Walt Disney World.) It rains daily in the summer and periodically throughout the year, so pack a collapsible umbrella that fits in your tote bag (rain ponchos can be a nuisance when wet).

TOURING ESSENTIALS: Bring a roomy, lightweight tote bag with a shoulder strap — you will find it invaluable for carrying around brochures, entertainment schedules, sunblock, purses, small purchases, and bottled water. Self-closing plastic bags are good for stashing wet bathing suits or food in your tote bag while you're touring. Pack a lightweight flashlight such as a penlight, which is useful for reading maps and entertainment schedules after dark, consulting guidebooks while waiting in line at dark attractions, and reading menus in dimly lit restaurants. To pass the time while waiting in lines, you might want to bring a book to read or a cassette player with headphones for audio books or music tapes.

UPON ARRIVAL: On your drive to Walt Disney World, you may want to pick up a few amenities for your room. If you're approaching on I-4 (from the Orlando airport), take Exit 27B and head for Gooding's Supermarket at Crossroads Shopping Center. Purchase enough bottled water for your stay (WDW water isn't very tasty), including some small bottles of water you can refill and carry with you as you tour. (Most people don't realize how dehydrated they can get here and how tired it can make them feel.) This is also a good time and place to purchase fresh fruit and snack items for your room, as well as juice, soft drinks, beer, or wine (spirits are available at Espresso Liquor, next door); in the mornings, and when you return to your room to relax midday, you'll thank yourself. Most resort rooms have mini bars where you can store your beverages, and what you've purchased will cost much less than the hotel-stocked treats. ◆

DISCOUNT TRAVEL CLUBS

Visitors vacationing at Walt Disney World can take advantage of discounts offered to a variety of travel clubs that help members take the bite out of vacation budgets. The clubs include national organizations such as the American Automobile Association, as well as Orlando-based or Disney-sponsored associations. Most of these organizations offer discounts on accommodations, restaurants, vacation packages, and car rentals.

MAGIC KINGDOM CLUB GOLD CARD

The Magic Kingdom Club, operated by The Disney Company, has been around for more than thirty-five years. Club members receive an embossed card that entitles them to a number of benefits and discounts at Walt Disney World in Orlando, Disneyland in Anaheim, and Euro Disneyland Resort in France.

WDW HOTEL DISCOUNTS: A 10 to 30 percent discount at Disney-owned hotels year round; a 10 percent discount at independently owned hotels on Disney property, such as the Swan, Dolphin, and Hotel Plaza resorts; and a wide selection of all-inclusive Walt Disney World vacation packages at discount rates.

ADMISSION DISCOUNTS: A slight (about 5 percent) discount on park admission tickets; a 10 percent discount on golf greens fees at selected times throughout the year; and a 10 percent discount on some dinner shows.

ADDITIONAL BENEFITS: A 10 percent discount at Disney Merchandise Stores in the United States; a toll-free WDW Reservations telephone number for Magic Kingdom Club members; restricted discounts with Delta Airlines and National Car Rental; a two-year subscription to Disney News, a members-only magazine; and membership in Travel America at HalfPrice, a hotel discount club.

MEMBERSHIP FEE: The fee for a two-year family membership is about $49.

REVIEWERS' COMMENTS: An excellent value for those who want to stay on property at WDW. The admission ticket discounts are small, but frequent visitors will save on telephone calls to Walt Disney World Reservations. The 10 percent Delta Airlines discount applies only to the higher fares, so it is of questionable value. Disney fans will appreciate the member gifts, which include a key chain, luggage tags, and a travel bag.

CONTACT: Magic Kingdom Club Gold Card, P.O. Box 3850, Anaheim, CA 92803 (800 248-2665).

DISNEY'S MAGIC YEARS CLUB

The Magic Years Club is a version of the Magic Kingdom Club designed for people age sixty and over. It includes many of the same benefits and discounts at Walt Disney World and Disney properties throughout the world, plus a few additional benefits.

WDW HOTEL DISCOUNTS: A 10 to 30 percent discount at Disney-owned hotels year round; a 10 percent discount at independently owned hotels on Disney property, such as the Swan, Dolphin, and Hotel Plaza resorts; and a wide selection Walt Disney World vacation packages at discount rates.

ADMISSION DISCOUNTS: A slight (about 5 percent) discount on park admission tickets; a 10 percent discount on golf greens fees at selected times throughout the year; a 10 percent discount on some dinner shows; discount parking tickets; and a 50 percent discount on admission to Discovery Island.

ADDITIONAL BENEFITS: Discount dining coupons for use at Walt Disney World and Disneyland; a 10 percent discount at Disney Merchandise Stores throughout the United States; a toll-free Walt Disney World Reservations telephone number for Disney's Magic Years Club members; restricted discounts with Delta Airlines and National Car Rental; discounts on selected luxury cruises.

MEMBERSHIP FEE: The fee for a five-year individual membership (which includes one guest) is about $35.

REVIEWERS' COMMENTS: Because the length of membership is five years, this is a good value for seniors who travel to Walt Disney World frequently. The 10 percent Delta Airlines discount applies only to the higher fares, so it is of questionable value. Disney fans will appreciate the member gifts, which include a key chain, luggage tags, and a travel bag.

CONTACT: Disney's Magic Years Club, P.O. Box 4709, Anaheim, CA 92803 (714 490-3250).

ORLANDO MAGICARD

The Orlando Magicard is sponsored by the Orlando/Orange County Convention and Visitors Bureau, and offers visitors discounts on attractions, dinner shows, car rentals, factory outlet merchandise, and hotels throughout the area, including hotels on Walt Disney World property.

WDW HOTEL DISCOUNTS: A 40 percent discount at Hotel Royal Plaza; a 25 percent discount at Grosvenor Resort; a 20 percent discount at Buena Vista Palace, Guest Quarters Suite Resort, and Howard Johnson Resort Hotel.

ADMISSION DISCOUNTS: $2 off the regular admission to Pleasure Island.

ADDITIONAL BENEFITS: A 10 percent discount on Alamo, Avis, and Hertz rental cars; a $1 discount per person on Mears shuttle, which provides transportation between Orlando International Airport and Walt Disney World.

MEMBERSHIP FEE: The Orlando Magicard is offered free of charge and can be used for groups of up to six persons.

REVIEWERS' COMMENTS: Be sure to call well ahead of your visit. It takes about three weeks to receive your discount card.

CONTACT: Orlando Magicard (800 255-5786).

DISNEY'S FOOD AND WINE SOCIETY

Disney's Food and Wine Society offers its members restaurant discounts and other benefits at Walt Disney World. Society membership is available to Florida residents, although frequent visitors to Walt Disney World will probably have little trouble securing a membership if they wish to apply.

RESTAURANT DISCOUNTS: A 20 percent discount at most restaurants in Disney-owned resorts; a 20 percent discount at Disney Village Marketplace restaurants; a 20 percent discount at selected Epcot Center and Disney-MGM Studios restaurants; a 20 percent discount at most WDW dinner shows.

ADMISSION DISCOUNTS: Society members and one guest receive a 50 percent discount on admission to Pleasure Island as frequently as they wish for one year.

ADDITIONAL BENEFITS: Reduced prices for members and one guest at wine tastings, vintner and celebrity chef dinners, and other events at Walt Disney World; a subscription to Disney's Food and Wine Society newsletter, *The Vine,* which lists gastronomic events, wine tastings, wine reviews, and member benefit updates.

MEMBERSHIP FEE: The fee for a one-year individual membership (which includes all guests in the member's party) is about $45.

REVIEWERS' COMMENTS: Considering the costs of food at Walt Disney World restaurants, this is a very good value for frequent visitors who stay at WDW and eat in the resort restaurants. Restaurant discounts include alcoholic beverages.

CONTACT: Disney's Food and Wine Society, The Walt Disney World Co., P.O. Box 10,000, Lake Buena Vista, FL 32830 (407 828-5792). Membership forms are available at Village Spirits in Disney Village Marketplace.

NATIONAL TRAVEL CLUBS

A number of national travel clubs and other organizations, such as the American Association of Retired Persons, offer members travel discounts throughout the United States, including discounts on selected Walt Disney World accommodations, vacation packages, and car rentals. Those listed here are among the most frequently used at Walt Disney World.

AMERICAN AUTOMOBILE ASSOCIATION: A 10 percent discount at Hotel Royal Plaza, Howard Johnson Resort Hotel, Grosvenor Resort, Guest Quarters Suite Resort, Travelodge Hotel, and the Hilton Resort; Walt Disney World vacation packages; and discounts at most car rental agencies. Periodically, AAA members also receive discounts at Disney-owned resorts. There's an AAA car-service center on site.

MEMBERSHIP FEE: The fee is about $55 for the first year and about $40 thereafter.

CONTACT: Call your local chapter of the American Automobile Association for an application.

ENCORE: A 50 percent discount at Hotel Royal Plaza and Howard Johnson Resort Hotel; discount vacation packages to Walt Disney World; and discounts at most car rental agencies.

MEMBERSHIP FEE: The fee for a one-year membership for an individual or family is about $50.

CONTACT: ENCORE Preferred Traveller Program, ENCORE Travel, 4501 Forbes Boulevard, Lanham, MD 20706 (800 638-0930).

ENTERTAINMENT PUBLICATIONS: A 50 percent discount at Hotel Royal Plaza, Howard Johnson Resort Hotel, and Travelodge Hotel; discounts on Pleasure Island admissions; and discounts at most car rental agencies.

MEMBERSHIP FEE: An Entertainment Publications discount book, good for one year, is about $25.

CONTACT: Entertainment Publications, P.O. Box 1014, Trumbell, CT 06611 (800 374-4464).

AMERICAN EXPRESS: American Express, the official charge card at Walt Disney World, offers card members Disney Family Vacation Packages, which include accommodations in a WDW resort, admissions, three hundred free Disney Dollars, and other amenities.

MEMBERSHIP FEE: Annual membership fee is about $55.

CONTACT: American Express Customer Service (800 528-4800). ◆

ORLANDO INTERNATIONAL AIRPORT

This large, futuristically designed airport has a variety of interesting shops and restaurants, along with a first-class hotel located inside the main terminal. Automated trams transport passengers from the outlying gates to the main terminal, where ticketing areas, baggage claim, and ground transportation are located.

Travelers arriving from different destinations who plan to rendezvous at the airport may find the layout confusing. The main terminal is divided into two mirror-image service areas: Landside A and Landside B. Each Landside is used by specific airlines, and each side has its own ticketing area, baggage claim, car rental counters, and ground transportation. Therefore, mixups can easily occur when visitors arriving separately decide to meet at Hertz, for instance, since there is a Hertz counter at each Landside.

MEETING ON LEVELS ONE OR TWO: At each Landside, car rental counters are on Level One; baggage claim and ground transportation services are on Level Two. There is no direct route between Landsides A and B at these levels, and travelers must return to the ticketing area on Level Three to cross over. If you plan to meet on Levels One or Two, be sure to specify Landside A or Landside B. Airlines serviced at Landside A include America West, American, Continental, and TWA. Airlines serviced at Landside B include Delta, Northwest, U.S. Air, and United. (For additional terminal information, call 407 825-2001.)

MEETING ON LEVEL THREE: Ticketing areas, shops, and restaurants are located on Level Three. If there is considerable time between your arriving flights, you may want to meet on Level Three after retrieving your luggage. (The airport does not have rental luggage carts.) Meeting spots on Level Three include Beauregard's Restaurant (on the mezzanine) and the adjacent Beauregard's Lounge (closes between 8 and 9 PM); Mort's Deli (closes between 8 and 9 PM); and the adjacent Orlando Marketplace lounge, which is open later (tables at this lounge can be used as a meeting spot even after it closes). On the other end of Level Three, near the Hyatt, is Glades Bar and Grill (closes at 7 PM) and, just beyond it, near the escalator to the Hyatt, is an atrium rotunda and fountain surrounded by several comfortable seating areas. The paging telephone number from outside the airport is 407 825-2000.

HYATT REGENCY ORLANDO INTERNATIONAL AIRPORT

If you are arriving in Orlando in the evening, it may be more convenient to spend that night at the Hyatt Regency, located inside the airport, rather than renting a car and trying to find your way to Walt Disney World in the dark. Upon arrival, you simply proceed from your gate to the Hyatt reception desk; the bellhops will retrieve your luggage at baggage claim, bring it to your room, and load it in your rental car or shuttle when you're ready to leave the next day. The hotel is centered around a spacious indoor atrium, and the rooms overlook either the atrium or the runways. Those overlooking the runways have balconies, and the soundproofing in the hotel is state-of-the-art.

RATES: Standard rooms start at about $150. (Weekend rates are lower.)

AMENITIES: Twenty-four-hour room service, pool, health club, in-room coffee maker, in-room safe, newspaper delivery, turndown service, business center, voice mail, and valet parking.

FEATURES: McCoy's restaurant serves seafood and steaks; Hemispheres restaurant features Italian specialties. The hotel has its own parking area, valet service, and a carport for departing guests.

RESERVATIONS: First call Hyatt Central Reservations (800 233-1234), then call the hotel directly (407 825-1234) to compare rates. Inquire about weekend rates and corporate rates. ◆

LOCAL TRANSPORTATION & PARKING

Most of the thirty million visitors to Walt Disney World this year will arrive in their own cars. About a third of them will fly into the Orlando International Airport. Visitors who arrive via the airport have a number of transportation options available to them, including rental cars, shuttle services, taxis, and limousines. It is not necessary to have a car at Walt Disney World, since its internal transportation system is an efficient network of buses, ferries, trams, and monorails. However, the transportation system can also be crowded, slow, and tiring for visitors who are staying at out-of-the-way resorts. Resorts with the most convenient WDW transportation are the Beach Club, Yacht Club, Swan, Dolphin, Grand Floridian, Contemporary, and Polynesian.

AIRPORT TRANSPORTATION SERVICES: Walt Disney World is a thirty-minute drive from the Orlando International Airport and lies to the south of Orlando. Several independent transportation services provide around-the-clock transportation to Walt Disney World from the airport.

SHUTTLE SERVICE: Mears Transportation provides twenty-four-hour mini-van transportation from the airport to all WDW resorts. Vans leave every fifteen to twenty minutes from the baggage claim areas. No reservations; about $15 per person one way, $25 round trip.

TAXIS: Private taxis from the airport to WDW cost about $25. If you have a party of two or more, it may be less expensive to take a taxi. Taxi service is also available at all resorts.

LIMOUSINES: Mears provides limousine service from the airport to WDW. The limousines are also available for travel within WDW and to other attractions in the area. Towncars start at about $50 per hour, stretch limousines at about $80 per hour. Reserve in advance (407 423-5566). Another limousine company, Coast to Coast, features fully equipped late-model limousines and will confirm your choice. Rates are competitive with other services in the area and reservations are suggested (407 282-5466). Tips for limousine drivers are customarily about 15 to 20 percent.

RENTAL CARS: Although WDW provides internal transportation for as many as 200,000 guests each day, it is often more convenient to drive your own car, especially if you would like to see and do a lot in just a few days.

WHERE TO RENT: Car rental companies that are not at the airport generally (but not always) offer better prices than those at the airport; however, the convenience of the airport location is considerable, especially upon return. The car rental companies located at the airport are Hertz, Avis, Budget, National, and Dollar. Visitors can also rent cars once they arrive at Walt Disney World and drop them off at the airport at no extra charge. Car rental companies located at Walt Disney World include National (Car Care Center, Dolphin, and Swan), Avis (Hilton), Budget (Guest Quarters), Value (Howard Johnson), Alamo (Buena Vista Palace), and Thrifty (Grosvenor).

TIPS: Confirm reservations before you arrive. Contact your insurance agent before leaving home to find out whether you are already covered for rental car collision and liability insurance, and ask your credit card company if you are covered for the collision deductible. Florida rental car companies push heavy insurance fees, and the long lines at the rental counters are primarily due to lengthy (and sometimes heated) explanations about these additional fees (which can add up to $20 per day to rental fees). Rental car companies offer the option of a full tank of gas at reasonable prices, prepaid, so you do not need to refill. If you are planning to stay at WDW for up to five days and will be using an economy car mostly on property, be aware that it is unlikely that you will use more than one-third of a tank of gas (perhaps more in the summer when air-conditioning is used).

DIRECTIONS TO WDW FOR RENTAL CAR DRIVERS: WDW is located about twenty miles from the airport. As you leave, follow the exit signs until you come to a green exit sign that reads "West – Area Attractions." Exit on the right at a sign that says "Tampa West – 528 and Area Attractions." On 528 (the Beeline Expressway), you'll go through two tollbooths (75¢ and 50¢), so it pays to have change on hand. Exit at Interstate Highway 4 and follow the signs that read "Tampa" and "Disney World." Depending on your resort destination, take one of the following exits:

EXIT 27: Guests at the Hotel Plaza Resorts and Disney Village Resort (turn left at Hotel Plaza Boulevard, where the sign reads "Walt Disney World Shopping Village").

EXIT 26B: Guests at Dixie Landings, Port Orleans, Vacation Club, and all Epcot Resorts.

EXIT 25B VIA HIGHWAY 192: Guests at all Magic Kingdom Resorts and at the All-Star Resorts.

FLORIDA TRAFFIC: Florida traffic laws permit right turns at a red light after a complete stop (unless posted otherwise). A seat belt must be worn by the driver and front-seat passenger, car seats are required for children under the age of four and under forty pounds, and headlights must be on whenever windshield wipers are in use. If you are bumped by a car from behind, lock your doors, crack your window, and tell the other driver to proceed to the nearest police station or tollbooth.

CAR TROUBLE: If you have problems with your rental car, call the rental agency for a replacement. If you have rented from a company with an office at WDW, you can exchange your car on the property. Otherwise, a car will be brought to you, or you may need to drive to a nearby office. If you're experiencing problems with your own car, you can drop it at the Exxon Car Care Center, near the Magic Kingdom (824-4813). Shuttles to attractions are provided for visitors so they're not stuck waiting for repairs. AAA cards are accepted for towing services. Carry any car warranty information with you.

PARKING: Overall, the parking system at Walt Disney World is well run and convenient. If you plan to move from place to place in a single day, however, a little parking strategy is required.

THEME PARK PARKING: The parking lots at the major theme parks are free to guests staying at WDW resorts. Day visitors are charged a nominal fee (about $5), which entitles them to park in all of the WDW parking lots for one day. The major theme park lots are serviced by trams that carry visitors from their parking area to the main entrance. To survive the parking experience at the theme parks, there are two things you *must* remember: your car's row number and your car's license plate number, especially if you've rented a car. The rental cars that fill the lots all look the same.

RESORT PARKING: All resorts have free self-parking lots and many have valet parking services. At the WDW-owned resorts, valet parking is free, and guests merely tip the valet a dollar or so when they pick up their car. Valet parking fees (ranging from $4 to $8) are charged at the independently run resorts. Sometimes it can be more convenient to park at a resort near the theme park you are visiting than in the theme park lot, especially if you are planning a short visit or plan to move on to other recreation or dining destinations in the vicinity. Resorts that neighbor theme parks have very convenient transportation options. Resorts with the most convenient WDW transportation to Epcot Center (trams) and Disney-MGM Studios (ferries) include the Swan, Dolphin, Yacht Club, and Beach Club (which is within walking distance). Resorts with the most convenient WDW transportation to the Magic Kingdom include the Contemporary (monorail), Polynesian (monorail and ferry), and Grand Floridian (monorail and ferry). The Contemporary resort has the most convenient WDW transportation to Discovery Island and Fort Wilderness. ◆

GROUPS, REUNIONS, AND WEDDINGS

The enormous variety of activities, attractions, entertainment, and sporting events at Walt Disney World make it an ideal vacation destination for groups. WDW offers an array of options for private groups, including special tours, private parties, and group lodging, and the WDW resorts offer conveniences that are especially useful to groups, such as resort-wide transportation, reservations services, voice mail, and child care.

ACCOMMODATIONS: Because of the hundreds of conventions held at Walt Disney World each year, the WDW resorts are equipped with amenities that also make them ideal for private groups that visit for family reunions, weddings, anniversaries, and vacations. In addition to standard hotel room accommodations, WDW offers several unique lodging options for groups, including campsites or vacation homes with full kitchens, which give groups the option of preparing their own meals and dining together (see "Hotels," page 143). Groups requiring ten or more adjacent rooms should book through Disney Group and Convention Services (800 327-2989).

VACATION HOMES: One- two- and three-bedroom condominium-style and detached vacation homes with fully equipped kitchens are available at Disney Vacation Club and Disney's Village Resort. Groups looking for a rustic outdoors setting may enjoy the less-expensive Wilderness Homes at Disney's Fort Wilderness Resort and Campground. These one-bedroom trailer homes include full kitchens and outdoor grills.

EFFICIENCY SUITES: Suites with separate bedrooms and mini kitchens equipped with refrigerators, coffee makers, and microwaves are available at the Guest Quarters Suite Resort, Buena Vista Palace Suites, and Disney's Village Resort in the Clubhouse Suites.

BUDGET RESORTS: WDW's limited-amenity resorts provide exceptional value for groups lodging together on a budget. Rooms may be booked together in the following resorts: Dixie Landings (refrigerator upon request), Port Orleans (refrigerator upon request), Caribbean Beach (mini bar), All-Star Resort (mini bar), Howard Johnson (mini bar and coffee maker), Travelodge (mini bar and coffee maker), and Grosvenor (refrigerator).

CAMPSITES: The Fort Wilderness campsites offer the most economical stay at a WDW resort. Groups may reserve adjoining campsites for tents and RVs, equipped with electrical outlets, charcoal grills, picnic tables, water, and cable TV hookup. A private area, Creekside Meadow, provides groups of twenty or more with a back-to-nature setting (no hookups), and can be reserved through Group Camping Reservations (407 354-1856). Showers, rest rooms, and laundry facilities are adjacent to all campsites; tents and cots can be rented through Fort Wilderness Guest Services (407 824-2900).

TOURING IN GROUPS: The guided tours at the WDW theme parks allow groups to enjoy the sights and attractions together, and are especially useful for orienting first-time visitors. WDW also offers groups a selection of private, special-interest, and behind-the-scenes tours.

THEME PARK TOURS: The Guided Tour of the Magic Kingdom presents an overview of the Magic Kingdom attractions and highlights the history of Walt Disney World. The Guided Tour of Epcot Center takes groups to attractions in both Future World and the World Showcase. Many of the attractions at Disney-MGM Studios are tours in and of themselves, which explore the diverse aspects of movie and television production (see "Attractions," pages 19, 55, and 36).

SPECIAL-INTEREST TOURS: Two special-interest tours focusing on the World Showcase are staged on alternate days at Epcot Center. "Hidden Treasures of the World Showcase" looks at the design and construction of the international pavilions, and "Gardens of the World" explores the horticultural efforts behind the gardens imported from the various nations. The tours must be reserved in advance; for details, see "World Showcase," page 29.

VIP TOURS: VIP Tours are limited to the groups that book them and have itineraries designed to meet the groups' special interests. VIP Tours may be reserved by individuals or groups of up to ten people per guide, and cost about $35 per hour per guide for a four- to eight-hour tour of one or more theme parks. (Groups touring for more than four hours must have a meal at a full-service restaurant; theme park admission is not included in the price of the tour.) VIP Tours may be booked from forty-eight hours to six months in advance through Park Special Activities (407 560-6233).

BEHIND-THE-SCENES PROGRAM: The Behind-the-Scenes tours take groups "backstage" to see how the Walt Disney World experience is created and maintained. The tours include "Architheming: The Story of Themed Architecture at the Walt Disney World Resort," "Innovation in Action: Behind the Scenes at the Walt Disney World Resort," and "Planting Ideas: The Art and Science of Gardening at the Walt Disney World Resort." Tours are available for private groups of fifteen or more; each tour lasts approximately $3^1/_2$ hours and costs about $50 per person. Behind-the-Scenes tours must be booked in advance through Walt Disney World Seminar Productions (407 828-1480).

TOURING SEPARATELY: Individuals traveling in groups often have divergent interests and energy levels, and touring the theme parks and recreation areas separately is a simple solution that satisfies everyone. Walt Disney World provides a number of innovative ways for group members touring separately to coordinate meals and shared activities, or to stay in touch in case of an emergency or a change in plans.

MESSAGE CENTER: Message centers are located at Guest Relations in the Magic Kingdom, Epcot Center, and Disney-MGM Studios. Here, visitors can leave and retrieve messages on a computer network that connects the three parks.

VOICE MAIL: Voice-mail systems are available in all WDW resort rooms (with the exception of some resorts at Hotel Plaza). Using voice mail, guests can leave personal outgoing messages and retrieve incoming messages from any phone. For example, a group organizer may leave rendezvous instructions on the outgoing message for individuals calling in; individuals may leave messages for the group organizer about delays or a change in plans.

CELLULAR PHONES AND POCKET PAGERS: Cellular phones and pocket pagers can be reserved in advance through Guest Services at any Walt Disney World resort. Cellular phones rent for about $10 a day plus call charges; pocket pagers rent for about $10 a day or $30 a week.

PRIVATE PARTIES AT WALT DISNEY WORLD: Groups have several options for private celebrations at Walt Disney World. WDW's catering and banquet services take care of all the work and arrangements so guests can enjoy the festivities.

RESORT RESTAURANTS: Groups can call resort restaurants directly to reserve a large seating and make special requests (a birthday cake, for example). Groups can also reserve a private room in a resort restaurant for a buffet or sit-down meal through WDW Accounts Services (828-2048). All resort restaurants take reservations for groups. The Garden Gallery's Summer Room at the Disney Inn and the Lake Buena Vista Restaurant's banquet room at the Village Resort provide especially pleasant settings.

GROUP VACATIONS

PLEASURE ISLAND: Private parties can be arranged in any of Pleasure Island's seven nightclubs, which offer a range of interesting atmospheres. Pleasure Island caters parties in the clubs from 5 until 7 PM (average cost is about $1,000); after 7 PM, the clubs open their doors to other Pleasure Island guests. Private parties on Pleasure Island can be arranged through WDW Accounts Services (828-2048).

DISNEY VACATION CLUB: Groups staying at the Vacation Club can have parties catered in their vacation homes or arrange for private cookouts in the Vacation Club's Family Tree recreation area. Catering arrangements can be made through Disney Food and Beverage Service (407 827-1191).

ORGANIZING TIPS: Groups meeting at Orlando International Airport should carefully plan where to meet, depending on the arrival times of flights. The airport has a mirror-image layout with duplicate services, which can cause some confusion (see "Orlando International Airport," page 253). Groups scheduled to arrive in the evening might consider spending the night at the Hyatt Regency, located inside the airport, and then traveling to WDW together the next day (see "Hyatt Regency," page 253).

HOLIDAYS: Holidays are the most festive – and the most crowded – times at Walt Disney World. Groups, however, must frequently arrange their trips around holidays. If you have a choice between traveling during the summer months or during holiday periods, then holidays are certainly preferable. The best time for group vacations is during the three weeks following Thanksgiving, which has the lowest attendance of the year, yet offers a variety of holiday entertainment and events. The best holidays for groups, considering attendance and weather, are Thanksgiving, Presidents' Day, Easter, and spring break. The most difficult holidays for group vacations are Memorial Day, Labor Day, the week between Christmas and New Year's, and the Fourth of July (see "Holidays," page 259).

DISCOUNTS: There are a number of discount clubs and vacation packages available at Walt Disney World that offer savings on accommodations, admissions, car rentals, airfares, meals, and merchandise (see "Discount Travel Clubs," page 250). Many of these discounts require only one person in a group to be a member of the club. Disney Group and Convention Services (800 327-2989) also offers discounts on blocks of ten or more rooms; discounts do not apply at the budget resorts.

BABYSITTING: There are abundant babysitting and child care services at Walt Disney World, affording groups the opportunity to enjoy adult-oriented activities and evening entertainment while their children are entertained by child care professionals in hotel rooms or centers equipped with toys, computers, video games, movies, arts and crafts, and books (see "Babysitting & Day Camps," page 263).

WEDDINGS AT WALT DISNEY WORLD: Destination weddings — where the bridal couple, family, and friends travel to a distant location for the event — are increasingly popular. Already the number-one honeymoon destination in the world, Walt Disney World is also becoming a premier wedding destination. Disney's Fairy Tale Weddings has a staff of full-service bridal consultants to help couples plan their wedding down to the last detail and tailor the arrangements to each couple's budget and taste. Walt Disney World weddings for the bridal couple and their guests start at about $8,000 for a ceremony with all the trimmings, including marriage license, invitations, welcome party, flowers, music, wedding cake, photographs, and catered reception (some wedding parties have spent as much as $250,000). A wedding for the bridal couple alone costs about $2,000, which includes the ceremony, four nights' accommodations, theme park admissions, dinner, and flowers. Fairy Tale Honeymoons are also available, ranging from $800 to $3,000 per couple. Walt Disney World weddings and honeymoons can be arranged through Disney's Fairy Tale Weddings (407 363-6333). ◆

HOLIDAYS AT WALT DISNEY WORLD

Any holiday is fair game for the entertainment designers at Walt Disney World, and no holiday goes unheralded. The holiday celebrations with entertainment of special interest to adult visitors include the following:

MARDI GRAS: Pleasure Island celebrates Mardi Gras with parties and parades, guest bands from Louisiana, and tasty New Orleans–style food. Mardi Gras music, dancers, stilt walkers, jugglers, costumes, floats, fireworks, and confetti all enhance this festive event.

JULY FOURTH: Flags are raised and bunting draped for Independence Day celebrations at WDW. The Magic Kingdom hosts the Salute America show featuring a daytime fireworks finale and, in the evening, presents an expanded fireworks show. Marching bands circle the World Showcase at Epcot Center, and there are expanded fireworks shows at IllumiNations, Disney-MGM Studios, and Pleasure Island.

THANKSGIVING: Beginning on Thanksgiving Day, Walt Disney World offers two holidays in one. Late Thursday night, Disney Cast Members work overtime to transform all of WDW into a Christmas wonderland. When the theme parks open on Friday, they are decked in full Christmas regalia and feature Christmas entertainment and tree-lighting ceremonies nightly. Selected full-service restaurants in the theme parks and resorts offer traditional Thanksgiving dinners. (Make your reservations early.)

CHRISTMAS: It's Christmas season from Thanksgiving Day on at Walt Disney World. The theme parks sport towering fir trees studded with lights that come alive in nightly tree-lighting ceremonies. On the weekends at the Magic Kingdom, Mickey's Very Merry Christmas Parade travels down Main Street, and on selected nights, Mickey's Very Merry Christmas Party presents a special evening celebration of holiday food, carolers, special entertainment, and fireworks for which the park reopens at 8 PM. Disney-MGM Studios re-creates Christmas in New York, with carolers, chestnut vendors, strolling musicians, and towering floats from Macy's Thanksgiving Day Parade. At Disney Village Marketplace, a forty-foot fir tree is lit nightly, followed by the Glory and Pageantry of Christmas, a living Nativity pageant.

The WDW resorts offer the Jolly Holidays vacation, with theme-decorated resorts and on-going entertainment. The Grand Floridian features a Victorian Christmas, the Yacht and Beach Club re-create the holiday festivities of the New England Coast, the Disney Inn presents a country inn–style Christmas, and Port Orleans celebrates Christmas with a Cajun flavor. The Contemporary resort puts on Christmas in the Southwest and hosts the Jolly Holidays dinner show (see "Jolly Holidays," page 213). Jolly Holidays vacation packages include accommodations, park admissions, and the Jolly Holidays dinner show.

NEW YEAR'S EVE: On New Year's Eve, the theme parks stay open into the wee hours with park-wide celebrations and midnight fireworks shows, and Pleasure Island stages the "REAL New Year's Eve," a special-admission party with food, favors, and celebrity performers. At the resorts, the Grand Floridian hosts a dinner and gala ball and the Hilton features a Carnivale Celebration followed by breakfast at 1 AM. The Grosvenor puts on a fifties-style New Year's Eve bash, and at Buena Vista Palace, Arthur's 27 presents a formal dinner party with live jazz.

At the dinner shows on New Year's Eve, the Polynesian Luau moves the party to the beach at midnight for a view of the Magic Kingdom fireworks, and at the Hoop-Dee-Doo Musical Revue, a country music band creates a down-home New Year's celebration. So that parents can be free to celebrate at one or several of the events, the Neverland Club entertains children until 2 AM, and KinderCare offers sleep overs (see "Babysitting & Day Camps," page 263). ◆

VISITORS WITH DISABILITIES

In keeping with the state-of-the-art technologies used throughout Walt Disney World, the facilities for visitors with disabilities are unparalleled in the travel industry. Both current and experimental technologies are brought into play — from closed-caption cable television in most resort rooms, to WDW's standard-wheelchair and motorized-wheelchair systems, the largest private fleet in the world. Many attractions are designed with antennas built into the ceilings that beam sound down to tiny FM receivers given to visitors with hearing impairments. Guests with visual impairments are given cassette players that help them tour the parks using sounds and smells to enhance their experiences. And, of course, all hotels and public transportation are outfitted with disability-friendly devices. Most of this is invisible to the general traveler, but visitors with disabilities will find WDW to be one of the most accessible vacation experiences anywhere in the world.

VISITORS WITH PHYSICAL DISABILITIES

When making hotel reservations, specify your needs — special requests are given every consideration. Ask that a complimentary copy of Walt Disney World's Guidebook for Guests with Disabilities *be mailed to you or that it be waiting for you when you check in. If you are driving and do not have special handicapped plates with you, ask your rental car company or hotel for a handicapped sticker.*

HOTELS: All WDW resorts have rooms for the physically disabled. The best facilities can be found at the following resorts: Vacation Club (lower beds, roll-in showers, handicapped parking near rooms), Caribbean Beach (handicapped parking near rooms), Dixie Landings (handicapped parking near rooms), Polynesian (automatic entrance doors, elevator access to the monorail), and Grand Floridian (door peepholes at wheelchair level, hand-held showers, elevator access to the monorail). Resorts presenting physical challenges include the Contemporary (no elevator access to the monorail), Port Orleans (many curbs and sidewalks throughout the resort), and Fort Wilderness (the trailer homes are narrow and accessed by stairs; the campsite grounds can be too soft for wheelchair operation).

WHEELCHAIRS: All WDW resorts have complimentary wheelchairs for guest use within the resort. The following theme parks and recreation areas have rental wheelchairs: Magic Kingdom (standard and motorized), Epcot Center (standard and motorized), Disney-MGM Studios, Disney Village Marketplace, and Fort Wilderness (electric carts). The following parks have a limited number of complimentary wheelchairs: Discovery Island, Typhoon Lagoon, and Fort Wilderness (through Guest Services).

PARKING AT THEME PARKS: All theme parks have handicapped parking areas. At the major theme parks, tell the tollgate attendant what your needs are and you will be issued a pass and directed to the handicapped parking lot (if you are immobile) or to handicapped-designated end spots in the main lot with easy access to the trams (if you can take a few steps and your chair folds). The smaller parks and recreation areas have handicapped parking near the entrance. Pleasure Island offers valet parking after 5 PM.

PARKING AT HOTELS: The following WDW resorts offer complimentary valet parking: Polynesian, Grand Floridian, Contemporary, Yacht Club, Beach Club, Hotel Royal Plaza, and the Disney Inn. Valets expect a tip when you pick up your car. Valet parking fees (ranging from $4 to $8) are charged at the following resorts: Swan, Dolphin, Hilton, Grosvenor, and Buena Vista Palace.

PUBLIC TRANSPORTATION: Many, but not all, WDW buses are wheelchair accessible. You may have to wait for more than one bus. All monorails and monorail stations are wheelchair accessible (except at the

Contemporary resort). All ferries are wheelchair accessible, except some that travel to Discovery Island and Fort Wilderness. You may have to wait for more than one ferry. Visitors with nonstandard or motorized wheelchairs can arrange at Guest Services for special vans to travel between theme parks and resorts.

TELEPHONES: All theme parks have wheelchair-accessible pay phones. Check with Guest Relations as you enter for a map showing telephone locations.

TOURING: The *Guidebook for Guests with Disabilities* explains which attractions are wheelchair accessible and which you must leave your chair in order to ride. WDW hosts and hostesses are not trained in transferring guests to and from wheelchairs, so plan on visiting with a companion who can assist you. Guests using motorized wheelchairs must transfer to standard wheelchairs before entering most attractions.

SIGHT-IMPAIRED VISITORS

When making hotel reservations, specify your needs — special requests are given every consideration. Sight-impaired guests with guide dogs should let the hotel know when making reservations. Guests may keep their animals with them in their room or can arrange to board them at one of the WDW kennels. Ask that a complimentary copy of Walt Disney World's Guidebook for Guests with Disabilities *be mailed to you, which shows which attractions can accommodate guide dogs.*

HOTELS: Braille-equipped elevators can be found at the following resorts: Polynesian, Contemporary, Grand Floridian, Port Orleans, Beach Club, Yacht Club, Dolphin, Swan, Grosvenor, and Buena Vista Palace. The high-rise hotels are the easiest to get around in, with the exception of the Dolphin, where the floor plan is very confusing. The Polynesian, Port Orleans, Dixie Landings, and Caribbean Beach resorts have sprawling layouts that may present a challenge to sight-impaired guests. The Grand Floridian also has rambling grounds, but offers a valet and trolley escort service from its outbuildings to the main lobby.

TOURING: Complimentary tape players and tour cassettes are available with a refundable deposit at Guest Relations in the Magic Kingdom, Epcot Center, and Disney-MGM Studios. The Magic Kingdom also offers a Braille touring text describing the park. Those traveling with guide dogs may want to bring a companion to take charge of the dog while enjoying attractions that restrict guide dogs. WDW hosts and hostesses are not permitted to take charge of guide animals.

GUIDED TOURS: Sight-impaired visitors may arrange for a complimentary guided overview tour of the major theme parks. The guide will provide a general sense of how to locate and enjoy the attractions. These tours are designed for visitors who wish to explore the parks on their own, and must be booked in advance through Parks Special Activities (407 560-6233). Guided tours are offered daily for a small fee at the Magic Kingdom and Epcot Center. These $3^{1}/_{2}$-hour tours present a more structured overview and experience of the parks, and are especially useful to first-time guests. At Disney-MGM Studios, many of the attractions are actually tours, and many involve sound as much as visuals. In addition, the World Showcase at Epcot Center offers two special-interest tours: Gardens of the World and Hidden Treasures of the World Showcase. These $3^{1}/_{2}$-hour tours provide rich descriptions of the varied cultures represented in the World Showcase pavilions. The tours cost about $20 per person and must be booked several weeks in advance (407 354-1855).

DISABILITIES

HEARING-IMPAIRED VISITORS

If you would like your hotel room fitted with special equipment for the hearing-impaired, make your request at the time you book your room. Ask that a complimentary copy of Walt Disney World Guide for Visitors with Disabilities *be mailed to you or that it be waiting for you when you check in.*

HOTELS: All WDW resorts can supply guest rooms with a telecommunications device for the deaf (TDD) and strobe lights. Guests can also use TDDs to make hotel reservations and special requests by calling 407 345-5984. Closed-caption television is available in guest rooms throughout WDW, with the exception of some Hotel Plaza resorts.

TELEPHONES: All theme parks have amplified and hearing aid–compatible pay phones. Check with Guest Relations as you enter for a map showing telephone locations. TDDs for hearing-impaired visitors are available at Guest Relations in the Magic Kingdom, Epcot Center, and Disney-MGM Studios.

TOURING: A complimentary written text of the narration of attractions is available at Guest Relations in the Magic Kingdom, Epcot Center, and Disney-MGM Studios. Epcot Center offers personal translator units (PTUs) to amplify the sound in attractions; they are available at Earth Station with a refundable deposit. Personal audio listening devices (PALs) are available at some of the attractions at Disney-MGM Studios. These must be requested at those attractions.

SIGNING TOURS: Hearing-impaired visitors can arrange for complimentary guided overview tours of the theme parks given in American Sign Language. These brief overviews provide guests with a sense of how to locate and enjoy the attractions, and are designed for those who wish to explore the parks on their own. Four- to five-hour signing tours are also available for a minimal fee, and offer a more structured experience. Both of these tours must be booked in advance through Parks Special Activities (407 560-6233).

TOURING COMPANIONS FOR VISITORS WITH DISABILITIES

While Walt Disney World is committed to providing the services and technology that make its attractions accessible to everyone, WDW employees are not trained to help guests physically. Visitors who require assistance to ride attractions may want to have a companion along to give them access to a broader range of activities. A number of independent services in Orlando provide trained companions for the physically challenged.

FRIENDS OF THE FAMILY: This comprehensive Orlando-based service provides helpers who guide visitors from the airport to the hotel and through the theme parks. Tour rates start at about $75 per hour and are based on ability to pay. Companions for dining or recreational activities are available for about $15 per hour (plus meals and park admissions), with a five-hour minimum (800 945-2045).

FAIRY GODMOTHERS: This local companion service is available twenty-four hours a day and offers assistance and companions to visitors with disabilities, provided lifting is not necessary. Rates vary, and there is a four-hour minimum (407 275-7326 or 407 277-3724).

OTHER RESOURCES: A recent and useful book, *Handicapped in Walt Disney World: A Guide for Everyone,* by Peter Smith (SouthPark Publishing Group, 800 669-5657), provides complete information for Walt Disney World visitors with physical disabilities. The author presents detailed descriptions of accessibility to all attractions and tips on lodging and transportation for handicapped travelers. ◆

BABYSITTING & DAY CAMPS

Walt Disney World provides visitors with children a wealth of child care options so they can get away and enjoy the many adult-oriented events and activities during the day and evening. While there are no Disney-operated services that include supervision within the theme parks, there is no need to feel guilty about leaving little tykes behind. The WDW clubs and camps create unique environments where children can feel entertained and not "sat." All drop-off programs require that children be completely toilet trained and able to dress themselves. No diapers, including pull-ups, are allowed.

KINDERCARE IN-ROOM BABYSITTING: KinderCare-trained sitters are available to all WDW resort guests for in-room child care. Sitters may not take children into the theme parks or on any transportation, but can take children to restaurants within walking distance of guests' rooms. Guests are asked to provide the sitter with a meal if the sitting hours are scheduled during mealtimes. In-room sitting is the only option for children who are too young for the day camps or who are not yet toilet trained.

> **HOURS AND FEES:** Twenty-four hours per day, four-hour minimum. About $8 per hour covers the first three children in the same family.
>
> **RESERVATIONS:** Necessary at least twenty-four hours in advance (827-5444).

KINDERCARE DAY CARE CENTER: Located in the Disney Village Resorts Area, this facility is a day care center for the children of Disney employees; however, children of guests are also accommodated when space permits. The KinderCare Learning While Playing Development Program provides a structured and educational environment, and guest children are placed in existing classes according to age. For toilet trained children ages two to twelve.

> **HOURS AND FEES:** 6 AM until 9 PM weekdays, and 6 AM until 8 PM on weekends. About $35 per day for a maximum of ten hours, a hot meal, and a snack. About $8 per hour for shorter stays.
>
> **RESERVATIONS:** Same-day reservations only (827-5437).

MOUSEKETEER CLUB: *Disney's Grand Floridian Beach Resort* — This pleasantly decorated small club accepts a maximum of twelve children at one time and provides an assortment of toys, board games, Nintendos, arts and crafts projects, books, and Disney movies. Available to children ages three to nine who are staying at any WDW-owned resort. Cookies and a beverage are provided; meals are not included.

> **HOURS AND FEES:** 4:30 PM until midnight. About $5 per hour for one child and $7 for two.
>
> **RESERVATIONS:** Recommended. Call Guest Services at the Grand Floridian (824-3000: hotel).

CAMP DOLPHIN: *Walt Disney World Dolphin* — This child care and activity center is designed for children ages five through twelve (ages three to five attend Toddler Dolphins). Activities include crafts, games, sporting activities, and a Dinner Club and movies in the evening. Available only to guests staying at the Dolphin and Swan hotels. Occupancy is limited to fifteen children at any one time.

> **HOURS AND FEES:** Camp is from 2 PM until 6 PM; toddlers from 3 PM until 5 PM. Dinner Club is from 6 PM until 10 PM for older children and from 5 PM until 8 PM for toddlers. About $5 per hour; Dinner Club and entertainment is about $25 for older kids and $20 for toddlers.
>
> **RESERVATIONS:** Drop-in basis. Dinner Club reservations accepted (934-4000: hotel).

CAMP SWAN: *Walt Disney World Swan* — Designed for children ages three to twelve, this child care and entertainment center offers both individual and group activities and a Disney movie in the evenings. Meals are not included but may be brought by parents or preordered from room service. While this program is offered to guests at the Swan and Dolphin resorts, guests from other resorts are accepted subject to availability. Club size is limited to a total of fifteen children at one time.

HOURS AND FEES: 4 PM until midnight. About $5 per hour for the first child and $3 per hour for each additional child from the same family.

RESERVATIONS: Reservations should be made prior to the evening requested (934-1621).

SANDCASTLE CLUB: *Disney's Beach Club Resort* — This child care and activity center is open to children ages three to twelve and features computers, television, Nintendos, arcade games, arts and crafts projects, and a library of children's books. Available to guests at the Yacht and Beach Club resorts; guests at other WDW resorts may use the facility on a drop-in basis after 4 PM if space is available.

HOURS AND FEES: 4:30 PM until midnight. About $5 per hour for the first child and $3 per hour for each additional child. Provision for a meal must be made for any child left more than four hours. Parents can provide the meal or preorder from room service.

RESERVATIONS: Suggested before the night desired (934-8000: hotel).

MOUSEKETEER CLUBHOUSE: *Disney's Contemporary Resort* — The Mouseketeer Clubhouse is basically a short-term facility with limited capacity and amusement value. Designed for children ages three to nine, it features video games, computers, and an assortment of toys. The Clubhouse is limited to twelve children at any one time, and accepts guests from any WDW resort.

HOURS AND FEES: 4:30 PM until midnight, with a four-hour maximum. About $5 per hour for the first child and $3 per hour for each additional child.

RESERVATIONS: Recommended at least two days before requested date (824-1000: hotel).

NEVERLAND CLUB: *Disney's Polynesian Resort* — Based on the story *Peter Pan,* this themed club is very popular. Guests enter the building and find themselves in Wendy's bedroom, where they sign in and watch as their child is sprinkled with pixie dust and climbs through the window into the wonderful world of Neverland. The fun includes a character visit with a photo session and an autograph, a visit from some of the feathered and scaly inhabitants of Discovery Island, unlimited video arcade games, and lots of Disney-themed toys, including a wealth of Disney plush toys. The children are supervised in both group and individual activities, and a kid-pleasing buffet dinner is included. Any toilet-trained child between the ages of three and twelve may attend.

HOURS AND FEES: 5 PM until midnight. Full buffet from 5:30 until 8 PM. Children arriving after the buffet can still get a peanut butter and jelly sandwich and dessert. About $8 per hour for each child, with a three-hour minimum.

RESERVATIONS: Strongly suggested, especially during peak seasons (824-2170).

HILTON YOUTH HOTEL: *The Hilton Resort* — In addition to the usual array of games, movies, and activities, this child care facility offers a mini-dormitory with small beds set off in a quiet area for children who wish to take a nap or go to sleep before Mom and Dad return. Don't let the name fool you though — this children's "hotel" is only open until midnight. Available to children ages four to twelve staying at any WDW resort.

HOURS AND FEES: 5 PM until midnight. About $5 per hour for one child, $7 per hour for two, and $8 per hour for three children. If you arrive to pick up your children after midnight, there is an additional charge of $25 per hour per child.

RESERVATIONS: Suggested a day in advance (827-4000: hotel). ◆

WHERE TO FIND IT

When it comes to supplying guests with everything they might need while on vacation, Walt Disney World has it pretty well covered. Forgotten or damaged items or articles of clothing can be replaced in one of the many stores located in Disney Village Marketplace, Crossroads Shopping Center, the resort shops, or a number of shops in the theme parks. Banking services and medical care are also offered in several locations.

✦ **BEAUTY AND BARBER SHOPS:** Hair-styling services can be found at the following resorts: Yacht Club and Beach Club (Periwig's Beauty/Barber Shop), Contemporary (Captain's Chair for men; American Beauty Shoppe for women), Polynesian (Alii Nui Barber Shop for men; Pretty Wahine Beauty Shop for women), and Grand Floridian (Ivy Trellis for men and women). Nikki Bryan's salons for men and women are at the following resorts: Swan, Dolphin, Hilton, and Buena Vista Palace.

    MAGIC KINGDOM: The Harmony Barber Shop, on Main Street, is open daily for men's haircuts.

✦ **BANKING AND MONEY:** The WDW resorts offer guests the following financial services: currency exchange, check cashing (up to $50), and money wires to and from WDW.

    DISNEY VILLAGE MARKETPLACE: There is an automatic teller machine (ATM) located outside of Guest Services. The Sun Bank (full service and foreign currency exchange) is located across the street.

    CROSSROADS SHOPPING CENTER: Sun Bank offers full-service banking, foreign currency exchange, and ATMs. Gooding's Supermarket has an ATM and also provides foreign currency exchange.

    THEME PARKS: Guest Relations at all theme parks will cash checks for visitors in the amount of $25. Epcot Center has a branch of the Sun Bank (full service and foreign currency exchange) and an ATM, an American Express Cash Machine, and American Express Travel Services (lost traveler's checks replacements). The Magic Kingdom has a branch of the Sun Bank (full service and foreign currency exchange) and an ATM. Disney-MGM Studios has an ATM.

✦ **BATHING SUITS:** Most resort shops carry bathing suits for men and women. The best selections can be found at the following resorts: Swan, Dolphin, Polynesian, Contemporary, and Buena Vista Palace.

    DISNEY VILLAGE MARKETPLACE: Resortwear Unlimited (women), Harrington Bay Clothiers (men), and Captain's Tower (men and women, seasonally).

    CROSSROADS SHOPPING CENTER: Sun Works Resortwear and Ken Done Fun and Sun Fashions.

    TYPHOON LAGOON: Singapore Sal's Saleable Salvage.

✦ **COMFORTABLE SHOES:** The premium resort shops carry walking and athletic shoes and sandals.

    DISNEY VILLAGE MARKETPLACE: Team Mickey's Athletic Club, Resortwear Unlimited (women), Harrington Bay Clothiers (men), and Captain's Tower (men and women, seasonally).

    CROSSROADS SHOPPING CENTER: Footlocker Athletic Shoes and Ken Done Fun and Sun Fashions.

✦ **COSMETICS:** Lancôme cosmetics can be found at the following resorts: Swan, Contemporary, Grand Floridian, Yacht Club, Beach Club, and Buena Vista Palace.

    DISNEY VILLAGE MARKETPLACE: Country Address and Resortwear Unlimited carry Lancôme.

    CROSSROADS SHOPPING CENTER: Gooding's Pharmacy carries Max Factor, Revlon, and Clarion.

    WORLD SHOWCASE: Guerlain Boutique in the French pavilion carries the complete line of Guerlain cosmetics and most fine French perfumes.

S H O P P I N G

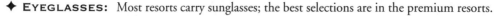
Shopping

◆ **EYEGLASSES:** Most resorts carry sunglasses; the best selections are in the premium resorts.
   CROSSROADS SHOPPING CENTER: Gooding's Pharmacy (reading and sunglasses), Ken Done Fun and Sun Fashions (sunglasses), Buena Vista Vision Centre (repairs, prescription glasses, and sunglasses).
   MAGIC KINGDOM: The Main Street Bookstore carries reading glasses.

◆ **EVENING WEAR:** The best selections in evening dress for men and women can be found in the shops at the following resorts: Swan, Dolphin, and Grand Floridian.
   DISNEY VILLAGE MARKETPLACE: Harrington Bay Clothiers (men), The City (trendy), Resortwear Unlimited (women), and Country Address (women).
   CROSSROADS SHOPPING CENTER: Chico's Ladies Clothing.

◆ **FLORIST:** Floral arrangements and fruit baskets can be ordered from the WDW Florist (827-3505).
   CROSSROADS SHOPPING CENTER: Gooding's Florists delivers to all WDW resorts (827-1206).

◆ **GROCERIES:** The following resorts offer a limited selection of groceries: Caribbean Beach, Port Orleans, Dixie Landings, Vacation Club, Grosvenor, and Fort Wilderness.
   DISNEY VILLAGE MARKETPLACE: Gourmet Pantry (limited groceries, bakery, and deli).
   CROSSROADS SHOPPING CENTER: Gooding's Supermarket.

◆ **LIQUOR:** Wine and beer can be found at the following resorts: Port Orleans, Dixie Landings, and Vacation Club. Wine, beer, and spirits are available at the following resorts: Caribbean Beach, Fort Wilderness, Contemporary, and Polynesian.
   DISNEY VILLAGE MARKETPLACE: Gourmet Pantry (wine and beer), Village Spirits (beer and spirits), and Vintage Cellars (wine).
   CROSSROADS SHOPPING CENTER: Gooding's Supermarket (wine and beer) and Espresso Liquor and Pizza (wine, beer, and spirits).
   WORLD SHOWCASE: La Maison du Vin (France) and Weinkeller (Germany) sell wine.

◆ **MEDICAL CARE AND MEDICATIONS:** HouseMed Service provides twenty-four hour physician house calls to all WDW resorts (648-9234). Guest Services at all resorts provide dental referrals.
   BUENA VISTA WALK-IN MEDICAL CENTER: Located in the Disney Village Resorts Area, the Medical Center is open daily from 9 AM until 8 PM. Free shuttle service is available to WDW resort guests (828-3434). WDW resort guests can have prescriptions filled and delivered to Guest Services through the Buena Vista Walk-in Medical Center pharmacy (828-8125).
   MEDICLINIC: This twenty-four-hour walk-in clinic is just west of WDW on Highway 192 (648-9234).
   HOSPITAL: Emergency services are provided by Sand Lake Hospital, just north of WDW on Interstate 4 at Exit 27 (351-8550).
   CROSSROADS SHOPPING CENTER: Prescriptions can be filled at Gooding's Pharmacy (827-1207).

◆ **SLEEPWEAR AND UNDERWEAR:** All resorts carry Disney-character night shirts. The Grand Floridian carries traditional nightwear. The Grand Floridian, Contemporary, Yacht Club, and Beach Club resorts carry a very limited supply of underwear. When available, it is kept behind the counter. All resorts carry Disney-character undershorts for men.
   DISNEY VILLAGE MARKETPLACE: Mickey's Character Shop, Harrington Bay Clothiers (men), The City (women, limited), and Country Address (women, limited).
   CROSSROADS SHOPPING CENTER: Gooding's Supermarket and Ken Done Fun and Sun Fashions. ◆

WALT DISNEY WORLD TELEPHONE DIRECTORY

The area code in Orlando and at Walt Disney World is 407. When dialing any of the numbers listed below
from outside the Orlando area, you must first dial 407 unless otherwise noted.
If you cannot find the number you need listed below, call Walt Disney World Information (407 824-4321).

HOTEL RESERVATIONS

Walt Disney World Reservations 934-7639
WDW Resorts Switchboard to All Hotels 824-2222
Hyatt Regency, Orlando International Airport.............. 825-1234

DINING AND ENTERTAINMENT RESERVATIONS

Dinner Show Reservations 934-7639
The Fireworks Factory 934-8989
MurderWatch Mystery Dinner Theater 800 624-4109
Park Special Activities (Special Meals) 560-6233
Resort Restaurant Reservations,
    WDW Resorts Switchboard................................ 824-2222
Theme Park Restaurant Reservatons 824-8800
Village Restaurant Reservations 828-3900

ATTRACTIONS INFORMATION

AMC Pleasure Island 10 Theatres, Show Times 827-1300
Discovery Island.. 824-2875
Disney-MGM Studios Production Office 560-3434
Pleasure Island 934-7781
River Country 824-2760
Typhoon Lagoon 560-4141
Walt Disney World Information................................... 824-4321

GENERAL INFORMATION

Hearing-Impaired Guest Information 827-5141
Hotel Services for Visitors with Disabilities.................. 345-5984
Lost and Found at Walt Disney World 824-4245
Orlando Airport Terminal Information......................... 825-2001
Orlando International Airport,
    Paging Telephone 825-2000
Walt Disney World Information................................... 824-4321
Weather, Disney 824-4104

SPORTS RESERVATIONS

Body by Jake Health Club,
    Walt Disney World Dolphin 934-4264
Fishing Excursion, Buena Vista Lagoon 828-2204
Fishing Excursion, Fort Wilderness.............................. 824-2757
Golf Reservations, Master Starter 824-2270

Golf Studio Lessons, Bonnet Creek Golf Club 824-2675
Golf Studio Lessons,
    Lake Buena Vista Clubhouse................................ 824-2270
Golf Studio Lessons, The Disney Inn............................ 824-2270
Olympiad Health Club,
    Disney's Contemporary Resort 824-3410
Ship Shape Health Club,
    Disney's Yacht and Beach Club Resorts 934-3256
St. John's Health Club,
    Disney's Grand Floridian Beach Resort.................. 824-2433
Swan Health Club, Walt Disney World Swan.............. 934-1360
Tennis Reservations,
    Disney's Grand Floridian Beach Resort................. 824-2433
Tennis Reservations,
    Disney's Contemporary Resort 824-3578
Tennis Reservations,
    Walt Disney World Dolphin and Swan 934-4396
Trail Ride, Fort Wilderness... 824-2832
Waterskiing Excursion, Fort Wilderness........................ 824-2621

GUIDED TOURS

Behind-the-Scenes Program 828-1480
Gardens of the World Tour 354-1855
Treasures of the World Showcase Tour 354-1855
VIP Tours 560-6233

SERVICES

Buena Vista Medical Center Pharmacy 828-8125
Buena Vista Walk-In Medical Center........................... 828-3434
Car Care Center, Exxon 824-4813
Gooding's Florist 827-1206
Gooding's Pharmacy 827-1207
HouseMed In-Room Medical Care 648-9234
Sand Lake Hospital 351-8550
Walt Disney World Florist.. 827-3505

TRANSPORTATION

Coast to Coast Limousine 282-5466
Mears Limousines 423-5566
Taxi Service at Walt Disney World 824-3360

READER SURVEY

Become part of our Walt Disney World for Adults Opinion Bank. Fill out this form and give us your opinion of the attractions, hotels, restaurants, dinner shows, tours, and more.

Was this your first trip to Walt Disney World?   YES   NO   If not, how many times have you visited? _____
    What time of year was your most recent visit? _____   How long did you stay? _____
    How many were in your party? _____   Any children?   YES   NO

Where did you stay? _____
    Did you agree with the hotel ratings?   YES   NO   If not, why? _____
_____

Did we overrate or underrate any of the restaurants where you dined?   YES   NO
    If so, which ones, and how would *you* rate them? _____
_____

Did we overrate or underrate any of the theme park attractions you visited?   YES   NO
    If so, which ones, and how would *you* rate them? _____
_____
_____

If you visited Pleasure Island, did you agree with the nightclub ratings?   YES   NO
    If not, which ones, and why? _____

If you attended any dinner shows, did you agree with the ratings?   YES   NO
    If not, which ones, and why? _____

Did you follow any of the attraction half-day tours?   YES   NO
    Which ones? _____
    Did they work for you?   YES   NO   If not, how would *you* change them? _____
_____

Did you follow one of the Vacation Itineraries?   YES   NO   Which one? _____
    Did it work for you?   YES   NO   If not, how would *you* change it? _____
_____

Did you engage in any sporting activities?   YES   NO   Which ones? _____
Was there a strategy or tip in the book that was especially helpful to you? _____
Did you discover any insider strategies that we should pass on to our readers? _____
_____

Other comments? _____
_____

Will you return to Walt Disney World?   YES   NO

OPTIONAL

Name: _____
Address: _____
_____

Send a copy of this survey to:

Walt Disney World for Adults, P.O. Box 1582, Sausalito, California 94966

Or fax your reply to 415 331-9359